South African War
BOOKS

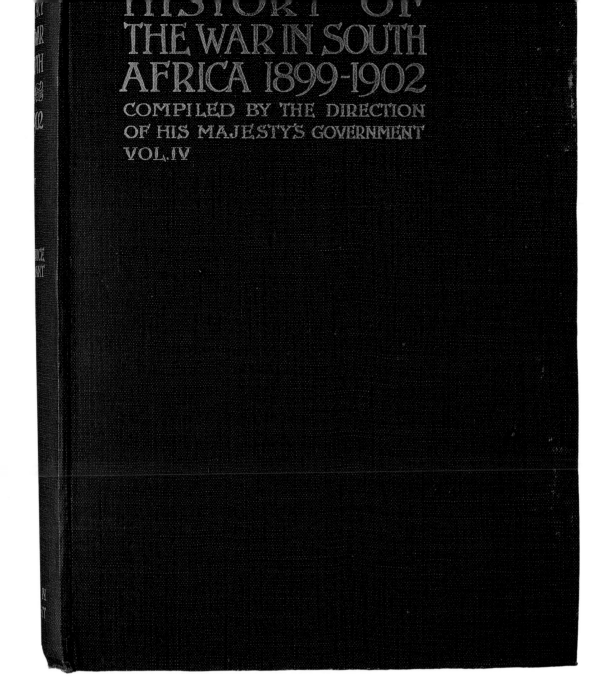

History Of The War In South Africa
1899–1902 Compiled By Direction Of His
Majesty's Government.
*Major-General Sir Frederick Maurice &
Captain Maurice Harold Grant. (With a staff
of Officers.)*
Hurst and Blackett Limited
London 1906–1910

Dark blue cloth. Front and spine blocked in
gold.
244×177mm

The official history of the war in South
Africa 1899–1902 complete in four volumes
together with four volumes of maps.
Volume one relates to war preparations, the
theatre of operations and the respective
armies. The record of the campaign is
drawn up to mid February 1900, prior to
Lord Roberts advance on Bloemfontein.
Volume two commences with the Relief of
Kimberley and ends with the final phase of
the Ladysmith siege (March 1900). Chapters
relate to the Paardeberg operations, the
occupation of Bloemfontein, the campaign
in the Orange Free State and operations in
Natal for the relief of Ladysmith. Volume
three embraces operations in Cape Colony
to July 1900, the advance from
Bloemfontein to Pretoria and further
operations in the Transvaal and Orange
River Colony. Volume four includes a
record of operations on all fronts (with the
exception of Natal) from Dec. 1900 to the
conclusion of peace. Extensive appendices
are common to all volumes and each is fully
indexed. Four volumes of loose maps and
freehand sketches complete the set. The
maps are numbered 1–64. (Some in multiple
sections.)
Vol.1. (1906) xvii+i+526pp.
Vol.2. (1907) xvi+701pp.
Vol.3. (1908) xiii+609pp.
Vol.4. (1910) xv+767pp. 1 plate.
Vol.1. (Maps) South Africa general map
and maps 1–17. With 6 freehand sketches.
Vol.2. (Maps) No.18–37. With 6 freehand
sketches.
Vol.3. (Maps) No.38–55. With 11 freehand
sketches.
Vol.4. (Maps) No.56–64.

South African War BOOKS

An illustrated bibliography of
English language publications
relating to the Boer War of
1899-1902

Compiled by
R. G. HACKETT

Privately Printed
LONDON
1994

Printed for P.G. de Lotz military bookseller
Primrose Hill Bookshop
134 Regents Park Road, London NW1 8XL

1200 copies printed

Printed in Great Britain by Lund Humphries Ltd, Bradford.
Bound in Great Britain by Hartnolls Ltd, Bodmin.

ISBN   0   9520039   0   2

Illustrated War Special
(Editor/compiler not shown.)
The Office of The Penny
Illustrated Paper
London 1899–1900

Crimson grained cloth. Front and spine
blocked in gold.
417×307mm

28 issues of a newspaper published weekly
from Nov. 21, 1899 to May 30, 1900.
Numbers 1–26 comprise vol.1 and numbers
27 and 28, vol.2. Content is predominantly a
mixture of war news combined with
dramatic illustration. Common to each issue
is a cover and double spread in colour
together with letterpress sections headed
'The war of the week' and 'War whispers'.
Among illustrations reproduced is the work
of S. Begg, J. R. Stewart, N. E. Wigfull,
G. Montbard and Dudley Cleaver. Number
5 of December 20, 1899 contains three
colour illustrations of cats by Louis Wain.
From number 1–6 each issue is of 16 pages.
Thereafter each issue numbers 12 pages.

332+24pp. Illustrated throughout.
Cover of issue No.1 shown

Contents

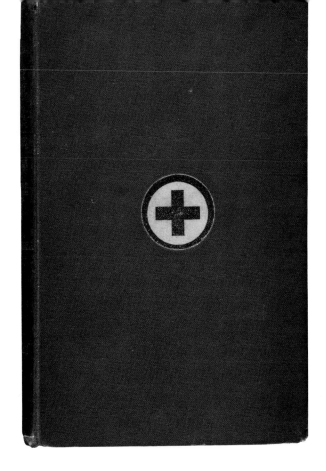

Author's note

The variance in spelling of place names follows a decision to adopt the form used in source material.

Orange Free State changed to Orange River Colony following annexation in May 1900. References to the western campaign, campaign in the west, western advance, etc. refer to the Kimberley and Mafeking relief operations and manoeuvres about the western borders of the Transvaal and Orange Free State.

The term northern advance is used in reference to Lord Roberts' march from Bloemfontein to Pretoria. General Buller's advance from Natal is termed the eastern advance.

On Active Service With The S.J.A.B. South African War, 1899–1902. A Diary Of Life And Events In The War Hospitals At Wynberg, Nourse Deep, Johannesburg, And Other Places, By The Late W. S. Inder, Orderly And 2nd Class Supernumerary Officer, Kendal Division, No.4 District, St. John Ambulance Brigade, Attached To The Royal Army Medical Corps.
W. S. *Inder*
Atkinson and Pollitt, printers
Kendal 1903

Dark green cloth. Front blocked in blind with paper onlay printed red laid down. Spine blocked in gold.
220×139mm *(Illustrated)*

Variant binding
Dark green cloth. Front and spine blocked in gold.
218×140mm

A campaign diary from November 1899 to December 1901 relating the author's experiences in the Royal Army Medical Corps and the Imperial Military Railways. Inder, a member of the St. John Ambulance Brigade, was employed at military hospitals near Cape Town and at Johannesburg. He describes fully the routine at the establishments and comments briefly on the prevailing war situation. In June 1901 he resigned the hospital service to join the staff of the Imperial Military Railways. He was engaged at Johannesburg but later moved to Bloemfontein. In the course of his duties in the Orange River Colony he was taken ill and died at Bloemfontein in January 1902. An active service roll of the Kendal Division S.J.A.B. is appended.

ix+318+iii pp. Illustrated.

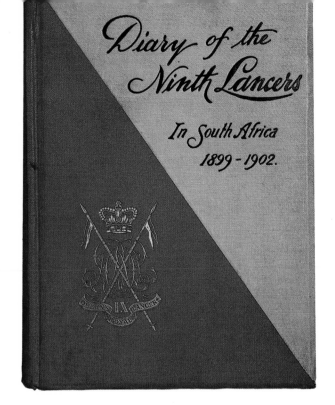

Acknowledgements

From among the many individuals who have kindly assisted in the preparation of this volume I wish to thank Mr P.E.Westra, Director of the South African Library Cape Town, for permission to quote from *A South African Bibliography To The Year 1925*. I have referred to the work, together with Mendelssohn's *South African Bibliography* in the absence of original material.

Thanks are also due to Miss T.A.Barringer of the Royal Commonwealth Society Library London, Dr. L.Washington of the National Army Museum London, and the Director of the National Library of Australia, all of whom supplied lists of Boer War holdings.

Mr M.M.Chapman of the Ministry of Defence Library London, compiled the list of War Office printings and Anna Hackett arranged the catalogue of HMSO publications. Both contributions are gratefully acknowledged.

Thanks are due to Kenneth Griffith for use of his extensive library and to Dr.Paul Dunn for supplying numerous volumes for inspection and patiently responding to many queries. In particular I wish to thank Neville Constantine who has generously made available his fine collection and, in other ways, contributed significantly to this publication.

Finally I would like to thank Peter de Lotz, publisher. It is largely due to his enthusiasm and support this once moribund project has been completed.

Diary Of The 9th (Q.R.) Lancers During
The South African Campaign, 1899 To 1902
*Bt.-Lieut.-Colonel F. F. Colvin and
Captain E. R. Gordon*
Cecil Roy
(London) 1904

Red and yellow cloth over bevelled boards.
Front blocked in black, gold, white and
blue. Spine blocked in gold.
204×151mm

A record of two and a half years service in
South Africa compiled from officers diaries
and other sources. The regiment joined
Lord Methuen's force in the advance to
Kimberley taking part in various
engagements to mid December 1899,
including Belmont, Modder River, and
Magersfontein. In the Orange Free State
from Feb.–May 1900 the 9th engaged in
operations near Paardeberg, at Poplar
Grove and Thaba' Nchu. In Transvaal, in
June 1900, they took part in the action at
Diamond Hill. Thereafter, to the end of the
campaign, the regiment was employed at
various times in western Transvaal, Orange
River Colony and Cape Colony. The
volume includes lists of honours,
promotions and casualties (officers and
other ranks). A large folding route map
showing battlegrounds is enclosed
separately.

xv+304pp. Map and illustrations.

for Angela who did much of the work

Introduction

A few lines concerning the origin of this volume seem appropriate. I began collecting Boer War books in the early Sixties after reading Rayne Kruger's fascinating account of the war *Good-Bye Dolly Gray*. My first purchase was an odd volume of *With The Flag To Pretoria*, then a bright copy of *Celebrities of The Army*, followed by De Wet's *Three Years War*. Thereafter the sequence of acquisitions is confused as it was prior to the time I kept records. Within a relatively short period, perhaps eighteen months, I had assembled over a hundred titles and considered progress excellent. Most of the books were bought from junk shops, market stalls or secondhand bookshops, which flourished in those days. Within half a mile of my north London home were four bookshops that I visited frequently. Cost was seldom a problem as most items were purchased for a few shillings. A volume priced over two Pounds was considered expensive. Two bargains of that time were a set of Amery's *Times History Of The War* bought for six Pounds ten shillings and a fine set of Creswicke's *South Africa And The Transvaal War*, purchased at four Pounds.

Early in my book buying forays I became aware of Kenneth Griffith. The actor was renowned for his numerous screen rôles but it appeared he was better known to dealers as a book collector. Booksellers all over London were pleased to inform you that he was a favoured customer and a similar response was met from traders at Portobello Road and other London markets. I met him in 1967 when he made a film on the siege of Ladysmith for BBC Television. Being unable to receive the broadcast I telephoned Griffith and asked if I might view the programme at the studios. The visit was arranged and that night I enjoyed a private viewing of 'Soldiers of the Widow', a personal view of the Ladysmith siege. The actor was elsewhere being entertained by BBC executives so we had the briefest of meetings, however he invited me to his home for tea the following day.

I arrived at the appointed hour expecting a discussion on the previous night's programme and to engage in chit chat about collecting. On entering the house I was surrounded by books, hundreds of books, all relating to the war. A quick calculation indicated some five or six hundred volumes. I was quite astounded by the display, surprised that the campaign should generate such a vast body of literature. Most of the titles were unknown to me and I spent an uncomfortable couple of hours trying to avoid direct reference to collecting lest I display my ignorance. Griffith allowed inspection of the books, identifying many important works and items of particular interest. For the first time I handled a set of *The Official History Of The War*, *The Commission Of Inquiry* volumes and a copy of Churchill's *London To Ladysmith Via Pretoria*. On subsequent visits, when the family had moved to a large house in north London and the collection was spread over the upper floor, I had better opportunity to view the books and found in excess of eight hundred titles in his library. In addition the collection included significant numbers of paintings, press illustrations, printed ephemera, artefacts and perhaps the

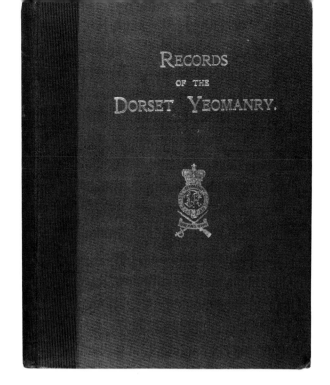

Records Of The Dorset Imperial Yeomanry, 1894–1905.
Edited by
Captain M. F. Gage
F. Bennett
Sherborne 1906

Dark blue and magenta cloth. Front and spine blocked in silver.
225×175mm

A second volume of records of the Dorset Imperial Yeomanry updating an earlier history of the regiment by Col. C. W. Thompson. The volume is arranged in three parts. The first is a regimental record from 1894 to August 1905. The second, (p.75–148) concerns the Dorset Yeomanry in South Africa and part three relates to regimental uniforms and organization of troops and squadrons from 1794 to 1905. The 26th (Dorset) Co., I.Y. arrived at the Cape in March 1900. During an active campaign lasting 16 months the Company served under various commanders in the Orange Free State and Transvaal. In April the Dorsets engaged in operations south of Bloemfontein under Generals Rundle and Brabizon. They were part of the force employed in the relief of Wepener and, for a short period, part of the garrison at Thabanchu. In May the Company entrained for Kroonstad to join Lord Roberts' army in the northern advance. The force entered Pretoria on June 5th. The Dorset I.Y. were present at the battle of Diamond Hill from 11–14 June but were not engaged. At this time Yeomanry units were reorganized and hereafter the Dorsets often served in composite squadrons. From July 1900 to May 1901 the Company took part in various treks in the Transvaal under Generals Mahon, Clements, Cunningham and other commanders. On 13th December 1900 the Dorsets were part of Clements' force attacked at Nooitgedacht by General Delarey. The British sustained severe casualties in the engagement. The Company operated in western Transvaal until recalled from active service in May 1901. Appendices include notes on equipment, a roll of the yeomanry who served in South Africa and a casualty list.

v+iv+265pp. Map and illustrations, including colour plates of uniforms.

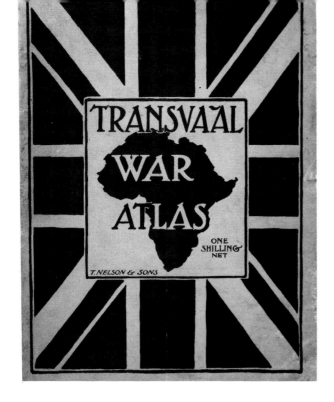

Transvaal War Atlas
(Author/editor not shown.)
T. Nelson & Sons
np./nd. (London c.1900)

White card cover. Front and back printed
red and blue.
281×220mm

An atlas published at the start of the war,
possibly printed in late 1899. Most of the
maps are of Africa including eight sectional
maps of South Africa prepared from the
latest surveys. The publishers state that the
atlas will be of advantage to all following
the present war and to further
understanding of recent events. The volume
includes an informative letterpress on 'The
Boers and Boerland' together with notes on
the South African Republic and the Orange
Free State.

40pp. (including cover). With some
illustrations.
Title from cover.

greatest assemblage of South African War correspondence
in private ownership.

Ken Griffith has described his library as an ancillary
development in support of the postal history archive. It is
nevertheless a resource of considerable importance and a
benchmark for collectors.

Meeting Ken Griffith transformed my attitude to collecting.
Thenceforward I curtailed the haphazard wanderings about
London, spent more time gleaning information about books
and sought the help of major bookdealers, an option
previously avoided on consideration of expense. I began
with Maggs Bros. whom, I was advised, were specialists in
military history. It was a pivotal decision. At the firm's
premises at Berkeley Square I was introduced to Ken
Wynn, a courteous man whose knowledge of military
literature appeared boundless. At the outset he suggested
development of a collection around a core of significant
works relative to major aspects of the campaign. Having
determined the requirement he proceeded to supply the
books. Within three years I had acquired many of the
standard works including various histories, regimental
records and personal accounts, together with manuscript
material and original photographs. My collection had grown
substantially to over four hundred titles and records show
that over half the books were supplied by Maggs Bros. Ken
Wynn left the company in the early Seventies to be
succeeded by Julian Browning with whom I continued
dealings but on a much reduced scale.

Other prominent suppliers of the period were Messrs. Chas.
J. Sawyer Ltd. and Francis Edwards. Sawyer's occupied
imposing premises at Grafton Street where, from a
comfortable office on an upper floor, Richard Sawyer
presided over one of the finest stocks of Africana in
London, much of it related to travel. Generally there were
few Boer War volumes on the shelves but those offered for
sale were always in exceptional condition, or in some
manner special copies. Sawyer's produced the most
interesting Boer War catalogues of the period. Few books
appeared in these lists but they contained the best of
original illustration, paintings, manuscript and printed
documents together with general memorabilia. Two
purchases I recall with particular pleasure. The first was a
group of War Office printings that included the uncommon
Military Notes On The Dutch Republics Of South Africa and
the other, a modern edition of Mendelssohn's *South African
Bibliography*. I reprinted 'Military Notes' in an edition of
120 copies in 1983 and sold most copies. The Mendelssohn
volumes have simply been indispensable from the day
purchased.

Francis Edwards was another bookshop universally
recommended. The firm was then based at Marylebone
High Street where the military book section was overseen
by Tony Gilbert. My acquisitions here were relatively
meagre but over the years I bought some uncommon
material from both the military and travel departments.
Other important sources of supply were the numerous
independent dealers operating postal businesses. For many
years I acquired books from foreign dealers while
maintaining profitable contacts locally. Among British
suppliers were Peter de Lotz and Victor Sutcliffe, both

occasionally invite buyers to his bookrooms. On my first visit I was surprised to find a stock to rival that of Maggs Bros, with an entire section devoted to the The South African War. I bought a number of volumes on that occasion and have remained a customer ever since. Victor Sutcliffe I first encountered in the Seventies, he issued regular catalogues with an emphasis on Victorian campaigns. India was his primary interest together with regimental history but he maintained a regular output of South African material. He supplied many rare items over the years some of which are illustrated herein.

The hectic programme of acquisitions begun in 1968 could not be sustained on my income as an illustrator and the decision was made to finance the operation by bookselling. In 1969 I secured a bank loan, registered the name 'Boer War Books' and embarked on my first catalogue, a typewritten list reproduced in 75 copies. The content was a mixture of Boer War and miscellaneous works relating to Southern Africa, a combination maintained to the present time.

Business was brisk from the outset, most of it originating in South Africa. Between 1969 and 1989 some two dozen catalogues and shortlists were issued. The earlier lists were numbered and the rest named after Boer commanders. From the latter group the most successful was BOTHA, issued in the mid Eighties. Of the 238 items listed over eighty percent was sold, a success rate never since attained. Perusal of the catalogue now reveals an unusual mix of books, printed ephemera, pictorial material and general memorabilia. Amongst significant items were a large fabric wallhanging depicting an armoured train and observation balloon, and a typescript document signed by Lord Roberts, subsequently published by the Military Government as Proclamation No.1. Printed books included a good selection of regimental history, a set of Howe's *Imperial Yeomanry Hospitals*, a bound volume of *The Mafeking Mail Siege Slips* and a presentation copy of Hobhouse's *The Brunt Of The War And Where It Fell*. Today it would be difficult to compile catalogues of similar content on a regular basis.

The collection expanded until the late Seventies during which time I made cursory attempts at gathering bibliographic information. *Mendelssohn* was my mainstay together with the booklist from *The Times History* and Griffin's bibliography from *Selected Translations Pertaining To The Boer War*. Later I acquired a copy of *White's Regimental Bibliography* and added a substantial list of titles extracted from dealer's catalogues, a valuable source of information. Simultaneously I assembled a photographic record of covers and title pages with the intention of producing an illustrated register. Progress was slow until matters came to a head in 1975 when I simply ran out of funds sufficient to maintain the collection and continue dealing. The collection was offered for sale and following protracted negotiations, was purchased by Bill Wright in partnership with Henry Lloyd, both military booksellers. Over eight hundred volumes were sold including some manuscript documents and original photographs. On removal of the books to London I retained a photographic record and reams of disjointed notes most of which have since been amended. Messrs. Wright and Lloyd

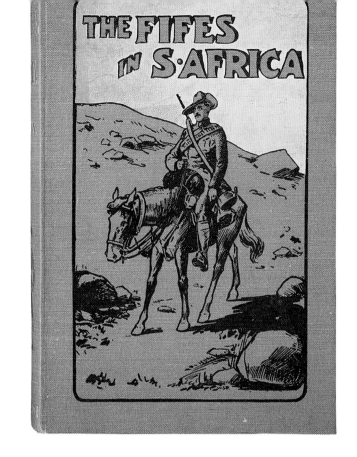

The Fifes In South Africa Being A History Of The Fife And Forfar Yeomanry In The South African War, 1900–1901 By 9176 I.Y.
(J. P. Sturrock)
A. Westwood & Son
Cupar-Fife 1903

Light brown cloth. Front blocked in gold and black. Spine blocked in gold.
225×148mm

A record of the 20th Company Imperial Yeomanry in South Africa from April 1900 to June 1901. The Fifes served under various commanders including Generals Hunter, Hutton, Clements and Cunningham. They engaged in drives against De Wet and Delarey and took part in numerous farm clearing operations in the Transvaal and Orange River Colony. In December 1900 the 20th Co. was part of Clement's force attacked at Nooitgedacht. The British sustained heavy casualties and the Fife yeomanry reduced to half strength. The remnant of the Company joined General Cunningham's force to the end of January 1901 and was then attached to Col. Benson's column. In active operations about south western Transvaal the corps harassed guerilla forces, cleared farms and captured numbers of the enemy. Of all the commanders under whom the Fifes served Benson was considered the best. In April 1901 the Fifes regrouped. A new contingent joined at Bloemfontein bringing them up to full strength. The Company, now about 150 strong, joined Col. Pilcher's column operating in Orange River Colony. In late May 1901 the members of the original 20th Co. returned home. The volume contains a nominal roll and campaign itinerary.

xii+197pp. Folding map and illustrations.

History Of The 1st Batt. Sherwood
Foresters (Notts. and Derby Regt.) In The
Boer War, 1899–1902.
Capt. C. J. L. Gilson
Swann Sonnenschein & Co., Ltd.
London nd. (1908)

Red cloth. Front and spine blocked in gold.
221×142mm

A complete record of the 1st Batt. in South
Africa, updating an earlier record published
in Hong Kong in 1904. The regiment took
part in Lord Roberts' march through the
Orange Free State and, at various times
thereafter, served in southern and western
Transvaal. Chapters relate to actions at
Vlakfontein and Moedwil where the
conduct of the 1st Batt. was especially
distinguished. A service record of nos.1 and
2 companies Derbyshire Mounted Infantry
is included. Appendices to the volume
include a casualty list, embarkation lists and
a list of 'mentions and awards'.

xviii+v+236pp. Two folding maps in
separate pocket, various plans and
photographic plates.

the best. Their list of 1978 entitled *The Great Boer War*
contained 734 items and is, I believe, the most
comprehensive catalogue of South African War books
issued during the last quarter century. It is still used by
some dealers as a basic reference. I tried to recover certain
items when the list was circulated, in particular the
typescript of Col. Godley's Mafeking letters and some rare
pamphlets, but the material was previously sold.

From the late Seventies I have concentrated on bookselling
contributing to collections in Britain and abroad. Mindful of
my early experience at Maggs Bros. my general advice to
new collectors is to obtain professional help at the outset.
Many of the dealers who assisted me in the past continue in
business. Sutcliffe, de Lotz, Gilbert and Browning all
operate from London, as do Maggs Bros. and Francis
Edwards. Richard Sawyer is now based in Kent. In addition
a host of new dealers have appeared on the scene.
Collectors applying to Derek Hayles Military Books of
Maidenhead will receive a list of secondhand bookshops and
booksellers in Britain specialising in military history. Other
suppliers will be found in trade directories such as *Cole's
Register of British Bookdealers* and *Sheppard's Book
Dealers In The British Isles*. Foreign sources should likewise
be considered. A considerable output of Boer War material
emanates from America, Canada, Australia and New
Zealand. In South Africa, Clarke's Bookshop of Cape
Town, is a major supplier. For over a decade the firm has
issued Africana catalogues incorporating South African War
material of exceptional rarity.

The pictorial section of this volume is derived from a full
range of contemporary publications. I am fascinated by
period bindings, many of which are fine examples of design.
The elegance of *A Military History Of Perthshire* (p.99) or
The Work Of The Ninth Division (p.43) is in stark contrast
to the crude typography of *Letters From South Africa
1900–1901* (p.33) and *69th Battery R.F.A.* (p.59), yet all are
typical of the era. Other notable examples are *Souvenir Of
The Siege Of Mafeking* (p.97) and *On The Heels Of De Wet*
(p.91) both covers strongly evocative of the war years. The
illustrations are a personal selection intentionally striking a
balance between the rare and the commonplace. All the
covers depicted are from private collections and the finest
copies that I could find.

Compiling this record has rekindled much of the excitement
I experienced as a young collector. Should the reader be
similarly moved the exercise will have been worthwhile.

R. G. Hackett / York 1994

The Times History

of

The War in South Africa

1899–1900

Edited by L. S. Amery

Fellow of All Souls

With many Photogravure and other Portraits, Maps, and Battle Plans

Vol. I.

LONDON

Sampson Low, Marston and Company, Ltd,

St. Dunstan's House

1900

The Times History Of The War In South
Africa 1899–1902.
*L. S. Amery (Editor) (Vols. IV & V edited
by Basil Williams)*
Sampson Low, Marston and Company
Limited
London 1900–1909

Bright red cloth. Front and back blocked in
blind. Spine blocked in blind and gold.
232×154mm

A comprehensive history of the war in seven
volumes published in the years 1900–1909.
A complete account of military operations
in South Africa from 1899–1902 together
with chapters on the political and historical
background to the conflict and the work of
reconstruction following hostilities. Volume
VII (Index and Appendices) contains much
useful information including a chronological
table of events from 1899–1909, regimental
casualties with period of service of each
regiment and engagements at which present,
official table of casualties with summary and
an extensive bibliography. An important
and well produced work. Possibly the
foremost general reference pertaining to the
second Boer War.

Vol.I. (1900) xxiv+392pp. Pocket map and
various plates.
Vol.II. (1902) xviii+467pp. Various maps
and plates.
Vol.III. (1905) xviii+597pp. Various maps
and plates.
Vol.IV. (1906) xviii+597pp. Pocket maps,
various other maps, plans and plates.
Vol.V. (1907) xxviii+614pp. Pocket maps,
various other maps, plans and plates.
Vol.VI. (1909) xvi+622pp. Various plates.
Vol.VII. (1909) vii+209pp.
Title page shown

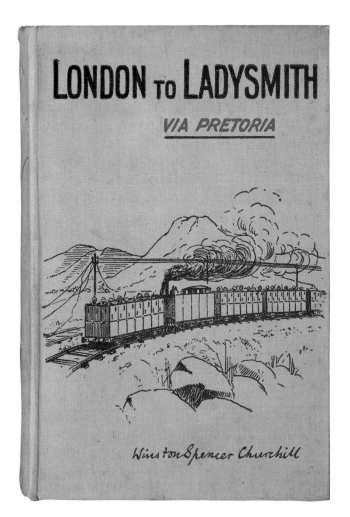

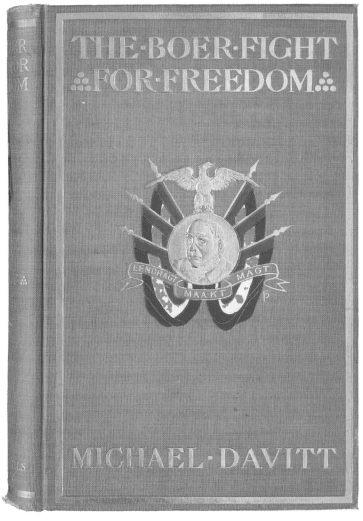

London To Ladysmith Via Pretoria
Winston Spencer Churchill
Longmans, Green and Co.
London 1900

Khaki cloth. Front blocked in black and red. Spine blocked in red and gold.
197×130mm

A correspondent's experiences in South Africa during the first five months of war described in a series of letters addressed to the *Morning Post* newspaper from Oct. 1899 to March 1900. The author recounts his capture near Estcourt, his period of imprisonment at Pretoria and subsequent escape to Delagoa Bay. Thereafter the correspondence concerns the campaign in Natal and operations for the relief of Ladysmith. The narrative is continued in a second volume entitled *Ian Hamilton's March** being letters to the same newspaper from March to June 1900. The latter volume relates to the campaign in the Orange Free State and the advance from Bloemfontein to Pretoria (*Not illustrated)

xiv+498pp. Various maps and plans, some folding.

The Boer Fight For Freedom
Michael Davitt
Funk & Wagnalls Company
New York and London 1902

Orange cloth. Front and spine blocked in gold, green, red, white and blue.
227×150mm *(Illustrated)*

Variant binding
Orange cloth. Front blocked in green and gold. Spine blocked in gold.
226×152mm

The author embarked on a fact finding tour of South Africa late in 1899. He travelled extensively through the Boer Republics and northern Natal gauging public opinion in regard to the crisis. He met many republican leaders and was officially assisted in his journey through Boer lines. The volume affords a full account of military operations to the end of May 1900 when the author returned home. Throughout the narrative Boer conduct is acclaimed and Britain reviled for prosecuting an unjust war. Concluding chapters comprise a diary of the campaign from June 1900 to March 1902.

xii+603pp. Folding map and numerous illustrations.

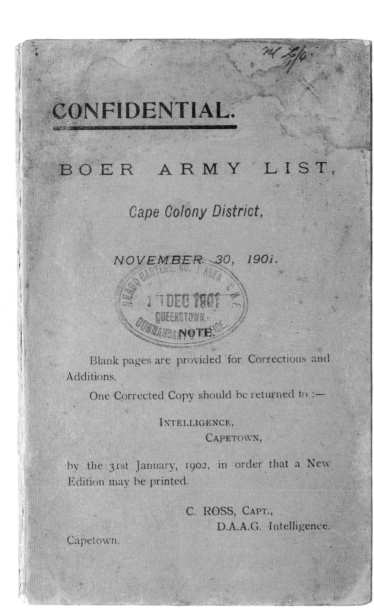

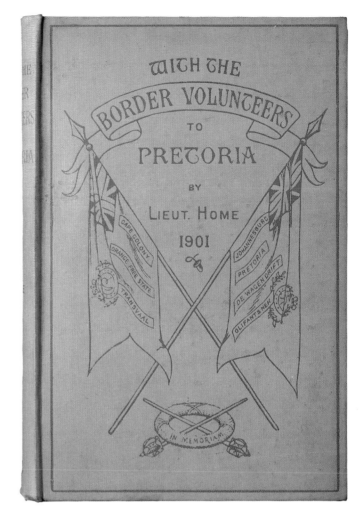

Confidential. Boer Army List, Cape Colony
District, November 30, 1901.
Intelligence Dept. (Publisher?)
Capetown 1901

Light green card cover. Black letterpress to
front only.
161×103mm

An index of Boer Commandos,
Commandants, Field Cornets and other
subordinates. With alphabetical index of
names and descriptions of commandants
and subordinates. The volume contains
blank pages throughout for corrections and
additions.

37 numbered rectos (with 2pp
unnumbered).

With The Border Volunteers To Pretoria
Lieutenant William Home
W. & J. Kennedy
Hawick 1901

Ochre cloth. Front and spine blocked in
red.
189×126mm

Record of a volunteer in the First Service
Company of the Kings Own Scottish
Borderers. The unit arrived at the Cape in
March 1900 and, in May, entrained for the
Orange Free State to join Lord Roberts'
force in the advance to Pretoria. For
approximately five months the volunteers
served in the Transvaal. Under General
Hamilton they took part in drives against
Boer commandos led by Botha and De Wet.
At other times they were employed in
guarding rail lines from Belfast to Pretoria.
The record extends from March to
November 1900. A company roll is included
and a list of camping grounds.

viii+203pp. Folding map and two plates.

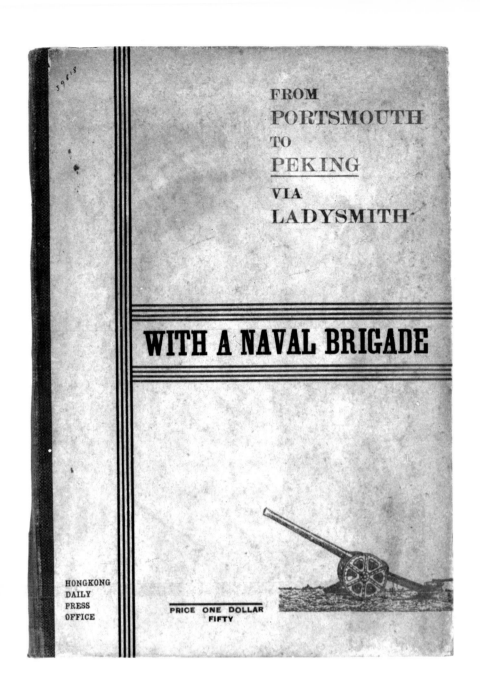

FROM
PORTSMOUTH
TO
PEKING
VIA
LADYSMITH

WITH A NAVAL BRIGADE

HONGKONG
DAILY
PRESS
OFFICE

PRICE ONE DOLLAR
FIFTY

From Portsmouth To Peking Via Ladysmith
With A Naval Brigade.
George Crowe
'Hongkong Daily Press' Office
Hongkong 1901

Grey/green paper covered boards backed in
dark blue cloth. Front printed navy, red and
ochre. Back printed navy and red.
233×167mm

Narrative of events connected with H.M.S.
Terrible at the Cape and China stations.
Part 1 relates to the Naval Brigade in the
Ladysmith relief operations.
(For a complete account see Crowe – *The
Commission of H.M.S. Terrible 1898–1902.*)

viii+151pp. With two maps.

The 'Mexican' Mercury No.1 Vol.1 Week
Ending March X 1900. Kharki Edition.
A Quick & Quizical Racy Record And
Pleasant Probe Of Our Daily Doings.
*Gordon Daniell / Dicky Church /
E. E. Brandon and Owen Harris*
(Editors and Publishers)
Printed on the High Seas crossing the Line
1900

Dull grey/green limp card cover printed
black to front and back.
290×185mm

A magazine produced on board the S.S.
'Mexican' transporting troops to South
Africa, among them Loch's Contingent
(Loch's Horse). The compilation includes
verse, articles, a review of the war, an
account of the raising of Loch's Horse,
notes and news. Much is written in
humorous vein and various illustrations and
caricatures are reproduced.

32pp (including cover).

No 1 Vol 1 Week ending March ? 1900

KHAKI EDITION

THE MEXICAN MERCURY

A Quick & Quizical
Racy Record And
Pleasant Probe
of our
Daily Doings

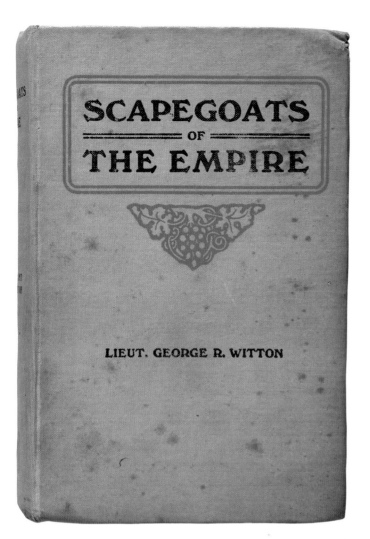

Scapegoats Of The Empire
The Story Of The Bushveldt Carbineers.
Lieutenant George R. Witton
D. W. Paterson Co.
Melbourne 1907

Fawn cloth. Front and spine blocked in
black and red.
190×126mm

An account of the campaign in northern
Transvaal in the latter part of 1901 and of
events leading to trial by courts-martial of
Australian officers involved in the killing of
Boer prisoners. A report from Lord
Kitchener, C.I.C. South Africa, to the
Governor-General of Australia stated that
Lieutenants Morant, Handcock and Witton
of the Bushveldt Carbineers were charged
with twenty separate murders including that
of a German missionary. From the evidence
it appeared that Morant was the originator
of the crimes which were carried out in a
cold-blooded manner. The officers were
convicted after most exhaustive trial and
sentenced to death. In the case of Lieut.
Witton the sentence was commuted to penal
servitude for life. Morant and Handcock
were executed on 27 Feb. 1902. Witton was
transported to England where he served less
than three years imprisonment prior to
release in August 1904.

x+240pp. Illustrated.

The Imperial Yeomanry Hospitals In South
Africa 1900–1902.
Edited by
The Countess Howe
Arthur L. Humphreys
London 1902

Royal blue cloth backed in maroon
buckram. Front blocked in yellow and gold.
Spine blocked in gold, red and white
(Three vols.)
283×218mm *(Illustrated)*

Variant bindings
Similar to above. (Three vols. bound in
one.)
283×218mm

Maroon cloth. Front blocked in red and
white. (Three vols. bound in one.)
283×218mm

A record of the inauguration and working of
the Imperial Yeomanry Hospitals in South
Africa.
Three volumes.
Vol.1. Organisation and administration.
viii+194pp.
Vol.2. With the Imperial Yeomanry Field
Hospital and Bearer Company. xv+266pp.
Vol.3. Medical and Surgical Reports.
xi+274pp.
Illustrated throughout with folding plans,
photographs and maps.

The Leaguer of Ladysmith
Captain C. M. Dixon
Eyre and Spottiswoode
London nd. (c.1900)

Illustrated paper covered boards backed in
green cloth. Front printed in full colour,
back printed brown.
238×304mm

Humorous sketches in colour by Capt.
Dixon of the 16th. Lancers, A.D.C. to Gen.
Sir George White. A souvenir of the siege
with brief text preceding each illustration.

39pp. (Unnumbered) Illustrated.

REPORT

OF

HIS MAJESTY'S COMMISSIONERS

APPOINTED TO INQUIRE INTO THE MILITARY

PREPARATIONS AND OTHER MATTERS CONNECTED

WITH THE

WAR IN SOUTH AFRICA.

Presented to both Houses of Parliament by Command of His Majesty.

LONDON:
PRINTED FOR HIS MAJESTY'S STATIONERY OFFICE,
BY WYMAN AND SONS, LIMITED, FETTER LANE, E.C.

And to be purchased, either directly or through any Bookseller, from
EYRE AND SPOTTISWOODE, EAST HARDING STREET, FLEET STREET, E.C., and
32, ABINGDON STREET, WESTMINSTER, S.W.; or
OLIVER AND BOYD, EDINBURGH; or
E. PONSONBY, 116, GRAFTON STREET, DUBLIN.

1903.

[Cd. 1789.] *Price 2s 7d.*

Report Of His Majesty's Commissioners
Appointed To Inquire Into The Military
Preparations And Other Matters Connected
With The War In South Africa. (Cd. 1789).
His Majesty's Stationery Office
London 1903

Blue paper cover. Black letterpress to front,
back and spine.
332×211mm

The report of the Elgin Commission
appointed to inquire into the military
preparations for the war in South Africa,
and into the supply of men, ammunition,
equipment and transport by sea and land in
connection with the campaign, and into the
military operations up to the occupation of
Pretoria. The Commission sat on 55 days to
take evidence and heard 114 witnesses
among whom were Gen. Sir Redvers Buller
and Field Marshal Earl Roberts, together
with many other senior officers, civil and
military. Numerous documents bearing
upon the proceedings are reproduced as

appendices. The volume is fully indexed.

viii+316pp.

The Report, together with three other
volumes, comprise the 'Royal Commission'
set. The volumes are – 'Minutes of Evidence
Taken Before The Royal Commission On
The War In South Africa' (Vols.1+2) and
'Appendices To The Minutes Of Evidence
Taken Before The Royal Commission,
Etc.'. See entries under H.M.S.O.
(Cd.1790.) (Cd.1791.) and (Cd.1792.).

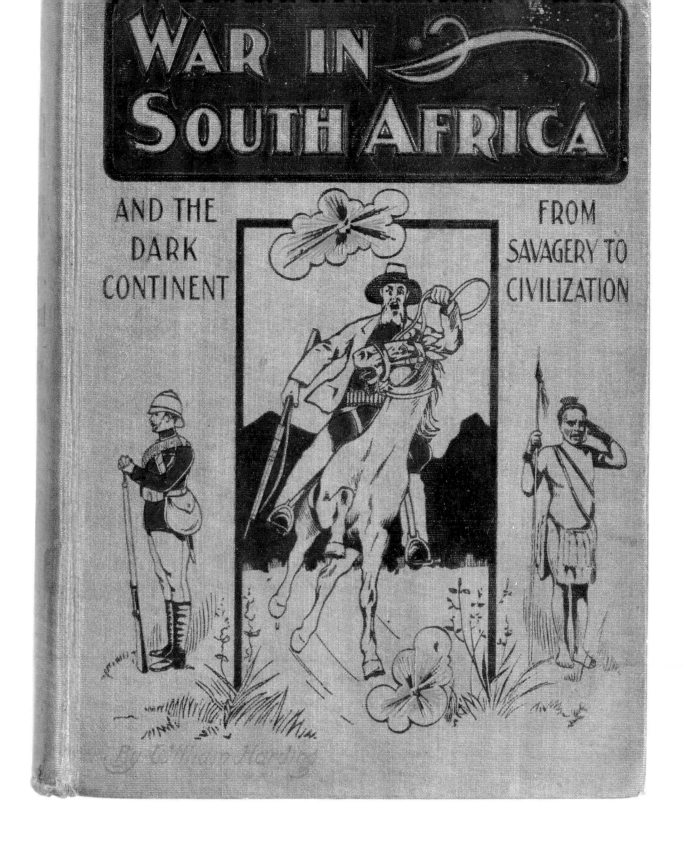

War In South Africa And The Dark
Continent From Savagery to Civilization
The Strange Story Of A Weird World From
The Earliest Ages To The Present,
Including The War With The Boers
Embracing The Explorations And
Settlements, Wars And Conquests, Peoples
And Governments, Resources And
Produces, Of This The Least Known, Yet
By Nature Endowed As The Richest And
Most Wonderful Of Continents, And
A Detailed History Of The Causes And
Events Of The British-Boer War.
William Harding
Butler & Alger
New Haven, Conn. nd. (c.1900)

Grey cloth. Front and spine blocked in gold,
black and red.
243×178mm

The story of South Africa and a review of
the political situation leading to war, with
chapters on other African countries. The
narrative of the war is brought down to July
1900.

534pp. With numerous illustrations.

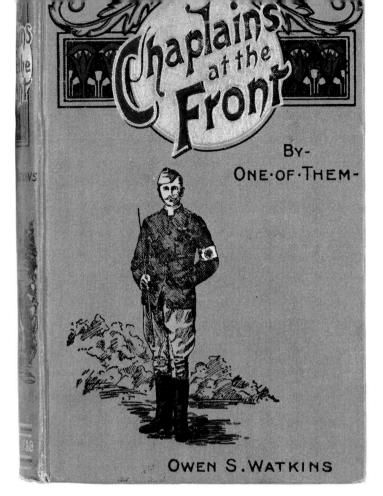

Owen Spencer Watkins
S. W. Partridge & Co.
London 1902

Dull blue cloth. Front blocked in red, black, gold, dark brown, light brown, ochre and white. Spine blocked in red, black, gold, light and dark brown.
189×124mm *(Illustrated)*

Variant binding
Red and brown cloth bindings recorded. Similar design and size to copy shown.

A Wesleyan chaplain's experiences at Ladysmith during the siege and on the march with Gen. Buller's army in Natal and south eastern Transvaal. The record includes accounts of the battles at Lombards Kop in October 1899 and Allemans Nek in June 1900. The narrative ends with the break up of the Natal Field Force in October 1900.

334pp. Sketch maps and various illustrations.

In The Web Of A War
H. F. Prevost Battersby
Methuen & Company
London 1900

Red cloth. Line border blocked in blind to upper and lower covers. Front and spine blocked in gold.
196×130mm

An account of the advance to Bloemfontein and Pretoria by a correspondent of the *Morning Post*. The narrative is followed by chapters on 'The remaking of an army'. Appendices include – The march of the 6th Division from Modder River to Bloemfontein, statistics in reference to killed and wounded, notes on climate, etc.

xii+297pp. Portrait and maps.

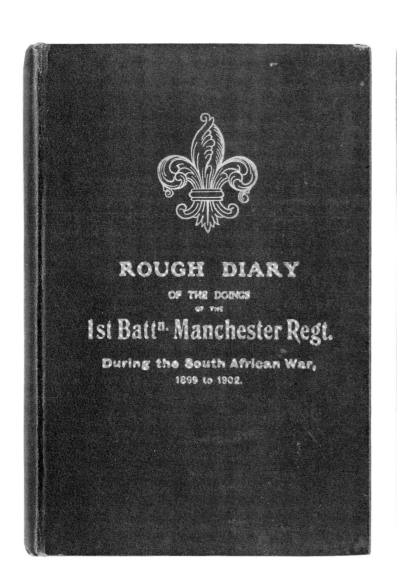

ROUGH DIARY

OF THE DOINGS

OF THE

1st Batt^{n.} Manchester Regt.

During the South African War,
1899 to 1902.

THE GHASTLY BLUNDERS

OF THE WAR.

A Guide to the Report of the
Royal Commission on the South African War,
1899-1900.

"If anybody has to be hung, it is the Secretary of State
for War."—Evidence of Lord Lansdowne.

LONDON:
"DAILY MAIL" OFFICES, CARMELITE STREET, E.C.

PRICE THREEPENCE.

Rough Diary Of The Doings Of The 1st
Battn. Manchester Regt. During The South
African War, 1899 To 1902.
Compiled by
Major A. W. Marden and Capt. & Adjt.
W. P. E. Newbigging
John Heywood
Manchester nd. (c.1903)

Dark green cloth. Front blocked in red and
gold. Spine blocked in red
188×126mm *(Illustrated)*

Variant binding
Dark brown cloth. Front blocked in gold
and black.
188×126mm

The Battalion was present at the battle of
Elandslaagte on Oct. 21. At the investment
of Ladysmith the Manchesters were
stationed on Caesar's Camp where they
experienced heavy fighting on November 11
and again on Jan. 6 (1900). In the latter
engagement losses were severe. Following
the relief of Ladysmith the Battalion formed
part of General Buller's force in the
advance on Lydenburg. From late 1900 to
the close of the campaign the unit served
under various commanders in eastern
Transvaal. A casualty list is included for
each action at which the Battalion was
present.

151pp. Folding maps.

The Ghastly Blunders Of The War.
A Guide To The Report Of The Royal
Commission On The South African War,
1899–1900.
'Daily Mail' Offices (Publishers)
London nd. (c.1903)

Blue paper cover. Black letterpress to
front only.
268×186mm

A catalogue of errors political and military
occasioned by the British in South Africa.
The volume is published as a guide to the
Report issued by His Majesty's
Commissioners appointed to inquire into
the military preparations and other matters
connected with the war in South Africa.
Contents include a list of chief witnesses
examined and a diary of the principal events
connected with South Africa from the date
of the Bloemfontein Conference to the
occupation of Pretoria.

48pp.

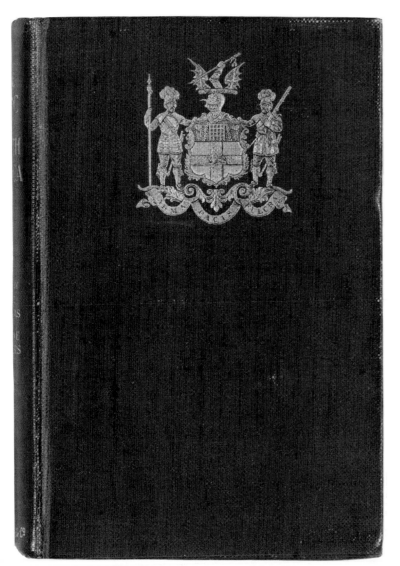

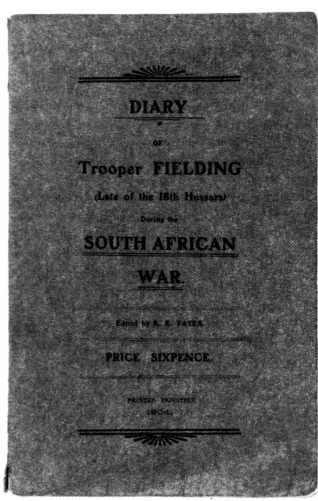

The H.A.C. In South Africa
A Record Of The Services Rendered In
The South African War By Members Of
The Honourable Artillery Company.
Edited by
Basil Williams and Erskine Childers
Smith, Elder & Co.
London 1903

Black buckram. Front and spine blocked
in gold.
199×130mm

A record of the 193 members of the
Honourable Artillery Company who served
in South Africa with the City Imperial
Volunteers, the Imperial Yeomanry and
various other corps. Of the H.A.C.
members incorporated in the C.I.V., most
served in the Field Battery and various
chapters relate to its formation and war
service. The volume contains a list of all
H.A.C. members in South Africa showing
rank and branch of service.

x+234pp. With a folding map.

Diary Of Trooper Fielding (Late Of The
18th Hussars) During The South African
War.
R. E. Yates (Edited by)
Printed privately
'Gazette' Co. Ltd.
Darwen 1904

Blue/Grey limp card cover, printed dark
blue to front only.
185×120mm

A diary of the campaign in Natal and later
operations in eastern Transvaal. The 18th
took part in the Talana Hill engagement
before the retirement on Ladysmith where
they remained throughout the siege. In the
subsequent eastern advance they joined
General Buller's force on the march to
Lydenburg. From late 1900 to cessation of
hostilities the regiment was chiefly
employed in eastern Transvaal.

120pp.

THE GRAPHIC
HISTORY OF THE SOUTH AFRICAN WAR

A COMPLETE NARRATIVE OF THE CAMPAIGN

CONTAINING ABOUT 300 ILLUSTRATIONS

Together with Special Chapters by the following Authorities:—
THE SIEGE OF LADYSMITH. By Lieutenant M. F. McTaggart, 5th Lancers.
THE SIEGE OF KIMBERLEY. By Mr. G. M. C. Luard.
THE SIEGE OF MAFEKING. By Major F. D. Baillie.
WITH ROBERTS TO BLOEMFONTEIN. By Mr. G. D. Giles.
THE VOLUNTEERS IN THE CAMPAIGN. By Colonel Sir Howard Vincent.
THE CARE OF THE WOUNDED IN THE FIELD. By Sir William MacCormac.

PRICE FIVE SHILLINGS.
THE GRAPHIC, 190, STRAND.
SIMPKIN, MARSHALL, HAMILTON, KENT & Co., Limited.

The Graphic History Of The South African War 1899–1900 Complete Narrative Of The Campaign By Wentworth Huyshe With Special Chapters
The Siege of Ladysmith. By Lieut. M. F. McTaggart, 5th Lancers, who took part in the Defence.
The Siege Of Kimberley. By G. M. C. Luard, Reuter's Correspondent during the Investment.
The Siege Of Mafeking. By Major F. D. Baillie, Correspondent of the 'Morning Post' during the investment.

With Roberts To Bloemfontein. By G. D. Giles, Special Artist-Correspondent of 'The Graphic'.
The Volunteers In The Campaign. By Colonel Sir Howard Vincent, K.C.M.G., C.B., M.P.
The Care Of The Wounded In The Field. By Sir William MacCormac, Bart., K.C.V.O., P.R.C.S.
Illustrated By Sketches And Photographs From W. T. Maud, C. E. Fripp, G. D. Giles, And R. Thiele, Special Artists Of 'The Graphic' And From Officers At The Front.
Wentworth Huyshe (and others)
The Graphic Office
London 1900

Blue paper covered boards backed in white buckram. Illustrated paper onlay to front board. Black letterpress to front only. 417×308mm

The 'Chronicle of the War' by Huyshe is brought down to Oct. 1900. In addition to the 'special chapters' contents include a 'Diary of the chief events of the war' to mid Oct. 1900. Approximately 300 illustrations are reproduced.

108pp. Illustrated throughout.

Shurey's Pictorial History Of The War
(Shurey's Pictorial Budget)
(Printer/publisher not shown.)
(London) 1900

Pictorial wraps, approx. 265×180mm.
This set bound in contemporary half calf
and dark green pebble grain cloth. Black
label to spine blocked in gold.
270×182mm

An illustrated record of the war published
in 12 parts, similar to *Black And White
Budget*. Following issue 12 the title was
incorporated with *Shurey's Illustrated*.
Among artists listed in issue 1 are
N. B. Wollen, Stanley Berkley,
J. Finnemore and C. H. Taffs. Photographs
by Earl De La Warr and other
correspondents are included.

26pp. to each issue, illustrated throughout.
Cover of issue No.1 shown

For The Flag Or Lays And Incidents Of The
South African War.
Mrs. E. S. Macleod
Archibald Irwin (Printer)
Charlottetown, Prince Edward Island 1901

Maroon calf. Front, back and spine blocked
in gold.
222×145mm

A volume in praise of patriots who followed
the flag to South Africa. Contents include a
record of the war, incidents of battle,
Generals in the war, and a chapter on the
Victoria Cross and those who gained it.
Reference to Canadians and their part in
the conflict appears throughout.

viii+185pp. Illustrated.

AUSTRALIAN CAVALRY:

THE NEW SOUTH WALES LANCER REGIMENT

AND

FIRST AUSTRALIAN HORSE

BY

FRANK WILKINSON

WAR CORRESPONDENT, SYDNEY "DAILY TELEGRAPH,"
AUTHOR OF " AUSTRALIA AT THE FRONT "

SYDNEY & MELBOURNE
ANGUS AND ROBERTSON
1901

Australian Cavalry
The New South Wales Lancer Regiment
And First Australian Horse.
Frank Wilkinson
Angus and Robertson
Sydney & Melbourne 1901

Green card cover. Red letterpress to
front only.
250×186mm

An account of the formation and early
history of the New South Wales Lancers and
First Australian Horse. Together with the
South African War record, nominal rolls
and lists of casualties.

x+64pp. Coloured frontispiece and other
plates.

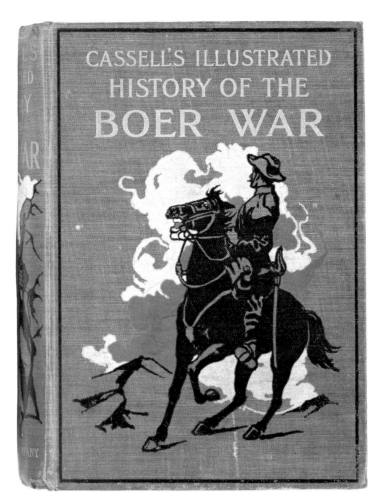

Cassell's History Of The Boer War
1899–1901.
Richard Danes
Cassell and Company, Limited
London, Paris, New York & Melbourne
1901

Olive green cloth. Front and spine blocked
in orange, white, black and gold. Back
blocked in black only.
231×164mm

A general history of the war up to June
1901, originally published in 49 parts. In this
edition the title is changed and the author's
name appears on the title page. Some copies
contain colour plates.

viii+1560pp. Numerous illustrations.

Cassell's Illustrated History Of The Boer
War 1899–1902.
(Author/editor not shown.)
Cassell & Company Limited
London, Paris, New York & Melbourne
nd. (c.1902)

Pale green wraps. Red letterpress to front
and back.
247×186mm

A complete history of the war published in
30 parts, each with illustrated cover (Part 5
shown). Paper quality is superior to that
used for earlier editions. Title from cover.

1903pp. Fully illustrated.

(See entry under *Cassell and Company
Limited* for 2 vol. revised and enlarged
edition published 1903.)

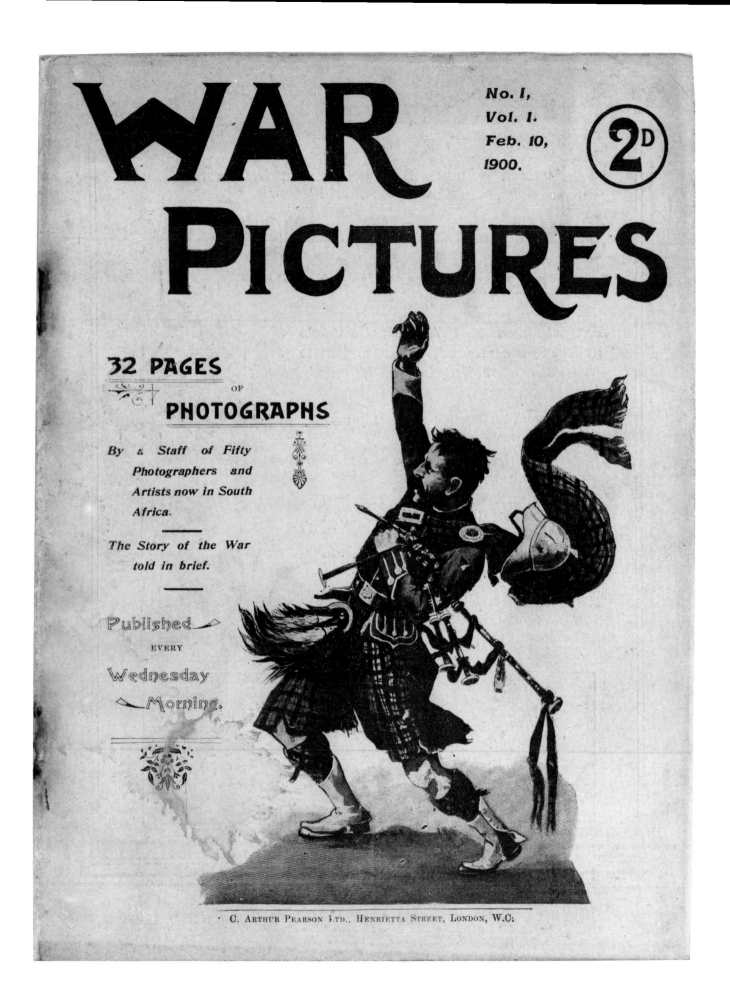

WAR PICTURES

No. 1,
Vol. 1.
Feb. 10,
1900.

2D

32 PAGES
OF
PHOTOGRAPHS

By a Staff of Fifty
Photographers and
Artists now in South
Africa.

The Story of the War
told in brief.

Published
EVERY
Wednesday
Morning.

C. ARTHUR PEARSON LTD., HENRIETTA STREET, LONDON, W.C.

War Pictures
(Author/editor not shown.)
C. Arthur Pearson Ltd.
London 1900

White wraps printed dark blue.
245×185mm

A pictorial record of the war published in 16
parts from Feb. 10 to May 26, 1900.
Contents include 'The story of the war' and
'War notes'. Each issue 32pp.

512pp. Illustrated throughout.

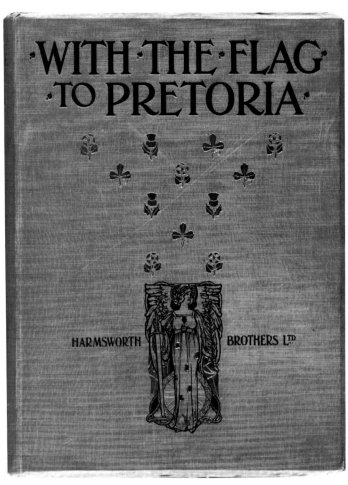

On The Eve Of The War A Narrative Of Impressions During A Journey In Cape Colony, The Free State, The Transvaal, Natal And Rhodesia September 1899 To January 1900.
Evelyn Cecil
John Murray
London 1900

Ochre cloth. Front blocked in white, green, black, red and gold. Spine blocked in red and gold.
197×129mm

An assessment of the local situation based on interviews with prominent British and Boer representatives.

viii+147pp. Folding map and illustrations.

With The Flag To Pretoria A History Of The Boer War Of 1899–1900.
H. W. Wilson
Harmsworth Brothers Limited
London 1900 (Vol.2 1901)

Green cloth over bevelled boards. Blocked in black and gold to front and spine. Back blocked in black only.
330×247mm *(Illustrated)*

Variant binding
Red cloth over bevelled boards. Front and spine blocked in black and gold, back in black only.
332×248mm

(Various other bindings recorded including orange cloth with decorative Union Jack design, publishers half morocco gilt and publishers half calf gilt. Also issued in 72 parts each with an illustrated paper cover. (Parts 31–72 being *After Pretoria: The Guerilla War*.)

An illustrated history of the Boer War in four volumes. *With The Flag to Pretoria* (Vols.1 & 2) comprise a record of the campaign to October 1900 and *After Pretoria: The Guerilla War* (Vols.1 & 2) complete the record to June 1902. The set is illustrated throughout.

Vol.1.viii+364pp. Folding map and illustrations.
Vol.2.viii+pp365–716. Folding map and illustrations.
After Pretoria: The Guerilla War. The Supplement To 'With The Flag To Pretoria'.
The Amalgamated Press, Limited, London 1902.
Vol.1.viii+528pp. Illustrated.
Vol.2.vi+2+pp.529–1008. Illustrated.

18

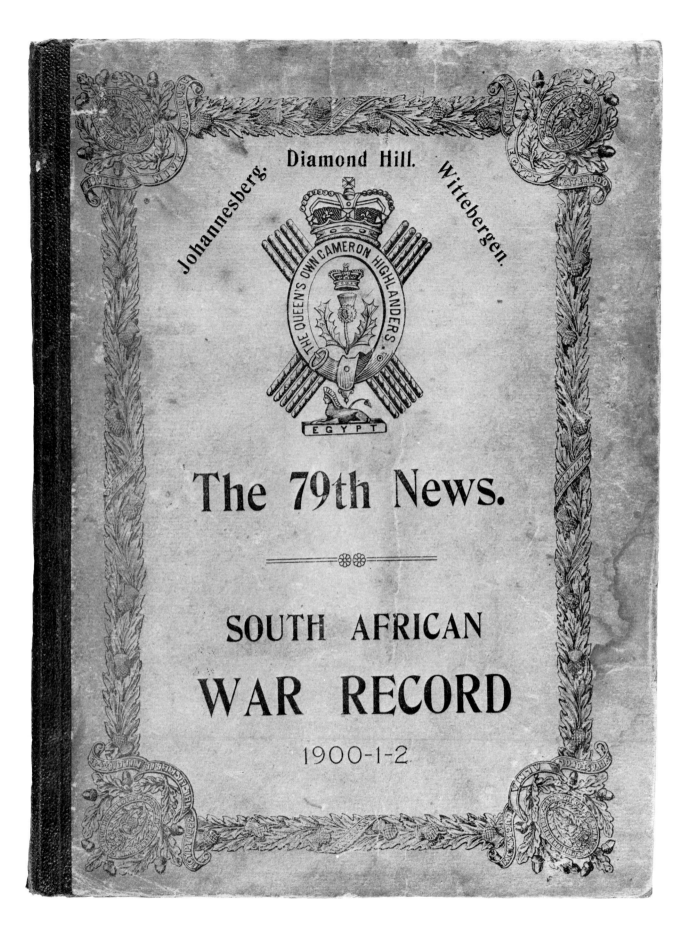

Johannesberg. Diamond Hill. Wittebergen.

The 79th News.

SOUTH AFRICAN
WAR RECORD
1900-1-2

South African War Record Of The
1st Battalion Queen's Own Cameron
Highlanders 1900–1–2.
Compiled by
Major N. G. Cameron
The Northern Counties Printing and
Publishing Company, Limited
Inverness 1903

Light green paper covered boards backed in
dark blue cloth. Black letterpress to front
and back.
245×185mm

A special edition of *The 79th News* being a
record of the 1st Battalion in South Africa
with contributions by various officers of the
regiment. The Cameron Highlanders took
part in the northern advance from
Bloemfontein. Following the occupation of
Pretoria they were employed, at various
times, in northern Orange River Colony and
in wide ranging patrols in Transvaal. The
volume contains various appendices
including notes on Lovat's Scouts,
mentioned in despatches, an itinerary of the
campaign and a nominal roll of all who
served in South Africa.

vii+258pp. Illustrations and folding maps.

ARMY ORDERS.

Cape Town,
January 10th, 1900.

1—Command—
Field-Marshal the Rt. Hon. F. S., Lord Roberts, V.C., K.P., G.C.B., G.C.S.I.. G.C.I.E., having arrived this day assumes command of the troops in South Africa.

2—Appointments—
The following appointments are made to the Head-Quarter Staff of the Army :—
Private Secretary to the Field-Marshal Commanding in Chief :—
    Col. Neville Chamberlain, I.S C.

Aides de Camp : —
    Col. Viscount Downe, C.I.E.
    Capt A. C. M. Waterfield, I.S.C.
    Capt. Lord H A. Montagu Scott, 3rd Bn. Royal Scots.
    Capt. Lord Settrington, 3rd Bn. Royal Sussex Regt.

Naval A.D.C. :—Commander the Hon. F. Fortescue, R.N.
Military Secretary :—Maj.-Gen. Sir W G. Nicholson, K.C.B.
Asst. Military Secretary :—Lieut.-Col. H. V. Cowan, R.A.
Commandant Head-Quarters :—Maj.-Gen. G. T. Pretyman, C.B.
Chief of Staff :—Maj.-Gen. Lord Kitchener of Khartoum, G.C.B., K.C.M.G.

Aides de Camp to Chief of Staff :—
    Brevet Major J. K. Watson, D.S.O., King's Royal Rifle Corps.
    Brevet Major G. F. Gorringe, D.S.O., R.E.

D.A.A.Gs. :—
    Major R. B. Gaisford, Royal Scots Fusiliers.
    Major H. I. W. Hamilton, D S.O., The Queen's Royal West Surrey Regt.
    Major R. C. C. Haking, Hampshire Regt.

Director of Supplies :—Colonel W. D. Richardson, C.B.
Dir. of Intelligence :—Lieut.-Colonel (local Colonel) G. F. R. Henderson, York and Lancaster Regt.

D.A A.Gs. :—
    Brevet Major C. J. Mackenzie, Seaforth Highlanders.
    Major C. V. Hume R.A.
    Major F. J. Davies, Grenadier Guards.

Director of Railways :—Brevet Major (Local Lieut.-Colonel) E. P. C. Girouard, D.S.O., R.E.
Staff Officers to Director of Railways :—
    Captain H. G. Joly de Lotbiniere, R.E.
    Lieut. M. G. E. Manifold, R.E.

Principal Medical Officer—Surgeon General W. D. Wilson.
Medical Officer :—Major W. G. A Bedford, R.A M.C.
Chief Ordnance Officer :—Colonel R. F. N. Clarke, A.O.D.
Commanding Royal Artillery : —(Major Gen. on Staff), Colonel (Local Major General) G. H. Marshall.
Staff Officer R.A. :—Major H. C. Sclater, R.A.
A.D.C., R.A. :—Capt. A. D. Kirby, R.F.A.
Chief Engineer :—(Major General on Staff), Colonel (Local Major General) E. Wood, C.B.
Staff Officer, R.E. :—Major E. H. Bethell, R E.
A.D.C., R.E. : —Brevet-Major R. S. Curtis, R.E.
Staff Officer for Colonial Contingents : —Brevet Lieut.-Colonel J. Adye, R.A.
Asst. Staff Officer for Colonial Contingents :—Lieut. W. Cowan, D.S.O., R.N.
Director of Signalling :—Major (Local Lieut.-Colonel) E. Rhodes, D S.O., Royal Berkshire Regt.
Director of Army Telegraphs :—Lieut.-Colonel R. L. R. Hippisley, R E.
Provost Marshal :— Brevet Major R. M. Poore, 7th Hussars.
Principal Chaplain :—Rev. E. H. Goodwin, B.A.
Press Censors :—
    Major Lord Edmund Talbot, 11th Hussars.
    Major H. J. Evans, The King's (Liverpool Regt.)
Deputy Judge Advocate :—Colonel J. L. C. St. Clair.
Army Post Master :—Captain (local Major) G. W. Treble, 24th Middlesex V.R.C. (Army Post Office Corps).

By Order,
KITCHENER OF KHARTOUM,
Major General,
Chief of Staff.

Army Orders Issued By Field Marshal Lord Roberts And Gen. Lord Kitchener Of Khartoum From 10th January 1900 To 23rd June 1902.
(Govt. Printer Pretoria)

Issues 1–19 published at Cape Town. Issues 19A–91 published at various locations on the line of march to Pretoria. Issues 92 to 566 inclusive published at Pretoria, with the exception of *Special Army Order* No.233 published at Johannesburg on 29th Nov. 1900. (Lord Roberts' farewell address on relinquishing command of the Army in South Africa.)

A set specially bound in three volumes. Half bottle green morocco with green cloth. Front, back and spine decorated in gold. Red morocco label blocked in gold to front of each volume.
334×208mm

Orders issued by the Commander in Chief of the Army in South Africa. Contents include Staff, and other appointments. Telegraph and postal services. Promotions, courts martial, and field intelligence reports. Decorations conferred. Operation of civil and military services. Army discipline and general news. Notes on military law and numerous other matters relating to the administration of an army in the field. The orders are fully indexed and bound together with notices numbered 1–68. Many of them marked *Confidential*.

Unpaginated except for index pages.

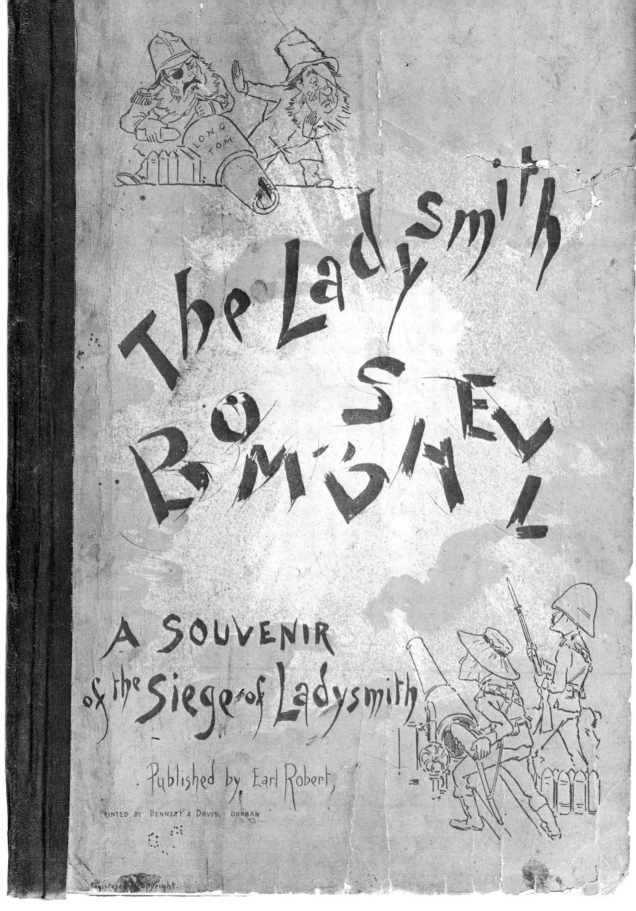

The Ladysmith Bombshell
A Souvenir Of The Siege Of Ladysmith
Published by Earl Robert.
(Editor/compiler not shown.)
Durban nd. (1900)

Card cover backed in cloth. Front printed
brown and grey.
337×238mm

A reprint of *The Ladysmith Bombshell* a
humorous magazine published at Ladysmith
during the siege. Eight issues are
reproduced dated Nov. 18, 1899 – Jan. 8,
1900. Each issue has an illustrated cover.
The Christmas Number of Dec. 23, contains
other illustrations.

Unpaginated. (50 printed rectos, including
explanatory note and dedication sheet.)
Illustrated.

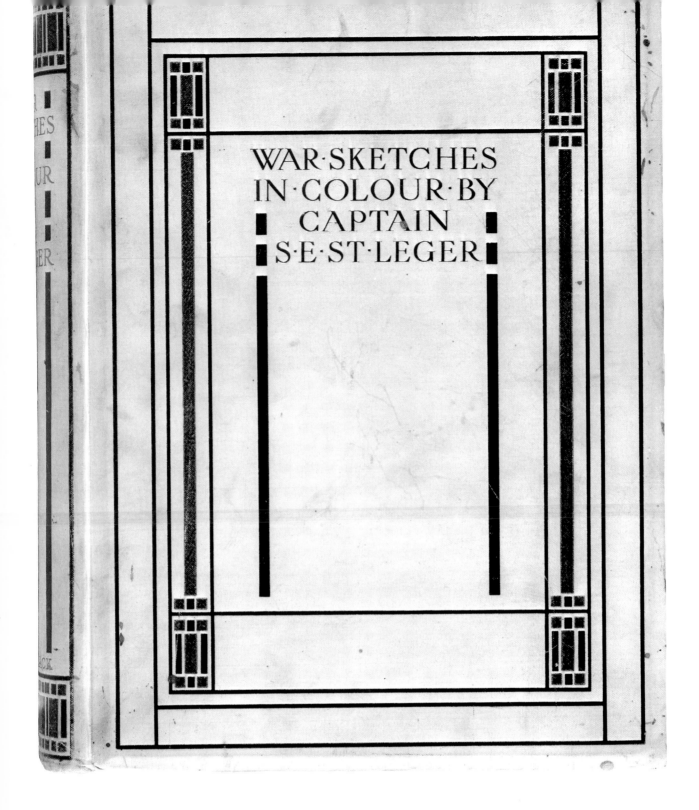

War Sketches in Colour
Captain S. E. St. Leger
Adam & Charles Black
London nd. (1903)

Royal blue cloth. Front and spine blocked
in orange, red and gold.
230×164mm

Variant binding
De luxe edition of 250 numbered copies.
White buckram over bevelled boards. Front
and spine blocked in red, blue and gold.
276×215mm

Campaign record compiled by an officer of
Mounted Infantry attached to Gen. French's
1st Cavalry Brigade. The content is drawn
from a sketch book kept up from day to day
during the war. Chapters relate to the siege
and relief of Kimberley, Events at Sanna's
Post, the crossing of the Vaal, etc. An
account of life on commando is based on
data supplied by a Transvaal Boer. The
volume contains 66 full page illustrations
and numerous other drawings.

xiii+274pp. Illustrated throughout.
De luxe edition shown.

22

Ten Months In The Field With The Boers
An Ex-Lieutenant of General
de Villebois-Mareuil
William Heinemann
London 1901

Orange cloth. Front and spine blocked in
black.
195×130mm

Recollections of six months service with the
republican armies. The author, Olivier
d'Etchegoyen, a French officer, joined Col.
(later General) de Villebois-Mareuil near
Kimberley, then besieged by the Boers. He
gives a lucid account of the campaign in the
western sector and of subsequent battles in
the Orange Free State at which the 'Foreign
contingent' was present. The French
General is much praised for his leadership
of European volunteers but the Boer
commanders censured for lack of military
organization. Following the death of
Villebois-Mareuil in action near Boshof
(April 5) the writer continued service in the
'Foreign corps' until disbandment in May
1900. He was captured in the Transvaal
about a month later and permitted to leave
South Africa.

v+248pp. Frontispiece and folding maps.

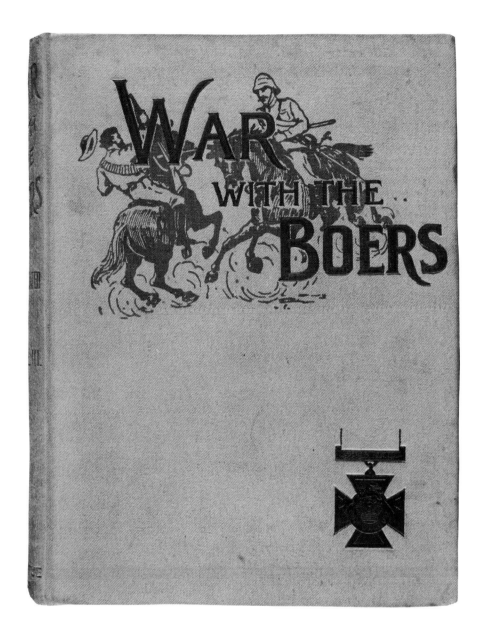

The Art Annual, 1900
The Work Of War Artists In South Africa.
A. C. R. Carter
'The Art Journal' Office
London 1900

Green cloth over bevelled boards. Front
blocked in gold.
340×260mm
Variant bindings
Turquoise cloth blocked in gold.
331×252mm

Grey paper covers, front and back printed
brown.
336×260mm *(Illustrated)*

Special edition of 250 copies printed on
Japan paper. Blue cloth blocked in gold.
355×280mm

Separately bound edition of *The Art Annual*
Xmas number displaying the work of war
artists active during the South African
campaign. Among the pictures reproduced
are those of Melton Prior, Frank Dadd,
Ernest Prater and R. Caton-Woodville.

32pp. Illustrated throughout.

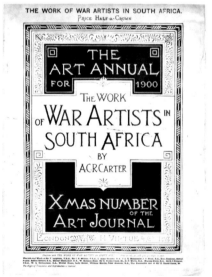

War With The Boers An Account Of The
Past And Present Troubles With The South
African Republics.
Harold Brown and E. Sharpe Grew
H. Virtue and Company, Limited
London nd. (c.1902)

Khaki cloth. Front blocked in bronze,
brown and red. Spine blocked in gold.
250×190mm

Subscribers edition
Pink paper covers, dark blue letterpress to
front and back.
259×193mm

A general history of the war in five
volumes. Volume 1 deals with the early
history of South Africa, the Boer States, the
first Boer War and events leading to the
conflict of 1899–1902. Volume 2 deals with
events in Natal to the relief of Ladysmith.
Volume 3 relates to the western campaign,
the invasion of the Free State and the
surrender of Cronje. Volume 4 is concerned
with the fall of the Boer capitals and the
advance to Komati Poort. Volume 5 relates
to the clearing of Natal, the guerilla war
under Roberts and Kitchener, the
blockhouse system and events leading to
peace negotiations. The history was also
published in a subscribers edition consisting
of 20 parts.

Vol. 1. vi+248+viii pp.
Vols. 2–5. vi+248pp.
Illustrated throughout.

With Lumsden's Horse Agin The Boers
J. H. Burn-Murdoch
Barnicott & Pearce (Printers)
Taunton 1901

Tan cloth. Front blocked in black and gold.
225×175mm

Experiences of a trooper in a volunteer
corps raised in India. The author gives an
account of the battle of Houtnek and of
medical services during the campaign.
A complete record of the corps in South
Africa is given in *'The History of Lumsden's
Horse'* by H. H. S. Pearse.

vii+157pp. Illustrated.

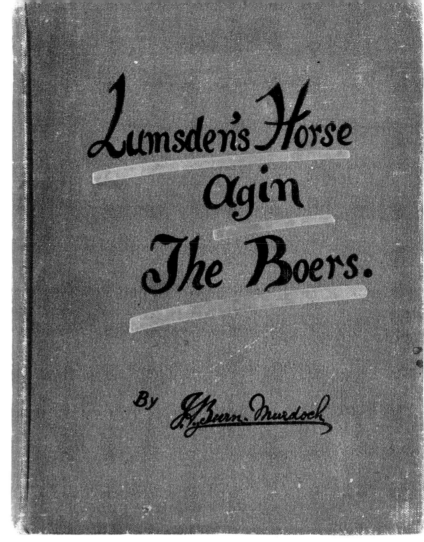

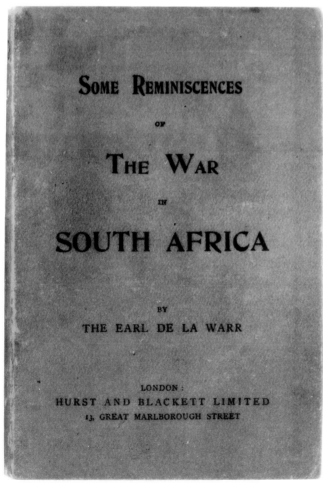

Some Reminiscences Of The War In
South Africa.
The Earl De La Warr
Hurst and Blackett, Limited
London 1900

Red pebble grain limp card cover. Front
printed black.
183×123mm

Letters from South Africa originally
published in the 'Globe'. De La Warr
arrived at Cape Town in October 1899 and
proceeded to Modder River Camp. For over
two months he reported Lord Methuen's
western operations. Letters relate to events
at Belmont and Modder River and include a
poignant account of the battle of
Magersfontein. In January the writer
travelled east to report General Buller's
campaign in Natal. He joined Col. Bethune's
Mounted Infantry and witnessed the Tugela
operations. A letter of Jan. 26 relates the
sad affair of Spion Kop, another of March 5
records the relief of Ladysmith. The writer
gives a short account of conditions in the
town at the time of British entry. In March
Bethune's Horse was ordered via Zululand
to displace Boers from Helpmakaar. After
successive attempts the area was cleared of
enemy forces. In the subsequent advance
towards Vryheid a section of the Corps was
ambushed and destroyed. The author was
wounded in this engagement and invalided
home in May 1900.

xvi+120pp.

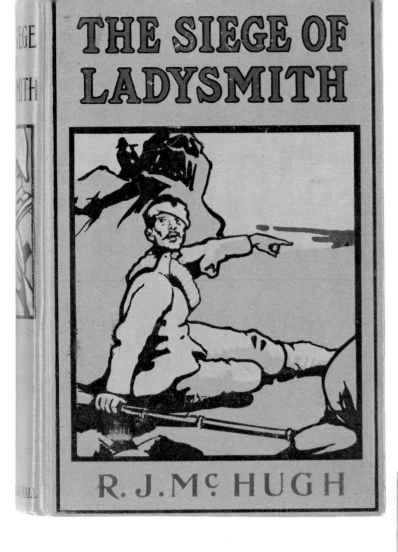

R. J. McHugh
Chapman & Hall Ld.
London 1900

Olive green cloth. Front and spine blocked
in khaki, red and black.
194×132mm

An account of the siege in a series of letters
sent home by the accredited representative
of the *Daily Telegraph*.

viii+213pp. Illustrated.

Cape of Good Hope
Proclamations And Government Notices
Issued During The Period October, 1899,
To June, 1900, Having Reference To And
Consequent On The Outbreak Of
Hostilities In South Africa.
W. A. Richards & Sons (Government
Printers)
Cape Town 1900

Buff coloured limp card cover. Black
letterpress to front.
330×202mm

Copies of proclamations and notices issued
by Sir Alfred Milner, W. P. Schreiner, Lord
Roberts and others.

v+23pp.

CAPE OF GOOD HOPE.

PROCLAMATIONS

AND

GOVERNMENT NOTICES

Issued during the period October, 1899, to June,
1900, having reference to and consequent on
the outbreak of hostilities in South Africa.

Presented to both Houses of Parliament by Command of His Excellency the Governor.
1900.

CAPE TOWN:
W. A. RICHARDS & SONS, GOVERNMENT PRINTERS, CASTLE STREET.
1900.
[G. 62—1900.]

Letters And Diary Of Lieutenant G. E. S.
Salt During The War In South Africa,
1899–1900.
(G. E. S. Salt)
Printed for private circulation
John Murray
London 1902

Dull blue paper covered boards backed in
vellum. Front blocked in gold and red, spine
blocked in gold.
221×176mm

Extracts from the letters and diary of Lieut.
Salt of the 1st Batt. Royal Welch Fusiliers
chiefly relating events in Natal from Oct.
1899 to April 1900. Salt witnessed the battle
of Colenso and reports comprehensively of
other engagements in operations about the
Tugela. Most of the correspondence
pertains to military matters with some
criticism expressed in respect of General
Buller. Soon after the relief of Ladysmith
the writer was taken ill with enteric fever.
He died at the base hospital near Modder
Spruit on April 3. The last two letters are
addressed to his father from an officer of
the regiment.

vii+119pp. Map and two plates.

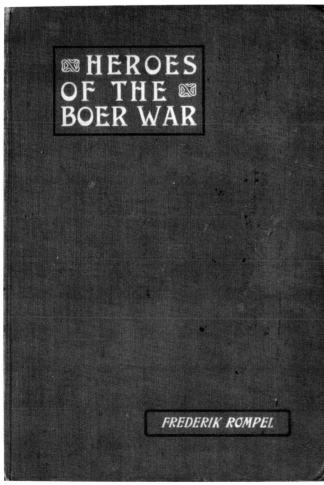

Heroes Of The Boer War
Frederik Rompel
'Review of Reviews' Office/London
The 'Nederland' Publishing Co.
The Hague and Pretoria
1903

Dull blue cloth. Front and spine blocked in
red and white.
244×170mm *(Illustrated)*

Variant binding
Apple green cloth. Front and spine blocked
in red and white.
244×170mm

An account of the Boers and their leaders
by the war correspondent of the *Volksstem*,
Pretoria. The brief memoirs of political and
military personalities include presidents
Kruger and Steyn (Steijn), Messrs. Reitz,
Leyds, Wolmarans and Wessels. Of military
personnel Generals Joubert, Cronje, Botha,
De Wet and De la Rey are included. The
introduction by Maj.-General A. Pfister is a
brief history of South Africa to the outbreak
of hostilities on Oct. 11, 1899. All preceded
by a laudatory preface by W. T. Stead.

xxviii+196pp. Folding maps and numerous
illustrations.

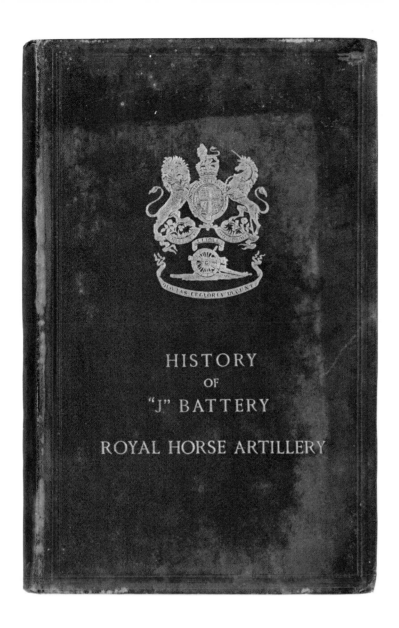

The Anglo-Boer War, 1899–1900.
An Album Of Upwards Of Three Hundred
Photographic Engravings. A Picture Record
Of The Movements Of The British,
Colonial And Boer Forces Engaged In The
Conflict.
(Editor/compiler not shown.)
Dennis Edwards & Co.
Cape Town nd. (c.1900)

Maroon pebble grain cloth. Front blocked
in gold and black.
251×310mm
Variant bindings
Dull green cloth. Front blocked in black,
dark blue, red, white and gold.
252×311mm

Beige cloth. Front blocked in dark blue,
red, white and black.
252×312mm *(Illustrated)*

Maroon pebble grain cloth. Front blocked
in gold and blind (Sunrise design).
251×311mm

A photographic record of the campaign in
South Africa with short letterpress and a
'Summary of the War 1899–1900'.
Pagination, and content, varies between
editions. An extended edition (c.1902)
contains over five hundred photographs
with the Summary of the War brought down
to termination of hostilities. In addition this
volume includes certain war statistics and a
list of V.C. recipients.

iv+192+22pp. Illustrated.
 v+228+xvi pp. Illustrated.
iv+200+xxi+iii pp. Illustrated.
vi+260+xxi+iii pp. Illustrated.
iv+204+xxii pp. Illustrated.
(Last edition listed is the *Kimberley Edition*
which includes a drawing by Cecil Boult)

The History Of 'J' Battery Royal Horse
Artillery (Formerly A Troop, Madras Horse
Artillery) Compiled From Private And
Official Records.
Major Guilbert E. Wyndham Malet
Charles Good and Co. (Printers)
London nd. (c.1903)

Royal blue cloth. Front blocked in gold and
blind, back blocked in blind only.
220×140mm

A record of 'J' Battery R.H.A. in South
Africa being a diary of events from Dec.
1899 to July 1903. The Battery arrived at
Port Elizabeth on Jan. 29, 1900, serving in
Cape Colony for a short period prior to
joining Lord Roberts force in the advance
from Bloemfontein to Pretoria. From Sept.
1900 to the close of the campaign the
Battery served under various commanders
in the Transvaal, northern Natal and
northern Orange River Colony. In Jan. 1902
orders were received for the force to be
converted to mounted rifles. After short
training at Elandsfontein the unit returned
to active service as the Royal Horse
Artillery Mounted Rifles. At the close of
hostilities they were part of a column
operating in south western Transvaal. The
record includes a short history of the
Battery from 1756 to 1899.
A list of principal engagements in the South
African War and various lists of officers are
appended.

x+133pp. Frontispiece and folding map.
(S.A. war diary pp.30–102.)

Fifty-Six Portraits Of Our Heroes' Orphans.
Children Of Fathers Who Lost Their Lives
In The South African War, 1899–1900.
W. L. N.
The Leadenhall Press, Ltd.
London nd. (1900)

Buff paper cover. Front printed dark blue
and red. Back printed dark blue only.
102×160mm

Commercial advertising purporting to be a
tribute to 'those valiant men who laid down
their lives in the cause of empire'. The
portraits (two per page) depict children of
soldiers who died, or were disabled in South
Africa, now being fed gratis by the
generosity of the proprietors of Mellin's
Food. It is claimed the 'patriotic' firm
realized that England would need strong
and healthy sons to fight her battles of the
future.

32pp. Illustrated.

SOUTH·AFRICAN·WAR·
·1899~1900·

Fifty-six Portraits

OF

Our Heroes' Orphans

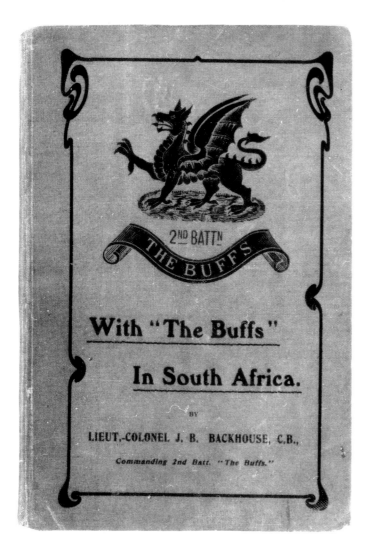

With 'The Buffs' In South Africa
Lieut.-Colonel J. B. Backhouse
Gale & Polden Ltd.
Aldershot (1903)

Limp red cloth printed black to front only.
182×122mm

A record of the 2nd Battalion East Kent Regiment based on the campaign diary compiled by their commanding officer Lieut.-Colonel Backhouse. In February 1900 the Battalion was active in the western theatre taking part in operations at Paardeberg, Poplar Grove and Abraham's Kraal prior to the occupation of Bloemfontein. In August 1900 the Buffs were in the Transvaal patrolling the Delagoa railway line. They formed part of Col. Benson's column when it was attacked at Bakenlaagte on Oct. 30th 1901. In this action the conduct of the regiment was considered less than heroic. For the remainder of the campaign the Battalion was chiefly employed in eastern Transvaal. The record includes various casualty lists.

xi+162pp. Illustrated.

On Active Service With The Northumberland And Durham Yeomen, Under Lord Methuen. (South Africa, 1900–1901.)
Karl B. Spurgin
Printed for the author by
The Walter Scott Publishing Co., Ltd.
London and Newcastle-On-Tyne
nd. (c.1902)

Dark green fine ribbed cloth over bevelled boards. Front blocked in gold, black and red. Spine blocked in gold.
188×125mm

A record of approximately 16 months service with the 14th and 15th Squadrons of Imperial Yeomanry under Lord Methuen. The account is based on the author's campaign diary. The corps was chiefly employed in the western sector operating in British Bechuanaland, Orange River Colony and western Transvaal. A roll of the companies is included.

xx+323pp. Illustrated.

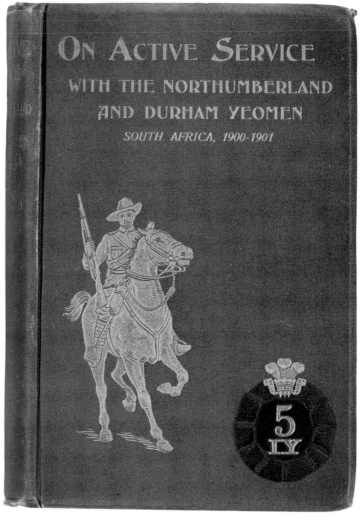

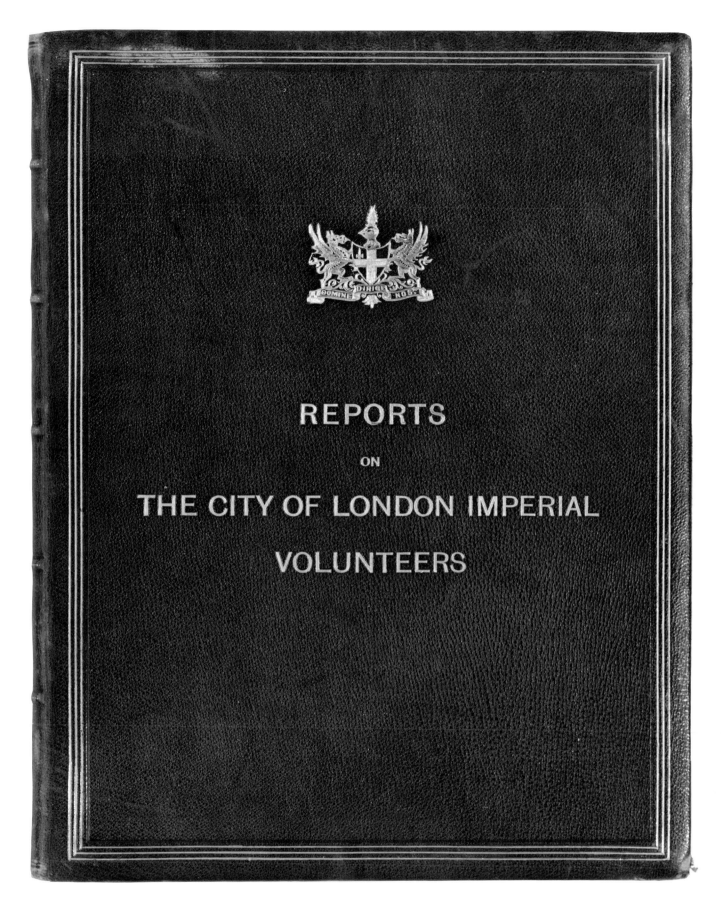

Official. Reports On The Raising,
Organising, Equipping And Despatching
The City Of London Imperial Volunteers
To South Africa.
Sir Alfred J. Newton
Blades, East & Blades, Printers
London 1900

Full dark blue morocco over bevelled
boards. Front, back and spine blocked in
gold and blind.
286×229mm

Standard edition
Ochre cloth over bevelled boards.
(No other details)
269×210mm

Four reports relating to the despatch of the
Regiment to South Africa published by
order of The Right Hon. The Lord Mayor
Sir Alfred J. Newton, Bart. The papers
relate to the formation of the Regiment,
selection of volunteers (with nominal rolls)
and to the supply of clothing and
equipment. The volume shown is one of the
superior edition, a presentation copy from
Sir Alfred J. Newton to C. W. Bartholomew
Esq.

v+61pp.

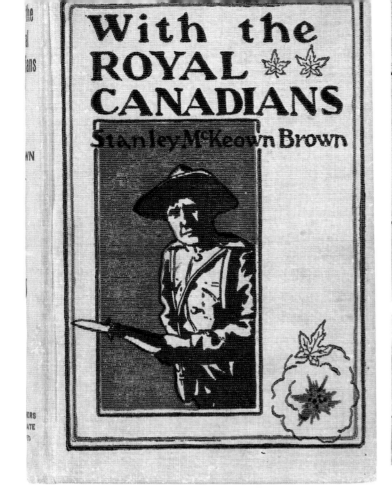

BULLETS

EXPANSIVE, EXPLOSIVE
AND POISONED

BY

ALFRED MARKS

Reprinted from THE WESTMINSTER REVIEW, *June 1902*

With The Royal Canadians
Stanley McKeown Brown
The Publishers' Syndicate, Limited
Toronto 1900

Light green cloth. Front blocked in red and
black, spine blocked in black.
190×125mm

A war correspondent's account of the First
Canadian Contingent on active service in
South Africa. Chapters relate to Cronje's
surrender at Paardeberg and the subsequent
march on Bloemfontein and Pretoria.

vi+291pp.

Bullets Expansive, Explosive And
Poisoned.
Alfred Marks
Reprinted from The Westminster Review
(London) 1902

Grey/green limp card cover. Black
letterpress to front only.
237×160mm

A pamphlet in reference to illegal
ammunition used in the war. The author
refutes claims that the Boers used
'poisoned' or 'explosive' bullets stating that
the latter did not exist. A short account is
given of the development of small arms
ammunition and of the production of the
'dum-dum' or 'explosive' bullet. At the
Hague Peace Conference held in 1899 it was
proposed that the delegates adopt a
declaration not to use such ammunition in
warfare. Great Britain was the only power
to object to the prohibition and finally
refused to accept the decision of the
Conference. Consequently, from July 1899,
when the subjugation of the Boer Republics
had already been determined, quantities of
Mark IV and Mark V (expansive) bullets
were shipped to South Africa. In conceding
that expansive bullets had been used by the
Boers it is stated that some had been of
British manufacture and taken from British
troops in the field. The author concludes
with a short account of revolver ammunition
with particular reference to Webley's patent
man-stopping bullet adopted by H. M.
Government.

19pp.

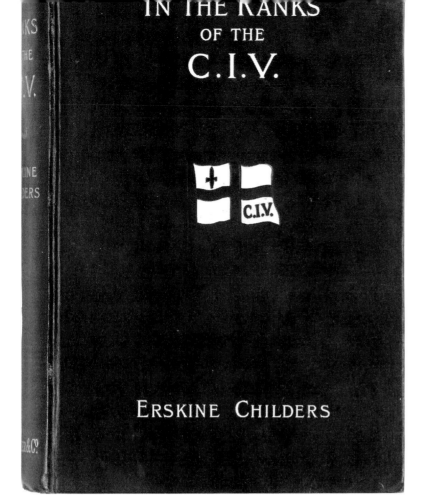

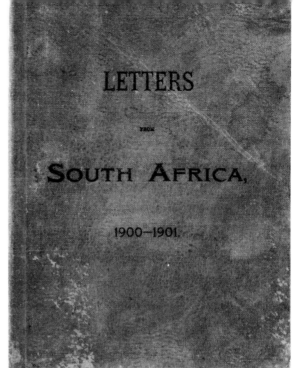

In The Ranks Of The C.I.V.
A Narrative And Diary Of Personal
Experiences With The C.I.V. Battery
(Honourable Artillery Company)
In South Africa.
By Driver Erskine Childers
Smith, Elder & Co.
London 1900

Red cloth. Front blocked in black and
white. Spine blocked in gold.
198×130mm

A narrative based on a campaign diary
(Feb.–Oct. 1900). The Battery was chiefly
employed in column work and garrison duty
along lines of communication in the Orange
River Colony and central Transvaal.

vii+301pp. With frontispiece.

Letters From South Africa 1900–1901.
Printed For Private Circulation.
H. Farr
J. W. Moore (Printer)
Chichester nd. (c.1902)

Red pebble grain cloth, blocked in black to
front only.
185×125mm

Letters home from Lance-Corporal H. Farr
of the Special Service Company 1st Batt.
Royal Sussex Regiment. Most of the letters
are addressed to his mother and father from
locations on line of advance. The volunteers
sailed to South Africa in March 1900 aboard
S.S. Tintagel Castle (See McLean &
Shackleton – *O.H.M.S.*). From April to
July they operated in the Orange Free State
and the Transvaal. By August they were
back in Orange River Colony chiefly
employed in convoy and garrison duties.
During an active campaign the corps took
part in various engagements including Zand
River, Diamond Hill and Retiefs Nek. The
writer, who was seriously ill on occasions,
gives a substantial account of hospital
services. The final letter, addressed from
Cape Town, is dated April 23, 1901.

106pp. With a diagram.

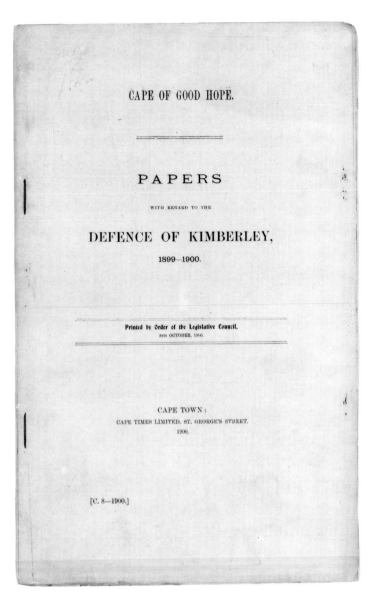

Cape Of Good Hope. Papers With Regard
To The Defence Of Kimberley, 1899–1900
[C.8–1900.]
(Editor/compiler not shown.)
Cape Times Limited
Cape Town 1900

Unbound (stapled sections).
345×216mm

Correspondence and official papers relative
to the defence of Kimberley. The document
is comprised of 31 numbered entries dated
22/5/99 to 5/10/99. Much of the content
deals with the inadequate state of local
defence and with acquisition of arms and
ammunition.

39pp.

Order Book Of The 26th (Dorset) Company
I.Y. For About A Year In South Africa.
Compiled From What Remains Of The
Company's Order Books, For Private
Circulation Among The Members Of The
Company.
Capt. Sir Elliott Lees
Henry Ling
(Dorchester 1903)

Full brown calf. Front and spine blocked
in gold.
223×141mm

A transcription of the Company order
books from April 1900–March 1901. The
corps joined Lord Roberts' army in the
advance through the Orange Free State and,
from May 1900 to conclusion of service,
served in the Transvaal under various
commanders. The record includes a list of
casualties, honours and mentions in
despatches and names and addresses of
officers, n.c.o.'s and men of the 26th
Company Dorset I.Y. (7th Battalion).

xvi+224pp. Folding map and illustrations.

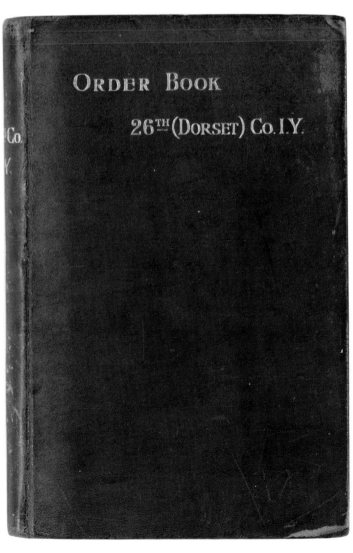

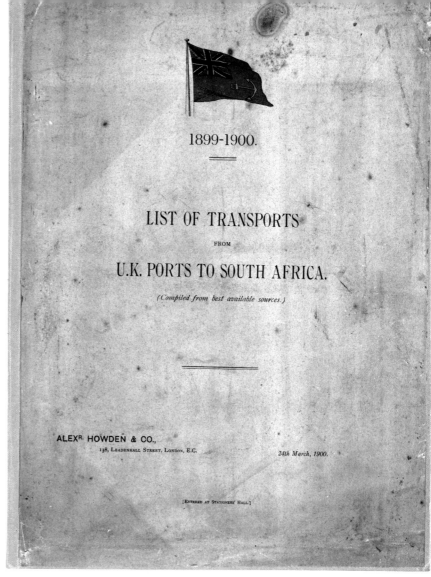

Canadians In Khaki South Africa, 1899–
1900 Nominal Rolls Of The Officers, Non-
Commissioned Officers & Men Of The
Canadian Contingents And Strathcona's
Horse With Casualties To Date And Also
R.M.C. Graduates With The Army In
South Africa.
(Author not shown)
The Herald Publishing Co.
Montreal 1900

Buff paper covered boards backed in brown
cloth (rebacked copy). Front only printed
black, ochre and red.
221×146mm

Information relating to Canadian
participation in the war. The record includes
nominal rolls of the First and Second
Contingents, Artillery Corps, Strathcona's
Horse, etc., together with casualty lists and
details of embarkation. An introductory
chapter contains an account of Canadian
endeavour at Paardeberg.

127pp. Illustrated.

1899–1900 List Of Transports From
UK Ports To South Africa (Compiled From
Best Available Sources)
(Editor/compiler not shown.)
Alexr. Howden & Co. (Publishers)
London 1900

Grey paper covered boards, front printed
red, yellow, blue and black.
373×276mm

A list of transports and freight ships (men)
departing for South Africa between
September 1899 and April 1900. The record
shows dates of departure and arrival, total
numbers carried listed by regiment or unit
and duration of voyage.

i+8pp. (Printed rectos only)

The profits accruing from this publication will be devoted to the Transvaal War Funds.

2/6

THE TRANSVAAL WAR ALPHABET

PRICE 6ᴰ

The Transvaal War Alphabet
Dedicated To Our Soldiers' Children
By A Soldier's Wife.
Celia Congreve
George Falkner & Sons
John Heywood
Manchester 1900
Simpkin Marshall, Hamilton, Kent
& Co. Ltd.
George Falkner & Sons
London 1900
John Menzies & Co.
Edinburgh 1900

Limp card cover. Front printed red, blue
and ochre. Back printed ochre and blue.
206×164mm

An illustrated rhyming alphabet published
as an interesting memento for younger
members of families. (The entire proceeds
of the publication to be devoted to
charitable objects in connection with the
Transvaal War.) The item is similar in
content to Hassall's *An Active Army
Alphabet.*

29pp. Illustrated.

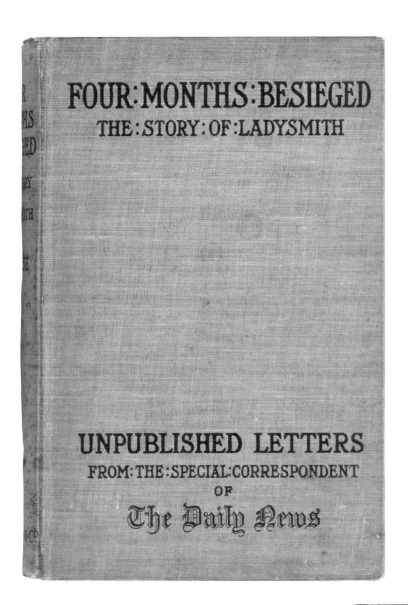

Four Months Besieged The Story
Of Ladysmith Being Unpublished
Letters From H. H. S. Pearse The
'Daily News' Special Correspondent.
H. H. S. Pearse
Macmillan And Co. Limited
London 1900

Fawn cloth. Front and spine blocked in red.
203×132mm

The story of Ladysmith under siege based
on a journalist's letters and diaries. Some of
the material was first published in the *Daily
News*.

xiv+244pp. Maps, plans and illustrations.

The History Of Lumsden's Horse
A Complete Record Of The Corps From Its
Formation To Its Disbandment.
Edited by Henry H. S. Pearse
Longmans, Green, And Co.
London/New York and Bombay 1903

Bright red cloth over bevelled boards. Front
blocked in gold. Spine blocked in gold, dark
blue, green and white.
257×185mm

Detailed record of a volunteer contingent
raised in India. The corps took part in the
advance from Bloemfontein to Pretoria and
thereafter engaged in various drives in the
Transvaal during the early phase of the
guerilla campaign. Appendices include a
regimental roll and a list of honours and
decorations awarded.

xii+506pp. Folding route map and various
illustrations.

'Ikona Sketches'
H.T.C. (H. T. Crispin?)
St. George's Press
Dover nd. (c.1902)

Off white limp card cover. Dark green
letterpress to front and back.
214×282mm

Sketches relating to 'Mounted Infantry' in
the campaign together with verse by
Rudyard Kipling. A volume, without title-
page, comprising 15 plates (printed rectos)
and 1 blank. The cover bears the insignia of
the Northumberland Fusiliers.

32pp. Illustrated.

38

The Canadian Contingents And Canadian
Imperialism A Story And A Study.
W. Sanford Evans
T. Fisher Unwin
London 1901

Orange cloth. Front blocked in black and
gold. Spine blocked in black.
208×138mm

An examination of the nation's response to
events in South Africa. The author alludes
to political agitation in Canada as a result of
the war, particularly among French
Canadians. News of volunteers in South
Africa is derived from reports of officers
on active service, from letters of
correspondents with the contingents and
other contemporary accounts.

xii+352pp. Maps and illustrations.

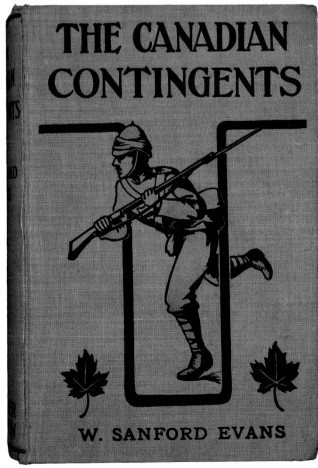

Khaki In South Africa. An Album Of
Pictures And Photographs Illustrating The
Chief Events Of The War Under Lord
Roberts. With A Chronological History.
(Author/editor not shown.)
George Newnes Limited
London 1900

Red cloth over bevelled boards. Front and
spine blocked in gold.
275×346mm

A pictorial record of the war with
descriptive letterpress being a narrative of
events to the occupation of Pretoria.
Originally published in 6 parts.

iv+140pp. Illustrated.

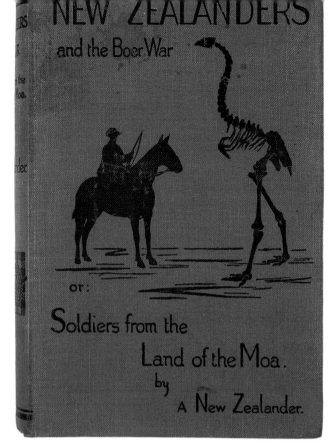

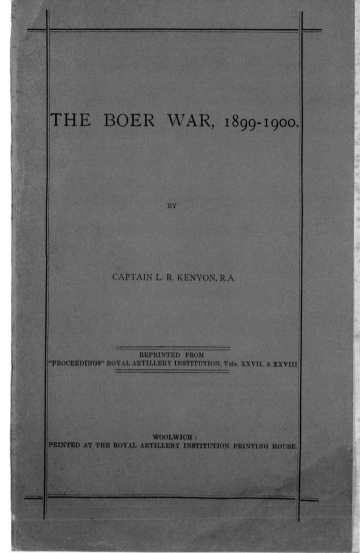

New Zealanders And The Boer War Or
Soldiers From The Land Of The Moa.
A New Zealander
Messrs. Gordon and Gotch
Christchurch nd. (c.1910)

Red cloth blocked in black to front and
spine.
189×128mm *(Illustrated)*

Variant binding
Red limp card cover printed black to front
and spine.
183×123mm

A narrative of New Zealand's part in the
war compiled chiefly from press reports and
private correspondence, being a record of
the ten Contingents that embarked for
South Africa between October 1899 and
April 1902. Some 6,500 men took part in
the campaign. New Zealanders served in
Cape Colony and the Orange Free State,
they joined Lord Roberts' army in the
northern advance and engaged in wide
ranging moves in the Transvaal. The 4th
and 5th Contingents arrived at Beira and
joined the Rhodesian Field Force under
General Carrington. The writer outlines the
work of each Contingent following, where
possible, the movements of detached units
and combined forces. Scant attention is paid
the 9th and 10th Contingents that arrived
too late for active service. Many troopers
tales are related and a short account given
of New Zealand volunteers in the hospital
service. The volume is attributed to Mrs.
Hawdon whose name does not appear on
the title page.

xi+287pp. With two plates.

The Boer War, 1899–1900
Captain L. R. Kenyon
Royal Artillery Institution
Woolwich nd. (c.1901)

Blue paper cover printed black to front
only.
247×155mm

A diary of military operations in South
Africa together with various statistics
relating to the war. Contents include an
official table of casualties, a list of
transports with principal units carried and
notes respecting British and Boer forces.
The volume is reprinted from *'Proceedings'
Royal Artillery Institution, vols. xxvii
& xxviii.*

206pp.

The Connaught Rangers
Regimental Records 1899–1902.
(Author/compiler not shown.)
W. & A. Richards & Sons
Cape Town 1902

Red and green morocco. Front and spine
blocked in gold. Back blocked in blind.
202×164mm

The 1st Battalion joined the Natal army
taking part in battles at Colenso, Venters
Spruit and Hart's Hill from Dec. 1899 to
Feb. 1900. In April the Rangers served for
a short period in Cape Colony before being
railed to the Transvaal where they engaged
in column work under various commanders
for approximately six months. In the
autumn of 1900 the Battalion returned to
Cape Colony operating in the Aliwal North
district to the end of the war. The record,
presented as a diary of events, includes lists
of casualties.

137pp. Various folding maps.

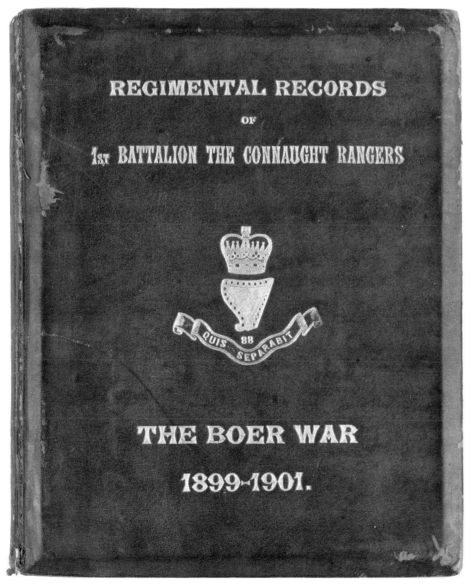

Regimental Records Of 1st Battalion The
Connaught Rangers The Boer War 1899–
1901.
(Author/compiler not shown)
Publisher/printer not shown

Full dark green calf over bevelled boards.
Front blocked in gold.
206×167mm

A regimental diary from Oct. 9, 1899 to
June 11, 1901 together with casualty lists,
being the first section of the full Boer War
record. Bound without a title page, the title
is drawn from the cover.

70pp. With four folding maps.

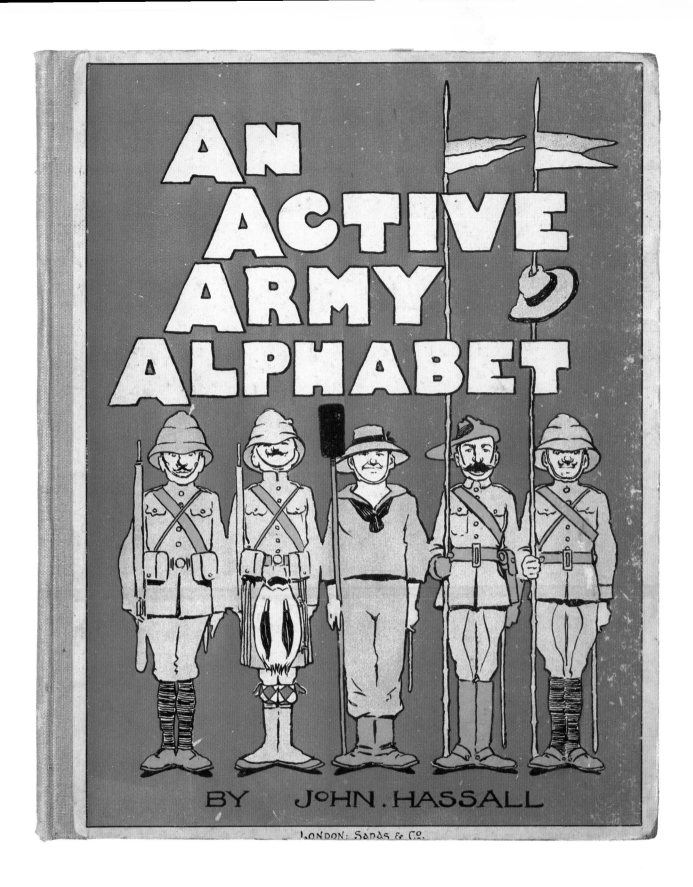

An Active Army Alphabet
John Hassall
Sands & Co.
London 1900

Paper covered boards backed in ochre
buckram. Colour illustration to front cover.
298×240mm

Lighthearted verse with bold illustrations
based on the prevailing situation. The title
page is dated Nov. '99 indicating the work
was completed within the first weeks of
hostilities.

53pp. Illustrated.

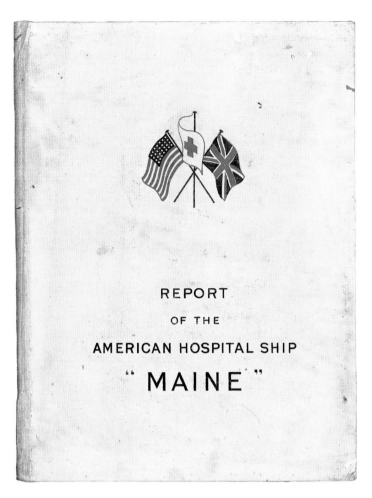

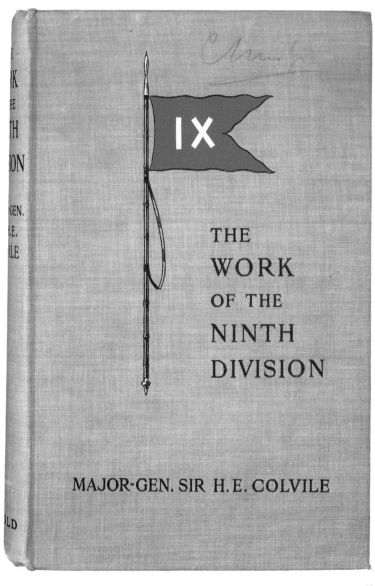

The Work Of The Ninth Division
Major-General Sir H. E. Colvile
Edward Arnold
London 1901

Fawn cloth. Front blocked in red, black and white. Spine blocked in black only.
229×146mm

A record of the campaign in the Orange Free State from Feb.–June 1900. The corps took part in operations at Paardeberg, Poplar Grove and Sanna's Post and, for a short period thereafter, engaged in column work in the area between Ventersburg and Heilbron. Gen. Colvile was dismissed from command in acrimonious circumstances. The Commander in Chief Lord Roberts, in correspondence with the War Office, made known that the Officer had on two occasions shown 'a want of initiative and military capacity'.

xiii+247pp. Folding maps and plans.

The American Hospital Ship 'Maine' Fund. Reports, List of Subscriptions, Donations, Etc. From October 27th, 1899, To April 30th, 1900.
Lady Randolph Churchill
(Chairman of the Executive Committee)
Wightman Mountain & Andrews, Ltd.
(Printers)
London nd. (c.1901)

Paper covered boards (imitation vellum). Front blocked in gold, black, red and dark blue.
289×217mm *(Illustrated)*

Variant binding
Red card cover. Black letterpress to front only.
266×206mm

Reports and accounts relating to the American hospital ship 'Maine' a vessel equipped and maintained by American subscription for service in the South African War. The 'Maine' completed three voyages from Dec. 1899 to Jan. 1901, the last voyage to the China station to aid allied forces in the China war. The reports present a coherent account of hospital arrangements, equipment and patient care. Lists of the executive and general committees and a list of medical and nursing staff are included. The card covered edition is of 56pp.

72+11pp. Illustrated.

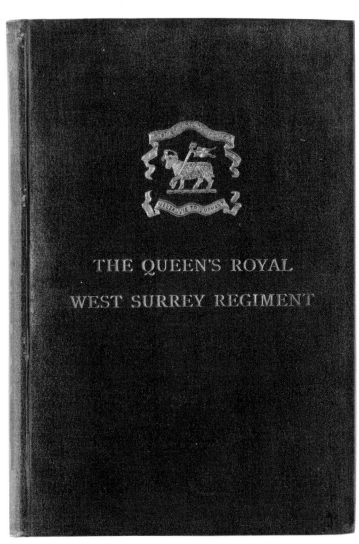

THE QUEEN'S ROYAL

WEST SURREY REGIMENT

Some Notes On The Queen's Royal West Surrey Regiment Together With An Account Of The 2nd And 3rd Battalions In The Late South African Campaign And Guildford's Aid To The Troops During Peace And War.
J. Davis/Sergeant-Major J. Woulds/ Sergeant H. R. Harrison
Frank Lasham
Guildford 1904

Vermilion cloth. Front blocked in gold.
189×125mm

An historical sketch of the regiment precedes an account of the 2nd and 3rd Battalions in South Africa. The 2nd Batt. took part in practically all the engagements in the Ladysmith relief operations and accompanied Buller's army in the northward march. In later stages of the campaign the 2nd Queen's operated in southern Transvaal with a detachment joining Col. Rimington's column in the north of Orange River Colony. The 3rd Battalion arrived at the Cape in March 1900 and, for the duration of the war, was chiefly employed in garrison and escort duties in various parts of the colony. The volume contains a list of honours gained and a chapter on memorials to the regiment.

94pp. Illustrated.

Boer War Diary Of Captain Eyre Lloyd, 2nd Coldstream Guards. Assistant Staff Officer, Colonel Benson's Column, Killed At Brakenlaagte, 30th October, 1901.
Captain T. H. Eyre Lloyd
(Printed for private circulation amongst the family)
Army and Navy Co-operative Society Limited
London 1905

Off white paper covered boards. Front blocked in maroon, dark blue and gold. Back and spine blocked in maroon and dark blue.
203×131mm

The diary of an officer of the 2nd Coldstream Guards from 12th November 1899 to 29th October 1901, being a record of operations in the western theatre and subsequent operations in the Transvaal. The author joined Col. Benson's force in March 1901 and died of wounds received in action near Bakenlaagte later that year. Some of Lloyd's letters from South Africa are reproduced together with other correspondence.

300pp. Illustrated.

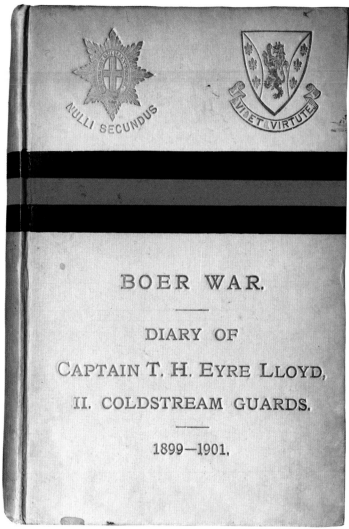

BOER WAR.

DIARY OF

CAPTAIN T. H. EYRE LLOYD,

II. COLDSTREAM GUARDS.

1899—1901.

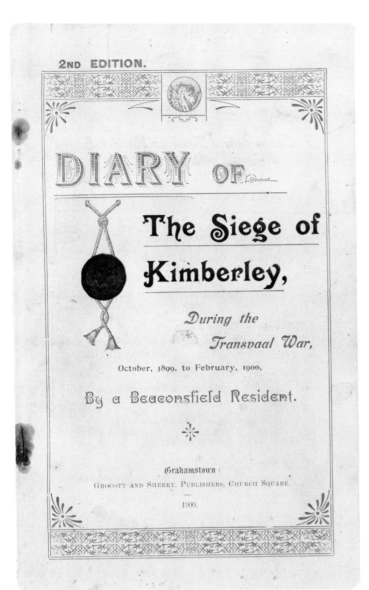

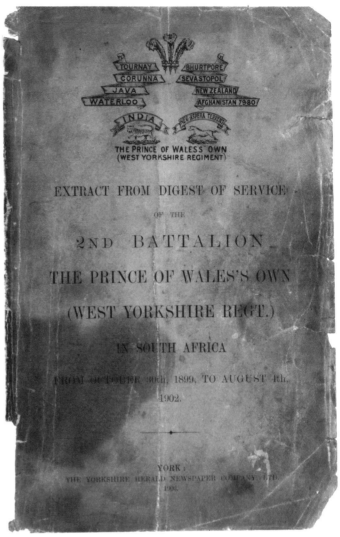

Diary Of The Siege Of Kimberley During
The Transvaal War, October, 1899
To February, 1900.
By a Beaconsfield Resident
Grocott and Sherry
Grahamstown 1900

White wraps. Red and blue letterpress to
front and back
214×133mm

A diary of the siege commencing October
14th, 1899 to February 18th, 1900. Together
with an extract from a speech – Mr Rhodes
on the siege.

89pp.

Extract From Digest Of Service Of The 2nd
Battalion The Prince Of Wales's Own (West
Yorkshire Regt.) In South Africa From
October 30th 1899, To August 4th, 1902.
(Author/editor not shown.)
The Yorkshire Herald Newspaper Company
Ltd.
York 1903

Light brown wrap. Black letterpress to front
only.
212×137mm

A diary of the campaign in South Africa.
The Battalion experienced severe fighting in
Natal in the first months of war taking part
in battles at Willow Grange, Vaal Krantz,
Monte Cristo and Railway Hill. Following
the occupation of Pretoria the West Yorks
remained in the Transvaal chiefly employed
in escort and garrison duties. At various
times they were at Rustenburg in the west
and Wakkerstroom and Piet Retief in the
south east. The record includes a list of
casualties.

106pp.

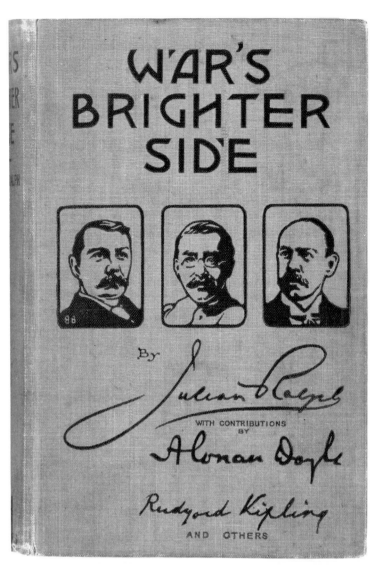

War's Brighter Side
The Story Of 'The Friend' Newspaper
Edited By The Correspondents With Lord
Roberts's Forces, March–April, 1900.
Julian Ralph
D. Appleton and Company
New York 1901

Fawn cloth. Front and spine blocked in
black.
194×126mm

An account of *The Friend* newspaper
established under military authority in
Bloemfontein soon after British occupation
in March 1900. For one month the paper
was edited by correspondents with Lord
Roberts' force before being turned over to
the proprietor of the *Johannesburg Star*.
Among contributors were Rudyard Kipling,
A. Conan Doyle and *The Times*
correspondent, Perceval Landon.

xvii+471pp. Illustrated.

The Petticoat Commando
Or Boer Women In Secret Service.
Johanna Brandt
Mills & Boon Limited
London nd. (1913)

Brown cloth. Front blocked in black, light
green and bottle green. Spine blocked in
black only.
197×124mm

An account of work done by Boer women
patriots during the struggle for
independence. The narrative is based on a
war diary relating events in the district of
Pretoria, then under martial law.

xv+376pp. Illustrated.

The War Against The Dutch
Republics In South Africa
Its Origin, Progress, And Results,
Annotated With . . . Extracts From Books,
Newspapers, Pamphlets, And Speeches By
Members Of Parliament And Other Leaders
Of Public Opinion.
H. J. Ogden
National Reform Union
Manchester nd. (1901)

(Presentation Copy)
Red cloth. Front and spine blocked in gold.
262×178mm *Illustrated.*

Variant bindings
Orange wrap. Black letterpress to front and
spine.
246×175mm

Red paper covered boards backed in red
buckram. Black letterpress to front. Spine
blocked in black.
246×175mm

Red paper covered boards backed in red
buckram. Black letterpress to front only.
251×171mm

A compilation of printed references
concerning the war in South Africa in
general support of the Boer republics.
With index.

344pp.

Echoes From The Battlefields Of
South Africa.
Dudley Kidd
Marshall Brothers
London 1900

Light green cloth. Front blocked in gold,
orange, black, white and red. Spine blocked
in black and gold.
198×128mm *(Illustrated)*

Variant binding
Maroon textured cloth. Front and spine
blocked in gold and blind.
201×130mm

An account of work undertaken by the
South Africa General Mission to aid soldiers
in the field. The narrative is primarily
concerned with events during the second
Boer War but includes reference to the
Jameson Raid and earlier work amongst the
Cape Mounted Riflemen.

xvi+192pp. Illustrated.

Recollections Of A Boer Prisoner-Of-War
At Ceylon.
J. N. Brink
Hollandsch-Afrikaansche Uitgevers-
Maatschappij, v/h Jac. Dusseau & Co.
Amsterdam/Cape Town 1904

Olive green textured cloth. Blind embossed
panels to front and spine with titles blocked
in gold. Paper onlay to front cover.
Decorative coat of arms embossed in blind
to rear cover.
230×151mm

An historical and descriptive sketch of the
island of Ceylon, with an account of the
outward journey from South Africa and of
life as experienced by Boer prisoners-of-war
at Diyatalawa and Ragama camps.

v+220pp. Illustrated.

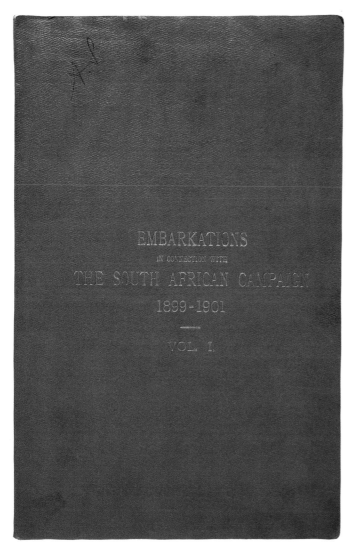

Embarkations In Connection With The
South African Campaign, 1899–1901.
(Up To 19th October 1900) Volume I.
(Compiler not shown.)
War Office
London 1901

Limp pebble grain red cloth. Front and
spine blocked in gold.
320×206mm

Papers relative to embarkations in
connection with the campaign in South
Africa. The volume contains an index to
units and drafts transported, index of ships
(with transport number), embarkations
from home and Mediterranean ports,
embarkations of troops, horses and mules
from India, embarkations of troops from
Mauritius and of colonial contingents.
Statement showing total number of troops
embarked for, and landed in, South Africa,
together with sundry information.

xxix+166pp.
(A second volume with supplement was
published in 1903.)

With The Scottish Rifle Volunteers At
The Front.
Godfrey H. Smith
William Hodge & Company
Glasgow/Edinburgh 1901

Tan cloth. Front blocked in red and black
with tartan fabric onlay. Spine blocked in
gold.
188×128mm

The record of K Company, the 2nd Scottish
Rifles, for approximately a year. The corps
arrived in South Africa in March 1900 and
joined Buller's army in Natal. Following the
eastern advance the volunteers served in
south eastern Transvaal, and later, in
northern Natal.

xvi+139pp. Various illustrations.

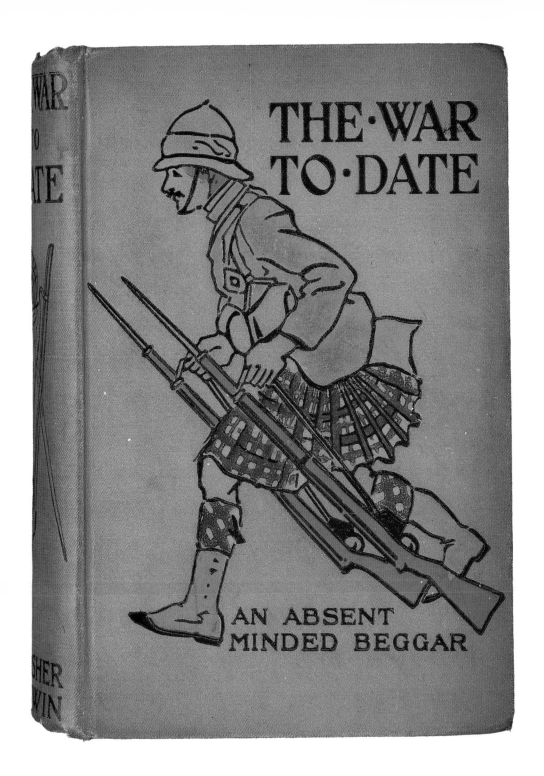

The War To Date (March 1, 1900)
Arthur H. Scaife
T. Fisher Unwin
London 1900

Light brown cloth. Front blocked in khaki,
black, blue, green and brown. Spine
blocked in brown and black. Back blocked
in blue and black.
192×125mm *(Illustrated)*

Variant binding
Olive green cloth blocked in black to front
and spine.
188×129mm

An outline of South African history and the
story of the war up to March 1900 with a
chapter on the political situation in Britain.
Appendices include a diary of the war,
biographical notes of British and Boer
officers, and a list of British officers killed,
wounded and missing from commencement
of hostilities to the relief of Ladysmith.

xii+372pp. Illustrated.

50

Le Livre D'Or (The Golden Book) Of The
Canadian Contingents In South Africa With
An Appendix On Canadian Loyalty
Containing Letters, Documents,
Photographs.
Gaston P. Labat
Montreal 1901

Red cloth. Front blocked in black, spine
blocked in gold.
230×156mm

A patriotic tribute published in English and
French. A volume consisting of stories,
letters and biographical notices of
Canadians involved in the war. With lists of
corps embarked for South Africa,
reinforcements and a list of casualties.

xii+178pp & xii+200pp & 66pp. Various
illustrations.

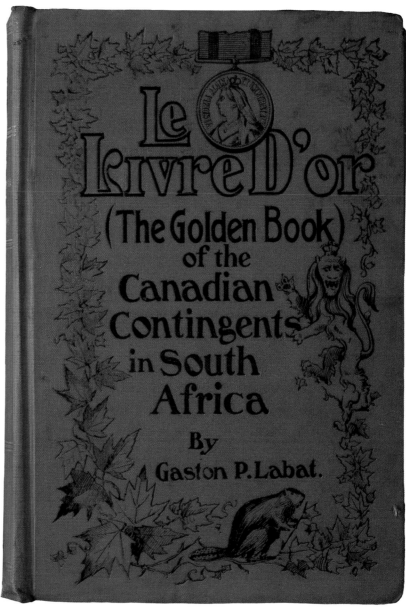

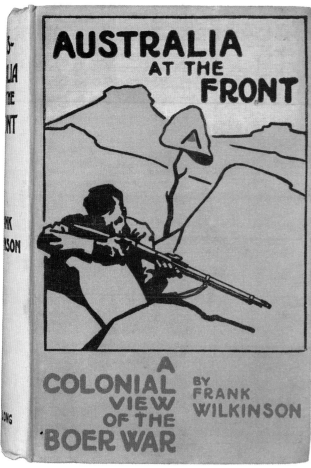

Australia At The Front
A Colonial View Of The Boer War.
Frank Wilkinson
John Long
London 1901

Khaki cloth. Front blocked in blue, red and
black. Spine blocked in black only.
196×125mm

Experiences of a war correspondent
contributing to the *Sydney Daily Telegraph*,
the *Adelaide Advertiser* and *Melbourne Age*.
The record covers ten months association
with Australian forces at the front and is
primarily concerned with events on the
march from Modder River to Pretoria, and
later operations in the Transvaal and
Orange River Colony.

xi+286pp. Folding map and illustrations.
(Illustrator – Norman H. Hardy.)

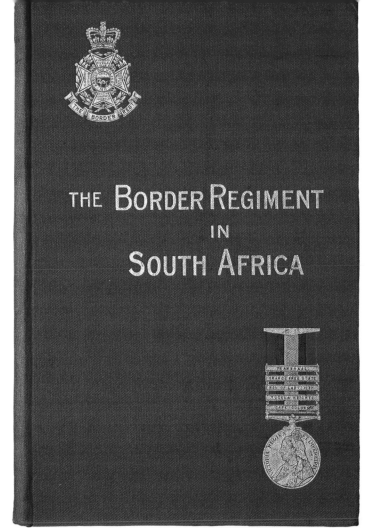

The Border Regiment In South Africa
1899–1902 From Photographs By Officers
Of The Regiment.
(Author/editor not shown.)
Eyre & Spottiswoode (Printers)
London nd. (c.1902)

Red cloth. Front blocked in silver, gold and
blue.
220×145mm.

A pictorial record of the 1st Battalion
Border Regiment in South Africa. The 128
captioned photographs reflect the
movements of the Regiment in Natal, Cape
Colony and Transvaal. For most of the
campaign the Battalion served in the
Transvaal, at various times operating about
Pretoria, Krugersdorp, in the Magaliesberg
and along the Ventersdorp-Lichtenburg
blockhouse line. Apart from titles and
captions the volume is devoid of letterpress.

Pages unnumbered (132pp. 66 printed
rectos).

With The Naval Brigade In Natal 1899–
1900. Journal Of Active Service Kept
During The Relief Of Ladysmith And
Subsequent Operations In Northern Natal
And The Transvaal, Under General Sir
Redvers Buller, V.C., G.C.B.
Lieutenant Burne, R.N.
Edward Arnold
London 1902

Dull blue/grey cloth, front blocked in
black. Spine blocked in gold.
230×147mm

The diary of a gunnery officer during ten
months service with the Naval Brigade in
South Africa. Burne joined Gen. Buller's
force in Natal taking part in operations at
Chieveley, Colenso, Spion Kop and Vaal
Krantz between December 1899 and
February 1900. Following the relief of
Ladysmith the naval detachment was
broken up. The men of *H.M.S. Powerful*
and *H.M.S. Terrible* being recalled for
service elsewhere. Burne was taken ill with
dysentery and sent to recuperate near
Maritzburg. On return to service in April he
was given command of a naval detachment
in General Hildyard's brigade. The writer
gives a personal account of the eastern
advance with reference to the engagement
at Almonds Nek in June 1900. Following a
second bout of illness in July the author
returned to his unit near Sandspruit in the
Transvaal until recalled from active service
in October 1900. The volume contains notes
on field gunnery together with a diary of the
war up to October 25, 1900. Extracts from
despatches and hints on clothing and
equipment for active service are appended.

xi+156pp. Folding map and plates.

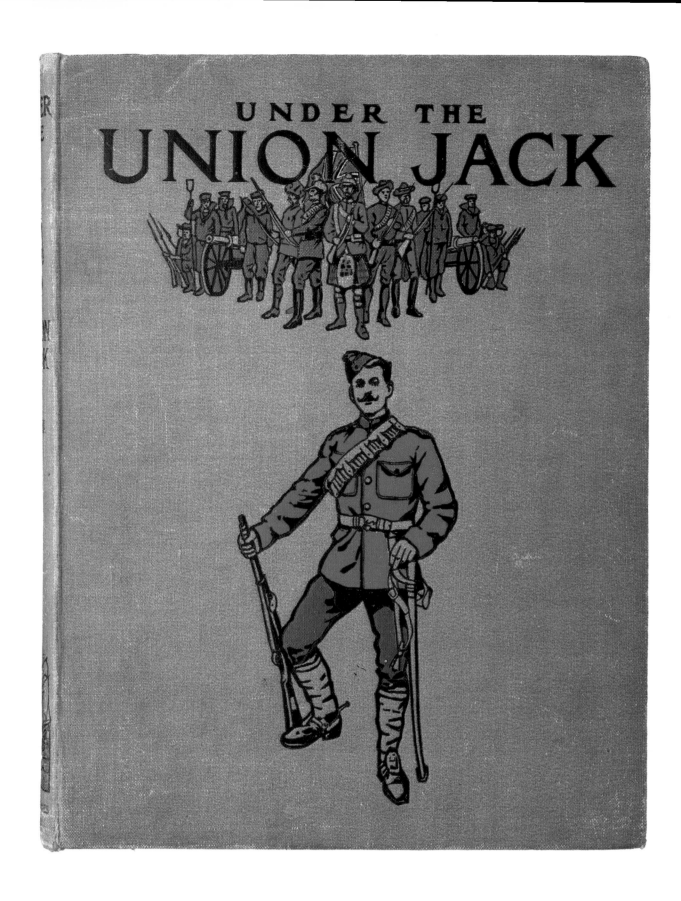

Under The Union Jack (Published Weekly)
Descriptive And Illustrative Of The
Campaign In South Africa The Second Boer
War. Vols. I & II.
(Author not shown)
George Newnes Limited
London nd. (1900)

Ochre cloth. Front and spine blocked in
blue, white, red and black.
294×228mm

A weekly survey of the war from Nov. 11,
1899 to July 14, 1900 being a pictorial
record of events in South Africa with notes
on war celebrities. News of the campaign is
related in ongoing articles 'Battling for
Empire' and 'Points on the war news'. 36
issues of the magazine comprise the record,
Vol. 1 includes numbers 1–18 from 11 Nov.
1899, to March 10, 1900. Vol. 2 includes
numbers 19–36 of March 17 to July 14,
1900. The magazines are bound without the
original covers, some were bound in one
volume of 36 issues.

Vol. 1. viii+432pp. Illustrated throughout.
Vol. 2. viii+pp.433–856. Illustrated
throughout.

A South African Journal, 1900
Captain H. I. Nicholl
For private circulation only
The Beds. Times Publishing Co. Ltd.
Bedford nd. (c.1908)

Fawn paper covered boards backed in dark
blue cloth. Edges trimmed flush. Front
printed dark blue and red. Back printed
dark blue only.
220×142mm

Soon after arrival at Cape Town in Feb.
1900 the author was appointed to command
of a Company in de Lisle's 2nd Mounted
Infantry Corps. In the advance from
Bloemfontein the volunteers were
frequently engaged. Between April 30 and
May 29 they were in action at Houtnek,
Zand River and Doornkop. Following the
capture of Johannesburg and Pretoria the
2nd M.I. took part in the battle of Diamond
Hill. By late June the unit had returned to
Orange River Colony, operating about
Heilbron. The writer was wounded in an
engagement with De Wet's force at
Paadeplatz the following month. He
remained some weeks in hospital at
Kroonstad and Wynberg before passage
home.

47pp. Map and illustrations.

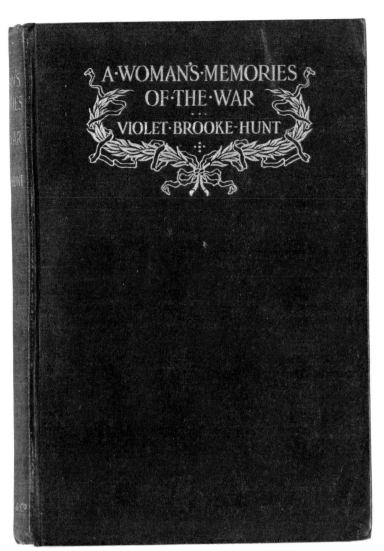

A Woman's Memories Of The War.
Violet Brooke-Hunt
James Nisbet & Co. Limited
London 1901

Maroon cloth blocked in gold to front and
spine.
196×133mm

A record of philanthropic endeavour during
the war. The author embarked for South
Africa in March 1900 determined to assist in
the war effort. She was initially employed at
convalescent camps at Naauwpoort and
Bloemfontein before proceeding to Pretoria
to establish a soldiers institute. The
narrative covers a period of nine months to
Nov. 1900 when the writer returned home.
Much of the content originally appeared in
The Lady.

vii+244pp. With frontispiece.

War Horses Present And Future: Or,
Remount Life In South Africa.
Sydney Galvayne
R. A. Everett & Co.
London 1902

Crimson cloth with paper onlay. Front and
spine blocked in white.
188×127mm

A volume pertaining to the supply and
management of horses during the war. The
author is critical of the Army Remount
Department suggesting a great deal of
money was wasted on purchase of
unsuitable animals. The merits of various
breeds are considered relative to conditions
prevailing in South Africa. In the writer's
opinion Arab and Australian ponies were
the most suitable. An interesting account is
given of work at the 'breaking department'
at the Stellenbosch remount depot, the
principal centre for remount distribution
during the war. Galvayne concludes with
suggestions for reorganization of the
department and attendant services.

202pp.

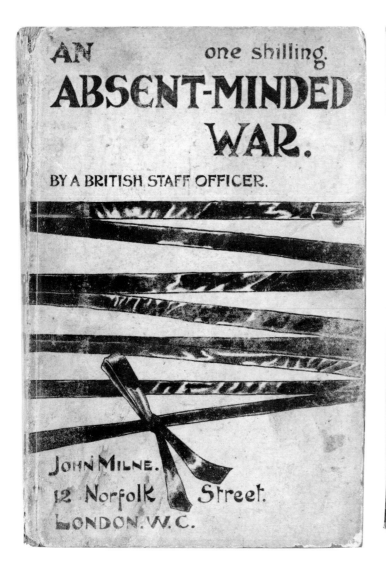

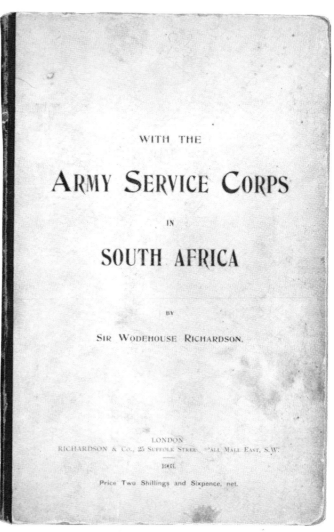

An Absent-Minded War Being Some
Reflections On Our Reverses And The
Causes Which Have Led To Them.
A British Staff Officer
John Milne
London nd. (1900)

White paper covered boards printed red to
front, back and spine.
181×121mm *(Illustrated)*

Variant binding
Dark blue cloth. Front and spine blocked in
gold.
188×127mm

An attack upon the British military system
in general and a call for the reorganization
of the army following the present war. The
writer is critical of the War Office and Staff
College suggesting both establishments
share responsibility for the predicament in
South Africa. With reference to war
despatches many commanders are criticized,
among them generals Buller, Methuen and
Gatacre. Anticipating future requirement
the author advocates a 'professional' army
led by highly trained, adequately paid
officers. A postscript relates to publication
of *The Spion Kop Despatches*, a source of
embarrassment to certain officers who
served in South Africa.

vii+183pp.

56

With The Army Service Corps In South
Africa By Sir Wodehouse Richardson,
K.C.B., Colonel (Late Army Service
Corps), Deputy Adjutant-General For
Supplies And Transport In South Africa,
1899–1900.
Sir Wodehouse Richardson
Richardson & Co.
London 1903

White paper covered boards backed in dark
blue cloth. Blue letterpress to front only.
213×140mm

An account of the organization and
distribution of supplies and transport
services to the army in South Africa, with
extracts from the authors' diary chiefly
relating to the first year of the campaign.

161pp.

A Fight To A Finish.
Major C. G. Dennison D.S.O.
Longmans, Green, and Co.
London, New York and Bombay 1904

Fawn cloth. Front blocked in brown. Spine
blocked in gold.
196×130mm

A colonial officer's account of the campaign
in the western sector, preceded by
reminiscences of the Boer War of 1881.
At the onset of hostilities in 1899 the author
left his home at Vryburg to assist in the
defence of Kuruman. The town fell to the
Boers in January 1900 and he was
imprisoned at Pretoria for a period of five
months. On liberation in June 1900
Dennison gained military appointments at
Rustenburg and Zeerust, transitory posts as
both towns were later evacuated when
threatened by enemy commandos. In
September the author received permission
to form a corps of scouts for local
operations. Initially he recruited fifty men
from the Vryburg area but the force later
expanded to over one hundred and fifty. At
various times Dennison's Scouts operated in
western Transvaal, Orange River Colony
and Bechuanaland under Generals Settle,
Parsons and various other commanders. For
over a year they were attached to the
Kimberley Column taking part in numerous
patrols and convoy operations in the
western districts under Colonel Milne, and
later, Major Paris. The author relates many
adventures and gives an account of his
capture at Paardeberg when ambushed by
enemy forces. He was fortunately released
some days later and rejoined the Kimberley
Column. In December 1901, following a
meeting with Lord Kitchener, Dennison was
offered a separate command. Recruitment
was well advanced in the new corps when
orders were received to disband the force.
An explanation was not offered leaving the
author resentful of the Imperial authorities.
To the end of the campaign Dennison
served under Major Paris in a newly formed
regiment, The Western Light Horse.

viii+192pp. Illustrated.

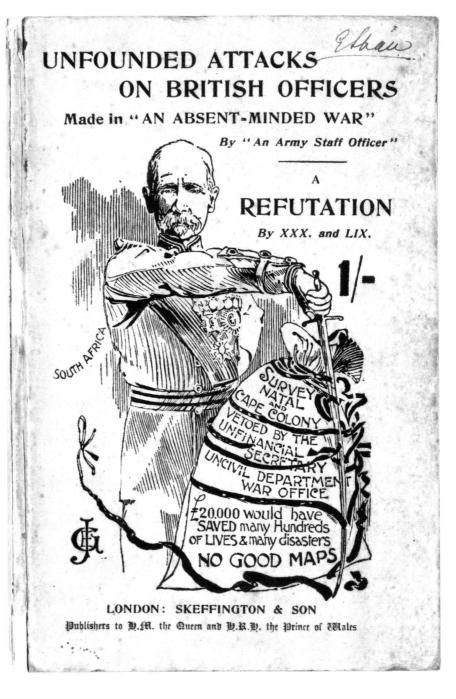

Unfounded Attacks On British Officers
Made In 'An Absent Minded War' By
'An Army Staff Officer'.
A Refutation by XXX and LIX.
XXX & LIX
Skeffington & Son
London 1901

Paper covered boards printed red to front
only
182×123mm

A refutation of allegations made in *An
Absent Minded War* concerning officers in
Her Majesty's Army serving in South
Africa, and a defence of War Office
departments involved in the present
conflict.

xiv+104pp.

HOW TO READ WAR NEWS

A VADE-MECUM
OF
NOTES AND HINTS
TO READERS OF DESPATCHES
AND INTELLIGENCE FROM
THE SEAT OF WAR WITH A
COLOURED WAR MAP AND
A GLOSSARY
OF
MILITARY
TECHNICAL TERMS,
LOCAL, AFRICAN & DUTCH
PHRASES ETC.

ALSO A SUPPLEMENTARY CHAPTER ON THE
SITUATION BY DR. G. M. THEAL

T. Fisher Unwin

XIII Hussars, South African War,
October, 1899–October 1902.
Compiled by Capt. J. H. Tremayne
May & Co. (Printers)
Aldershot nd. (c.1905)

Dark blue and white cloth over bevelled
boards. Front blocked in gold.
188×127mm

The regiment arrived in South Africa in
early December 1899, taking part in the
battle of Colenso and other engagements for
the relief of Ladysmith. From August 1900
to the close of that year the regiment was
chiefly employed along the Standerton-
Newcastle line. In 1901 the 13th Hussars
were brought to western Transvaal and
employed near Klerksdorp. They later
operated east of Pretoria under Brigadier-
Gen. G. Hamilton and other commanders.
The record includes a casualty list and a list
of honours gained.

ii+202pp.
(The South African War section of C. R. B.
Barrett's *History of the XIII Hussars* [2 vols.
London 1911] is based on Tremayne's
account.)

How To Read War News
A Vade-Mecum Of Notes And Hints To
Readers Of Despatches And Intelligence
From The Seat Of War With A Coloured
War Map And A Glossary Of Military
Technical Terms, Local, African And Dutch
Phrases Etc. Also A Supplementary
Chapter On The Situation By
Dr. G. M. Theal.
(Author/editor not shown.)
T. Fisher Unwin
London 1900

Grey paper covered boards printed black to
front and spine.
147×96mm *(Illustrated)*

Variant binding
Light blue paper covered boards printed
black to front and spine.
147×96mm

A handbook of useful information in
reference to the war, together with an
extract from Dr. Theal's 'South Africa'.

140pp. With a folding map.

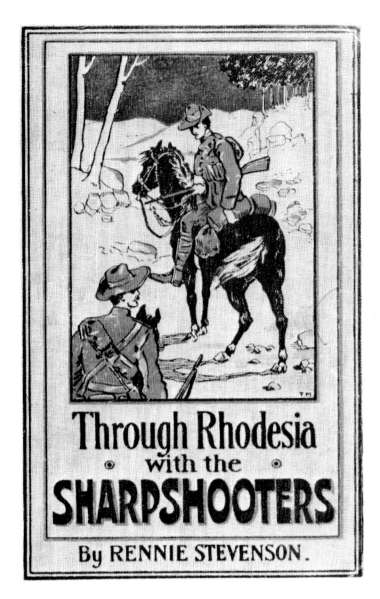

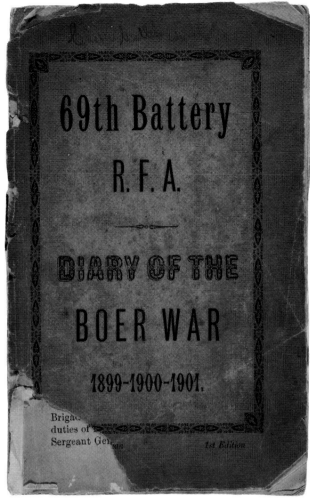

Through Rhodesia With The Sharpshooters
Rennie Stevenson
John Macqueen
London 1901

Light brown cloth. Front blocked in black,
red and ochre. Spine blocked in red and
black.
199×133mm

Experiences of a member of the 18th Battn.
Imperial Yeomanry. The corps arrived at
Beira in May 1900. Following a short delay
a squadron was entrained for the southward
journey to assist in the relief of Mafeking
but was too late to be of service. The
narrative concentrates on the various treks
undertaken by the force in Rhodesia and on
the brief excursion to the Zoutpansberg
area of the Transvaal.

199pp.

69th Battery R.F.A.
Diary Of The Boer War 1899–1900–1901.
(Author not shown.)
Blooming Press
Multan 1902

Grey/green wrap. Black letterpress to
front only.
218×135mm

A brief record of 69th Battery to November
1901. The battery was present at Talana Hill
at the outset of war and active in Ladysmith
throughout the siege. In April 1900 the 69th
joined Gen. Buller's force in the advance on
the Transvaal where, for much of 1901, the
battery was employed in the south-eastern
sector. A short account is given of
operations in Zululand where a section of
the battery served. A list of casualties
during the campaign is included.

84pp.

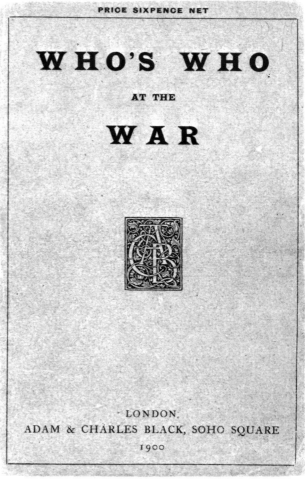

My Experiences Of The Boer War.
Translated From The German With
An Introduction By Lieut.-Colonel
G. F. R. Henderson.
Count Sternberg
Longmans, Green, and Co.
London 1901

Sienna cloth. Front blocked in blind and
gold. Spine blocked in gold.
201×133mm

A narrative of travel in the Boer states
during the war. The author, an Austrian,
met Presidents Kruger and Steyn during
visits to the Boer capitals prior to joining
the republican army at the western front
near Jacobsdal. As an accredited war
correspondent Sternberg was allowed free
movement within the war zone. He gives a
description of camp life on the Modder
River, recounts a visit to Boer forces
surrounding Kimberley and reports events
from Gen. Cronje's camp near Paardeberg.
The author was taken prisoner at
Paardeberg drift shortly before Cronje's
surrender.

xliii+268pp.

Who's Who At The War
(Author not shown.)
Adam & Charles Black
London 1900

Red paper cover, printed black to front and
back.
186×123mm

Biographical notes of war personalities with
a list of officers wounded and killed and a
short bibliography.

55pp.

60

The 'Last Post': Being A Roll Of All
Officers (Naval, Military Or Colonial) Who
Gave Their Lives For Their Queen, King
And Country, In The South African War,
1899–1902.
Mildred G. Dooner
Simpkin, Marshall, Hamilton,
Kent & Co. Ltd.
London nd. (1903)

Dark grey cloth, front and spine blocked in
gold.
228×147mm

A memorial to officers who lost their lives
in the war together with information, where
available, in regard to their careers and
services. A list of war correspondents and
nursing sisters who died during the conflict
is included.

viii+446pp. With frontispiece.

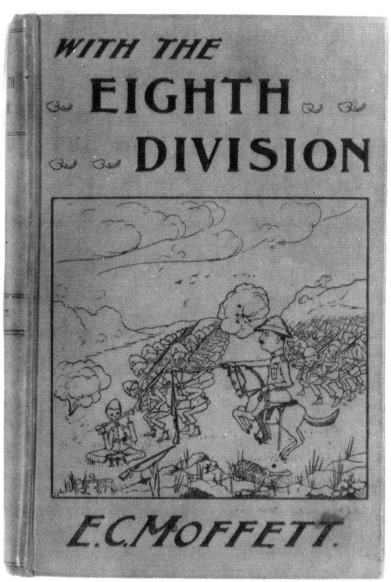

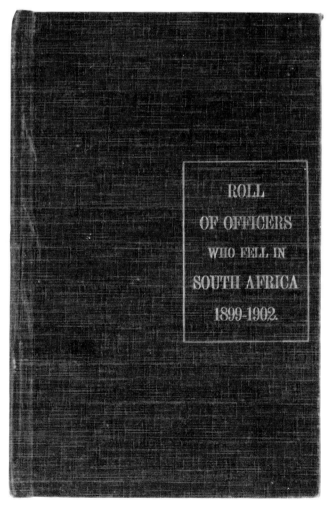

With The Eighth Division: A Souvenir Of
The South African Campaign.
Private E. C. Moffett
Revised by *Sergt. F. J. B. Lee*
Knapp, Drewett & Sons Ltd.
Kingston-On-Thames and Westminster 1903

Red buckram. Front and spine blocked in
black.
192×128mm

A record of operations of the force
commanded by Maj.-Gen. Rundle. Details
are given of the composition of the corps
together with accounts of engagements and
marches from mid-April 1900 to the close of
the campaign. Much of the narrative relates
to events in the eastern sector of Orange
River Colony. An extensive casualty list by
regiment is included, compiled from official
records.

xiv+222+ii+xlvii.pp. Folding map and
plates.

With Seven Generals In The Boer War
A Personal Narrative.
Major A. W. A. Pollock
Skeffington & Son
London 1900

Green cloth. Front and spine blocked in
dark blue and white, back blocked in dark
blue only.
193×130mm

Campaign experiences from October 1899
to July 1900. The author accompanied
several forces during nine months of war
reporting operations from various fronts
including Stormberg, General Methuen's
operations about Boshof, and the relief of
Mafeking. The narrative incorporates
material originally published in *The Times*.

viii+292pp. Maps and illustrations.

With The Guards' Brigade From
Bloemfontein To Koomati Poort And Back.
Rev. E. P. Lowry
Horace Marshall & Son
London 1902

Olive green cloth. Front blocked in black
and yellow ochre. Spine blocked in black.
208×137mm *(Illustrated)*

Variant binding
Dull red cloth. Front blocked in ochre and
black. Spine blocked in black only.
208×138mm

A record compiled by the senior Wesleyan
chaplain attached to the Guards' Brigade.
Most of the narrative concerns the march
through the Orange Free State and later
operations in the Transvaal. A chapter, on
clergy in general, is included. Some of the
material was first published in *The
Methodist Times*, *The Methodist Recorder*
and other papers.

xii+277pp. Illustrated.

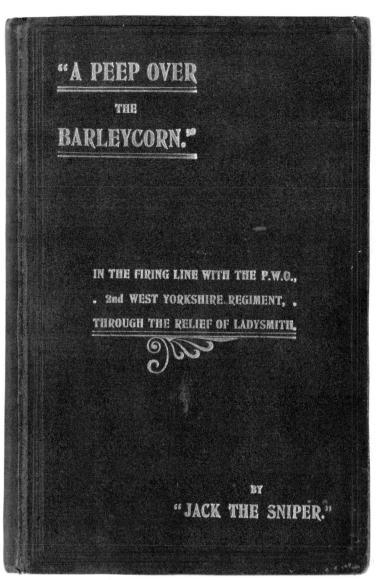

'A Peep Over The Barleycorn' In The
Firing Line With The P.W.O., 2nd West
Yorkshire Regiment, Through The Relief
Of Ladysmith.
'Jack The Sniper'
(Charles James O'Mahony)
John T. Drought (Printer)
Dublin 1911

Blue fine grain cloth. Front blocked in blind
and gold.
190×124mm

Recollections of service with the 2nd Batt.
West Yorkshire Regiment in South Africa.
The 'barleycorn' mentioned in the title
refers to the foresight of a Lee-Metford
rifle. (An account of regimental operations
is given under *Extract From Digest Of
Service Of The 2nd Battalion P.W.O. West
Yorkshire Regt.* p.45.)

214pp. Illustrated.

On Commando
Dietlof Van Warmelo
Methuen & Co.
London 1902

Crimson cloth. Front blocked in blind and
gold. Spine blocked in gold, back blocked in
blind only.
198×130mm

War experiences of a Transvaal Boer.
A short account of events in Natal precedes
a narrative of the guerilla campaign in the
Transvaal. The author was taken prisoner in
1901 and shipped to India.

viii+183pp. With portrait frontispiece.

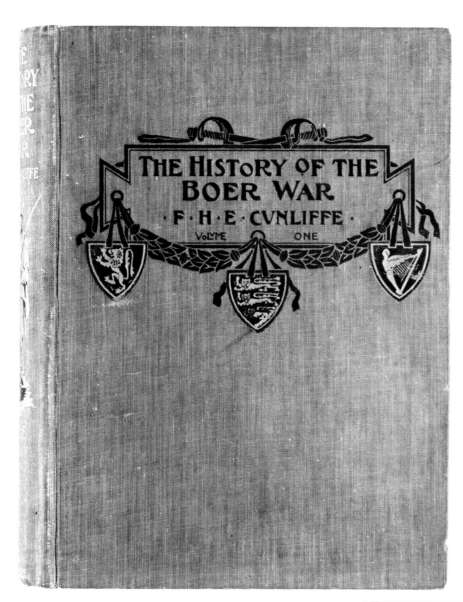

The History Of The Boer War
F. H. E. Cunliffe
Methuen and Co.
London 1901

Crimson cloth. Front blocked in navy blue and cream. Spine blocked in navy blue and gold.
254×190mm

A general history of the war in two volumes. Vol.1 published in 1901 outlines events to the relief of Ladysmith. Vol.2 of 1904 is titled 'The History Of The Boer War To The Occupation Of Bloemfontein'. Appendices to the second volume include notes on the defence of Ladysmith and reference to volunteer forces.

viii+520pp. & xiii+646pp. Maps and illustrations throughout.

A Mule-Driver At The Front Being Transport Experiences In Natal.
Roland Cecil Billington
Chapman & Hall Ltd.
London 1901

Maroon cloth blocked in white to front and spine.
196×128mm

Proposals for improvement of the transport system and better animal management based on practical experience gained in the war. The author was employed in the ambulance service transporting casualties to field hospitals during the Ladysmith relief operations. He was later promoted to sub-conductor in charge of a group of wagons conveying supplies to the Transvaal. The record extends to August 1900.

xii+92pp. Illustrated.

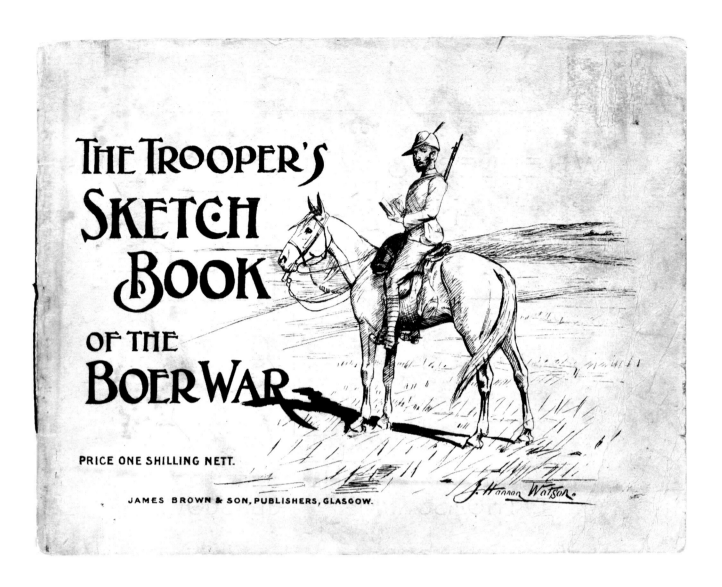

The Trooper's Sketch Book Of The
Boer War.
J. Hannan Watson
James Brown & Son
Glasgow nd. (c.1900)

Yellow card cover. Red and black
letterpress to front. Back printed black
only.
215×280mm

Sketches of the Boer campaign compiled by
trooper Watson of the Imperial Yeomanry,
being a record of sixteen months active
service. The volume is comprised of thirty
sketches depicting mundane incidents in the
life of a trooper on the veldt. The
illustrations include scenes of camp life,
outpost duty, foraging and field ablutions.
Each drawing is accompanied by a
descriptive text.

Unnumbered. (80pp. Including 3 pages of
advertisements and some blanks.)

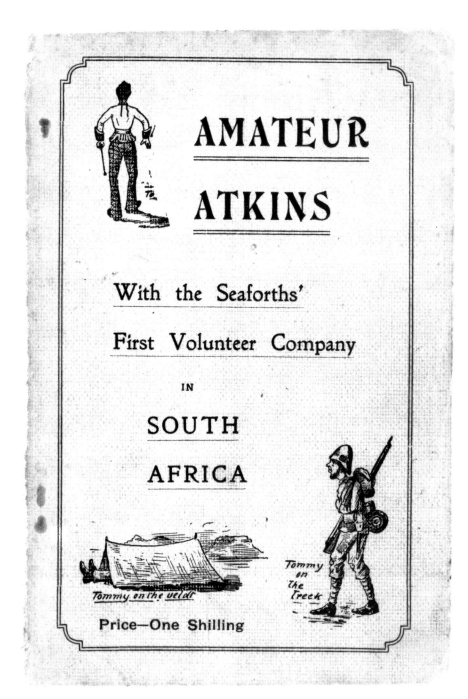

Amateur Atkins On Active Service With
The Seaforths' First Volunteer Company
In South Africa.
Private William Cowper
Peter Reid & Coy.
Wick 1902

Beige paper cover. Front printed red.
183×125mm *(Illustrated)*

Variant binding
Red cloth. Front blocked in black.
184×123mm

A campaign diary compiled by a volunteer
in K company 2nd Seaforth Highlanders.
During an active campaign from March 1900
to Feb. 1901 the volunteers made wide
ranging moves in the Orange Free State.
At various times they were at Frankfort and
Heilbron in the north and Jagersfontein and
Rouxville to the south. The corps
experienced little fighting throughout the
campaign but took part in the battle for
Retiefs Nek on July 24. In all engagements
losses were light. For a brief period in
August/September 1900 the Seaforths were
left to garrison Heilbron. At other times
they were employed in escorting convoys.
The writer gives a disturbing account of the
evacuation of Jagersfontein on Christmas
day 1900 and of a farm burning mission in
the Zastron area in January 1901. Shortly
thereafter he was taken ill with enteric fever
and removed to hospital in Aliwal North
prior to being shipped home. A list of
officers and men of K (Volunteer) Company
2nd Seaforths is appended.

110pp.

French's Cavalry Campaign
J. G. Maydon
C. Arthur Pearson Ltd.
London 1901

Crimson cloth. Front and spine blocked in
white.
191×127mm

A record of operations in the western
sector. Chapters relate to events at Modder
River, Magersfontein, to Gen. French's
cavalry operations in northern Cape Colony
and the relief of Kimberley. The narrative is
brought down to the capture of
Bloemfontein, including an account of
Cronje's surrender at Paardeberg.

xxix+pp.31–198. Illustrated.

The Boer War, 1899–1900. From The
Ultimatum To The Occupation Of
Bloemfontein. Compiled From Authentic
Sources.
(Author/compiler not shown.)
R. E. King Limited
London 1900

Tan cloth. Front and spine blocked in black
and gold. Back blocked in blind.
242×180mm

A narrative of the war up to the fall of
Bloemfontein, preceded by a chapter on the
origin of the Boer Republics and the causes
of the war.

ii+316pp. Illustrated.

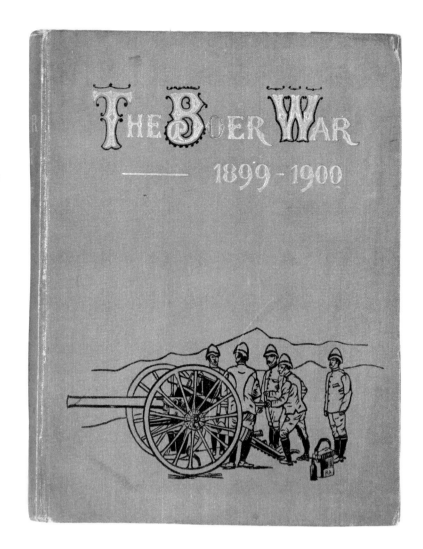

For Remembrance And In Honour Of
Those Who Lost Their Lives In The South
African War 1899–1902 Lest We Forget.
Colonel Sir James Gildea
Printed by Eyre and Spottiswoode Ltd.
London 1911

Red cloth blocked in gold to front and
spine.
313×252mm

A short description of some 900 memorials
to the fallen in the South African War. The
content is divided into two parts. The first
deals with monuments in the British Isles
and the second relates to the colonies,
including memorials in South Africa.
Various indices show names, places,
regiments and sculptors.

xv+429pp. Illustrated throughout.

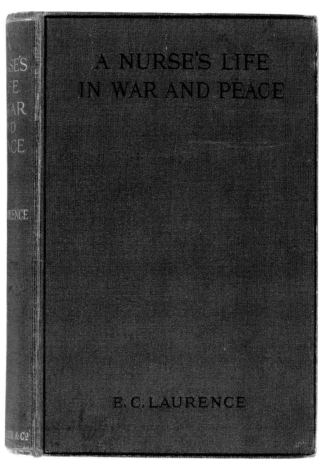

Diary Of An Edinburgh Trooper Being
A Series Of Letters Written During The
South African Campaign, 1901–2.
R. Paterson Hay
Printed for private circulation
Bishop & Sons
Edinburgh 1903

Crimson cloth blocked in gold to front and
spine.
191×124mm

Diary of a volunteer in the 19th Company
Imperial Yeomanry. Much of the narrative
relates to operations along the Orange
River Colony and Basutoland border.

vi+137pp. Illustrated.

A Nurse's Life In War And Peace
E. C. Laurence
Smith, Elder & Co.
London 1912

Dark blue ribbed cloth. Front blocked in
black, spine blocked in gold.
192×125mm

An account of nursing experiences
presented in a series of letters. Some of the
correspondence is addressed from South
Africa and Egypt prior to Oct. 1899 but
most of the content relates to medical work
during the Second Boer War.

xi+311pp.

"O.H.M.S."

or

HOW
1200 SOLDIERS
went to
TABLE BAY

'Troopin, Troopin, Troopin To The Sea'
'O.H.M.S.' An Illustrated Record Of The
Voyage Of S.S. 'Tintagel Castle' Conveying
Twelve Hundred Soldiers From
Southampton To Cape Town March 1900.
Recorded and illustrated by
W. McLean and E. H. Shackleton
Simpkin Marshall, Hamilton, Kent & Co.,
Limited.
London 1900

Paper covered boards. Front and back
printed black and light blue.
287×195mm

An account of the ship and her officers
precedes a narrative of the voyage to South
Africa. The log of the voyage is reproduced
together with a nominal roll of every
regiment represented and a list of
occupations of the 1200 troops aboard.

59pp. Illustrated.

NOTES ON THE CONSTRUCTION OF

"LONG CECIL,"

A 4·1-INCH RIFLED BREECHLOADING GUN,

IN KIMBERLEY, DURING THE SIEGE, 1899–1900.

BY

South

EDWARD GOFFE, A.M.I.MECH.E. *Africa*

———◆———

EXCERPT MINUTES OF PROCEEDINGS
OF THE MEETING
OF THE

INSTITUTION OF MECHANICAL ENGINEERS,

IN LONDON, 28TH JUNE 1900.

SIR WILLIAM H. WHITE, K.C.B., LL.D., D.Sc., F.R.S.,
PRESIDENT.

———

BY AUTHORITY OF THE COUNCIL.

———

PUBLISHED BY THE INSTITUTION,
STOREY'S GATE, ST. JAMES'S PARK, WESTMINSTER, S.W.

———

The right of Publication and of Translation is reserved.

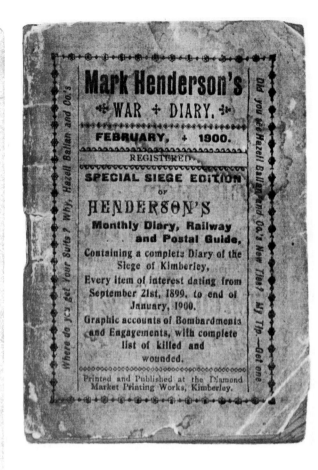

Notes On The Construction Of 'Long
Cecil', A 4·1-Inch Rifled Breechloading
Gun, In Kimberley, During The Siege,
1899–1900. By Edward Goffe, A.M.I.Mech.E.
Excerpt Minutes Of Proceedings Of The
Meeting Of The Institution Of Mechanical
Engineers In London, 28th June 1900.
Sir William H. White, K.C.B., LL.D.,
D.Sc., F.R.S., President.
By Authority Of The Council.
Edward Goffe
Published by the Institution
Westminster nd. (1900)

Dull brown paper cover printed black to
front only.
216×140mm

Notes relating to the construction of a gun
in the workshops of the De Beers Company.
The work progressed under direction of Mr.
G. Labram who was unfortunately killed by
a Boer shell during the siege.

pp.359–374. Photographic plate and
drawings.

Mark Henderson's War Diary. February,
1900. Special Siege Edition Of Henderson's
Monthly Diary, Railway And Postal Guide,
Containing A Complete Diary Of The Siege
Of Kimberley, Every Item Of Interest
Dating From September 21st, 1899, To End
Of January, 1900. Graphic Accounts Of
Bombardments And Engagements, With
Complete List Of Killed And Wounded.
Mark Henderson
Diamond Market Printing Works
Kimberley 1900

Light green wrap. Printed black to front and
back.
111×76mm

Principally a diary of local events during the
siege of Kimberley, together with accounts
of the battles of Modder River,
Magersfontein, and the battle of Tugela in
Natal. Pages 36 to 49 comprise a diary for
February 1900. Several advertisements for
local firms appear throughout.

98pp.

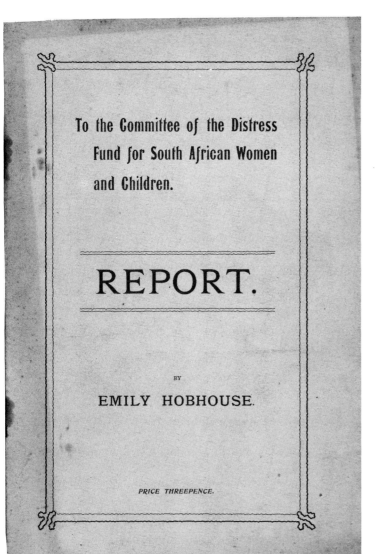

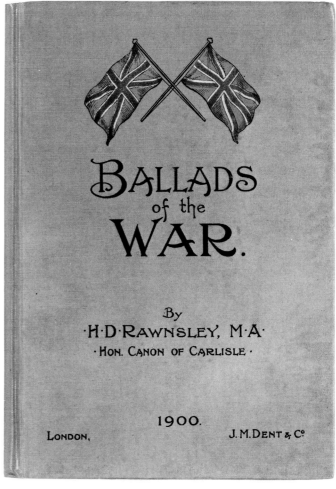

To The Committee Of The South African
Distress Fund. Report Of A Visit To The
Camps Of Women And Children In The
Cape And Orange River Colonies.
Emily Hobhouse
Friars Printing Association Limited
London nd. (c.1901)

Buff limp card cover, printed black to front
only.
244×163mm

Report and extracts from letters concerning
visits to concentration camps in the Cape
and Orange River Colony. A list of
recommendations for improvement of the
camps is included together with appendices
comprised of personal records of inmates,
applications for release, etc. A fuller
account of internment camps is given in the
volume *The Brunt Of The War And Where
It Fell.*

39pp.

Ballads Of The War
H. D. Rawnsley
J. M. Dent & Co.
London 1901

Ochre cloth. Front blocked in red, white,
black and blue.
193×134mm *(Illustrated)*

Variant bindings
Light grey/green cloth. Front blocked in
dark green. Spine blocked in dark green and
gold.
197×134mm

Brown wrap printed red, blue and black to
front only.
200×135mm

A record in verse of some golden deeds and
incidents of the war. Contents include
'Death aboard our transports', 'To Winston
Churchill', 'To De Wet', etc. The enlarged
second edition with illustrations.

xiv+219pp. Illustrated.

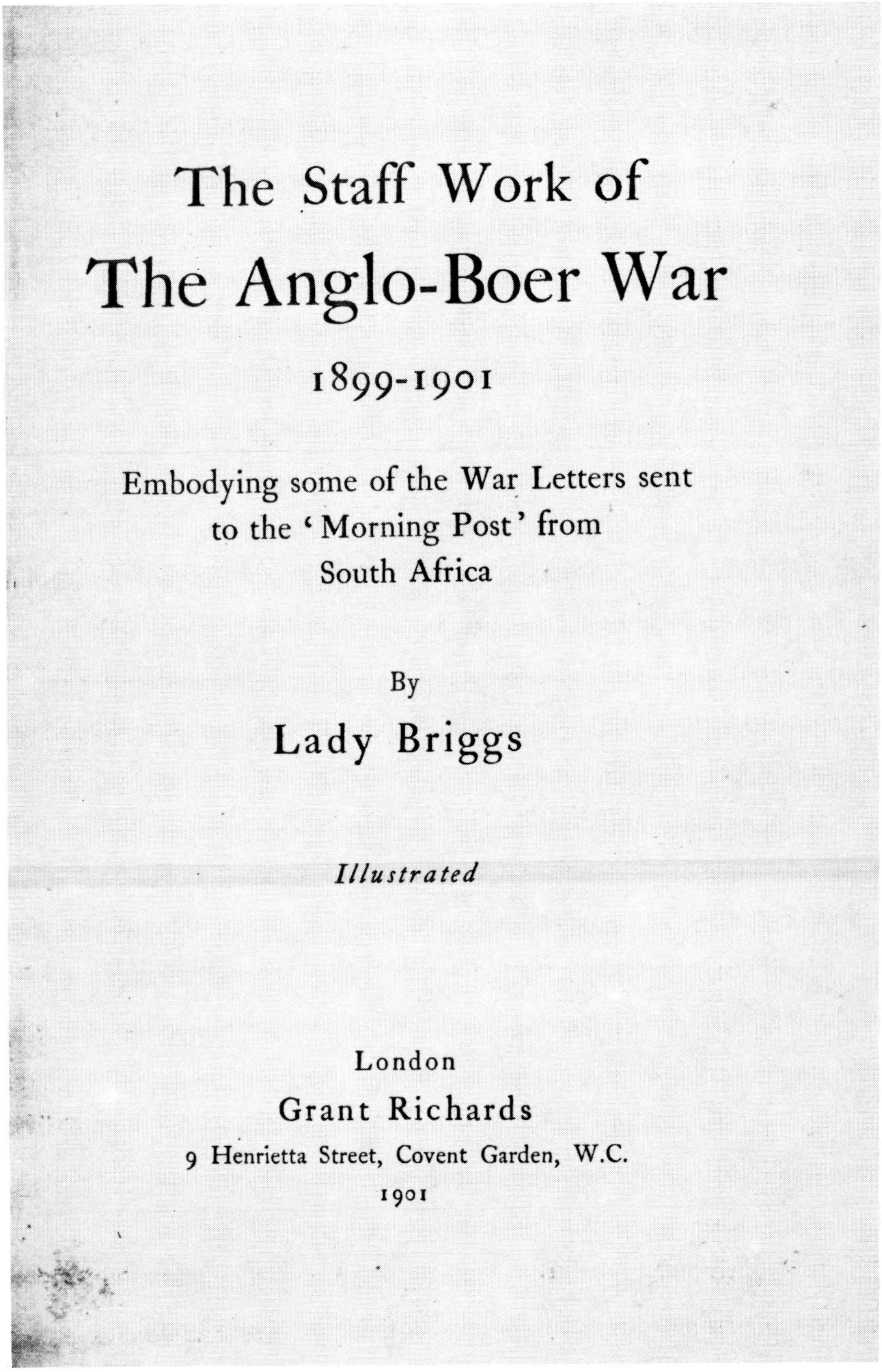

The Staff Work of
The Anglo-Boer War

1899-1901

Embodying some of the War Letters sent
to the 'Morning Post' from
South Africa

By

Lady Briggs

Illustrated

London

Grant Richards

9 Henrietta Street, Covent Garden, W.C.

1901

The Staff Work Of The Anglo–Boer War
1899–1901 Embodying Some Of The War
Letters Sent To The 'Morning Post' From
South Africa.
Lady Briggs
Grant Richards
London 1901

Crimson cloth. Front and spine blocked in
gold.
233×154mm

An account of work done by non-combatant
branches of the army and other
administrative departments. Chapters relate
to the Remount Department, Transport
Department, Government Railways, Field
Post Office, Press Censors, etc., together
with information in reference to medical
services, official and private.

xi+503pp. Illustrated.
Title-page shown

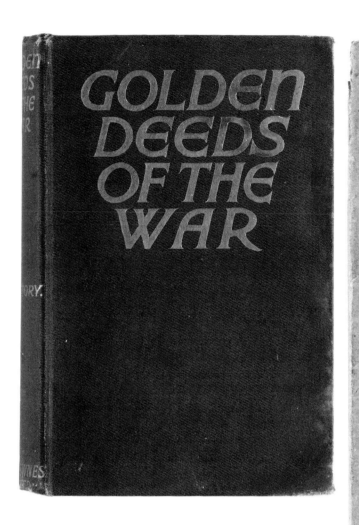

Golden Deeds Of The War
Alfred Thomas Story
George Newnes Limited
London 1900

Bright red cloth blocked in gold to front and
spine.
189×124mm

Variant binding
Dark blue cloth blocked in gold to front and
spine.
189×124mm *(Illustrated)*

A record of brave and daring deeds
performed in battle. The events described
occurred in the first year of the campaign.

xii+315pp. Illustrated.

Boer War, 1899–1900
Chart Showing Organization And
Distribution Of The British Forces With
A List Of Military And Naval Officers And
An Account Of The Organization And
Administration Of The Boer Forces Etc.
Lieut.-Colonel H. M. E. Brunker
William Clowes and Sons, Limited
London 1900

Red wrap. Printed black to front and back.
215×140mm

Statistics relative to military forces in South
Africa with a diary of the present campaign
and lists of casualties. The volume contains
a large folding chart showing the
arrangement of British forces.

125pp. Folding map.

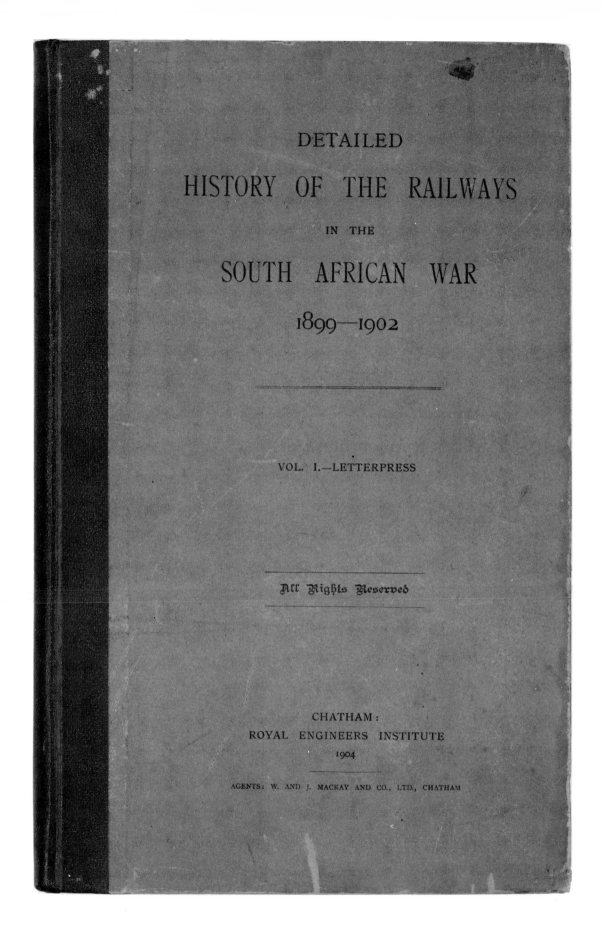

DETAILED

HISTORY OF THE RAILWAYS

IN THE

SOUTH AFRICAN WAR

1899—1902

VOL. I.—LETTERPRESS

All Rights Reserved

CHATHAM:

ROYAL ENGINEERS INSTITUTE

1904

AGENTS: W. AND J. MACKAY AND CO., LTD., CHATHAM

Detailed History Of The Railways In The South African War 1899–1902.
Royal Engineers Institute
(W. and J. Mackay and Co., Ltd.) Agents Chatham 1904

Blue paper covered boards backed in blue cloth. Black letterpress to front cover of both volumes.
340×218mm

A record of railway operations during the war abridged from the four volume official record compiled by the War Office. Due to considerations of expense only the first volume of the original history was published, i.e. – (*History Of The Railways During The War In South Africa, 1899–1902 By Lieut.-Colonel Sir E. P. C. Girouard, K.C.M.G., D.S.O., R.E., Director Of Railways, South Africa Field Force. London 1903.*) The present work is drawn from the last three volumes of the original compilation and issued under the title – Detailed History Of The Railways, Etc., in two volumes.

Volume 1. Letterpress. xxvi+275+xxvii–xli. pp. With map and folding charts.
Volume 2. Illustrations. viii+61pp. photographs. Together with 93 plates and a map.

The Kirkcaldy War Album Containing
Portraits Of Over Two Hundred Fife Men
Serving In South Africa And Groups And
Views Connected With The War.
(Author/editor not shown.)
The 'Fifeshire Advertiser' Office
Kirkcaldy 1901

Red grained cloth, front blocked in gold.
283×223mm

A compilation of photographs and drawings
in celebration of local men serving in South
Africa.

64pp. Illustrated.

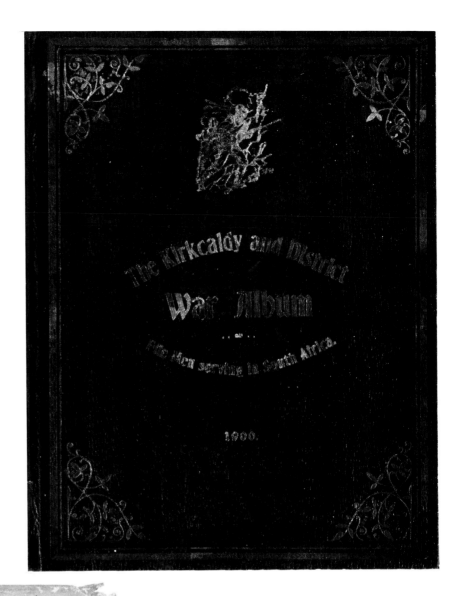

5,000 Miles With The Cheshire Yeomanry
In South Africa. A Series Of Articles
Compiled From Letters And Diaries
Written By Officers, Non-Commissioned
Officers And Men Of The 21st And 22nd
(Cheshire) Companies Of Imperial
Yeomanry, Relating Their Experiences
During The South African War In The
Years 1900–1901; Also Articles From 'The
Times', 'The Times History Of The War',
And Other Papers Relating To The
Marches, Movements And Operations
Of The Two Companies.
Compiled by
John H. Cooke
Mackie & Co. Ltd, Warrington
Phillipson & Golder, Chester
1913–1914

Red cloth blocked in black to front and
spine.
252×188mm

Variant binding
Superior edition. Red half calf. Front and
spine blocked in gold.
253×188mm

A comprehensive record compiled from
diverse sources. The 21st and 22nd
(Cheshire) companies of Imperial
Yeomanry operated in the Orange River
Colony and Cape Colony, the record
includes nominal rolls of both companies
together with an itinerary. Five hundred
copies of the book were printed, many of
them numbered and signed by the compiler.

xxxiii+434pp. Folding map in separate
pocket. Numerous illustrations.
*Standard edition in original dust-jacket
shown*

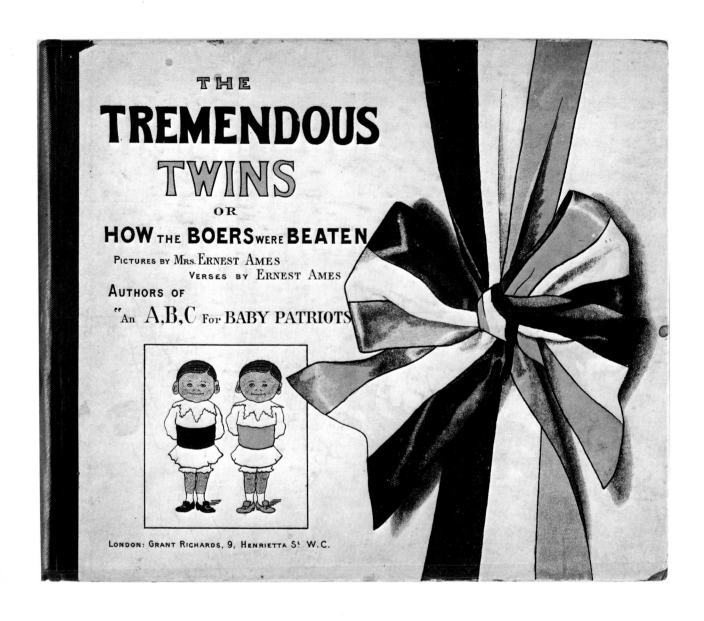

The Tremendous Twins Or How The Boers
Were Beaten.
Pictures by *Mrs. Ernest Ames*
Verses by *Ernest Ames*
Grant Richards
London 1900

White paper covered boards backed in red
cloth. Front printed black, red, yellow and
blue. Back printed black, red and blue.
211×250mm

The story of four-year-old twins (appointed
Commanders-in-Chief by the Queen) who
embark for South Africa to bring the war to
a close. By the end of the adventure they
have shown the Generals how to beat the
Boers and chased Mr Kruger from Pretoria.
Typical of many juvenile publications of the
period.

95pp. Illustrated.

2nd Battalion South Wales Borderers South
African War 1899–1902.
(Author/editor not shown.)
Swiss & Co. Army printers
Devonport nd. (c.1902)

Dark green cloth backed in white cloth.
Front blocked in gold.
137×110mm

Campaign record from Oct. 11th, 1899 to
May 31st, 1902. The Battalion joined Lord
Roberts' force at Ramdam in February 1900
and took part in subsequent operations to
the fall of Pretoria. In Transvaal the 2nd
Batt. engaged in column work and garrison
duties mainly in the south-western sector.
The Borderers were the main part of a
detachment forced to surrender at
Modderfontein, of which action a full
account is given. The record includes a
summary of services of the Mounted
Infantry sections, lists of casualties, deaths
from disease, names of officers on active
service and a list of honours and awards
gained.

125pp. With folding map.

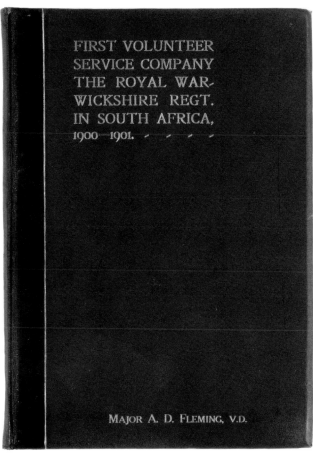

Record Of The First Volunteer Service
Company The Royal Warwickshire
Regiment In South Africa 1900–1901.
Major A. D. Fleming
The Midland Counties Herald Limited
Birmingham 1907

Red cloth over bevelled boards backed in
red calf. Front and back blocked in gold.
255×181mm

The volunteers arrived at Cape Town in
March 1900. During an active campaign of
thirteen months they took part in operations
in Cape Colony, Orange Free State and
Transvaal. The Company moved north from
Bloemfontein with the 11th Division in May
1900. In Transvaal, between June 4 and
Aug. 26, the Warwicks were in action at Six
Mile Spruit, Diamond Hill and Belfast.
They were later employed along the
Pretoria–Koomati Poort rail line between
Balmoral and Waterval Boven. By
December the volunteers were stationed in
Cape Colony in the vicinity of Bethulie
Bridge. In March they moved to Bethulie
town in the Orange River Colony, where
they formed part of the garrison for a brief
period prior to returning home in April
1901. The record appears as chapter X in
Col. C. J. Hart's book entitled *The History
Of The 1st Volunteer Battalion The Royal
Warwickshire Regiment And Its Predecessors*
(Birmingham 1906). A calendar of events
and nominal roll are included.

vi+66+ii. pp. Coloured map and
illustrations.

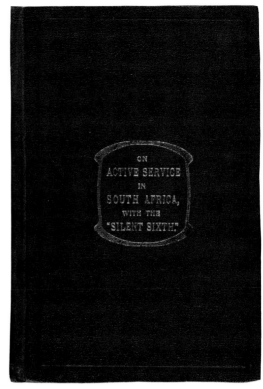

On Active Service In South Africa With
'The Silent Sixth'. Being A Record Of
Events, Compiled By The Writer, From
The Time Of The Formation Of The
Regiment In New Zealand Until Its Return
From South Africa.
Joseph Linklater
McKee & Co., printers
Wellington nd. (1902)

Purple pebble grain cloth. Front blocked in
blind and gold.
189×128mm

The New Zealand 6th Contingent arrived at
East London in March 1901 and entrained
for Pretoria. The regiment was attached to
General Plumer's force and, for over a year,
engaged in widespread operations in the
Transvaal and Orange River Colony.
Between March and July the regiment took
part in a trek to Pietersburg and was active
in southern and eastern Transvaal.
Thereafter the force was railed to
Bloemfontein and embarked in clearing
operations in sections of Orange River
Colony. At various times the contingent was
at Poplar Grove, Modder River, Wepener
and Rouxville. In October 1901 the New
Zealanders were transported to south
eastern Transvaal where they patrolled the
country about Wakkerstroom. Though
frequently engaged with the enemy
casualties were few until January 1902 when
they were overwhelmed by a Boer force at
Spitskop. In the encounter the New
Zealanders sustained significant casualties
and had 28 men captured. The writer
describes the event as the regiment's most
serious reverse of the campaign. The 6th
continued operations in eastern Transvaal
until recalled from active service in March
1902 . The record includes a death-roll of
the Contingent up to the time of leaving
South Africa.

102pp. Illustrated.

Fighting For The Empire
The Story Of The War In South Africa.
James Otis
Dana Estes & Company
Boston nd. (1900)

Fawn cloth. Front blocked in dark blue,
red, white and green. Spine blocked in dark
blue.
203×142mm

A short history of South Africa from 1806
precedes a chronological record of the
campaign from the Boer ultimatum to the
annexation of the Transvaal in September
1900. Accounts of the besieged towns are
included together with profiles of the
opposing commanders Lord Roberts and
Gen. Joubert. The volume is illustrated by
Frank Merrill and other artists.

xxi+pp.11–466. Map and illustrations.

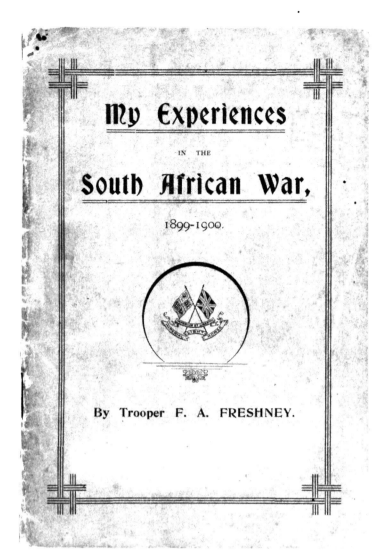

My Experiences In The South African
War 1899–1900.
Trooper F. A. Freshney
Gazette and Echo Printing Works
Lincoln nd. (1902?)

Blue wrap printed black to front only.
184×124mm

The account of a volunteer in the Imperial
Light Horse. The author was severely
wounded at Colenso in December 1899.
Much of the narrative relates to military
medical services.

44pp. With portrait.

Black And White Budget
(Editor/compiler not shown.)
Black and White Publishing Company,
Limited.
London 1900

Dark green cloth. Front and spine blocked
in blind and gold.
282×187mm

Bound issues of the weekly magazine dated
October 1899–Sept. 1900 of which numbers
1 to 13 are subtitled 'Transvaal Special'.
Essentially a pictorial record of the war with
short letterpress content including a
summary of recent events and reports from
the front. The magazine continued to report
war news until the end of the campaign but
the South African content is greatly reduced
beyond August 1900.

Three vols. bound in two. Illustrated
throughout. (Each issue 32pp.)

South Africa And The Transvaal War
Louis Creswicke
T. C. & E. C. Jack
Edinburgh 1900–1901
(Supplementary vols.VII & VIII published
by The Caxton Publishing Co. London
[c.1902])

Fawn cloth. Front and spine blocked in red
and black.
251×177mm *(Illustrated)*

Variant bindings
Red grained cloth. Front and spine blocked
in gold, back blocked in blind.
251×175mm

Dark blue fine ribbed cloth over bevelled
boards. Front blocked in gold and blind.
Spine blocked in gold.
251×176mm

Half red morocco and red cloth. Line
borders blocked in gold to front and back.
Spine blocked in gold.
251×175mm

A comprehensive history of the war in six
volumes, with supplementary vols.VII & VIII
dealing with the guerilla campaign and
South Africa and its future. Vols.I–VII
contain a chronological table of events and
various appendices, including extracts from
official correspondence, casualties, deaths
from disease, biographical notes of eminent
persons engaged in the war, and a list of
recipients of the Victoria Cross. Vol.VII has
a table showing composition and
distribution of columns operating in various
sectors from Feb. 1901. The volumes are
illustrated throughout with folding (and
other) maps, photographs and drawings,
including numerous colour plates. An
attractive and informative work.

Vol.I – From the foundation of Cape
Colony to the Boer ultimatum of 9th Oct.
1899. xii+200pp.
Vol.II – From the commencement of the
war to the battle of Colenso, 15th Dec. 1899
viii+201+ii. pp.
Vol.III – From the battle of Colenso, 15th
Dec. 1899, to Lord Roberts' advance into
the Free State, 12th Feb. 1900. viii+200pp.
Vol.IV – From Lord Roberts' entry into the
Free State to the battle of Karree.
viii+216pp.
Vol.V – From the disaster at Koorn Spruit
to Lord Roberts' entry into Pretoria.
viii+199pp.
Vol.VI – From the occupation of Pretoria to
Mr. Kruger's departure from South Africa,
with a summarised account of the guerilla
war to March 1901. viii+216pp.
Vol.VII – The guerilla war. From February
1901 to the conclusion of hostilities. The
development of peace negotiations from
February 23, 1901, to May 31, 1902.
xvi+214pp.
Vol.VIII – South Africa and its future.
(Edited by Louis Creswicke.)
viii+199pp.
Illustrated throughout.

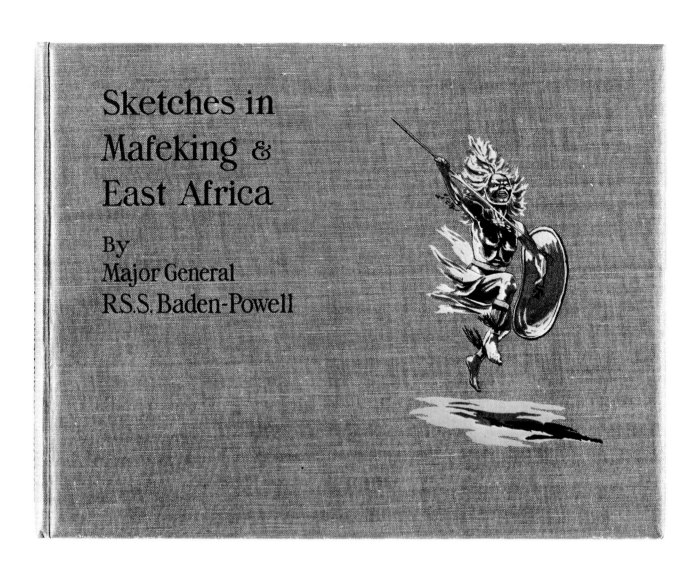

Sketches In Mafeking And East Africa
Major-General R. S. S. Baden-Powell
Smith, Elder & Co.
London 1907

Light brown cloth over bevelled boards.
Front blocked in dark brown, light brown
and grey. Spine blocked in dark brown.
240×313mm *(Illustrated)*

Variant binding
Grey paper covered boards backed in light
brown cloth. Front blocked in black and
brown. Spine blocked in black.
242×315mm

A record of a brief visit to South Africa,
Rhodesia and East Africa compiled from
diaries, letters and sketchbooks. Together
with reminiscences of Mafeking during the
siege (pp.23–72).

xii+183pp. Colour plates and other
illustrations.

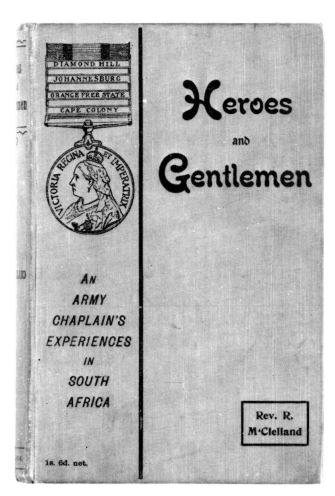

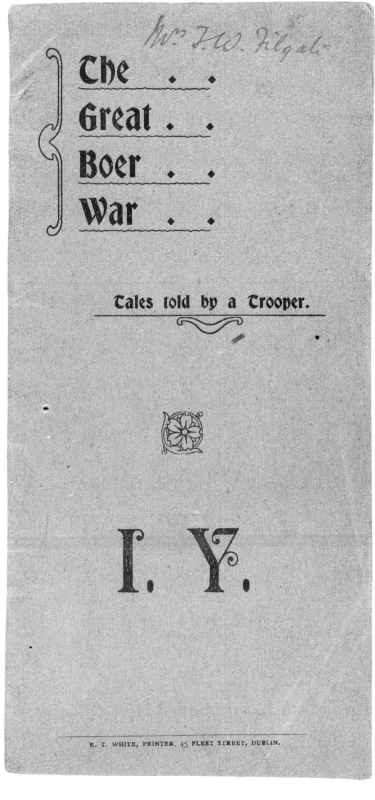

Heroes And Gentlemen An Army
Chaplain's Experiences In South Africa.
Rev. Robert M'Clelland
J. and R. Parlane/Paisley
John Menzies and Co./Edinburgh and
Glasgow
Houlston and Sons/London 1902

Red cloth blocked in black to front and
spine.
188×126mm

A chaplain's account of the march to
Bloemfontein and Pretoria. The narrative
relates to operations in the western theatre
and to the writer's association with the
Highland Brigade and 1st Battalion Queen's
Own Cameron Highlanders. A glossary of
words in use at the front is included
together with a list of camps en route.

159pp. Frontispiece and map.

The Great Boer War
Tales Told By A Trooper I.Y.
(Author/editor not shown.)
R. T. White (Printer)
Dublin nd.

Dull green wrap. Black letterpress to front
only.
206×100mm

Anecdotes relating to Imperial Yeomanry
in South Africa. The incidents described
chiefly concern Irish companies, i.e. the
46th and 54th (Belfast) and the 74th Co.
(Dublin) I.Y. Stories include 'Two narrow
shaves at Lindley', 'Lord Methuen and the
Boers' and 'Nooitgedacht'.

26pp.

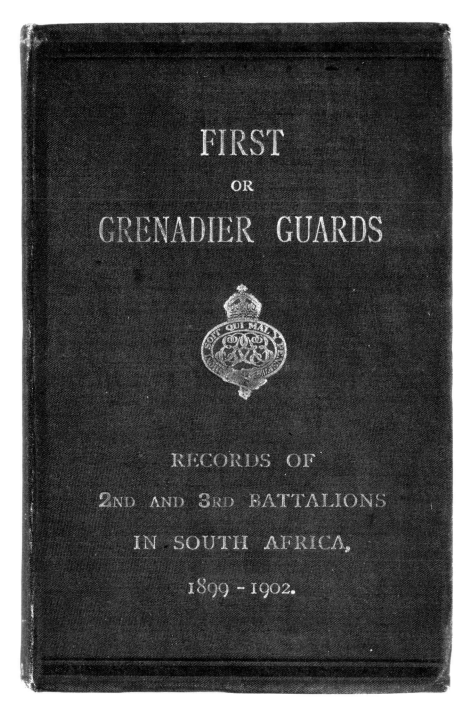

First Or Grenadier Guards In South Africa
1899–1902 Records Of The Second
Battalion Compiled By
Brigadier-General F. Lloyd, C.B., D.S.O.
Records Of The Third Battalion Compiled By
Brevet-Major Hon. A. Russell
J. J. Keliher & Co. Limited
London 1907

Dark blue cloth over bevelled boards. Front
blocked in gold and blind. Spine blocked in
gold.
217×140mm

The first section has the title page common
to both parts. The record of the 2nd Batt. is
compiled by Brigadier-Gen. F. Lloyd. The
2nd Grenadiers formed part of General
Rundle's 8th Division. They arrived in the
Orange Free State in late April 1900 and
continued operating in this area to the end
of the campaign. During an arduous tour of
25 months the Battalion was frequently on
trek and often engaged. On May 29, 1900
the 2nd sustained significant losses in the
action at Biddulphsberg. Thereafter
casualties were never severe. The diary of
events from March 1900 to Oct. 1902 is
succeeded by a list of officers who served
during the war.

114pp.

The second section, dealing with the 3rd
Batt., is compiled by Brevet-Major Hon.
A. Russell. The 3rd Grenadiers formed part
of the Guards' Brigade under Gen. Colvile.
They advanced with Lord Methuen's force
from Orange River Bridge in Nov. 1900,
taking part in operations at Belmont,
Modder River and Magersfontein.
Thereafter the 3rd marched with Lord
Roberts' army through the Orange Free
State and Transvaal, arriving at Komati
Poort on the eastern border by late Sept.
1900. In Nov. of that year the Grenadiers
were brought down to Cape Colony to
guard drifts on the Orange River. To the
end of the campaign they were employed in
the Colony in suppressing Boer insurgency.
Casualty lists, a campaign itinerary, nominal
rolls and other statistics are included.

138pp. Folding charts and map.

War Notes The Diary Of Colonel De
Villebois-Mareuil From November 24, 1899,
To March 7, 1900. Authorised Translation
From The Paris *Liberté* By Frederic Lees.
With A Preface By E. M. De Vogüé
Member Of The Académie Française.
(Frederic Lees. Translator.)
Adam and Charles Black
London 1901

Cream buckram. Front and spine blocked in
brown. Paper onlay to front cover.
197×130mm

Translation from the diary of a French
officer serving in the Boer army. The entries
relate to events in Natal, the siege of
Kimberley and the campaign in the Orange
Free State. The author was killed in action
near Boshof in April 1900.
(See – Ex Lieutenant – *Ten Months In The
Field With The Boers.*)

xx+283pp.

Historical Record Of The 3rd County Of London (Sharpshooters) Imperial Yeomanry 1900–1905.
(Author/editor not shown.)
W. P. Griffith & Sons Ltd. (Printers)
London nd. (c.1905)

Dark green buckram, front blocked in gold.
140×110mm

Campaign record of the 18th, 21st and 23rd Battalions of Imperial Yeomanry during the Boer War, with an account of the Home Service Regiment raised in 1901.

72pp. Coloured frontispiece.

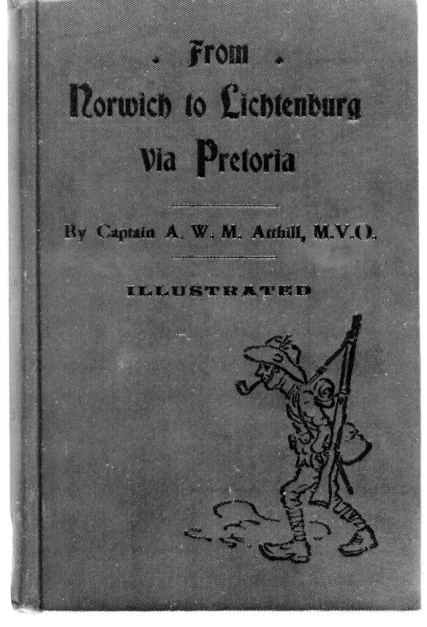

From Norwich To Lichtenburg Via Pretoria Being Some Personal Experiences With The 2nd Norfolk Volunteer Active Service Company In South Africa, 1901–2 Together With Extracts From Letters Written By Colin G. Cubitt Between June And December, 1901.
Captain A. W. M. Atthill, M.V.O.
A. E. Soman & Co., St. Andrew's Printing Works.
Norwich 1909

Brown cloth blocked in black to front and spine.
190×127mm

Campaign diary from March 1901 to May 1902 compiled by the Company commander. The narrative is chiefly concerned with events in western Transvaal. Two shipboard magazines *The Chit* and *The Orcana Oyster* are reproduced in appendices.

vii+166pp. Illustrated.

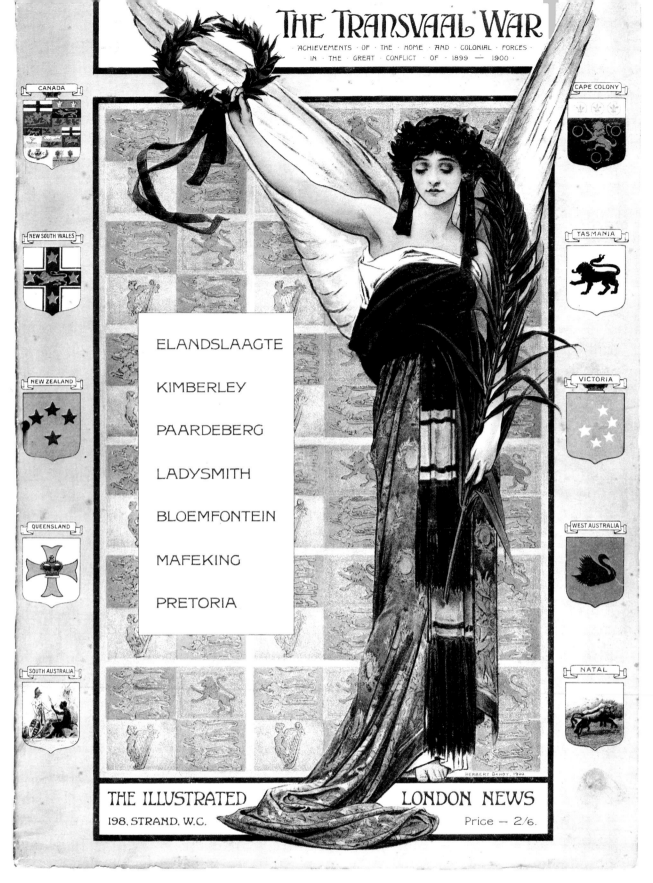

THE TRANSVAAL WAR

· ACHIEVEMENTS · OF · THE · HOME · AND · COLONIAL · FORCES ·
· IN · THE · GREAT · CONFLICT · OF · 1899 — 1900 ·

CANADA

CAPE COLONY

NEW SOUTH WALES

TASMANIA

NEW ZEALAND

VICTORIA

QUEENSLAND

WEST AUSTRALIA

SOUTH AUSTRALIA

NATAL

ELANDSLAAGTE

KIMBERLEY

PAARDEBERG

LADYSMITH

BLOEMFONTEIN

MAFEKING

PRETORIA

HERBERT GANDY, 1900

THE ILLUSTRATED   LONDON NEWS

198, STRAND, W.C.   Price — 2/6.

The Illustrated London News Record
Of The Transvaal War, 1899–1900 The
Achievements Of The Home And Colonial
Forces In The Great Conflict With The
Boer Republics.
(Spenser Wilkinson.)
The Illustrated London News and Sketch
Limited.
London nd. (1900)

Limp card cover printed in colour to front
and back.
414×305mm

A record of the campaign to Oct.14,1900.
Chapters relate to British and Irish
regiments, the Colonies in the war, the
Cavalry, the Navy, the Medical Staff, etc.
The volume contains various photogravure
plates and numerous other illustrations by
prominent artists, including Melton Prior,
R. Caton Woodville and S. Begg.

84pp. (Including advertisements.)
Illustrated throughout.

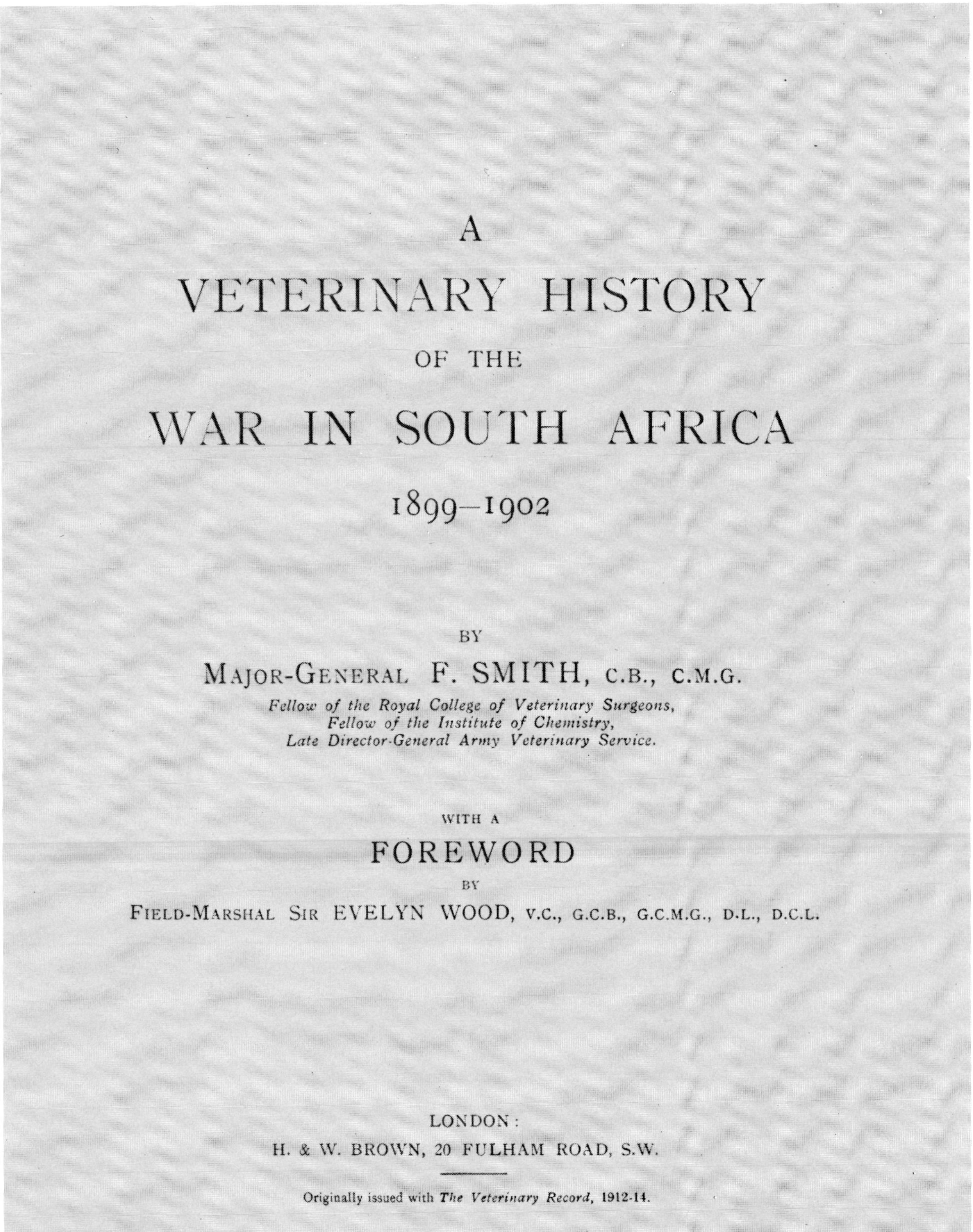

A

VETERINARY HISTORY

OF THE

WAR IN SOUTH AFRICA

1899–1902

BY

MAJOR-GENERAL F. SMITH, C.B., C.M.G.

Fellow of the Royal College of Veterinary Surgeons,
Fellow of the Institute of Chemistry,
Late Director-General Army Veterinary Service.

WITH A

FOREWORD

BY

FIELD-MARSHAL SIR EVELYN WOOD, V.C., G.C.B., G.C.M.G., D.L., D.C.L.

LONDON:

H. & W. BROWN, 20 FULHAM ROAD, S.W.

Originally issued with *The Veterinary Record*, 1912-14.

A Veterinary History Of The War In South Africa 1899–1902.
Major-General F. Smith
H. & W. Brown
London nd. (1919)

Maroon cloth over bevelled boards. Front and back blocked in blind. Spine blocked in gold.
276×218mm

A history of the war originally issued with *The Veterinary Record* 1912–1914. The author censures the army for ill treatment of animals, the Remount Department for supplying horses unfit for service, and the authorities responsible for the inadequate veterinary establishment despatched to South Africa. He states that during 32 months of war there was an appalling loss of animal life amounting to nearly 600 beasts a day. A situation exacerbated by the lack of adequate reserves of medical and surgical materials throughout the campaign. The volume is comprised of three parts. The first covers the period October 1899 to December 1900. The second embraces the period January 1901 to May 1902 and the third deals with general and technical matters and related services. Chapters relate to the working of veterinary hospitals and debility farms.

viii+321pp. Maps, plates and folding chart.
Title page shown.

The Aftermath Of War An Account Of The
Repatriation Of Boers And Natives In The
Orange River Colony 1902–1904.
G. B. Beak
Edward Arnold
London 1906

Brown cloth. Front blocked in black, spine
blocked in black and gold.
222×144mm

Impressions gained in South Africa in the
course of five years service from 1900–1904.
The volume is a private account of the
repatriation scheme carried out in the
Orange River Colony by an official of the
Government Relief Department.
Appendices include 'Terms for land-
settlers' 'Statements of expenditure' etc.

x+296pp. Folding map and various
illustrations.

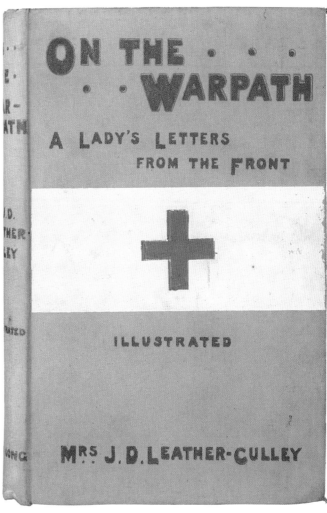

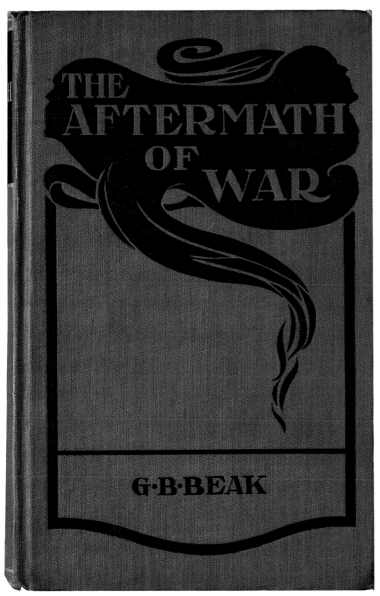

On The War Path A Lady's Letters
From The Front.
Mrs. J. D. Leather-Culley
John Long
London 1901

Khaki cloth blocked in white, red and blue
to front. Spine blocked in blue and red.
198×126mm

Travel diary of the author who visited South
Africa for approximately three months to
distribute medical comforts to military
hospitals. The record includes a list of goods
delivered and place of delivery.

vii+133pp. Illustrated.

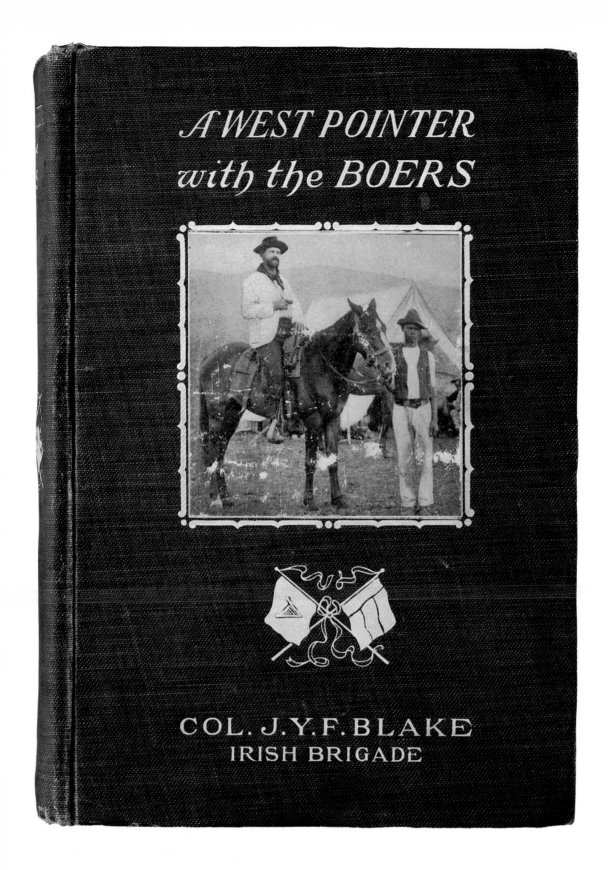

A WEST POINTER with the BOERS

COL. J. Y. F. BLAKE
IRISH BRIGADE

A West Pointer With The Boers
Personal Narrative Of Colonel J. Y. F.
Blake Commander Of The Irish Brigade.
Colonel J. Y. F. Blake
Angel Guardian Press
Boston 1903

Dark green ribbed cloth with paper onlay.
Front blocked in white, spine blocked in
gold. (Some copies with front and spine
blocked in white.)
209×144mm

Variant binding
Dull blue cloth with paper onlay. Front and
spine blocked in white.
207×146mm *(Illustrated)*

Experiences of an American officer in
service of the Boer Republics. Blake
commanded a group of Irish patriots
numbering about 350 at onset of hostilities.
The 'Irish Brigade' was active in Natal
taking part in the Tugela operations. In May
1900 the volunteers were employed in the
Orange Free State and soon thereafter were
fighting in the Transvaal. By late August
1900, with both republics under British
control, the Irish Brigade was disbanded.
Many volunteers departed South Africa via
Koomati Poort, others joined various
commandos to continue the war. Col. Blake
remained active with Boer forces to the end
of the campaign.

xii+pp.13–411. Illustrated.

Rhodesia – And After Being The Story
Of The 17th And 18th Battalions Of
Imperial Yeomanry In South Africa.
Sharrad H. Gilbert
Simpkin Marshall, Hamilton, Kent
& Co. Ltd.
London 1901

Cream cloth. Front and spine blocked in red
and dark blue.
210×138mm

War record of a member of the 65th
Squadron Imperial Yeomanry. The
narrative is divided into three parts. The
first concerns service in Rhodesia, the
second is an account of the campaign in
Cape Colony and the third section relates to
stories from the squadrons (50th I.Y., the
Irish Yeomanry, 65th I.Y. and Dunraven's
Sharpshooters). A list of casualties and a
glossary of South African names are
included.

350pp. Mounted frontispiece, folding maps
and numerous illustrations.

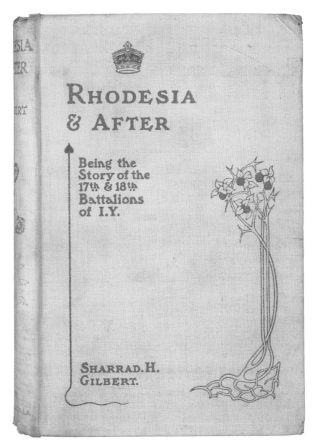

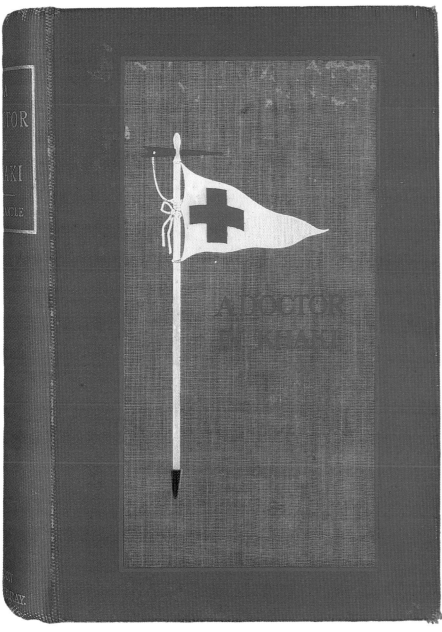

Impressions Of A Doctor In Khaki
Francis E. Fremantle
John Murray
London 1901

Dark red cloth, spine blocked in gold.
Khaki cloth inlay to front cover blocked in
light red, white and black.
208×135mm *(Illustrated)*

Variant binding
Murray's Imperial Library edition. Green
cloth. Front blocked in red and gold. Spine
blocked in gold.
208×135mm

Experiences of a civil surgeon employed in
the RAMC. During twelve months' army
service the author worked at No.1 General
Hospital at Wynberg, made two homeward
voyages aboard hospital ships *Avoca* and
Spartan tending casualties, and served in the
Field Hospital and Bearer Company
attached to the 19th Brigade operating in
the Orange Free State and Transvaal.
Fremantle was summoned to give evidence
before The Hospitals Commission Of
Inquiry before leaving South Africa in Oct.
1900.

xvi+549pp. Maps and illustrations.

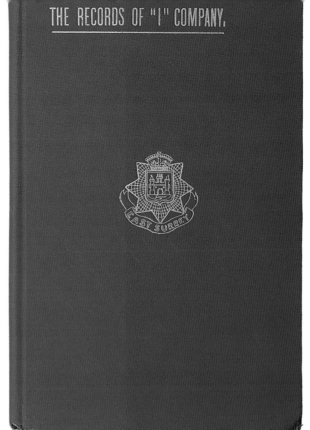

With Methuen's Column On An Ambulance
Train.
Ernest N. Bennett
Swan Sonnenschein & Co. Ltd.
London 1900

Light brown cloth blocked in red, black and
white to front and spine.
194×130mm

Narrative of a volunteer in the RAMC
engaged in transporting casualties from the
front. The author relates incidents from the
battles of Belmont, Graspan and
Magersfontein, with reference to medical
work in the field.

v+127pp.

The Records Of 'I' Company. A Brief
History Of The East Surrey Volunteers'
Service In The South African War.
A. G. Garrish
Walbrook & Co. Limited
London 1901

Royal blue cloth. Front blocked in gold.
222×145mm

Campaign record of the Volunteer
Company the East Surrey Regiment in
South Africa from April 1900–May 1901.
The unit joined Gen. Buller's force in the
northern advance from Ladysmith.
Thereafter the Company was stationed for
several months at Van Reenen's Pass on the
Natal/Orange River Colony border.
A company roll is included.

xvi+103pp. Folding map and illustrations.

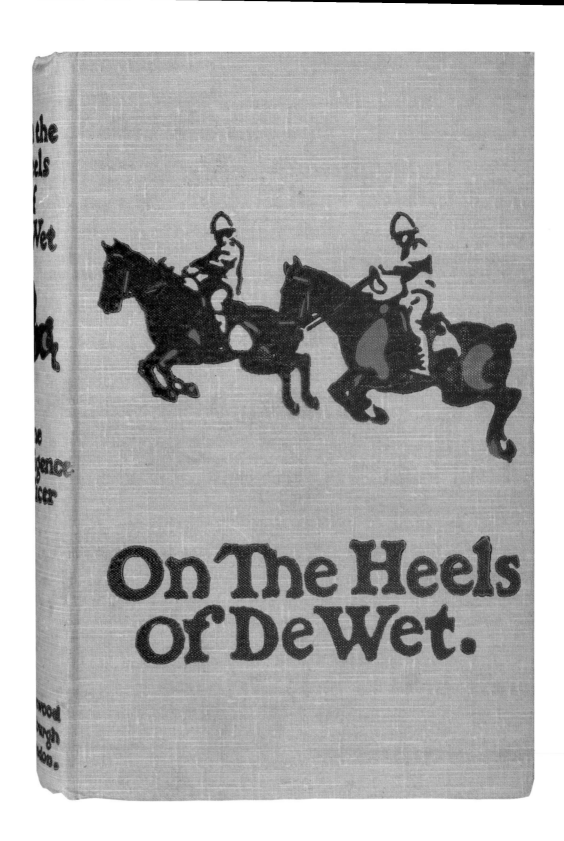

On The Heels Of De Wet
The Intelligence Officer
William Blackwood and Sons
Edinburgh and London 1902

Fawn cloth. Front and back blocked in
black and dark brown. Spine blocked in
black and ochre.
198×128mm

An account of operations to suppress the
Boer invasion of Cape Colony in 1901. The
author took part in various drives chiefly in
pursuit of the Boer commander De Wet.
The narrative, based on the writer's war
diary, was first published as a series of
papers in *Blackwood's Magazine*.

vii+346pp.

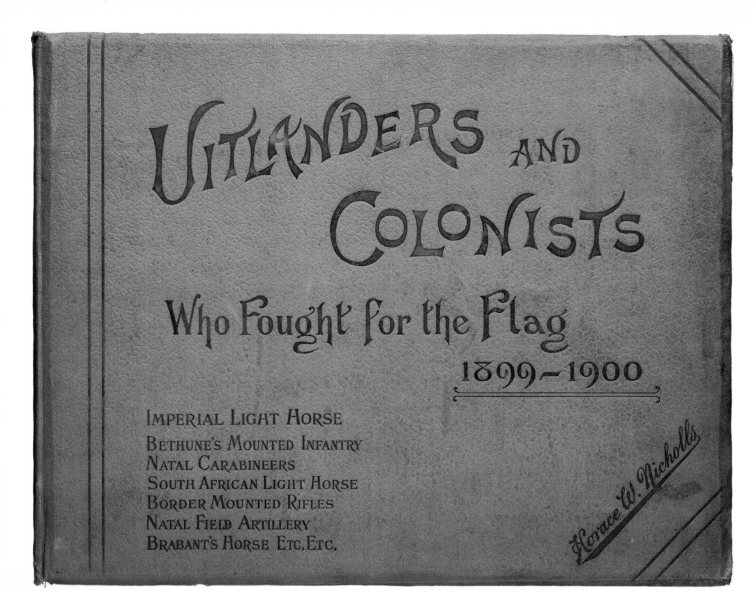

Uitlanders And Colonists Who Fought
For The Flag, 1899, 1900. A Series Of 110
First-Class Collotype Photographs,
Illustrating Life With The Imperial Light
Horse And Other South African Volunteer
Regiments.
Horace W. Nicholls
The Goch Studio
Johannesburg nd. (c.1900)

Textured grey/green cloth over bevelled
boards. Front blocked in green.
218×285mm

A photographic record of volunteer corps
engaged in the conflict, with introductory
letterpress. Among regiments shown are
Bethune's Mounted Infantry, South African
Light Horse and Border Mounted Rifles.

64pp. (Unnumbered.) Illustrated
throughout, including two large foldout
plates.

Outposts And Convoys With The Ayrshire
Volunteers In South Africa.
Robert M'Caw
Dunlop & Drennan (Printers)
Standard Office.
Kilmarnock 1901

Red cloth over bevelled boards. Blind
embossed panel with paper onlay to front
cover. Blocked in gold to front and spine.
192×127mm *(Illustrated)*

Variant binding
Grey paper cover. Magenta letterpress to
front and spine.
184×124mm

A record of the Volunteer Service Company
the Royal Scots Fusiliers in South Africa.
The volunteers arrived at Cape Town in
March 1900. Following a brief period at the
Natal front they returned to Cape Colony
concentrating, with other units, north of
Kimberley. For thirteen months thereafter
they operated about south western
Transvaal and Orange River Colony, at
various times trekking to Vryberg,
Christiana, Lichtenburg, Ventersdorp and
Potchefstroom. For a few months to Oct.
1900 the Company joined the garrison at
Krugersdorp, and for six months to May
1901 formed part of the garrison at
Smaldeel in the Orange River Colony.
Although not involved in any major battle
the volunteers engaged in numerous
skirmishes with the enemy to the close of
their tour of duty in May 1901.

ix+150pp. With two plates.

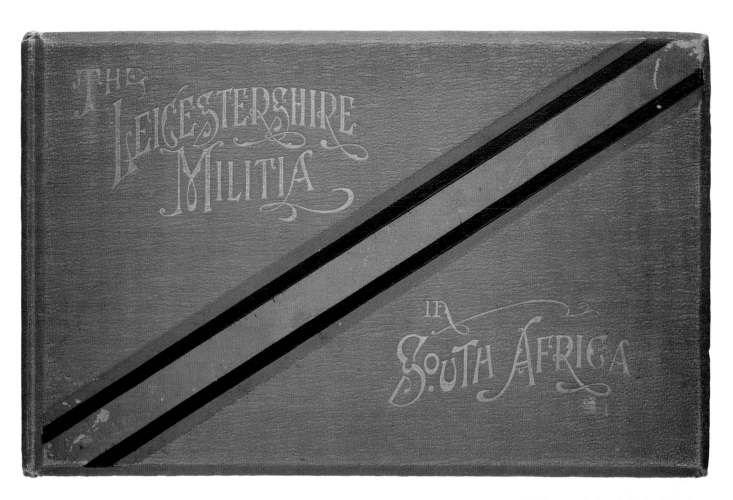

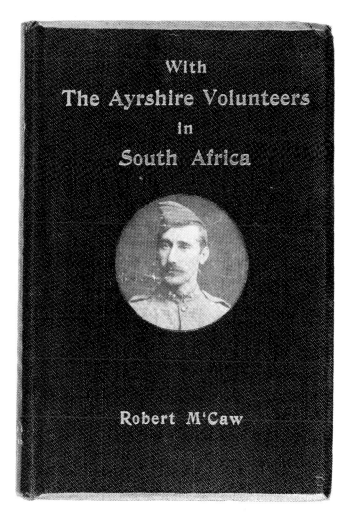

The Leicestershire Militia In South Africa
Major G. H. P. Burne
Clarke & Satchell
Leicester nd. (c.1902)

Ochre grained cloth over bevelled boards.
Front blocked in gold, red, black and orange.
158×252mm

An account of the 3rd Leicestershire Regiment from the day it was embodied in 1902 until its return from South Africa. The militia battalion arrived at Cape Town on April 14, 1902, too late to take a significant part in the war. From the start it was broken up into small detachments and dispersed along blockhouse lines in north eastern Cape Colony. The headquarters section was directed to Knapdaar close to the Orange River Colony border. In late May the detachment was brought down to Steynsberg in an effort to entrap Boer commandos being driven westwards, but the operation proved unnecessary as by June 1 peace was concluded. The Regiment sailed from East London on Sept. 9, 1902. Details are given in respect of other detachments and a medal roll of the 3rd Batt. included.

vii+116pp. Illustrated.

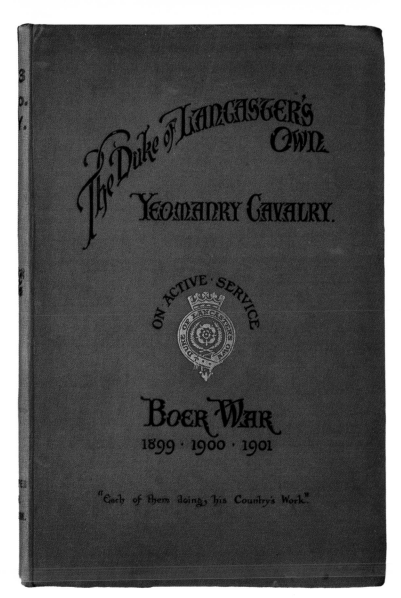

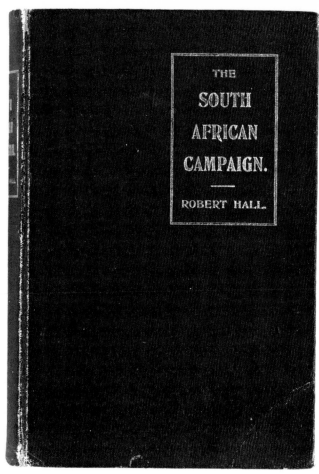

The Duke Of Lancaster's Own Yeomanry
Cavalry, 23rd Co., I.Y. A Record Of
Incidents Connected With The Services Of
The First Contingent Of The D.L.O.Y.C.
In The South African Campaign Of 1899–
1900–1901–1902; Of Interest Also To The
Westmorland And Cumberland Yeomanry,
24th Co., I.Y., Who Were Our Partners
And Comrades-In-Arms.
Trooper L. H. Johnson
(Published by the author)
Bolton nd. (1902)

Red cloth. Front blocked in black and gold.
Spine blocked in black.
223×150mm

Campaign record of the 23rd and 24th
companies I.Y. in South Africa. The
volunteers arrived at Cape Town in March
1900. During an active campaign extending
over a year they joined Gen. Warren's force
in operations about Griqualand West,
served in the Orange River Colony in
pursuit of De Wet, and in Cape Colony
from Dec. to April 1901. For three months
to mid Nov. 1900 a detachment joined Gen.
Settle's column in western Transvaal. The
companies were in action at Faber's Put in
May and near Hoopstad in Oct. 1900. The
record includes a nominal roll, casualty list
and a summary of the war.

158pp. Frontispiece, folding map and
various coloured illustrations.

The South African Campaign
Robert Hall
John K. Milne
Aberdeen 1901

Blue grained cloth. Front and spine blocked
in gold.
188×130mm *(Illustrated)*

Variant binding
Red cloth. Front and spine blocked in gold.
188×130mm

Experiences of the author, a builder from
Aberdeen. At the outbreak of war Hall left
the Transvaal for Pietermaritzburg. He later
found employment with H.M. Public Works
Dept. and was engaged in building projects
in areas under military occupation. The
narrative is drawn up to December 1900.

vii+285pp. Portrait frontispiece.

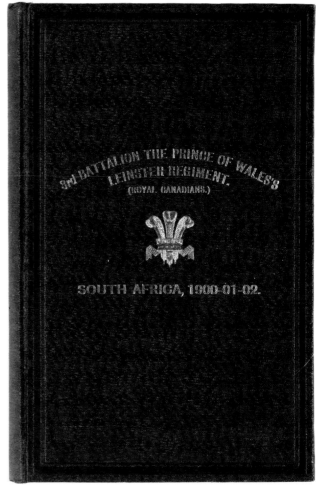

Record Of Services Of The 3rd Battn. The Prince Of Wales's Leinster Regiment (Royal Canadians) In The South African War, 1900, 1901, 1902.
Colonel F. Luttman-Johnson, D.S.O.
Army and Navy Co-Operative Society, Limited.
London 1913

Dark green grained cloth. Front blocked in blind and gold. Back blocked in blind.
221×142mm

The record of a militia battalion in South Africa based on regimental records, the author's campaign diary and other sources. The 3rd Leinsters arrived at East London in April 1900. They were first based at Queenstown in eastern Cape Colony before moving north to Stormberg where they were stationed for nine months. A detachment was posted to Aliwal North near the Orange Free State border. In late April 1901 the Leinsters regrouped at Stormberg and entrained for Kimberley where they stayed eight months primarily employed in blockhouse duties north and south of the town. A detachment joined the Kimberley Column, a local mounted force commanded by Col. Paris, and a company of Mounted Infantry was organized. The Column took part in convoy operations to Boshof in May 1900 and, in August of that year, was engaged by a Boer force at Wolvenkuil. In December the regiment was ordered to Modder River to reinforce the garrison. To the conclusion of active service, in April 1902, the 3rd Batt. engaged in blockhouse duties between Spytfontein and Honeynestkloof. Appendices include extracts from the author's diary, an account of the battle of Stormberg and notes on the early history of the Regiment.

148pp. Maps and illustrations.

With Paget's Horse To The Front.
Cosmo Rose-Innes
John Macqueen
London 1901

Blue cloth. Front blocked in red, dark blue and orange. Spine blocked in gold.
200×130mm

An account of the 19th. Batt. Imperial Yeomanry (Paget's Horse) in South Africa. The corps arrived at Cape Town in April 1900 and, for approximately a year thereafter, engaged in operations in Griqualand West and western Transvaal under Generals Warren, Carrington and other commanders. Although not involved in major battles the volunteers experienced frequent skirmishing throughout the campaign. The author recounts engagements at Fabers Put in May 1900 and at Elands River in August of that year. In the latter action the British were repulsed by a Boer force under Lemmer. The author fell ill during convoy operations near Schweizer Reneke early in 1901. He was referred to hospitals at Mafeking, Kimberley and Deelfontein prior to being invalided home.

v+180pp. With frontispiece.

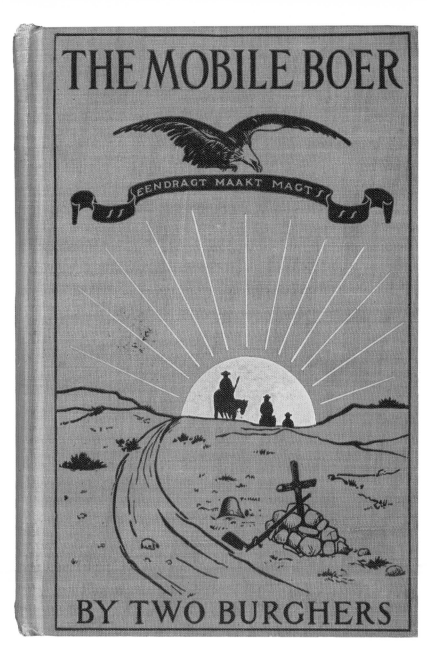

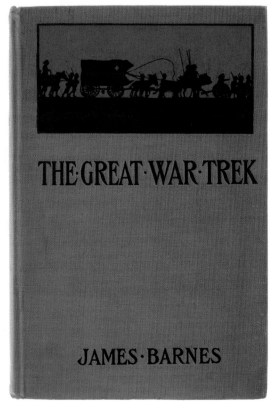

The Mobile Boer
Being The Record Of The Observations
Of Two Burgher Officers.
Alan R. I. Hiley and John A. Hassell
(Captains of Scouts in the Boer Army)
The Grafton Press
New York nd. (1902)

Orange cloth. Front blocked in dark green
and gold, spine blocked in gold.
192×129mm

A narrative of the campaign compiled by
American officers serving in the Republican
army. The authors draw comparisons
between the Anglo–Boer conflict and the
American War of Independence, accusing
the British of conducting the present war in
the same barbarous manner employed in the
earlier campaign. The narrative, which is
brought down to the arrival of British forces
at Koomati Poort, is based on personal
observation or information gained from
other eye-witnesses. The writers, at the
Natal front in the first months of war, give
frank accounts of the carnage at Colenso
and in later operations about Spion Kop.
The volume contains considerable
information in respect of the Republican
military organization, leadership and mode
of operation, together with notes on
ordnance and other equipment.

xvii+277pp. Folding map and illustrations.

The Great War Trek With The British
Army On The Veldt.
James Barnes
D. Appleton and Company
New York 1901

Ochre cloth. Front blocked in black and
red. Spine blocked in black only.
194×128mm

An American correspondent's narrative of
the western advance. Barnes accompanied
British forces from December 1899 giving
accounts of numerous battles from Modder
River and Magersfontein to the engagement
at Diamond Hill in June 1900. Many
incidents on the march are related together
with his impressions of various British
commanders. The writer visited Kimberley
at the end of the siege and witnessed the
entry of Bloemfontein and Pretoria,
reporting from both capitals during British
occupation. Barnes encountered many
Boers in the course of his travels and
formed a favourable opinion of the people.
He acknowledges their military prowess but
states they must eventually submit to British
supremacy. The author left South Africa in
October 1900 at the onset of the guerilla
campaign.

xii+372pp.

Souvenir Of The Siege Of Mafeking
Being Fac-simile Reproductions Of The
Most Interesting General Orders Issued To
The Garrison Of Mafeking By General
Baden-Powell During The Siege.
With introduction by
Chas. E. Hands
John Lewis & Compy., The Selkirk Press
London nd. (c.1900)

Olive green limp card cover. Front printed
black and pink, back printed black.
263×209mm

Facsimile reproductions of twenty-one
orders issued to the garrison from
commencement of hostilities to May 28th
1900. Together with an introduction by
C. E. Hands, war correspondent for the
Daily Mail, and an article on 'The
typewriter in warfare'. The manufacturers
of the *Smith Premier Typewriter* used at
Mafeking are co-publishers of the souvenir.
In some copies their name appears on the
title page above that of John Lewis &
Compy.

Unnumbered. (34pp.) With two illustrations.

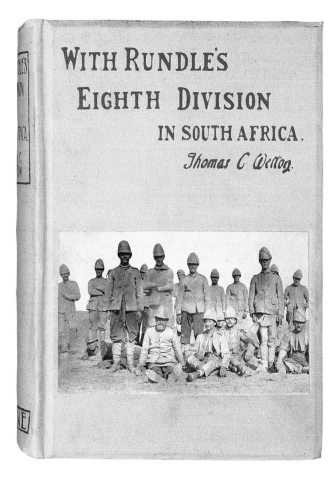

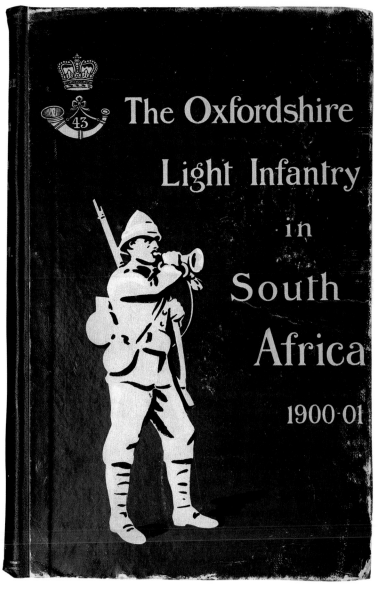

With Rundle's Eighth Division In South
Africa Being A Volunteer's Experience
With The Division, 1900–1902.
Thomas Charles Wetton
Henry J. Drane
London nd. (c.1902)

Ochre cloth. Front blocked in red and blind,
spine blocked in red. Paper onlay to front
cover.
185×126mm

A campaign record compiled from the
author's journal and various other sources.
Most of the narrative relates to events in the
Orange River Colony and to the writer's
experiences of hospital work with the
RAMC. Some of the material was first
published in English newspapers.

vii+pp.8–580. Illustrated.

The Oxfordshire Light Infantry In South
Africa. A Narrative Of The Boer War From
The Letters And Journals Of Officers Of
The Regiment, And From Other Sources.
Edited by
Lieut.-Colonel A. F. Mockler-Ferryman
Eyre and Spottiswoode
London 1901

Paper covered boards backed in dark green
cloth. Front printed green, cream and black.
Back printed black and green. Spine
blocked in gold.
218×141mm

An extensive record of the O.L.I. in South
Africa. The 1st Battalion joined
Lord Roberts' force in the march to
Bloemfontein taking part in operations at
Paardeberg in Feb. 1900. Thereafter the
Battalion moved to Kroonstad and
garrisoned various posts on lines of
communication. In August 1900 the
Regiment joined a column under Gen.
Knox operating along the railway from
Kroonstad to the Vaal. The Oxfords took
part in a most successful engagement at
Bothaville on Nov. 3 capturing over 100
Boers, guns and stores. From late 1900 the
O.L.I. were based at Heilbron with
companies on detachment doing column
work and garrison duty. The narrative is
complete to the spring of 1901. The volume
contains a comprehensive record of the
Mounted Infantry Company, a chapter on
the transportation of Boer prisoners to
Ceylon, together with despatches, casualty
lists and other statistical matter.

314pp. Folding maps and numerous
illustrations.

A Military History Of Perthshire 1899–1902
With A Roll Of The Perthshire Men Of The
Present Day Who Have Seen Active Service
Under The British Flag.
Compiled By The Editor & Jane C. C.
Macdonald.
Edited by
The Marchioness of Tullibardine
R. A. & J. Hay / Perth
J. Maclehose & Sons / Glasgow
William Brown / Edinburgh
1908

Full oxblood calf. Front and spine blocked
in gold.
252×190mm *(Illustrated)*
Variant bindings
Red buckram. Front and spine blocked in
gold.
260×198mm

Red cloth. Front blocked in blind, spine
blocked in gold.
262×198mm

A tribute to Perthshire men who served in
the South African War and earlier conflicts,
being a collection of brief records of 170
officers and 1,370 non-commissioned
officers and men, together with portraits.
The record extends to all Perthshire men
who saw active service under the British flag
from 1893 to 1903 thereby including men
who served in the Soudan Expedition of
1898 and those who participated in various
campaigns on the Indian frontier in the
decade preceding 1903. The majority of
entries are arranged according to regiment
with Imperial Yeomanry and Colonial units
included. All entries include details of
medals awarded. The volume contains
significant reference to the 1st and 2nd
battalions The Black Watch in South Africa
and to operations of The Scottish Horse.

xxi+316pp. Maps, portraits and other
illustrations.

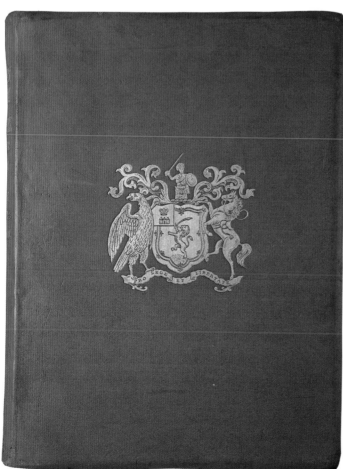

Side Lights On The War In South Africa
Being Sketches Based On Personal
Observation During A Few Weeks
Residence In Cape Colony And Natal.
Jessica Sykes
T. Fisher Unwin
London 1900

Red, white and blue cloth. Front blocked in
silver and dark blue, spine blocked in dark
blue.
189×127mm

An account of philanthropic work in Natal
during the initial phase of war. The writer
arrived in South Africa in November 1899
and proceeded to the hospital at Estcourt
Convent. During a stay of five weeks she
assisted the resident staff and provided the
establishment with supplementary
provisions and equipment. She gives a
sombre account of events following the
battle of Colenso when large numbers of
casualties were admitted. Army officials
generally elicit severe criticism and the
writer alludes to the incompetence of
certain generals then conducting military
operations. On the homeward voyage Mrs
Sykes visited the hospital ship *Lismore*
moored in Durban harbour. The Portland
Hospital and the Simon's Town Naval
Hospital were visited during her stay at
Cape Town.

vii+156pp.

THE GRAM

Edited by the

EARL OF

ROSSLYN.

OUR PRISON OUTSIDE PRETORIA.

WHERE THE GRAM WAS PUBLISHED.

The Gram A Social Magazine Founded By British Prisoners Of War In Pretoria Facsimile Edition.
Earl of Rosslyn (Editor)
Eyre & Spottiswoode
London nd. (c.1900)

Vellum over bevelled boards. Blind embossed panel to upper cover with pictorial onlay. Front only blocked in red and black.
267×210mm

Three issues of a magazine published at the officers prison at Pretoria, no.3 edited by Major Sturges. This facsimile edition of 500 copies is comprised of the original issues together with 'Notes for guidance in reading'. The content is mildly amusing with some cartoons and caricatures included in each issue. No.2 contains a list of officers and civilians detained. (This copy No.267, signed by Rosslyn.)

Unnumbered. (114pp.)

The Great Boer War 1899–1901. Letters
Captain Frank Denton Price
For private circulation
Andrew Reid & Company, Limited
Newcastle-upon-Tyne 1901

Oxblood morocco over bevelled boards. Front and back blocked in gold and blind. Spine blocked in gold.
187×128mm

Letters from Captain Price of the 1st Durham Royal Engineers (volunteers) while on active service in South Africa. Most of the letters are to the author's father addressed from various locations in the Orange River Colony and Transvaal. A diary of the campaign 1900–1901 is appended preceded by a roll of the Volunteer Detachment the 1st Durham R.E. Some copies are bound without the campaign diary.

v+150pp. Illustrated.

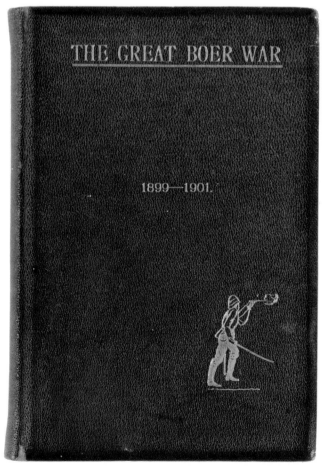

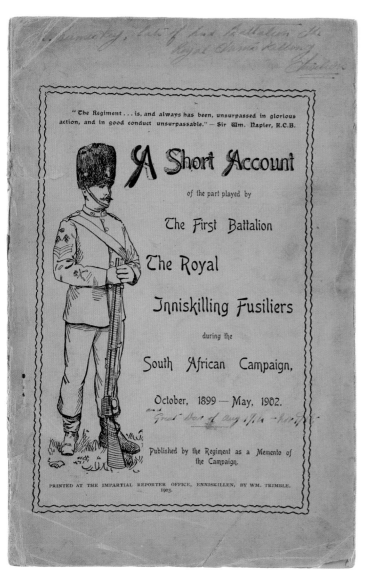

A Short Account Of The Part Played By
The First Battalion The Royal Inniskilling
Fusiliers During The South African
Campaign October 1899–May 1902.
Published By The Regiment As A Memento
Of The Campaign.
(Author/editor not shown.)
W. M. Trimble (Printer)
Impartial Reporter Office
Enniskillen 1903

White limp card cover. Front only printed
black.
210×136mm

A diary of services of the 1st Battalion from
Sept. 6, 1899 to 8th Feb. 1903. With a
record of the Mounted Infantry Section
during the same period. The Fusiliers joined
Gen. Fitzroy Hart's 5th Brigade in Natal
taking part in operations at Colenso,
Venters Spruit and Inniskilling Hill between
December 1899 and late February 1900.
After the relief of Ladysmith the Battalion
advanced with Gen. Buller's force to
Lydenburg. The Fusiliers led the attack at
Bergendal on 27 August. Thereafter they
served at various times in eastern Transvaal
(late 1900), central Transvaal (late 1901)
and in 1902 assisted in operations in Orange
River Colony. The volume contains a list of
memorials erected in South Africa and
Ireland, extracts from battalion orders and
war despatches, and a roll of officers and
men who served in South Africa.

109pp.

The Biograph In Battle Its Story In The
South African War Related With Personal
Experiences.
W. K.-L. Dickson
T. Fisher Unwin
London 1901

Sienna cloth. Front blocked in silver, black
and white. Spine blocked in black and gold.
199×141mm. *(Illustrated)*

Variant binding
Olive green cloth. Front blocked in silver,
black and white. Spine blocked in black and
gold.
199×138mm

Observations of a film pioneer in South
Africa. Dickson joined General Buller's
army in Natal and witnessed events at
Colenso, Spion Kop and the entry of
Ladysmith. He later joined Lord Roberts
force in the western advance filming the
annexation ceremony at Bloemfontein and
the hoisting of the British flag at Pretoria.

xx+296pp. Folding panorama and other
illustrations.

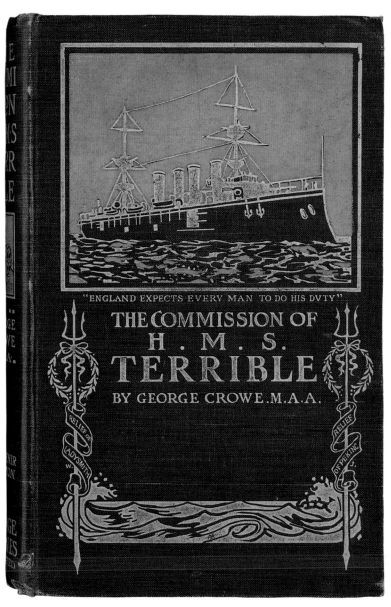

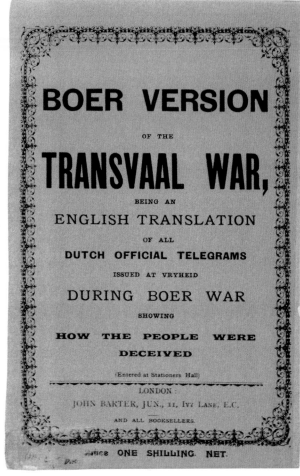

The Commission Of H.M.S. 'Terrible'
1898–1902.
George Crowe
George Newnes, Limited
London 1903

Dark blue cloth. Front and spine blocked in
light blue and gold.
222×142mm

A commentary of the principal events in
connection with H.M.S. Terrible and of
Naval Brigade participation in the South
African and North China wars. The Boer
War section includes accounts of defence
preparations at Durban and the Ladysmith
Relief Operations. Appendices include
nominal rolls and a list of officers and men
mentioned in despatches. The volume is an
extended version of *From Portsmouth To
Peking Via Ladysmith With A Naval
Brigade* published at Hong Kong in 1901.

xvii+370pp. Illustrated.

Boer Version Of The Transvaal War Or
An English Translation Of All Dutch Official
Telegrams Received At Vryheid During
Boer War Up To The Time When British
Troops Occupied Vryheid.
(Editor/compiler not shown.)
John Barter, Jnr. (Publisher)
London nd. (c.1901)

Pink paper cover. Black letterpress to front
and back.
212×138mm

An authentic translation of all the official
telegrams and proclamations issued by the
late government of the South African
Republic from Oct.3, 1899 until British
occupation of Vryheid on Sept.19, 1900.
Notwithstanding the flow of information
into Vryheid, it is claimed the Dutch people
were deceived and kept in ignorance of the
true state of affairs.

95pp.

THE

SEAFORTH HIGHLANDERS

ASSAYE

CUIDICH'N RIGH

SOUTH AFRICA
1899-1902

The Seaforth Highlanders South Africa 1899–1902.
Major H. Davidson (Editor)
W. & A. K. Johnston Limited
Edinburgh and London nd. (c.1904)

Paper covered boards backed in red cloth. Front printed red and black. Back printed red only.
252×186mm

South African war record of the 2nd Batt. Seaforth Highlanders compiled from letters, diaries and various other sources. At Magersfontein the Battalion sustained heavy casualties. At Paardeberg, in February 1900, losses were again severe. After the occupation of Bloemfontein the Seaforths operated in Orange River Colony to February 1901 when they entrained for Victoria West, the enemy being active in western Cape Colony at that time. From June 1901 to the close of the campaign the Battalion (or detachments) served in eastern and western Transvaal and on lines of communication in Orange River Colony. Notes concerning the three Volunteer Service Companies associated with the Seaforths are included. Appendices include casualty lists, mentioned in despatches and rewards, and a roll of officers and men who served in South Africa.

vii+86pp. Folding map and two plates.

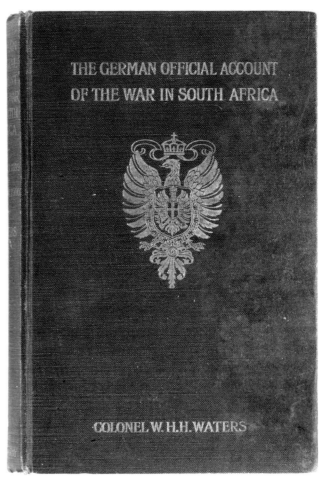

Convalescent Depot Gazette Germiston
(Author/Editor not shown.)
Publisher/printer not shown
Germiston. Transvaal 1901

Red cloth. Front blocked in black
205×130mm

Six issues (complete run) of a magazine
published at the Convalescent Depot,
Germiston from June to November 1901.
The original issues were paper covered, in
this cloth bound collection the wraps are
removed. Content is similar to that of other
magazines of the period such as *The Gram*
and *The Cossack Post*. Contributions
include poetry, articles of general interest
and local news. This copy lacks the title
page. The title is drawn from issue No.2.

138pp.

The War In South Africa. Prepared In The
Historical Section Of The Great General
Staff, Berlin.
Translation by Colonel W. H. H. Waters
John Murray
London 1905

Dark green buckram. Front and spine
blocked in gold.
226×146mm

An account of military operations in South
Africa prepared by the General Staff,
Berlin. Part I of the volume concerns the
campaign in Natal up to and including the
battle of Colenso, with an account of Lord
Methuen's campaign in the west concluding
with the battle of Magersfontein. Part II
relates to operations in the western theatre
from the assumption of command by Lord
Roberts until the surrender of Cronje at
Paardeberg. With appendices to each
section.

ix+280pp. Various folding maps and two
plates.

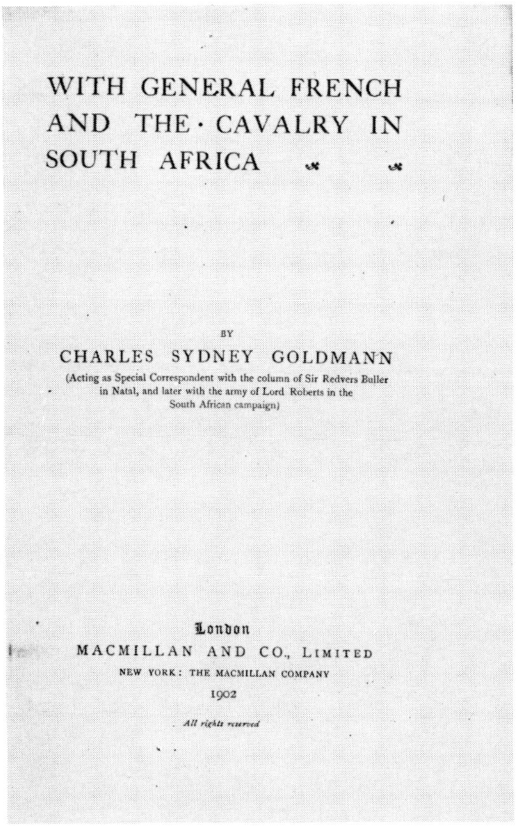

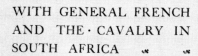

WITH GENERAL FRENCH AND THE · CAVALRY IN SOUTH AFRICA

BY

CHARLES SYDNEY GOLDMANN

(Acting as Special Correspondent with the column of Sir Redvers Buller in Natal, and later with the army of Lord Roberts in the South African campaign)

London
MACMILLAN AND CO., LIMITED
NEW YORK: THE MACMILLAN COMPANY
1902

All rights reserved

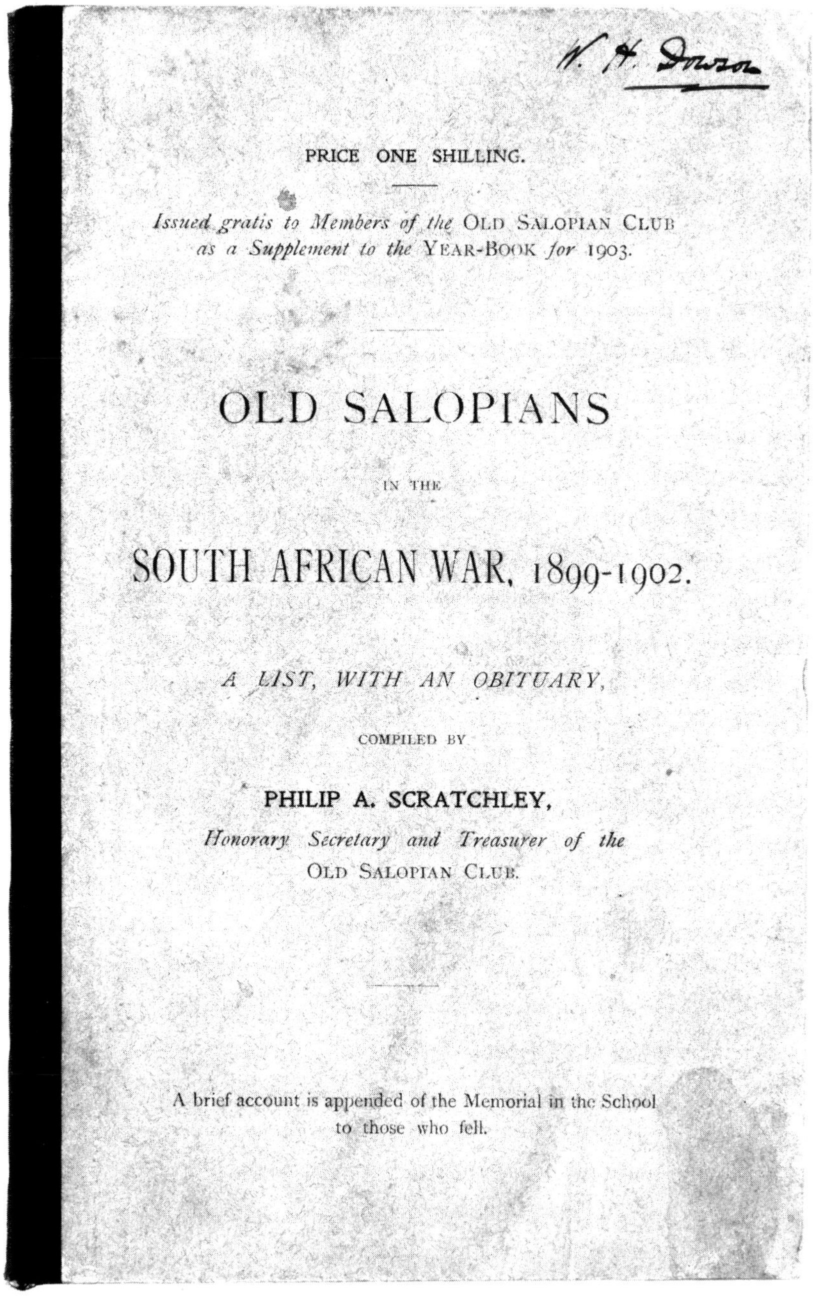

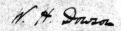

PRICE ONE SHILLING.

Issued gratis to Members of the OLD SALOPIAN CLUB *as a Supplement to the* YEAR-BOOK *for* 1903.

OLD SALOPIANS

IN THE

SOUTH AFRICAN WAR, 1899-1902.

A LIST, WITH AN OBITUARY,

COMPILED BY

PHILIP A. SCRATCHLEY,

Honorary Secretary and Treasurer of the OLD SALOPIAN CLUB.

A brief account is appended of the Memorial in the School to those who fell.

With General French And The Cavalry In South Africa.
Charles Sydney Goldmann
Macmillan and Co., Limited
London 1902

Black cloth backed in maroon cloth. Spine blocked in gold.
230×148mm

An account of French's cavalry operations excluding the campaign in Natal. Chapters relate to Colesberg operations, the relief of Kimberley, operations to the fall of Bloemfontein and Pretoria, and the campaign in eastern Transvaal to November 1900. The narrative is preceded by an informative introduction relating events to the investment of Ladysmith. Among appendices are observations on cavalry, notes on reconnaissance, on transport and remounts in war. The volume is liberally illustrated with folding maps, panoramas and plates. Loose sketches are contained in a separate pocket.

xix+462pp. Illustrated.
Title page shown

Old Salopians In The South African War, 1899–1902. A List, With An Obituary, Compiled By Philip A. Scratchley, Honorary Secretary And Treasurer Of The Old Salopian Club.
Philip A. Scratchley
Harrison & Sons (Printers)
London 1903

Grey paper covered boards backed in red cloth. Black letterpress to front only.
213×138mm

A record compiled by the Hon. Secretary of the 'Old Salopian Club' issued free as a supplement to the Year-Book for 1903. Being a list of students of Shrewsbury School who served in South Africa. Entries include – rank and regiment, brief description of service, casualties, promotions, mentioned in despatches, medals awarded, etc. The work includes an obituary and reference to the Old Salopian Memorial.

50pp.

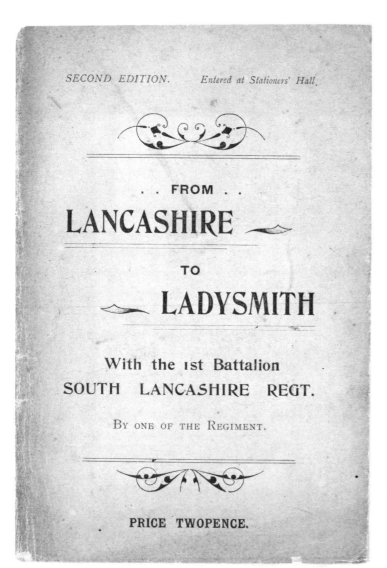

Boer War, 1899–1900. From Lancashire
To Ladysmith With The 1st Battalion South
Lancashire Regiment (Famous Fighting
Fortieth) Giving A Detailed Account Of
The Forced March From Estcourt To
Springfield, And A Graphic Description Of
The Battles Of Spion Kop, Potgieter's Drift,
And Pieter's Hill, The Sad Death Of Col.
O'Leary, And The Entry Of The Relieving
Force Into Ladysmith, Where, For Four
Months, British Soldiers Had Upheld The
Honour Of Great Britain. By One Of The
Regiment.
T. Neligan
Messrs. Neligan and Carter
Preston 1900

Buff coloured wraps. Black letterpress to
front only.
176×120mm

Personal experiences of the campaign in
Natal from 23 December 1899 to 3 March
1900.

48pp. With frontispiece.

With Both Armies In South Africa.
Richard Harding Davis
Charles Scribner's Sons
New York 1903

Bright red cloth. Front blocked in black,
white, green and blue. Spine blocked in
black only.
200×132mm

An American correspondent's account of
the war up to the fall of Pretoria. During his
travels the author joined the British army in
Natal and witnessed the Ladysmith relief
operations. He later interviewed President
Kruger at Pretoria and gives a description of
life in the Boer capital prior to British
occupation. Thereafter he proceeded to the
Orange Free State where he observed the
battle of Sand River south of Kroonstad.
The narrative concludes with an account of
the British advance into the Transvaal and
the exodus from Pretoria prior to British
occupation. The writer presents an unbiased
record of the conflict but questions British
motives and conduct of the war.

xi+237pp. Illustrated.

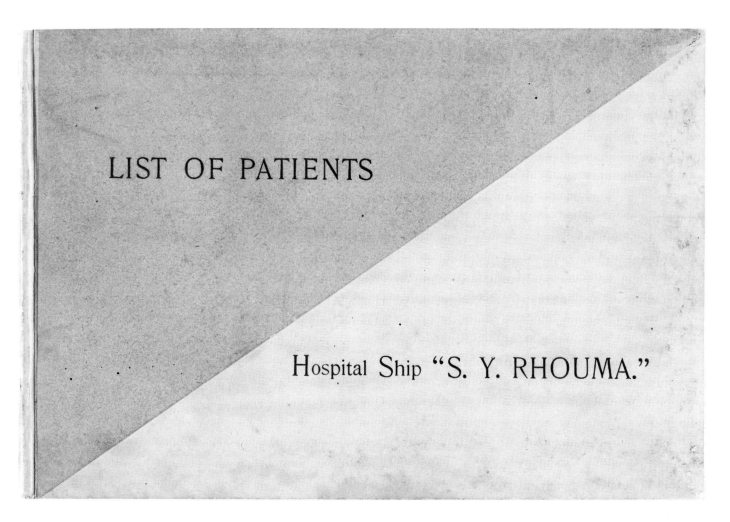

LIST OF PATIENTS

Hospital Ship "S. Y. RHOUMA."

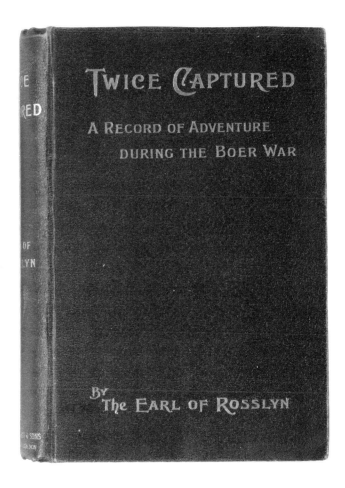

List Of Patients On Board Hospital Ship
S.Y. 'Rhouma' Cape Town, 1900.
(Editor/compiler not shown.)
Orr, Pollock & Co. Printers
Greenock nd. (c.1900)

Blue and white paper covered boards.
Brown letterpress to front only.
125×188mm

A list of patients treated aboard steam yacht
'Rhouma' off Cape Town, 1900. Case
details include name, official no., regiment,
date of entry and discharge, disease treated,
remarks and where wounded. Most patients
referred were from Portland Hospital, from
No.3 General Hospital and Wynberg
Hospital. S.Y. 'Rhouma' belonged to
industrialist George Bullough. For
providing the yacht to the nation for use as
a hospital ship, he was knighted in 1901.

36pp. Illustrated.

Twice Captured A Record Of
Adventure During The Boer War.
The Earl of Rosslyn
William Blackwood and Sons
Edinburgh and London 1900

Blue leather grained cloth. Front and spine
blocked in gold.
207×137mm

Adventures of the roving correspondent to
the *Daily Mail* and *Sphere*. The author was
twice taken prisoner by Boer forces, the
second occasion at Reddersburg where a
British detachment was overwhelmed by a
force led by De Wet. He gives a full account
of prison life at Pretoria and of setting up
The Gram, a camp magazine. Concluding
chapters relate to British occupation of
Pretoria and reflections on the campaign to
date.

xvi+477pp. Illustrated.

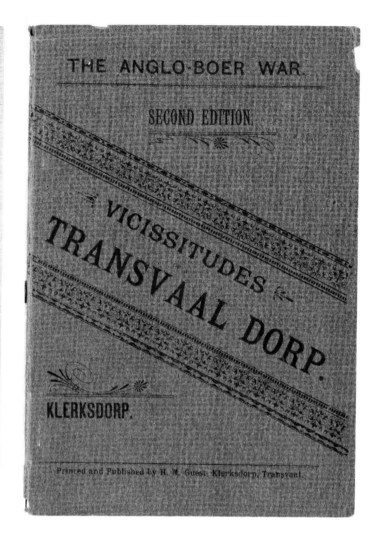

THE ANGLO-BOER WAR.

Incidents
In the
Western
Transvaal.

KLERKSDORP:
H. M. GUEST, PRINTER AND PUBLISHER, BOOKSELLER, STATIONER, &c.

1902.

The Anglo Boer War. Incidents In The
Western Transvaal.
H. M. Guest (Printer and Publisher)
Klerksdorp, Transvaal, 1902

Pale green textured wrap. Front lettered in
black.
204×137mm

A short history of Klerksdorp during the
war. With an account of operations of the
First Division under Lord Methuen,
descriptions of other engagements and notes
in respect of casualties.

63pp.

The Anglo-Boer War. Vicissitudes Of
A Transvaal Dorp. Klerksdorp.
H. M. Guest (Printer and Publisher)
Klerksdorp, 1901

Brown wrap. Black letterpress to front only.
201×140mm

A record of events at Klerksdorp during the
war with accounts of the British and Boer
occupations. Much of the narrative is based
on diaries kept by local residents. The
volume includes a list of British residents on
active service together with a roll of the
town guard and lists of local Boer losses.

47pp.

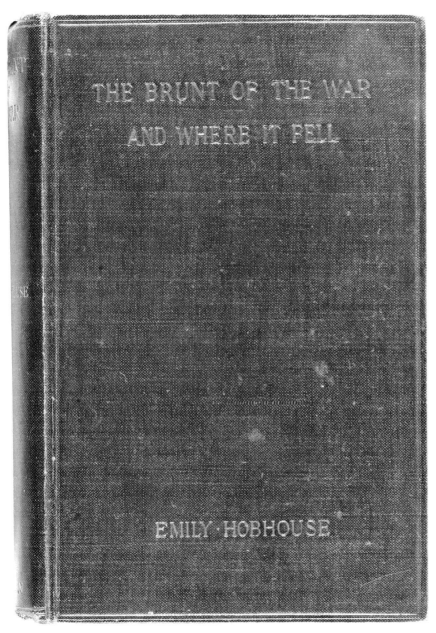

The Brunt Of The War And Where It Fell
Emily Hobhouse
Methuen & Co.
London 1902

Dark green cloth. Line border blocked in blind to upper and lower covers. Front and spine blocked in gold.
197×128mm

An account critical of British conduct of the war. The author censures the policy of farm burning and internment of Boer women and children in concentration camps. During the course of her visit to South Africa in 1901 she inspected some of the establishments describing the conditions then prevailing. The volume contains various independent reports relating to the camps together with information concerning issue of rations, mortality rates and farm destruction.

xvi+356pp. Map and illustrations.

Concentration Camps Commission. Report On The Concentration Camps In South Africa, By The Committee Of Ladies Appointed By The Secretary Of State For War; Containing Reports On The Camps In Natal, The Orange River Colony, And The Transvaal.
(Committee of ladies)
Printed for His Majesty's Stationery Office
London 1902

Blue wraps. Black letterpress to front, back and spine.
331×213mm

In response to national agitation over the question of concentration camps (much of it caused by Emily Hobhouse) the War Office appointed a Commission of Ladies to inspect the camps and report their findings. Under the presidency of Mrs. Fawcett the commissioners embarked for South Africa in July 1901. In a tour extending over four months they visited all the camps with the exception of that at Port Elizabeth. All aspects of camp organization and administration were examined including location, issue of rations, water supply, sanitation, medical facilities and education. The inspectors initiated many valuable reforms and, as a result of their recommendations, conditions at the camps steadily improved. By February 1902 the general death rate had reduced dramatically. The volume is comprised of separate reports on establishments under Natal, O.R.C. and Transvaal administration together with the general report and appendices.

i+208pp.

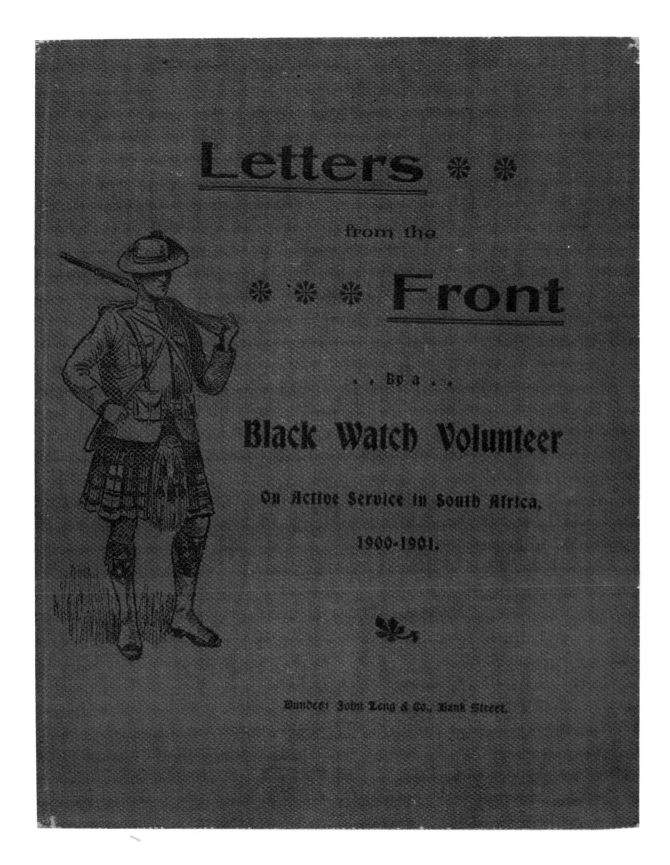

Letters From The Front By A Black Watch
Volunteer On Active Service In South
Africa, 1900–1901.
(Author not shown)
John Leng & Co. (Printers)
Dundee 1901

Ochre buckram over boards trimmed flush.
Front and back blocked in black.
211×168mm

Letters written by a Black Watch volunteer
to his mother presenting an unbroken
record of the work and marches of the
Active Service Company in South Africa
from March 1900 to April 1901. The letters
are reprinted from the Dundee *Evening
Telegraph* for private circulation. The Black
Watch, together with other volunteer
companies, joined the Highland Brigade
under General Hector Macdonald. For

approximately one year they campaigned in
the Orange Free State during which period
they marched over 1,400 miles. At various
times the Company was at Norval's Pont,
Bloemfontein, Winburg, Ventersburg,
Kroonstad and Reitz. The volunteers
experienced frequent skirmishing with the
enemy but were not seriously engaged until
the Retiefs Nek operations of July 22–24,
1900. In September 1900 they took part in
an attack on a Boer column near Winburg.
The following month they completed a short
spell of garrison duty at Ladybrand, and in
November, they were the occupying force at
Valentines Kop during operations to entrap
General De Wet. During the latter part of
their service, from January to the end of
March 1901, the volunteers operated in
south eastern Orange River Colony.

36pp. Frontispiece and folding map.

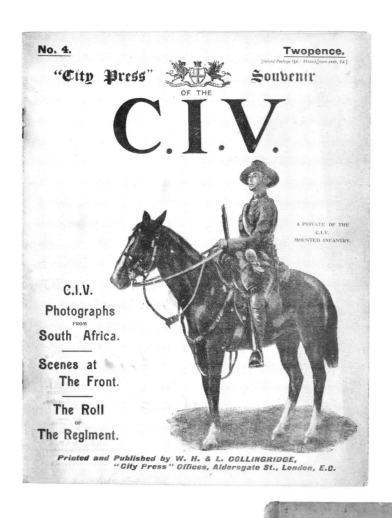

No.4. City Press Souvenir Of The C.I.V. C.I.V. Photographs From South Africa. Scenes At The Front. The Roll Of The Regiment.
(Author/editor not shown.)
W. H. & L. Collingridge (Publishers)
London 1900

Pale green wraps, printed red to front and back.
279×220mm

An account of the C.I.V. in South Africa with a list of contents for all four issues. The souvenirs were also published in a superior edition bound in card covers backed in cloth.

32pp. (including some pages of advertisements). Illustrated throughout.

The City Of London Imperial Volunteers In South Africa, A.D.1900. The 'City Press' C.I.V. Souvenir (Complete Edition).
(Author/editor not shown.)
W. H. & L. Collingridge
London 1900

Khaki cloth blocked in red to front and spine.
285×220mm

'Complete edition' of the C.I.V. war souvenir originally published in four parts. The issues bound are the 'fine paper' copies first published in pictorial card covers. Contents include organisation and enrolment, commissions, promotions, campaign notes and a list of casualties. Issue 3 contains the official roll of the C.I.V. and issue 4, the roll of C.I.V. reinforcement.

Issues 1–3 unpaginated. Issue 4–32pp. With supplement. Illustrated throughout.

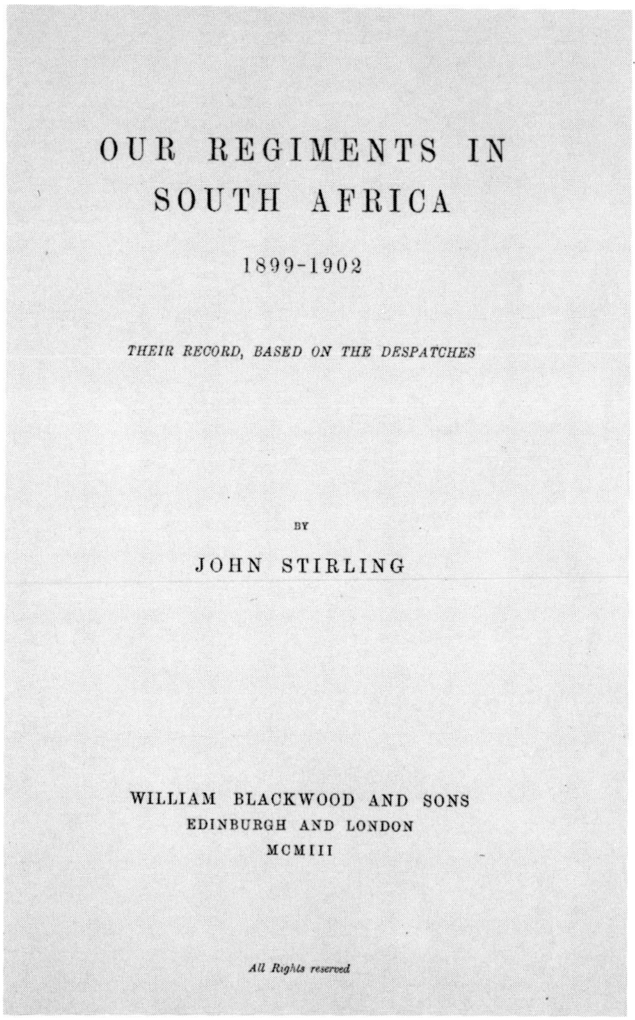
OUR REGIMENTS IN
SOUTH AFRICA

1899-1902

THEIR RECORD, BASED ON THE DESPATCHES

BY

JOHN STIRLING

WILLIAM BLACKWOOD AND SONS
EDINBURGH AND LONDON
MCMIII

All Rights reserved

Our Regiments In South Africa 1899–1902
Their Record, Based On The Despatches.
John Stirling
William Blackwood and Sons
Edinburgh and London 1903

Dull blue cloth. Line borders blocked in blind to front and back. Spine blocked in gold and blind.
230×145mm

A directory showing the movements and engagements of British regiments during the South African Campaign. The information is drawn from the chief despatches of the campaign, from regimental records and from unofficial sources. Records of the Royal Engineers, Army Service Corps, Medical Corps, Chaplain's Department, Ordnance and other departments, are included.

xiv+532pp.
Title page shown

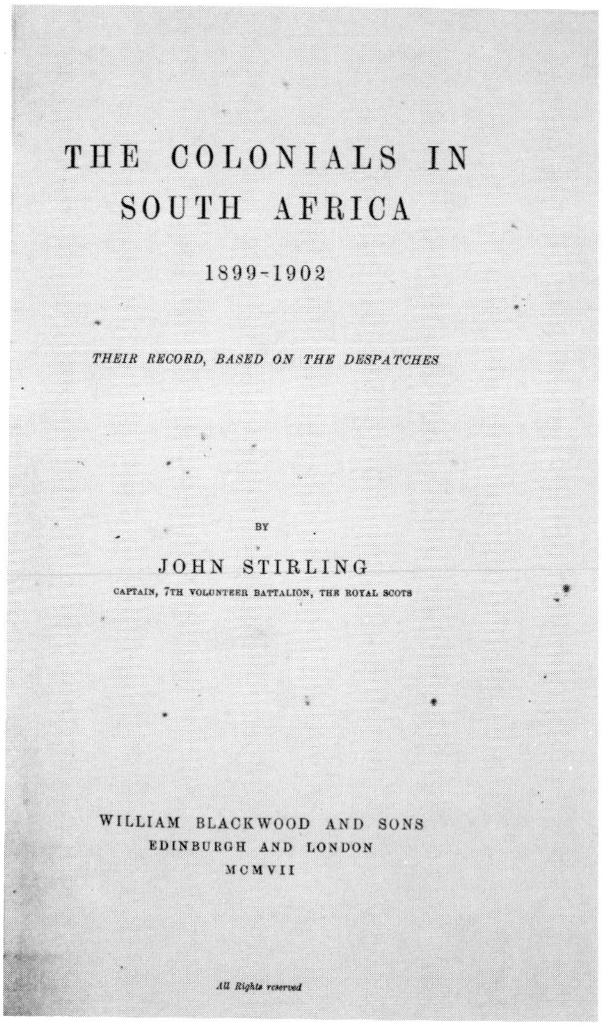
THE COLONIALS IN
SOUTH AFRICA

1899-1902

THEIR RECORD, BASED ON THE DESPATCHES

BY

JOHN STIRLING
CAPTAIN, 7TH VOLUNTEER BATTALION, THE ROYAL SCOTS

WILLIAM BLACKWOOD AND SONS
EDINBURGH AND LONDON
MCMVII

All Rights reserved

The Colonials In South Africa 1899–1902
Their Record, Based On The Despatches.
John Stirling
William Blackwood and Sons
Edinburgh and London 1907

Dull blue cloth. Line borders blocked in blind to front and rear. Spine blocked in blind and gold.
230×147mm

A record similar to the author's earlier volume *Our Regiments In South Africa.*
A directory of Colonial Volunteer Corps and their work in the South African campaign. The information is drawn from official despatches, other reliable published accounts and from private accounts furnished by officers in the field.

xii+497pp.
Title page shown

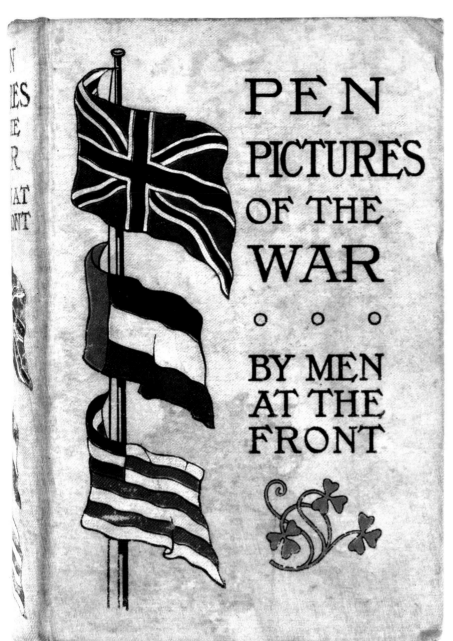

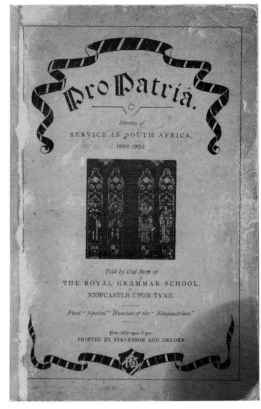

Pen Pictures Of The War By Men At The
Front Volume I. The Campaign In Natal To
The Battle Of Colenso.
(Men at the Front)
Horace Marshall & Son
London 1900

Ochre cloth blocked in black, green, red,
white, orange and blue to front and spine.
193×131mm

A narrative of the campaign interspersed
with letters relating the experiences of the
common soldier in battle, in camp and on
the march. The content relates primarily to
operations in Natal but includes some
episodes of the western campaign.
A chapter on 'The Laws and Usages of War'
deals with contentious issues such as abuse
of the white flag, refusing quarter and
looting of non-combatants. Of these charges
it is claimed both armies were often guilty.
The volume contains some maps and plans
together with a calendar of events to the fall
of Bloemfontein. The reference to Volume I
on the title page is misleading as a second
volume was not published.

vii+343pp. Frontispiece, maps and plans.

Pro Patriâ. Stories Of Service In South
Africa, 1899–1902. Told By Old Boys Of
The Royal Grammar School, Newcastle-
Upon-Tyne. First 'Special' Number Of The
'Novocastrian'.
(Author/editor not shown.)
Stevenson and Dryden, printers
Newcastle-upon-Tyne nd. (1902)

Off white paper covered boards trimmed
flush. Front printed black and red.
219×141mm

A volume published to commemorate the
patriotic services of 'Old Boys' who served
in South Africa. The stories, relating
personal experiences during the campaign,
include accounts of the battle of
Magersfontein, the campaign in Cape
Colony, the siege and relief of Wepener and
the chase after De Wet. The volume
includes a roll of 'Old Boys' and the Corps
in which they served.

88pp. Illustrated.

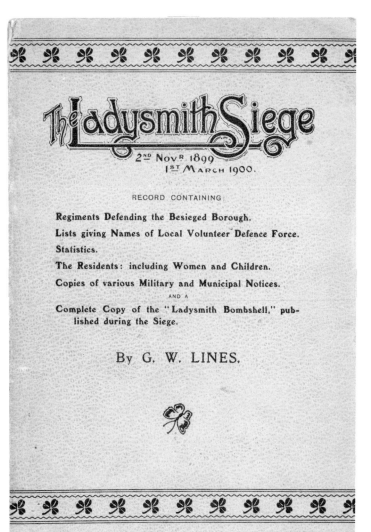

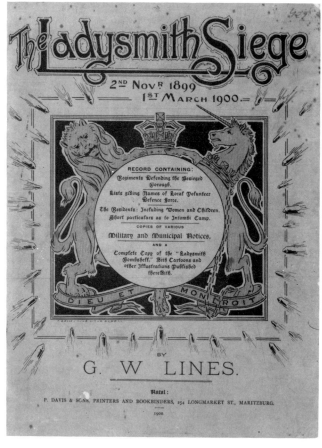

The Ladysmith Siege 2nd Nov. 1899–
1st March, 1900.
Record Containing: Regiments Defending
The Besieged Borough. Lists Giving Names
Of Local Volunteer Defence Force.
Statistics. The Residents: Including Women
And Children. Copies Of Various Military
And Municipal Notices. And A Complete
Copy Of The *Ladysmith Bombshell*
Published During The Siege.
G. W. Lines
Wilsons Music and General Printing Co.
Ltd.
London nd. (c.1900)

Light blue grained card cover. Dark blue
letterpress to front only.
201×136mm

Statistics and printed ephemera relating to
the siege.
96pp. Some cartoon sketches.

The Ladysmith Siege.
2nd November 1899–1st March 1900.
G. W. Lines
P. Davis & Sons
Maritzburg 1900

Pink wraps printed dark blue to front and
back.
302×238mm

Statistics relating to the siege of Ladysmith,
including particulars of Military Staff,
strength of defending forces, burials at
borough cemetery, lists of besieged
residents and copies of certain military and
municipal notices. Together with issues of
the *Ladysmith Bombshell*.

31pp. Advertisements+27pp.+8 issues of
Ladysmith Bombshell siege newspaper
(unpaginated). Some cartoon illustrations.

The True History of the War.   Part IV.

BEING THE

OFFICIAL DESPATCHES

FROM THE

GENERAL COMMANDING-IN-CHIEF

THE FORCES IN

SOUTH AFRICA

AND ENCLOSING

REPORT ON THE SIEGE OF MAFEKING

FROM

MAJOR-GENERAL BADEN-POWELL

PRICE SIXPENCE.

LONDON:

HARRISON & SONS, PRINTERS IN ORDINARY TO HER LATE MAJESTY,

45, 46 & 47, ST. MARTIN'S LANE, W.C.

The True History Of The War Being The Official Despatches And Enclosures From The General Commanding-In-Chief The Forces In South Africa.
(Editor/compiler not shown)
Harrison & Sons, publishers
London nd. (1900)

Salmon pink wraps backed in brown paper.
Front printed black.
315×194mm

Official Despatches reprinted from *The London Gazette*, published in five parts.
Part I. From November 9th, 1899 to December 28th, 1899. Reprinted from *The London Gazette* of January 26th, 1900.
Part II. Contents. Victoria Cross and Special Awards. Despatches of Lord Roberts, Lord Methuen, General Gatacre, Admiral Harris, Sir Redvers Buller, Sir C. Warren. List Of European deaths in Kimberley District. Synopsis of Part I. Reprinted from *The London Gazette* of February 2nd, March 13th, March 16th, March 30th, April 6th and April 17th, 1900.
Part III. Describing the Military Operations at Colesberg, Kimberley, Paardeberg, Bloemfontein, Kroonstadt and Pretoria.
Part IV. Enclosing Report on the Siege of Mafeking from Major-General Baden-Powell.
Part V. Enclosing an account of the Defence and Relief of Ladysmith. A list of contents to each issue is present in Part V.

186pp.

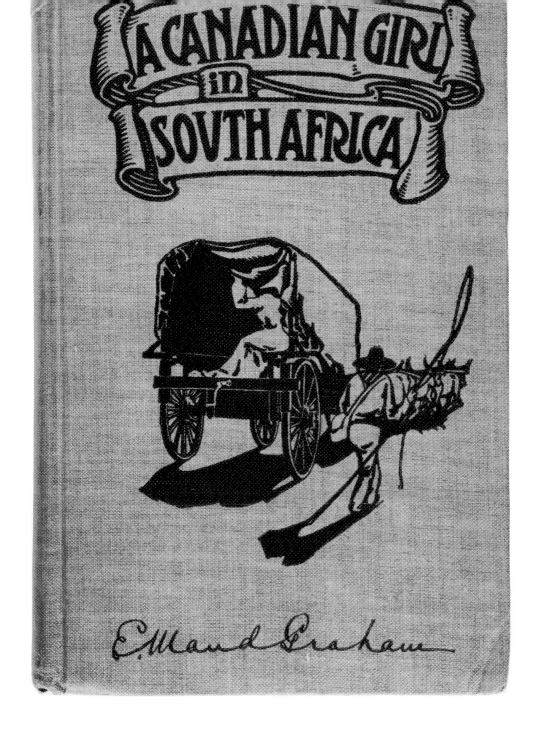

A Canadian Girl In South Africa.
E. Maud Graham
William Briggs
Toronto 1905

Ochre cloth. Front blocked in dark green,
spine blocked in gold.
199×130mm *(Illustrated)*

Variant binding
Ochre cloth. Front blocked in cream, spine
blocked in gold.
200×130mm

A schoolteacher's experiences in South
Africa from June 1902 to July 1904. At the
close of the war the Colonial Office called
for volunteers to assist in the education
service of the annexed territories. Women
teachers were recruited from Australia,
New Zealand, Great Britain and Canada.
The writer, a member of the Canadian

contingent, recounts her experiences at
schools at Norvals Pont, Fauresmith and
Kroonstad and comments briefly on social
conditions then prevalent. She perceives
that many at Cape Town profited from the
war while communities in parts of Orange
River Colony were brought to a state of
near ruin. The writer visited Johannesburg
and Pretoria during her stay and met many
Boer families. She formed a favourable
opinion of the people noting their desire for
education and their friendly disposition
despite recent deprivation. The prospects of
a united South Africa are considered in
relation to the current state of farming, the
native labour question, repatriation and the
vital work of the relief agencies. Miss
Graham completed two years service before
departing South Africa in July 1904.

192pp. Illustrated.

Celebrities Of The Army.
Chas. N. Robinson (Editor)
George Newnes, Limited.
London 1900

Bright red cloth over bevelled boards. Front
and spine blocked in gold.
358×268mm *(Illustrated)*

Variant bindings
Dark green cloth over bevelled boards.
Front and spine blocked in gold.
358×268mm

Ochre cloth over bevelled boards. Front and
spine blocked in red.
358×268mm

Set of 18 numbered parts. Limp card covers
printed black.
384×287mm

A collection of 72 coloured portraits of
prominent British army officers with brief
service records. Most of the officers
depicted were engaged in the South African
campaign. The portraits were originally
issued in 18 parts.

iii+144pp. Illustrated throughout.

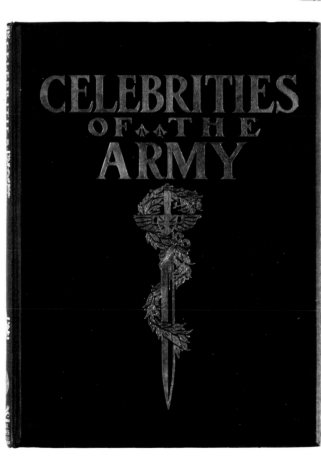

Seventy Days With The Troops From
Southampton To Ladysmith.
J. W. Moodie
John Thomlinson/Partick
John Menzies & Co./Glasgow and
Edinburgh.
1900

Limp card cover. Front only printed in
colour.
182×122mm

A record of evangelistic work during the
early phase of the campaign. The author
arrived at the Cape on Feb. 5, 1900
intending to join the Highland Brigade at
the western front. Being unable to obtain
travel warrants to join the western force he
remained at Cape Town administering to
troops at military camps and hospitals.
A few weeks later, in company of other
christian workers, the author embarked for
Durban, base of eastern operations. The
party travelled inland to Pietermaritzburg,
Mooi River and Colenso prior to Moodie
proceeding alone to Ladysmith. He entered
the town 26 days after the relieving force.
The narrative includes a short account of
Gen. Buller's Natal operations and of
events at Ladysmith during the siege and
the period thereafter.

71pp. Photographs and other illustrations.

Report Of The Work Of The Edinburgh
And East Of Scotland South African
Hospital.
*Edited by David Wallace and
Francis D. Boyd*
Oliver and Boyd
Edinburgh 1901

Brown buckram. Front blocked in red,
white and gold. Spine blocked in gold.
226×180mm

An account of the hospital opened at
Norval's Pont in May 1900. Chapters relate
to the organization and administration of
the establishment and to medical and
surgical cases treated. Editors Wallace and
Boyd were members of the professional
medical staff.

x+193pp. Folding plan, various charts and
other illustrations.

Australians In War. With The Australian
Regiment From Melbourne To
Bloemfontein.
Major W. T. Reay
A. H. Massina & Co.
Melbourne 1900

Fawn cloth. Front and spine blocked in
black.
190×125mm

A record of the First Australian Regiment
in South Africa from November 1899 to
April 1900. The force, comprised of
Victorian, South Australian, West
Australian and Tasmanian contingents, was
employed in the Kimberley relief operations
and later served in Cape Colony. In
December 1899 the regiment was stationed
on the De Aar-Modder River line. Units
occupied posts at Belmont and Enslin. In
January 1900 they were brought down to
Naauwpoort in Cape Colony and all units
converted to mounted infantry. The
following month the regiment was attached
to Gen. Clements' force engaged in
operations in the Colesberg area. In the
heavy fighting during February and March
the Australians sustained significant
casualties. As northern Cape Colony was
cleared of Boers British columns advanced
into the Orange Free State. The Australians
formed part of the force that reached
Bloemfontein on April 4. The narrative
ends with the reorganization of the regiment
in April 1900. Appendices include a list of
Victorian casualties up to September 1900.

xv+pp.9–382.

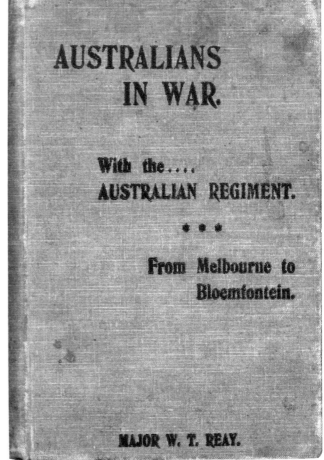

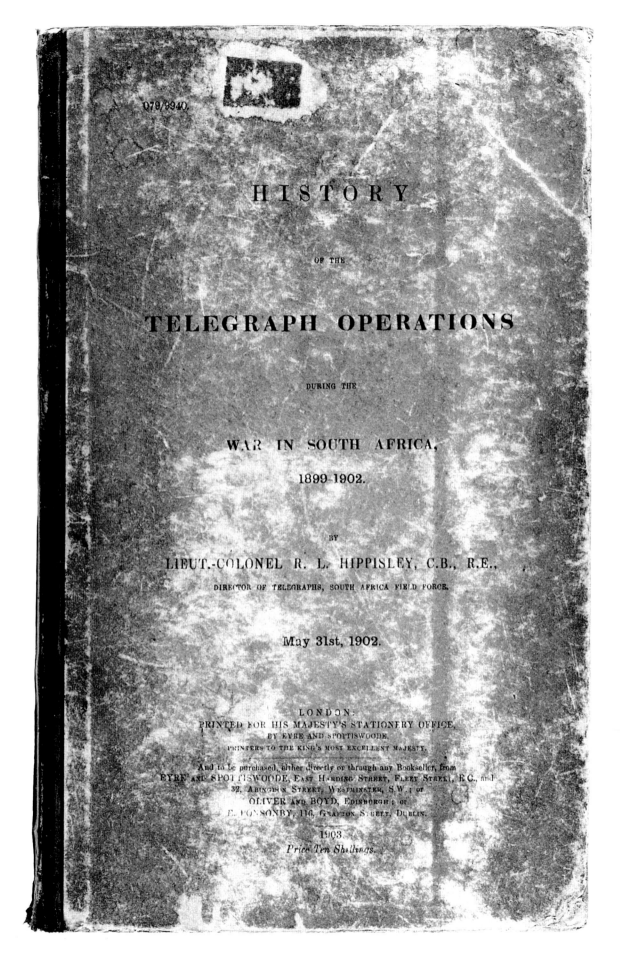

HISTORY

OF THE

TELEGRAPH OPERATIONS

DURING THE

WAR IN SOUTH AFRICA,

1899-1902.

BY

LIEUT.-COLONEL R. L. HIPPISLEY, C.B., R.E.,

DIRECTOR OF TELEGRAPHS, SOUTH AFRICA FIELD FORCE.

May 31st, 1902.

LONDON:
PRINTED FOR HIS MAJESTY'S STATIONERY OFFICE,
BY EYRE AND SPOTTISWOODE,
PRINTERS TO THE KING'S MOST EXCELLENT MAJESTY.

And to be purchased, either directly or through any Bookseller, from
EYRE AND SPOTTISWOODE, East Harding Street, Fleet Street, E.C., and
32, Abingdon Street, Westminster, S.W.; or
OLIVER AND BOYD, Edinburgh; or
E. PONSONBY, 116, Grafton Street, Dublin.

1903.
Price Ten Shillings.

History Of The Telegraph Operations During The War In South Africa, 1899–1902. By Lieut.-Colonel R. L. Hippisley, C.B., R.E., Director Of Telegraphs, South Africa Field Force. May 31st, 1902.
Lieut.-Colonel R. L. Hippisley
Printed for His Majesty's Stationery Office by Eyre and Spottiswoode
London 1903

Beige paper covered boards backed in crimson cloth. Black letterpress to front only.
332×208mm

Official account of the telegraph operations by the Director of Telegraphs. With 100 charts showing communication systems in various sectors, including blockhouse lines.

85pp. With 100 charts, some folding.

OFFICIAL RECORDS

OF THE

AUSTRALIAN MILITARY CONTINGENTS

TO THE

WAR IN SOUTH AFRICA.

COMPILED AND EDITED FOR THE DEPARTMENT OF DEFI
BY LIEUT.-COLONEL P. L. MURRAY, R.A.A. (RET.).

By Authority:
ALBERT J. MULLETT, GOVERNMENT PRINTER, MELBOURNE.

C.4720.

Official Records Of The Australian Military
Contingents To The War In South Africa.
Compiled And Edited For The Department
Of Defence By Lieut.-Colonel P. L.
Murray, R.A.A. (Ret.)
Lieut.-Colonel P. L. Murray
Albert J. Mullett, Government Printer
Melbourne nd. (1911)

Rebound copy.
248×191mm

A register of Australian military contingents
to South Africa grouped under Colonies.
The information includes details of
establishment, equipment, embarkation,
records of service, engagements,
promotions and honours. A nominal roll
completes each entry.

iii+607pp.
Title page shown.

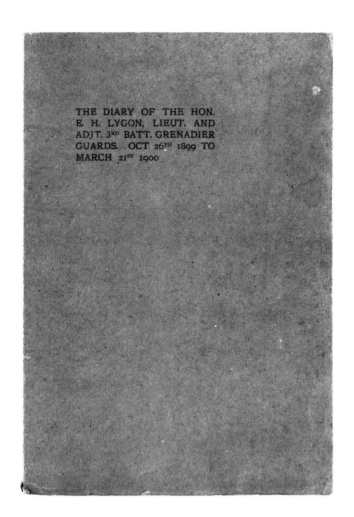

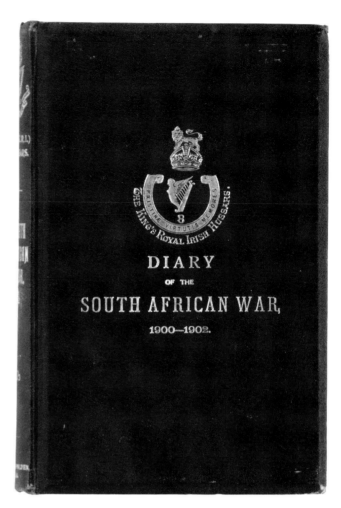

The Diary Of The Hon. E. H. Lygon,
Lieut. And Adjt. 3rd Batt. Grenadier
Guards. Oct. 26th 1899 To March 21st 1900.
E. H. Lygon
Privately printed by
Angus & Robertson
Sydney 1900

Brown card cover. Red letterpress to front
only.
289×200mm

Campaign diary of Lieut. Lygon of the 3rd
Batt. Grenadier Guards together with an
account of his death near Karee Siding
extracted from the *Bloemfontein Friend* of
March 27th 1900. The officer records his
experiences up to the occupation of
Bloemfontein with reference to the battles
of Belmont, Modder River and
Magersfontein. (The work of the 3rd
Grenadiers is outlined on page 83 of this
volume.) On March 23rd Lieut. Lygon,
together with three senior Guards officers
and an orderly, left their encampment north
of Bloemfontein to seek forage from
neighbouring farms. Returning from the
mission the group encountered a party of
Boers near Karee Siding. In the ensuing
action Lygon was killed and all the others
wounded. The Boers helped the wounded to
a nearby farm and Lygon's body was
retrieved for burial the following day. This
elegantly printed volume is a tribute from
members of the officer's family.

iii+iii+45pp.

8th (King's Royal Irish) Hussars, Diary Of
The South African War, 1900–1902.
J. W. Morton
Gale & Polden, Ltd.
Aldershot 1905

Dark green cloth over bevelled boards.
Front and spine blocked in gold.
217×143mm

The following account of the regiment in
South Africa is extracted from the columns
of the *Dublin Daily Express* of March 1st,
1905. – The regiment arrived at Cape Town
on March 10th, 1900. Together with the
14th Hussars and the 7th Dragoon Guards,
they formed the Fourth Cavalry Brigade.
Their first engagement took place near
Thaba'nchu, and they subsequently took
part in the main advance from Bloemfontein
to Pretoria, being present in the fighting
round Johannesburg and at the battle of
Diamond Hill in June 1900. The 8th were
next employed in the eastern advance to
Belfast and Barberton. In November they
joined the Second Cavalry Brigade
operating in the Rustenberg district under
General Broadwood and, early in 1901,
took part in an arduous trek under General
French to south eastern Transvaal. The
regiment then remained for some months at
Volksrust. Squadrons were attached to
various columns operating in eastern
Orange River Colony, south eastern
Transvaal, Natal and Zululand. In 1902 the
regiment was concentrated under its own
commander, Col. Duff, and took part in
various 'drives' until the close of the
campaign. The 8th remained in South
Africa after peace was declared, they were
stationed at Pretoria. The volume includes
nominal rolls by squadron and notes on the
South African War Memorial in St.
Patrick's Cathedral, Dublin.

xv+159pp. Double frontispiece and folding
plate.

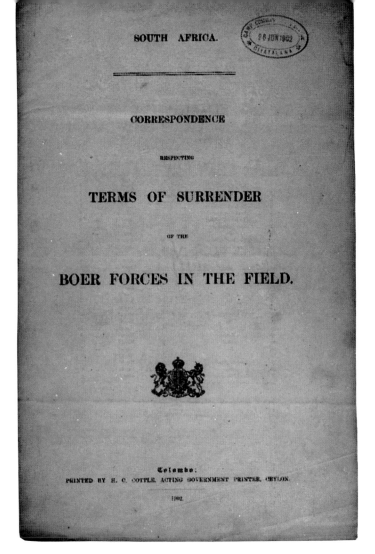

South Africa. Correspondence Respecting
Terms Of Surrender Of The Boer Forces
In The Field.
(Editor/compiler not shown)
Printed by H. C. Cottle
acting Government Printer, Ceylon
Colombo 1902

Paper covered. Letterpress to front only.
336×213mm

29 telegrams concerning the surrender of
Boer forces. The correspondence is
addressed between Lord Kitchener and The
Secretary of State for War and Lord Milner
and Mr. Chamberlain. The document is
similar to that published by HMSO
(Cd.1096) that extends to 13pp. Both
publications contain the Draft Agreement as
to Terms of Surrender of the Boer Forces in
the Field approved by His Majesty's
Government.

8pp.

The South African Boer War Exhibition.
The Greatest And Most Realistic Military
Spectacle Known In The History Of The
World Produced Under The Direction Of
Frank E. Fillis The Famous South African
Showman And Organizer Of Savage South
Africa In Greater Britain Exhibition, Earls
Court, London, Etc., Etc.
(Author/compiler not shown.)
South African Boer War Exhibition
Company (Published by)
St. Louis 1904

Limp card cover. Front printed in full
colour, back cover printed black.
240×171mm

The official program and historical libretto
of the Anglo-Boer War Exhibition at the
World's Fair, St. Louis, 1904. It is stated
that Captain A. W. Lewis, originator of the
spectacle, brought over six hundred men,
women and children from South Africa. The
program contains notes on the National
South African exhibit and a synopsis of the
three tableaux staged. The pageant featured
the Battle of Colenso and the loss of Col.
Long's guns, Battle of Paardeberg and
surrender of Gen. Cronje, and De Wet's
flight through a cordon of British troops.
Notes on the Boer generals Viljoen and
Cronje are included together with a list of
the Exhibition Company directors.

24pp. Illustrated.

Bibliography

Abbreviations

SABIB	A South African Bibliography To The Year 1925. London 1979
M	Mendelssohn's South African Bibliography. London 1968
WO	War Office
BM	British Museum Library
RE	Royal Engineers / Chatham
RCSL	Royal Commonwealth Society Library
THB	L.S. Amery / The Times History Of The War In South Africa 1899-1902. London 1900-1909
ROTE	R. Perkins / Regiments Of The Empire A Bibliography Of Their Published Histories. Newton Abbot 1989
BIM	Brent Mackrell Military Library
NAM	National Army Museum
CC	Collection. Neville Constantine
GC	Collection. Kenneth Griffith
DC	Collection. Dr. Paul Dunn
WS	Collection. Wayne Sheldrick
HC	Collection. Brian Hardy
SNH	Scottish National Heritage
W/L	Wright / Lloyd Catalogue 1978
CB	Clarke's Bookshop / Cape Town
W	A.S. White / A Bibliography Of Regimental Histories Of The British Army. London 1988
NL	National Library Of Australia
AWM	Australian War Memorial
ALH	Australian Library Holdings
BOPP	Annual Catalogue Of British Official And Parliamentary Publications 1894-1909. Bishops Stortford 1975
MOD	Ministry Of Defence
H	H.E. Haferkorn / The South African War 1899-1902. Washington 1924
GR	A.P.C. Griffin / Bibliography. List Of Works In The Library Of Congress On The Boer War. Selected Translations Pertaining To The Boer War. Washington 1905

Except for titles published by institutions which are grouped under corporate headings, entries are listed alphabetically under author. Where the author is not shown entries are listed by publisher or printer. Volumes without an imprint are catalogued under an appropriate heading.

Size is indicated in millimetres with height given first. Items drawn from published sources retain the original size shown, with the exception of titles extracted from HAFERKORN and SABIB, which herein are converted to millimetres. Titles illustrated are denoted by a page number at the end of the entry.

The provenance of each entry is shown excluding those drawn from my trade catalogues and personai collection .

War Office publications from the Ministry of Defence Library London, are numbered 1-162 for convenient reference.

A

Abadie (Lt. Eustace H.) – Military Pigeon Post. Operations. Etc. See WO. 110.

Abbott (J.H.M.) – Tommy Cornstalk Being Some Account Of The Less Notable Features Of The South African War From The Point Of View Of The Australian Ranks.
Longmans, Green, and Co.
London/New York/Bombay 1902
xi+264pp.
197×132mm

Abbott (J.H.M.) – Plain And Veldt. Being Studies, Stories, And Sketches Of My Own People, In Peace And At War.
Methuen & Co.
London 1903
viii+306
Cr.8vo.   M
Sketches of the South African War, the majority reproduced from the columns of various Australian journals.

Ackland (Joseph) – War And Christian Profession. With A Brief Enquiry As To The Causes Of The War In South Africa.
James Clark & Co.
London 1900
57pp.
12mo.   M

Adams (C. F.) – 1865–1900. The Confederacy And The Transvaal: A People's Obligation To Robert E. Lee. A Paper Read Before The American Antiquarian Society, At Its Annual Meeting In Worcester, Massachusetts, Wednesday, October 30, 1901.
Houghton, Mifflin & Co.
Boston 1901
26pp.
220mm   SABIB
See FISHER S.G. – The American Revolution and the Boer War. Etc.

Adams (C. F.) – 1865–1900. The Confederacy And The Transvaal: A People's Obligation To General Lee. Etc.
Gay and Bird
London 1902
28pp.
8vo.   M
A comparison of the situation in the Transvaal 1901/1902 and the United States, following the defeat of Confederate forces in 1865.

Adcock (A. St. John.) – In The Wake Of The War.
Hodder & Stoughton
London 1900
155pp.
12mo.   M
Short stories illustrative of the effects of the South African War on the lower and poorer classes of the British population. Possibly a work of fiction?

Adcock (A. St. John.) – Songs Of The War.
R. Brimley Johnson
London 1900
60pp. Including publishers advertisements.
12mo.   M
Verses dealing with events leading up to war and of early stages of the campaign.

A. D. L. (A. D. Lückhoff) – Woman's Endurance. By A.D.L., B.A., Chaplain In The Concentration Camp, Bethulie, O. R. C., 1901.
S. A. News Co., (Printers)
Cape Town 1904.
iii+67pp.
220×143mm

Adlington (E. H.) (Printer) – Concert In Aid Of The Scottish Horse Convalescent Camp, Johannesburg, March 15th, 1902: Book of Words.
E. H. Adlington, printer
Johannesburg 1902
6pp.
230mm   SABIB

('Africanus') – The Transvaal Boers. A Historical Sketch By 'Africanus'.
Horace Marshall & Son.
London 1899.
158pp.
Cr.8vo.
Recent history of the Boer Republic forming a comprehensive sketch of the causes of the war – M. & SABIB list author, Sir M. C. C. Seton. Two entries, i.e. –
1st Ed. 1899. xv+158pp. Folding map.
2nd Ed. Revised and enlarged, 1900. xvi+164pp. Folding map.

(Airlie, Earl of) – The Happy Warrior, Etc. See entry under JACOB and JOHNSON 'Hampshire Chronicle' office.

Aitchison (John) – A Christian Colour-Sergeant, Etc. See entry under BRODIE & SALMOND (Publishers).

Aitken (W. Francis) – Baden-Powell, The Hero Of Mafeking.
S. W. Partridge & Co.
London 1900
160pp. With portrait.
190×130mm
M. lists copy of 176pp. Much concerning the siege and relief of Mafeking.

Aked (Charles Frederic) – 'I Told You So!' A Sermon On Our Cowardly War Preached On Peace Sunday, December 23rd, 1900.
C. Tinling (Printer)
Liverpool (1900?)
11pp.
210mm   SABIB

Aked (Charles Frederic) – 'Who Was Right?' The Annual Sermon On Our Cowardly War, Preached On Peace Sunday, December 22nd, 1901.
Published by the author
Liverpool 1901
19pp.
210×110mm
Catalogued from cover.

Aked (C. F.) – 'Who Was Right?' The Annual Sermon, Etc. 2nd Edition, 10th Thousand.
E. Smith & Co., printers
Liverpool 1901
15pp.

Albertyn (Johannes Rudolph) – The Boer Prisoners In Bermuda. Photographs Taken At Bermuda By Rev. T. R. Albertyn, Of Wellington, Cape Colony, Chaplain To Boer Prisoners Of War. Description Also By Him. March 20th, 1902.
C. R. Trumbull
New York 1902
4pp. Illustrated.
170mm?   SABIB

Alderson (A. W.) – The Worst Tax Of All The Real Cause Of The South African War, Peace Or Polyglottism, The Great 'Race' Fallacy, Race, War, And Language. Why There Is Always Trouble In The Balkans. An Income Tax Up To 20/- In The £. Caste And Nepotism.
P. S. King & Son
London 1909
12pp.
216×130mm   RCSL

Allen (P.) – Mafeking Day. A Snap-Shot From Real Life.
S. P. C. K.
London (1901)
216pp. Illustrated.
200mm   SABIB

Allison (T. J.) – Della Dorn Or Struggles Of The Boers.
J. S. Hyland
Texas 1908
266pp. Illustrated.
185×130mm
Epic poem relating to the Anglo-Boer conflict. Anti British sentiment throughout.

Allpass (S. R.) – The Tick. A Weekly Publication By And For Prisoners Of War, Umbilo, Durban, June 1902.
Printer/publisher not shown
Durban 1902
4pp.
329×203mm

Alt (Brian) – Brian Alt.
Ballantyne, Hanson & Co. (Printed by)
London 1900
104pp. Illustrated.
194×132mm   CC
Memoir of W. B. L. Alt, of the C.I.V. killed in action at Diamond Hill, June 12th, 1900. A volume of letters home from South Africa together with a few letters from friends and fellow soldiers.

(American Academy Of Political And Social Science) (Publisher?) – Annals Of The American Academy Of Political And Social Science, The South African Conflict – Its Legal And Political Aspect.
The Academy?
np. 1900
40pp. With folding map.

(American Transvaal League) (Publisher?) – Constitution, Etc.
The League (Publishers)
Chicago 1901
ii+31pp.
240mm   SABIB
Objects are to diffuse information in the U.S. concerning the causes and conduct of the war in South Africa, promote the cause of peace, to raise funds to aid the widows, orphans and crippled soldiers of the Boer Republics, etc.

(American Transvaal League) (Publisher?) – The Chicago Chronicle And President Kruger.
The League
Chicago 1901
32pp. Illustrations and maps.
200mm   SABIB
Criticism of an editorial from the Chronicle directed against the Boers. Signed by John O'D Rennie.

Amery (L. S.) (General Editor) – The Times History Of The War In South Africa (1899–1902).
Sampson Low, Marston and Company, Ltd.
London 1900–1909 (7vols.)
232×154mm   p.1
Vol.1. – 1899–1900   xxiv+392pp. 1900
Vol.2. – 1899–1902   xviii+467pp. 1902
Vol.3. – 1899–1902   xviii+597pp. 1905
Vol.4. – 1899–1902   xviii+597pp. 1906
Vol.5. – 1899–1902   xxviii+614pp. 1907
Vol.6. – 1899–1902   xvi+622pp. 1909
Vol.7. – 1899–1902   vii+209pp. 1909
Vols.1, 4 & 5 – Pocket maps, other maps and plates.
Vols.2 & 3 – Folding maps and plates.
Vol.6 – Various plates

Ames (E. & E.) – The Tremendous Twins Or How The Boers Were Beaten.

Grant Richards
London 1900
95pp. Illustrated.
211×250mm   p.76
An example of juvenile fiction of the
period.

Andree (A. W.) – Illustrations Of Life In
The Boer Camp.
Colombo Apothecaries Co. (Printer)
Colombo (1901?)
2+1+19 leaves. 20 plates.
140×210mm   SABIB
Catalogued from cover. RCSL lists copy
printed Hopetown 1901.

(Anglo-Africander) – Africanderism, The
Old And The Young. Letters To John
Bull, Esquire, By Anglo-Africander.
Sampson Low, Marston & Company
Limited
London 1902
viii+86pp.
Cr.8vo.   M
Outline of the Boer character and the
cause of the conflict explained.

(Annalist) – Musings Without Method.
A Record Of 1900–01, By Annalist.
William Blackwood & Sons
Edinburgh and London. 1902
pp.10, 323.
Many references to the South African War
– M. & SABIB list authors name –
C. Whibley.

(Anon) – 1st. V.B. King's Own Yorkshire
Light Infantry. West Yorks Dragoons.
St. John Ambulance, Souvenir On
Return Of – From South Africa Nov.
26th, 1900.
Publisher/printer not shown
np./nd. (c.1900)
20pp. Illustrated.
207×278mm
Souvenir published in celebration of the
return of West Yorkshire volunteers from
South Africa.

(Anon) – The Bombshell Poems Grave
And Humorous. Printed At Ladysmith
During The Memorable Siege 1899–1900.
Publisher/printer not shown
nd. (1900)
12pp.
196×126mm   CC
Poems relating to Ladysmith under siege.

(Anon) – Intelligence, Organization And
Administration (South Africa) (1901).
Publisher/printer not shown
Pagination not shown
Entered under 'Army' in THB.

(Anon) – South African War, With The
23rd Imperial Yeomanry (Duke Of
Lancaster's Own) From Blackpool To
Fabers Putt, Cape Colony, 1900.
(For private circulation only)
Author/printer/publisher not shown
np./nd. (c.1901)
60pp. Plans and illustrations.
184×121mm
A record of Lancashire Yeomanry in
South Africa compiled from private
correspondence and other sources.

(Anon) – The Only Way Towards A
Settlement In South Africa. A Third
Letter Addressed To The Members Of
His Majesty's Cabinet By The Writer Of
The Pamphlet On The Settlement Of The
South African Question.
Publisher/printer not shown
np. (1901?)
1+ii+11pp.
220mm   SABIB

(Anon) – Extracts From Principal
Decisions On Various Subjects [Pay,
Conditions Of Service, Etc.] During The
South African Campaign, 10th Jan.
1900–31st May 1902.
Publisher/printer not shown
Johannesburg 1902
xii+48pp.
Item drawn from War Office list of
publications. WO. ref. – WH Loc: SA67.

(Anon) – The British Volunteers In South
Africa: Extracts From Orders.
Publisher/printer not shown
London (1903)
Pagination not shown
Entered under 'Army' in THB.

(Anon) – Conditions Of Service Of South
African And Oversea Contingents
Employed In The South African War
1899–1902.
Publisher/printer not shown
np. 1904
348pp.
Item marked 'Official Print' from War
Office list of publications. WO. ref. – WH
Loc: SA10. See HMSO. Non-Parliamentary
Publications.

(Anon) – The 1st Battalion Essex
Regiment In South Africa, 1899 To 1902.
Regimental Press
Thayetmo, (Burma) 1908
38, viii pp.
8vo.   W

Appleton (Captain Francis M.)
(Compiler) – The Volunteer Service
Company (1st South Lancashire
Regiment). In South Africa During The
Boer War. January, 1900–July 1901.
With Some Particulars Concerning The
Third Contingent.
Mackie & Co. LD., Guardian Office
Warrington 1901
xiv+178pp. Map and illustrations.
250×190mm

Appleton (Francis Martin) – The
Warrington Volunteers In South Africa.
Illustrated By Lantern Slides. A Paper
Read On Monday, October 14th 1901.
Warrington Library and Philosophical
Society (Publisher)
Warrington 1902
17pp.
210mm   SABIB

Appleton (Lewis) – Britain And The
Boers. Who Is Responsible For The War
In South Africa.
Simpkin, Marshall, Hamilton, Kent
& Co., Ltd.
London 1899
viii+109pp.
220×145mm

Archibald (James F. J.) – Blue Shirt And
Khaki A Comparison.
Silver, Burdett and Company,
New York, Boston, Chicago. 1901
269pp. Illustrated.
190×130mm
Notes on the war by an American officer.
The author draws a comparison between
the British and American armies and
operational methods.

(Argus Co.) (Printers) – The R.S.O.'s
Notebook. An Unvarnished Tale.
(Printed for private circulation)
Argus Co.
Cape Town 1901
17pp.
270mm   SABIB
Satirical account of the duties of Railway
Staff Officers during the war.

(Argus Co.) (Printers) – Report Of The
Deputation Sent To The Cape Colony,
By The Peace Committees In The
Orange River Colony.
Argus Co., printers
Bloemfontein (1901?)
pp.3–10
220mm   SABIB
Catalogued from cover.

(Argus Co.) (Publisher) – Service In
Memory And In Honour Of Those Who
Fell When Serving With The Imperial
Light Horse. Held At St. Mary's,
Johannesburg, On September 9th, 1909.
The Tenth Anniversary Of The
Formation Of The Regiment.
Argus Co.
Johannesburg 1909
10pp.
220mm   SABIB

**(Argus Co., Limited, Government
Printer)** (Printers) – Public Health
Department, Orange River Colony
Administration. Report On Mortality
Statistics, &c., Of Refugee Camps,
1902–3.
Argus Co., Limited, Government
Printers.
Bloemfontein nd. (1903)
Pagination not shown.
292×205mm   RCSL

(Argus Printing and Publishing Co.)
(Printers?) – Extracts From Orders And
Memoranda Published For The Guidance
Of Officers Commanding Columns And
Posts In The Orange River Colony.
Argus Printing and Publishing Co.
Bloemfontein 1901
41pp.
160mm   SABIB
17 extracts, irregularly interleaved, and
covering a variety of subjects, i.e.,
treatment of prisoners-of-war dressed in
British uniform, selection of posts and
their fortification, etc.

(Argus Printing and Publishing Co.)
(Printers) – List Of Free State Prisoners
Of War, 14th May, 1900, With Their
Descriptions. Lijst Van Vrijstaatsche
Krijgsgevangenen, 14 Mei, 1900, Met
Hunne Beschrijvingen.
Argus Printing and Publishing Co.
Bloemfontein 1900
49pp.
390mm   SABIB
Item catalogued from caption title.
Supplement to the Government Gazette of
the Orange River Colony, No.2. July 6th,
1900.

(Argus Printing and Publishing Co.)
(Printers) – Proclamations Issued In The
Orange River Colony From The Date Of
The Annexation To The Promulgation Of
The Constitution On The 23rd June,
1902. Printed By Government Authority.
Argus Printing and Publishing Co.
Bloemfontein (1902?)
xiii+131pp.
240mm   SABIB

(Argus Printing and Publishing Co.)
(Printers) – Farm List O.R.C. By
Districts. (Marked – Confidential).
Argus Printing and Publishing Co.
Bloemfontein 1902
iv+316pp.
185×140mm
Field Intelligence Dept. publication listing
farms in the Orange River Colony, name
of owner and value.

**(Argus Printing & Publishing Co., Ltd,
The)** (Printers) – Government Gazette Of
The Orange River Colony.

The Argus Printing & Publishing Co., Ltd.
Bloemfontein 1900
20pp.
375×250mm   DC
*Issue No. 1 of Friday, June 29th, 1900.
Thereafter to be published weekly on
Fridays. The name of the printer is taken
from a subscription rate notice on page
15. The paper, printed in English and
Dutch, contains proclamations and notices
of an official nature. It is similar to the
Pretoria paper 'Government Gazette
Extraordinary'. See entry under –
GOVERNMENT PRINTER.*

**(Argus Printing and Publishing Company
Limited)** (Printers) – Public Health
Department, Orange River Colony
Administration. Report On Mortality
Statistics Of Refugee Camps, 1901.
Argus Printing and Publishing Company
Limited.
Bloemfontein 1902
(Pagination not shown.)
292×205mm   RCSL

(Army And Navy Gazette, The)
(Publisher) – South Africa, 1899–1902.
Officers And Men Of The Army And
Navy Mentioned In Despatches. Also
List Of Honours And Rewards.
Containing All Mentions, Honours,
Promotions, &c., Gazetted Up To May
6th, 1902.
'The Army and Navy Gazette'
London 1902
2+1+104pp.
260mm   SABIB

(Army And Navy Gazette, The)
(Publisher) – South Africa, 1899–1902.
Officers And Men Of The Army And
Navy Mentioned In Despatches. Also
List Of Honours And Rewards.
Containing All Mentions, Honours,
Promotions, &c., Gazetted Up To
November 1902.
'The Army and Navy Gazette'
London 1902
iv+132pp.
256×183mm

(Army H.Q.) (Publisher?) – South
African Field Force. Republication Of
Principal Circulars Issued During 1900.
Army H.Q.
Pretoria 1901
23pp.   MOD
*Item from War Office Library. WO. ref.–
WH Loc: SA37C.*

(Army H.Q.) (Publisher?) – Circular To
Accompany Rules For Guidance Of Press
Censors In South Africa. June 1901.
Army H.Q.
Pretoria 1901
1p.   MOD
*Item from War Office Library. WO. ref.–
WH Loc: SA58.*

(Army H.Q.) (Publisher?) – Report On
Demobilization Of The South African
Field Force, From 1 June, 1902 To 28
Feb., 1903. Apr. 1903
Army H.Q.
Pretoria 1903
61pp.   MOD
*Item from War Office Library. WO. ref.–
WH Loc: SA13.*

(Army H.Q./Cape Colony) – Confidential.
Martial Law In Cape Colony, 1901.
H.Q. Cape Colony District
Cape Town. May 1901
60pp.
108×108mm   CC
*Pamphlet relating to administration of
Martial Law in the colony together with a
set of Martial Law Regulations. [C.R. No.
A/9842/141] Title from cover.*

(Army H.Q./Cape Colony) – Cape Colony
District. Martial Law Circular. No. 6.
H.Q. Cape Colony District
Cape Town. August 1901
12pp.
112×105mm   CC
C.R. No. A/9842/141. Title from page 1.

(Army H.Q./Cape Colony) – Cape Colony
District Martial Law Circulars. Nos. 1–5.
H.Q. Cape Colony District
Cape Town 1901
(Var. pag.)
*Item from War Office Library. WO. ref.–
WH Loc: SA37C.*

(Army H.Q./Cape Colony) –
Administration Of Martial Law.
Feb. 1901.
H.Q. Cape Colony District
Cape Town 1901
26pp.
*Item from War Office Library. WO. ref.–
WH Loc: SA37C.*

(Army H.Q./Cape Colony) – Martial Law
In Cape Colony, May 1901.
H.Q. Cape Colony District
Cape Town 1901
60pp.
*Item from War Office Library. WO. ref.–
WH Loc: SA37C.*

(Army H.Q./Cape Colony) – Martial Law
In Cape Colony. 3rd Ed. 1901–2.
May 1902.
H.Q. Cape Colony District
Cape Town, 1902
vi+89pp.
*Item from War Office Library. WO. ref.–
WH Loc: SA37D.*

(Army H.Q./South Africa) – Reprint Of
Circulars Issued By The Director Of
Supplies, Aug. 1901.
Army H.Q. South Africa
Pretoria 1901
69pp.   MOD
*Item from War Office Library. WO. ref.–
WH Loc: Camps Boer.*

(Army H.Q./South Africa) – Reprint Of
Circulars Issued By The Director Of
Supplies.
Army H.Q. South Africa
Johannesburg 1902
(99+iv pp.?)   MOD
*Item from War Office Library. WO. ref.–
WH Loc: Camps Boer.*

(Army Orders) – Reprint Of The
Principal Army Orders And Lines Of
Communications Orders Since The
Outbreak Of Hostilities To 31st Jan.
1900.
Publisher/printer not shown
np./nd.
70pp.   MOD
*War Office Library. WO. ref. – WH Loc:
Camps Boer.*

(Army Orders) – Additional Reprint Of
The Principal Army Orders, Lines Of
Communications Orders And Base
Orders From 1 Feb. 1900 To 31 Mar.
1900.
Publisher/printer not shown
np./nd.
51pp.   MOD
*War Office Library. WO. ref. – WH Loc:
Camps Boer.*

(Army Orders) – Additional Reprint Of
The Principal Army Orders, Lines Of
Communications Orders, Base Orders
And Circulars From 1 Apr. 1900 To 31
May 1900.

Publisher/printer not shown
np./nd.
67pp.   MOD
*War Office Library. WO. ref. – WH Loc:
Camps Boer.*

(Army Orders) – Additional Reprint Of
The Principal Army Orders, Lines Of
Communications Orders, Base Orders
And Circulars From 1 June 1900 To 31
Jul. 1900.
Publisher/printer not shown
np./nd.
42pp.   MOD
*War Office Library. WO. ref. – WH Loc:
Camps Boer.*

(Army Orders) – Additional Reprint Of
The Principal Army Orders, Lines Of
Communications Orders, Base Orders
And Circulars From 1 Oct. 1900 To 31
Dec. 1900.
Publisher/printer not shown
np./nd.
125pp.   MOD
*War Office Library. WO. ref. – WH Loc:
Camps Boer.*

(Army Orders) – Additional Reprint Of
The Principal Army Orders, Lines Of
Communications Orders, And Base
Orders From 1 Jan. 1901 To 28 Feb.
1901.
Publisher/printer not shown
np./nd.
80pp.   MOD
*War Office Library. WO. ref. – WH Loc:
Camps Boer.*

(Army Orders) – Additional Reprint Of
The Principal Army Orders, Lines Of
Communications Orders From 1 Mar.
1901 To 30 Apr. 1901.
Publisher/printer not shown
np./nd.
63pp.   MOD
*War Office Library. WO. ref. – WH Loc:
Camps Boer.*

(Army Orders) – Reprint Of The
Principal Army Orders, Cape Colony
District Orders And Circulars From
1 Aug. 1901 To 30 Sept. 1901.
Publisher/printer not shown
Cape Town nd.
53pp.   MOD
*War Office Library. [official print] WO.
ref. – WH Loc: Camps Boer.*

(Army Orders) – Reprint Of The
Principal Army Orders And Cape Colony
District Orders, From 1st October, 1901
To 31st December, 1901.
Publisher/printer not shown
np./nd. (1902?)
94pp.
240×155mm   CC
*pp.81–94 Errata and corrigenda, date
index and subject index. Possibly
published in South Africa.*

(Army Orders) – Local General Orders,
South Africa, Nos. 2489–2580, Jan.–Oct.
1899; Army Orders, South Africa, Nos.
1–472, Nov. 1899–Dec. 1901.
Publisher/printer not shown [official
print]
Cape Town nd.
(Var. pag.)   MOD
*From War Office Library. WO. ref. –
WH Loc: SA47–1.*

(Army Orders) – Lines Of
Communications Orders, Nos. 1–442,
Nov. 1899–Apr. 1901: Cape Colony
District Orders, Nos. 443–804, Apr.
1901–Dec. 1901.
Publisher/printer not shown [official
print]

Cape Town nd.
(Var. pag.)   MOD
*Item from War Office Library. WO. ref.–
WH Loc: SA47–2.*

(Army Orders) – Army Orders, South
Africa, Nos. 473–566, June 1902;
General Orders, Nos. 1–368, June 1902–
Dec. 1903.
Publisher/printer not shown [official
print]
Pretoria nd.
(Var. pag.)   MOD
*War Office Library. WO. ref. – WH Loc:
SA47–3.*

(Army Orders) – Cape Colony District
Orders, Nos. 805–1531, Jan. 1902–Mar.
1903; Cape Colony Orders Nos. 1532–
1970, Mar. 1903–Dec. 1903.
Publisher/printer not shown [official
print]
Cape Town nd.
(Var. pag.)   MOD
*War Office Library. WO. ref. – WH Loc:
SA47–4.*

(Army Orders) – Natal Field Force
Orders, Oct. 1899–Mar. 1900; Natal
Army Orders, Nos. 24–174, Mar. 1900–
Oct. 1900; Lines Of Communications
Orders, Nos. 1–20, Oct. 1899, Nos.
76–357, Jan. 1900–Oct. 1900; Natal
District Orders, Oct. 1900–Dec. 1900.
Publisher/printer not shown [official
print]
Partly typescript
Ladysmith/Maritzburg/Newcastle nd.
(Var. pag.)   MOD
*War Office Library. WO. ref. – WH Loc:
SA47–6.*

(Army Orders) – South Africa Revised
Reprint Of Principal Army Orders, Lines
Of Communications Orders And Cape
Colony District Orders From The
Outbreak Of Hostilities To The End Of
July 1901 With The Principal HQ
Circular Memoranda For 1900 And 1901.
Publisher/printer not shown [official
print]
Cape Town nd.
239+28pp.   MOD
*War Office Library. WO. ref. – WH Loc:
SA46.*

(Army Orders) – Army Orders Issued By
Field Marshal Lord Roberts And General
Lord Kitchener, Etc. See entry under
GOVERNMENT PRINTER, PRETORIA.

(Army Temperance Association)
(Publisher?) – 'Not Forgotton'. Work In
South Africa, 1900–1.
Ideal Publishing Union
London (1901?)
26pp. Illustrated
190mm   SABIB

Arnold-Forster (The Rt. Hon. H. O.) –
The War Office, The Army, And The
Empire. A Review Of The Military
Situation In 1900.
Cassell & Company Limited
London, Paris, New York and
Melbourne 1900
102pp.
Cr.8vo.   M

Ashdown (Charles H.) – The 'Old
Albanian' Roll Of Honour 1899–1902.
The Dangerfield Printing Co., Ltd.
London nd., (1904)
Unnumbered (78pp.) Illustrated
244×158mm
*A roll of those from St. Albans school
who served in South Africa with
particulars of service and portrait.
Together with a list of every 'Old Boy'*

*whose whereabouts, at time of
publication, could be ascertained.*

Ashe (E. Oliver) – Besieged By The
Boers. A Diary Of Life And Events In
Kimberley During The Siege.
Hutchinson & Co.
London 1900
xii+210pp. Illustrated
194×130mm

Ashe (E. O.) – Besieged By The Boers.
A Diary Of Life And Events In
Kimberley During The Siege.
Doubleday, Page & Co.
New York 1900
xii+175pp. Illustrated
192×126mm

Asher (G.) – The Settlement Of The
South African Question. A Suggestion.
Love & Wyman (Printers)
London (1901?)
16pp.
210mm   SABIB
Catalogued from cover.

Asquith (The Rt. Hon. Herbert H.) – The
Rt. Hon. Herbert Henry Asquith, K.C.,
M.P., On The Transvaal War And
Settlement.
Imperial South African Association
Westminster (1902?)
8pp.
8vo.
*See – IMPERIAL SOUTH AFRICAN
ASSOCIATION.*

Atkins (J. B.) – The Relief Of Ladysmith.
Methuen & Company
London 1900
xi+320pp. Illustrated
196×134mm
*Revised 2nd edition, xi+351pp. Map
plans and illustrations. SABIB lists
Methuens Colonial Library edition.*

(Atlas Press) (Publisher) – Souvenir Of
The Departure Of The Victorian And
Tasmanian Contingents For South Africa
From Melbourne, Saturday, October
28th, 1899.
Atlas Press
Melbourne 1899
(Pagination not shown) ALH

Atthill (Capt. A. W. M.) – From Norwich
To Lichtenburg Via Pretoria Being Some
Personal Experiences With The 2nd
Norfolk Volunteer Active Service
Company In South Africa 1901–2;
Together With Extracts From Letters
Written By Colin G. Cubitt Between
June and December, 1901.
A. E. Soman & Co., St. Andrew's
Printing Works
Norwich 1909
vii+166pp. Illustrated
190×127mm   p.84

Auchinleck (S. E.) – For The Honour Of
The Queen, And Other Verses.
Hodges, Figgis, & Co., Ltd./Dublin
Simpkin, Marshall, and Co., Ltd.
London 1900.
viii+44pp.
220×175mm
*Titles include – 'The Mail to Mafeking',
'The Boer Spy'. etc.*

(Austin, Stephen & Sons) (Printers) – The
Queenslanders At Elands River, August
1900. For Private Circulation Only.
Stephen Austin & Sons. Printers,
Hertford (1901?)
32pp.
8vo.   M
Extracts from newspaper articles and

*letters in reference to the Elands River
siege, August 4–16, 1900.*

Aveling (Frederick Wilkins) – Patriotism.
Berryman & Sons
London (1900?)
16pp.
180mm   SABIB
*Pamphlet written during the South African
War.*

(Average Observer, An.) – The Burden
Of Proof: Some Aspects Of Sir Redvers
Buller's Work During His Recent
Campaign In South Africa Considered
From An Ordinary Commonsense
Standpoint, By An Average Observer.
Grant Richards
London 1902
vii+154pp.
196×130mm

(Average Observer, An.) – The Burden
Of Proof: Or, England's Debt To Sir
Redvers Buller.
Grant Richards
London 1902 (2nd Edition)
123pp.
8vo.   M

(A. W. F.) – The Present Phase Of The
Boer War.
Langley & Sons, printers
London nd. (c.1900)
12pp.
210mm   SABIB
*No title page. Catalogued from caption
title: A pro-Boer pamphlet.*

B

('B') – A Protest Against The Cooking
Up And Dissemination Of Old And Stale
News, Etc. See – TYDEMAN. J. R.
printer.

(Bachelors Club) (Publisher?) – A List Of
The Members Of The Bachelors Club
Who Served In The South African War
1899–1902.
Privately printed
Printer/publisher not shown
np. 1904
27pp.
210mm

Backhouse (J. B.) – With 'The Buffs' In
South Africa.
Gale & Polden
Aldershot 1903
xi+162pp. Illustrated
182×122mm   p.30
*Account of the 2nd Batt. East Kent
regiment in South Africa.*

(Backsight Forethought) – The Defence
Of Duffer's Drift. A Few Experiences In
Field Defence For Detached Posts,
Which May Prove Useful In Our Next
War. Reprinted From The 'United
Service Magazine'.
Williams Clowes & Sons, Limited
London 1904
39pp. With maps
244×155mm
*Pertinent hints conveyed by the author, Sir
Ernest Swinton, to those who may have
been in charge of outposts during the
recent war. SABIB lists reprint editions up
to 1918.*

Bacon (A. O.) – Resolution Of Sympathy
For the South African Republics.
Remarks Of Hon. A. O. Bacon, Of
Georgia, Citing Speeches Of Eminent
Statesmen In The Senate Of The United
States, May 29th, 1900.

Govt. Printing Office
Washington D.C. 1900
16pp.
8vo.   M

Baden-Powell (Major B. F. S.) – War In
Practice Some Tactical And Other
Lessons Of The Campaign In South
Africa, 1899–1902.
Isbister & Company, Limited
London 1903
280pp. Diagrams and illustrations
188×129mm

Baden Powell (R. S. S.) – Report Upon
The Siege Of Mafeking, Sent To Field-
Marshal Lord Roberts, May 10th, 1900
And Forwarded By Him To The
Secretary For War, June 21st, 1900.
'Mafeking Mail'
Mafeking 1901
40pp.
260mm   SABIB
*Supplement to The Mafeking Mail, March
1st, 1901. Reprinted from the London
Gazette, 8th Feb., 1901.*

Baden-Powell (Major-General R. S. S.) –
Sketches In Mafeking And East Africa.
Smith, Elder & Co.
London 1907
xii+183pp. Colour plates and other
illustrations
240×313mm   p.81

Bagot (Dosia) – Shadows Of The War.
Edward Arnold
London 1900
xvi+214pp. Illustrated
230×150mm
*An account of work at the Portland
hospital at Rondebosch and
Bloemfontein.*

Baillie (Major F. D.) – Mafeking A Diary
Of The Siege.
Archibald Constable & Company, Ltd.
Westminster 1900
viii+299pp. With facsimile of Mafeking
Mail Siege Slip and other illustrations.
198×134mm
*Variant covers – Red cloth with paper
onlay./Pictorial cloth.*

Baker (Major C.) – Trekking With The
Royal Irish Rifles Mounted Infantry.
See – CLINTON-BAKER.

Baldock (Colonel T. S.) – Royal Artillery
Mounted Rifles In South Africa.
Royal Artillery Institution
np./nd.
(London c.1906?)
64pp. With various plans.
245×155mm

Ballyfrench (Morton) – The Lighter Side
Of War.
The Century Press
London 1909
215pp.
196×127mm   GC
*Campaign experiences of a volunteer in
the Devonshire Militia.*

(Banffshire Journal Office) (Publisher) –
Soldiers Of Banffshire, 1899–1900: Being
A List Of All Banffshire Men Who
Served Their Queen And Country In The
South African War.
Printed at the Banffshire Journal Office
Banff 1901
39pp. Illustrated.
240mm   SABIB

(Banffshire Journal Office) (Publisher) –
Soldiers Of Banffshire In South Africa
1899–1902 Being A List Of Banffshire
Men Who Served In The War Followed

By A Short Diary Of The War An
Article By J. W. F. And A Story By
'Linesman'
Printed and published at The Banffshire
Journal Office
Banff 1903
67pp. Illustrated.
255×190mm

(Banks, Claude M.) (Printer) – Souvenir
Of The Departure Of The N.Z.
Contingent For The Transvaal Sat. Oct.
21st 1899.
Claude M. Banks
Wellington (1899)
Cover+2pp.
140×220mm   BIM

Barnes (James) – The Great War Trek
With The British Army On The Veldt.
D. Appleton and Company
New York 1901
xii+372pp.
194×128mm   p.96

Barr (James) – Christianity And War:
A Series Of Lectures Delivered In
Rutherford United Free Church,
Glasgow, During The Course Of The
South African War.
Simpkin, Marshall, Hamilton, Kent
& Co. Ltd.
London 1903
C. L. Wright/Glasgow
191pp.
190mm   SABIB

Barrington (Col. J. T.) – Infantry
Equipment, Lessons From The South
African War.
Alex Ross & Co. Ltd.
London nd. (c.1903)
12pp. Illustrated.
178×121mm   CC
*Pamphlet promoting equipment designed
by Col. Barrington with reference to the
recent experience in South Africa.*

(Barter. John, jnr.) (Publisher) – Boer
Version Of The Transvaal War Or An
English Translation Of All Dutch Official
Telegrams Received At Vryheid During
Boer War Up To The Time When British
Troops Occupied Vryheid.
John Barter jnr.
London 1901
95pp.
212×138mm   p.102
*Also published by Simpkin, Marshall,
Hamilton, Kent & Co. Ltd., London
1901. See entry under WILTER. Frank,
(publisher).*

Bate (Henry) – Transvaal War. . . First
Canto.
George Stoneman (London)
Chorley & Pickersgill (Leeds) 1900
16pp.
C.8vo.
Ref. M/BM Library.

(Batson & Co. Ltd.) (Publisher) –
Souvenir, The Australian Bushmen's
Contingent.
Batson & Co. Ltd.
Sydney nd. (1900)
(Pages unnumbered.) Illustrated.
                 RCSL
*Second Souvenir and Final Souvenir
recorded. Batson & Co. Ltd./Sydney
1900. Correct spelling may be Bateson &
Co.*

Battaliou (H. A.) – Political Letters On
The South African Situation. By
A South African.
A. E. Heyer
Cape Town 1900
44pp.
8vo.   M

Battersby (H .F. Prevost) – In The Web
Of A War.
Methuen & Co.
London 1900
xii+297pp. Portrait and maps.
196×130mm   p.10

Battersea (Lord) – The South African
Settlement. Speech 2nd, March 1901.
Eighty Club.
(Eighty Club)
Place of publication not shown.
Pagination not shown.   THB

(Battle Smoke) – Battle Smoke,
A Pictorial Record Of The War.
Publisher/printer not shown.
Melbourne 1900
108pp. Illustrated. CB
*Six issues of an illustrated newspaper
published from March 28th to July 4th,
1900.*

Batts (H. J.) – Pretoria From Within
During The War 1899–1900.
John F. Shaw and Co.
London nd (1900)
viii+pp.9–231. Illustrated.
194×126mm

Batts (H. J.) – Pretoria From Within
During The War 1899–1900.
John F. Shaw and Co.
London nd (c.1900)
Darter Bros. and Walton
Cape Town
viii+pp.9–231. Illustrated.

Baty (Thomas) – International Law In
South Africa.
Stevens & Haynes
London 1900
xii+127pp.
215×140mm
*Reference to legal matters during
hostilities, i.e. – Passage of troops over
neutral territory, Limited companies in the
war, etc.*

Baynes (Rev. A. H.) – My Diocese
During The War Extracts From The
Diary Of The Right Rev. Arthur
Hamilton Baynes, D. D. Bishop Of
Natal.
George Bell and Sons
London 1900
xvii+266pp. Illustrated.
194×133mm

(Beaconsfield Resident) – Diary Of The
Siege Of Kimberley, Etc. See –
GROCOTT & SHERRY, Printers.

Beak (G. B.) – The Aftermath Of War
An Account Of The Repatriation Of
Boers And Natives In The Orange River
Colony 1902–1904.
Edward Arnold
London 1906
x+296pp. Folding map and plates.
222×144mm   p.87

Beck (Henry Houghton) – History Of
South Africa And The Boer-British War.
Blood And Gold In Africa.
The Matchless Drama Of The Dark
Continent From Pharaoh To 'Oom Paul.
The Transvaal War And The Final
Struggle Between Briton and Boer Over
The Gold Of Ophir, A Story Of Thrilling
Romance And Adventure Among Wild
Beasts And Wilder Men, In Search Of
Sport And Gems And Gold.
Profusely And Superbly Illustrated With
Photographs, Sketches, And Maps From
Official Sources.
Globe Bible Publishing Co.
Philadelphia 1900

505pp. Folding map and numerous illustrations.
238×173mm
SABIB lists copies of 487pp. and 496pp. Illustrated.

Beck (H. H.) – History Of South Africa And The Boer-British War, Etc.
Globe Bible Publishing Co.
Philadelphia 1900
159pp. Illustrated.
238×172mm
Copy of publisher's 'dummy'.

Beevor (Surgeon-Major W.) – With The Central Column In South Africa. From Belmont To Komatipoort.
Published at the office of the 'King And His Navy And Army'.
London 1903
81pp. Colour plates and other illustrations with a number of blank leaves bound in.
250×350mm
Compiled by W. Beevor, Scots Guards.

Begbie (A. R. G.) – The Experiences Of An Artillery Officer, Etc.
See – NORTH (Charles), printer.

Begbie (Capt. A. R. G.) – Letters On The Boer War, 1899–1902.
See – NORTH (Charles), printer.

Begbie (Edward Harold) – The Handy Man And Other Verses.
Grant Richards
London 1900
viii+116pp.
190mm

Bell (Major James) – Some Experiences With The Ayrshire Yeomanry In South Africa.
Printer/publisher not shown.
Privately printed?
np. nd (c.1916)
63pp. Portrait frontispiece.
217×143mm

Bell (J. J.) – Songs Of The Hour.
Scots Pictorial Publishing Co.
Glasgow 1900
25pp.
190mm   SABIB
Poems relating to Scottish soldiers in the war. Originally published in The 'Glasgow Evening Times' and the 'Scots Pictorial'.

Belleroche (E.) – Letters Reproduced From The 'Belgian Times And News' Of Brussels.
Imprimerie Anglo-Belge
Bruxelles
2pp.
Folio   M

Bellows (John) – Letter To Senator Hoar On The Transvaal War.
McCorquodale
London 1900
4pp.
220mm   SABIB
Item catalogued from caption. Publication of – Imperial South African Association. See entries under – ISAA.

Bellows (John) – The Truth About The Transvaal War: And The Truth About War.
Simpkin, Marshall, Hamilton, Kent & Co., Ltd.
London 1900
John Bellows
Gloucester 1900
16pp.
Quarto   M

Pamphlet written by a quaker citizen of Gloucester.

Bengough (Maj.-General H. M.) – Notes And Reflections On The Boer War.
William Clowes & Sons
London 1900
76pp.
Cr.8vo.   M

Bennet (N.) – The Little Bugler, And Other War Lyrics.
Elliot Stock
London 1900
24pp. Illustrated
190mm

Bennett (E. N.) – With Methuen's Column On An Ambulance Train.
Swan Sonnenschein & Co., Ltd.
London 1900
v+127pp.
194×130mm   p.90

(Bennett & Davis) (Printers) – Letters And Telegrams Of Condolence To Mrs. Royston, On The Death Of Her Husband, Colonel Royston, Commandant Natal Volunteers.
Bennett & Davis, printers.
Durban 1900
ii+59pp.
210mm   SABIB
Col. Royston was in Ladysmith throughout the siege, and died shortly after of enteric fever.

Benson (Maj.-General F. W.) – Report Of The Inspector-General Of Remounts, Etc. See – WO. 86.

Beresford (G. C.) (Publisher) – The Boer Plan Of Campaign. A Forecast Of Their Scheme Of Operations In The Second Theatre Of War. By An Officer On The Active List.
G. C. Beresford
London 1899
8pp. With a map.
Roy.8vo.   M
SABIB lists a 2nd Ed. – The Boer Plan Of Campaign. A Forecast. By An Officer On The Active List. Published by Simpkin, Marshall (1899?) 8pp. Folding map. Item catalogued from cover.

Bethell (Lieut. L. A.) – Outpost Duties As Learnt In South Africa.
William Clowes & Sons
London 1903
40pp.
16mo.
Boer war references? M records BM library copy.

(Bickers & Son) (Publishers) – The Scapegoat: Being A Selection From A Series Of Articles Which Have Appeared In 'The Review Of The Week' On The Case Of Sir Henry Colvile. With A Preface By The Editor.
Bickers & Son
London 1901
vi+77pp.
8vo.   M
Articles in reference to the dismissal of Gen. Colvile from command of the Ninth Division in South Africa.

Bidder (G.) – Britain At War.
Printer/publisher not shown.
Plymouth 1900
16pp.   CB
Paper covered.

Biggar (E. B.) – The Boer War Its Causes, And Its Interest To Canadians With A Glossary Of Cape Dutch And

Kafir Terms.
Biggar, Samuel & Co.
Toronto and Montreal 1900
40pp.
218×131mm
Seventh edition – revised and enlarged.

Billington (Roland Cecil) – A Mule-Driver At The Front Being Transport Experiences In Natal.
Chapman & Hall, Ltd.
London 1901
xii+92pp. Illustrated.
196×128mm   p.64

Birch (James H. Jr.) & Northrop (H. D.) – History Of The War In South Africa Containing A Thrilling Account Of The Great Struggle Between The British And The Boers Including The Causes Of The Conflict; Vivid Descriptions Of Fierce Battles; Superb Heroism And Daring Deeds; Narratives Of Personal Adventures; Life In Camp, Field And Hospital, Etc., Etc. Together With The Wonderful Story Of The Transvaal The Orange Free State; Natal And Cape Colony; The Kaffirs And Zulus; Richest Gold And Diamond Mines In The World, Etc., Etc.
Publisher not shown.
np./nd. (c.1900)
xvi+pp.17–708+80pp. Illustrated.
232×173mm
An extended edition containing an Appendix – Australian Colonies make a great record in the War. M lists an edition published by – National Publishing Co. Philadelphia 1900. vii+439pp.

Birkbeck (Lieut.-Col. W. H.) – Report On Remount Department. See WO. 84.

Birkbeck (Lieut.-Col. W. H.) – Remounts, Etc. See WO. 85.

Birkin (Lieut.-Col. R. L.) – History Of The 3rd Regiment Imperial Yeomanry, 28-1-00 To 6-8-02.
J&J Vice
Nottingham 1906
viii+144+84pp. Folding map and various illustrations.
210×340mm
A comprehensive history compiled by the corps commander. A superior edition was published printed on hand-made paper, bound in half-calf. 220×342mm

Black (Adam and Charles) (Publishers) – Who's Who At The War.
Adam and Charles Black
London 1900
55pp.
186×123mm   p.60
M lists copy of 76pp... Fifteenth thousand.

(Black And White Publishing Company Limited) (Printers) – Black And White Budget.
Black and White Publishing Company, printers.
London 1899/1900/1901/1902
Each issue 32pp. Illustrated.
282×187mm   p.79
Bound issues of the weekly magazine of which numbers 1 to 13 are subtitled 'Transvaal Special'.

Blackburn (D.) (Compiled by) – Times Of Natal War Number, Written And Compiled By Douglas Blackburn.
'Times of Natal'
Pietermaritzburg (1900)
48+?pp.
370mm   SABIB
Incomplete copy.

Blackmore (E. G.) – The Story Of The South Australian Bushmen's Corps 1900.
Hussey & Gillingham
Adelaide 1900
Pagination not shown.　ALH

(Black Watch Volunteer) – Letters From The Front, Etc. See LENG, John & Co.

(Blackwood & Sons) (Publishers) – A Short Account Of The Black Watch (Royal Highlanders) 1725–1907, Etc. See entry under WAUCHOPE, Capt. A. G.

Blake (Colonel J. Y. F.) – A West Pointer With The Boers Personal Narrative Of Colonel J. Y. F. Blake, Commander Of The Irish Brigade.
Angel Guardian Press
Boston 1903
xii+pp.13–411. Numerous illustrations.
207×147mm　p.88

Blake (Robert) – Trial And Triumph: A Coronation Ode.
Greening & Co., Ltd.
London 1902
32pp.
8vo.　M
Reference to the South African war and to Irish soldiers in particular.

Blakeney (Lt. R. B. D.) – Report On Work Done By 3rd Balloon Section, Etc. See WO. 51.

Bleloch (W.) – The New South Africa; It's Value And Development.
William Heinemann
London 1901
xvi+345pp. Maps and illustrations.
8vo.　M
Progress of the new South Africa with reference to the ongoing war.

(Blooming Press) (Publisher) – 69th Battery R. F. A. Diary Of The Boer War 1899–1900–1901.
Blooming Press
Multan 1902
84pp.
218×135mm　p.59

Bodington (P.) – 'I.Y.' Etc.
See – (CORPORAL, The)

(Boer Prisoners Of War) – Lists Of Boer Prisoners Of War. 24 Parts Bound In 1 vol.
Publisher/printer not shown [official print].
np./nd.
Var. pag.　MOD
War Office library. WO. ref:- WH Loc: SA6A.

(Boer Prisoners Of War) – Report On The Arrangements Made In India For Accommodation Etc., Of Boer Prisoners Of War.
Office of QMG.
Simla 1904
24pp.　MOD
War Office library. WO. ref:- WH Loc: SA6C.

See entries under – PRISONERS OF WAR and WO. 111–114.

(Boer Relief Fund) – Leaflets published New York 1900–1901 supportive of the Boer cause.
SABIB lists leaflets Nos.10, 13–29, together with other Boer Relief Fund pamphlets.
Size 240mm

(No.10) – 'Labor Leaders And The Boer War'... Reprinted from circular issued in London.

(No.13) – Appeal To The American People. Analysis Of The British Conditions Of Peace... By C. D. Pierce And, The South African War. Views Of The Presiding Judge... S. W. Penny-packer.　2pp.

(No.14) – A Very Remarkable Historical Parallel.　2pp.

(No.15) – The Boer Relief Fund Of America.　2pp.

(No.16) – British Barbarities In South Africa... By C. D. Pierce.　2pp.

(No.17) – Letters From The English People 'Drunk With Blood'.　2pp.

(No.18) – Roberts A Failure...　2pp.

(No.19) – The Despairing War...　2pp.

(No.20) – Consul General Pierce Of The Boer Republics In Denver On A Visit.　4pp.

(No.—?) – The Boer – His Church And His Attitude Toward The Black Race. By C. D. Pierce.　4pp.
Marked No.20 on the list advertising leaflets.

(No.21) – Thousands Cheer, That Boers May Fight On.
4pp. Illustrations, portrait.

(No.22) – The Boers Reach The Sea Near Cape Town.　2pp.

(No.23) – Two Years' War Has Cost England $1,000,000,000.　2pp.

(No.24) – England's Opposition To The Boer War.　2pp.

(No.25) – Jingo Government Bankrupt. Can't Pay The Troops.　2pp.

(No.26) – How The Boers Continue War.　2pp.

(No.27) – Boer Commandos In South Africa.　2pp.

(No.28) – The Absent-Minded Burgher. A Tribute From An American Friend Of The Boers.　2pp.

(No.29) – Maps Of South Africa, From Methuen's Great Book, 'Peace Or War In South Africa'.　2pp.
(3 maps.)

(Boer Relief Fund) (Publisher) – Looting And Burning A Boer Farm.
The Fund
New York (1900?)
2pp. Illustrated.
240mm　SABIB

(Boer Relief Fund) (Publisher) – National American Transvaal Leagues.
The Fund
New York (1900?)
4pp.
240mm
An appeal to American people to form leagues in every city to work for the Boer Republics.

(Boer Relief Fund) (Publisher) – The South African Republics: This Souvenir Is Published For And In Behalf Of The Boer Relief Fund To Aid The Widows And Children Of Those Brave Men Who Have Fallen In The War Brought By Great Britain Against The South African Republics.
The Fund
New York 1900
48pp. Illustrated.
Roy.8vo.
H attributes booklet to – PIERCE, Charles D.

(Boer Relief Fund) (Publisher) – The South African Republics, This Sheet Is Issued For And In Behalf Of The Boer Relief Fund To Aid The Widows And Children Of Those Brave Men Who Have Fallen In The War Brought By Great Britain Against The South African Republics.
The Fund
New York 1900
8pp.　SABIB
No title page. Catalogued from caption.

(Boer Relief Fund) (Publisher) – *New York, Woman's Auxiliary League.* National Relief Benefit To Aid The Widows And Orphans Of The Fallen Boers And Those Of The South African Republics Deprived Of Their Natural Protectors By The Anglo Boer War. Under The Auspices Of The Woman's Auxiliary League Of The National Boer Relief Fund Association... New York Metropolitan Opera House, Thursday, April 26th, 1900.
The Fund
New York (1900?)
40pp. Illustrated.
250mm　SABIB
Cover title – Grand National Relief Concert To Aid The Boer Widows And Orphans.

(Boer War 1899–1902) – The British Volunteers in South Africa: What They Did And How They Did It. Extracts From The Orders Of The General Officers And Colonels Commanding The Regular Battalions, Under Whom They Served.
Publisher/printer not shown
np. 1903
15pp.
Item from WO. Cat./1912.

(Boer Women And Children Clothing Fund) (Publisher) – Third Report Of The Committee.
The Fund.
London (1902?)
12pp.
210mm　SABIB
No title page. Catalogued from caption title.

Boissevain (Charles) – The Struggle Of The Dutch Republics. (Parts 1 & 2. Two Open Letters.)
'Handelsblad' Office
Amsterdam (1900)
56, 93, 1pp.
190mm　SABIB
The two parts were also published separately.

Boissevain (Charles) – The Struggle Of The Dutch Republics. (Part 1.) Open Letter To The Duke Of Devonshire.
'Handelsblad' Office
Amsterdam (1900)
16pp.
260mm　SABIB
Catalogued from cover.

Boissevain (Charles) – The Struggle Of The Dutch Republics. (Part 2.) Open Letter To An American Lady.
'Handelsblad' Office
Amsterdam (1900)
93pp.
199×133mm

Boissevain (Charles) – The Struggle Of The Dutch Republics. (Part 3.) A Great Crime. An Appeal To The Conscience Of The British Nation.
'Handelsblad' Office
Amsterdam (1900)
49pp.
201×130mm

(Border Regiment) See entry under – EYRE & SPOTTISWOODE, printers.

Borthwick (John Douglas) (Compiler) – Poems And Songs On The South African War. An Anthology From England, Africa, Australia, United States, But Chiefly Canada.
Gazette Publishing Co.
Montreal 1901
214pp.
220mm   SABIB

Boscawen-Wright (C.) – With The Imperial Light Infantry Through Natal.
W. Straker
London 1903
90pp.
217×146mm
Includes an extensive account of the battle of Spion Kop.

Botha (Paul M.) – From Boer To Boer And Englishman.
Hugh Rees, Ltd./London
J. C. Juta & Co./Cape Town
1901
43pp.
213×140mm
Various editions published, including that of Hugh Rees, Ltd./London 1900.

Boulton (S. B.) – Address On The War In South Africa, By Mr. S. B. Boulton, J.P., D.L. Given At A Conservative And Unionist Meeting Held At Copped Hall, Totteridge, On 15th February, 1900.
Printed at the *Barnet Press* Office
(London 1900?)
15pp.
186×118mm   RCSL

Bovill (Rev. John H.) – Natives Under The Transvaal Flag.
Simpkin, Marshall, Hamilton, Kent, & Co.
London 1900
82pp.
190×125mm
Limited Boer War interest.

Bowdler (Colonel C.) – St. John Ambulance Brigade. Report Of The Commissioner On The Mobilization Of The Brigade For Service In South Africa, 1899–1900.
Charles Cull & Son
London 1900
30pp.
212×155mm

Bowlby (A. A.) – A Civilian War Hospital. See – (PROFESSIONAL STAFF.)

Bowlby (Anthony) – Reminiscences Of The War In South Africa (Being The Opening Address Delivered Before The Abernethian Society, October 11th 1900).
Adlard and Son (Printers)
London 1900
27pp.
215×141mm
A lecture delivered by surgeon A. Bowlby late of the Portland hospital Bloemfontein. Reprinted from St. Bart's Hospital Journal of Oct. 1900.

Boyle (C.) – Cecil Boyle: In Memoriam.
(Printer/publisher not shown.)

np./nd. (c.1900)
Unpaginated.
240mm   SABIB
Tribute to Boyle, an Imperial Yeomanry officer killed at Boshof in April 1900. The work contains a reprint of his article "The Cavalry rush to Kimberley, and in pursuit of Cronje", from "The Nineteenth Century" of June 1900 (17pp.) together with biographical material. No title page. Catalogued from cover.

Brabazon (Maj. Gen. J. P. B.) – Report On The Imperial Yeomanry in South Africa. See – WO. 32.

(Bradley. C. W. & Co.) (Publishers?) – John Bull's Guinea-Pigs; Or, The World And The War. By A True Liberal Imperialist.
C.W. Bradley & Co.
London (1900?)
51pp.
8vo.   M

Bradley (J.) – A Pottery Man's Journal, Etc. See – LOONEY (J. C.) Printer.

(Braithwaite. Joseph) (Publisher?) – Fourth Contingent New Zealand Rough Riders From Otago And Southland.
Joseph Braithwaite (Published by?)
Dunedin 1900
27pp. (unnumbered) Illustrated.
Essentially a photographic record of local volunteers.

(Braithwaite. Joseph) (Publisher) – Fourth And Fifth Contingent New Zealand Rough Riders From Otago And Southland, March 1900.
Joseph Braithwaite
Dunedin nd. (1900)
32 leaves. (Unnumbered.) Illustrated.
193×268mm   GC
Printed rectos only. 32 leaves. Various photographs and nominal roll by sections. Including some advertisements.

Brandon (R. A. L.) – The Ladysmith Town Guard, 1899/1900.
C. W. Budge & Co., Printers
Ladysmith nd. (1900)
16pp.
183×121mm   CC
Paper covers.

Brandt (Johanna) – The Petticoat Commando Or Boer Women In Secret Service.
Mills & Boon Limited
London nd. (1913)
xv+376pp. Illustrated.
197×124mm   p.46

Briggs (Lady) – The Staff Work Of The Anglo-Boer War 1899–1901 Embodying Some Of The War Letters Sent To The "Morning Post" From South Africa.
Grant Richards
London 1901
xi+503pp. Illustrated.
233×154mm   p.72

Bright (Allan H.) – Is Liberty Asleep?
T. Fisher Unwin
London 1903
88pp.
12mo.   M
Reference to the "Peace" party during the South African War. "Militarism will soon have spent its force and the nation will once again turn its attention to peace, etc."

Brink (J. N.) – Recollections Of A Boer Prisoner-Of-War At Ceylon.
Hollandsch-Afrikaansche Uitgevers-Maatschappij.
v/h Jac. Dusseau & Co.

Amsterdam/Cape Town 1904
v+220pp. Illustrated.
230×151mm   p.48

(British And Foreign Bible Society) (Publisher) – The New Testament Of Our Lord And Saviour Jesus Christ, Translated Out Of The Original Greek: And With The Former Translations Diligently Compared And Revised By His Majesty's Special Command. Appointed To Be Read In Churches.
British and Foreign Bible Society
London 1902
240pp.   SABIB
On cover – New Testament, South Africa, 1900.

(British National Society) (Publisher?) – Report By The British National Society For Aid To The Sick And Wounded In War Of Its Operations In Connection With The Transvaal War, 1899–1902, Together With Statements Of Expenditure, Etc.
Publisher/printer not shown
np. 1902
101pp.   WO. Cat./1912.

(British Staff Officer, A.) – An Absent Minded War Being Some Reflections On Our Reverses And The Causes Which Have Led To Them By A British Staff Officer.
John Milne
London nd. (1900)
vii+183pp.
181×121mm   p.56
Author – W. E. Cairnes. An edition published in cloth cover c.1900 – 175×120mm.

Brodie (J.) (Editor) – The Muster Roll Of Angus, Etc. See – SALMOND J. B.

(Brodie & Salmond) (Publishers) – A Christian Colour-Sergeant Brief Memoir Of Col-Sergt. Macmillan Black Watch, Who Fell At Magersfontein, On 11th December, 1899.
Brodie & Salmond
Arbroath 1912
16pp.
165×107mm
Religious pamphlet by John Aitchison whose name does not appear on the cover. Being a short sketch of the life of Col-Sergeant Macmillan together with letters from South Africa and elsewhere and 'Tributes of respect'. A copy of the third edition. Two earlier editions were published in 1900 and 1911. Paper covered.

Bron (Alice) – Diary Of A Nurse In South Africa Being A Narrative Of Experiences In The Boer and English Hospital Service. Translated From The French By G. A. Raper.
Chapman & Hall, Ld.
London 1901
xiii+208pp. With frontispiece.
200×130mm

Brooke-Hunt (Violet) – A Woman's Memories Of The War.
James Nisbet & Co., Limited
London 1901
vii+244pp. With frontispiece.
194×130mm   p.55

Brooksbank (R. G.) – Letters From The Seat Of War, 1899–1900.
No other information.   THB

Broughton (Major E. C.) – A Continuation Of The Historical Records Of The First Regiment Of Militia Or Third West York Light Infantry, Now

The Third Battalion York And Lancaster Regiment, From 1875 to 1905.
William Clowes and Sons
London 1906
106pp.
8vo.   M
Particulars are given of the enrolment of the battalion for service in the South African War.

Brown (Sapper J. W.) – Diary Of The 1st Service Section Newcastle R. E. Volunteers During The Boer War, 1899–1902.
T. E. Harding, Doric Press
Gateshead-On-Tyne 1904
55pp. Illustrated.
176×123mm

Brown (Stanley McKeown) – With The Royal Canadians.
The Publishers' Syndicate, Limited
Toronto 1900
vi+291pp.
190×125mm   p.32

Brown (H.) and Grew (E. Sharpe) – War With The Boers An Account Of The Past And Present Troubles With The South African Republics.
H. Virtue and Company, Limited
London nd. (c.1902)
Five vols.
Vol. 1. – vi+248+viii pp.
Vol. 2. – vi+248pp.
Vol. 3. – vi+248pp.
Vol. 4. – vi+248pp.
Vol. 5. – vi+248pp.
Illustrated throughout.
Vols. 1. & 2. by Harold Brown.
Vols. 3. & 4. (Authors name/names omitted from title-page.)
Vol. 5. by Harold Brown and E. Sharpe Grew. (Both names appear on title page of Vol. 4 in some copies.)
250×190mm   p.24
See entry under VIRTUE & COMPANY. Paper covered subscribers edition in 20 parts.

Browne (Percy J.) – A Rough Diary Kept On The Veldt.
Bennetts Printing Works
Sherborne 1908
72pp. Portrait frontispiece.
190mm
Diary of O.C. the 7th Batt. I.Y. in South Africa 1900–1901.

Bruford (George) – A Wandering Quartette, By One Of Them.
S. S. Campion and Sons
Northampton (1902)
128pp.
8vo.   M
An account of travel in Africa in 1901. Limited war reference. Printed for private circulation only.

Brunker (Lieut.-Col. H. M. E.) – Boer War, 1899. Chart Showing Organization And Distribution Of The British Forces, With A Nominal List Of The Staffs Of All Units And Estimate Of Strength Of Our Available Forces, Etc.
William Clowes & Sons, Limited
London 1899
55pp. With map.
Cr.8vo.   M
Copy of the second edition, revised. Summary of events to November 8, 1899.

Brunker (Lieut.-Colonel H. M. E.) – Boer War, 1899–1900 Chart Showing Organization And Distribution Of The British Forces With A List Of Military And Naval Officers And An Account Of The Organization And Administration Of The Boer Forces, Etc.

William Clowes & Sons, Limited
London 1900
125pp. Folding map.
215×140mm   p.73

Brunker (Lieut.-Col. H. M. E.) – Formation For Attack, Night Operations, &c., Adopted In South Africa Compared With Formations As Previously Suggested And Carried Out.
Holbrook & Son, Ltd.
Portsmouth 1900
12pp. Illustrated.
16mo.   M

Bryant (Harold Josling) – The Autobiography Of A Military Great Coat, Etc. See – JOSLING.

Bryce (J.) Brooks (S.) Engelenburg (Dr. F. V.) and others – Briton And Boer Both Sides Of The South African Question. See (HARPER BROTHERS) Publishers.

Buchan (John) – The African Colony Studies In The Reconstruction.
William Blackwood and Sons
Edinburgh and London 1903
xviii+404pp.
220×143mm
An assessment of the political situation at the start of reconstruction, together with notes on travel.

Buel (J. W.) – Fighting In Africa England's Battles With The Boers In The Transvaal Including An Exhaustive History Of The Settlement Of Cape Colony, Wars With The Kaffirs, Matabeles, Zulus, The Diamond And Gold Mines Of South Africa And A History Of Exploration, Discovery, Conquest And Development By All The Famous Travelers That Have Traversed The Dark Continent Comprising The Story Of The Campaigns Led By General Gordon And Lord Kitchener Against The False Prophets Of The Soudan And A Full, Graphic And Authentic Description Of The War Between The British And The Dutch In South Africa.
Official Publishing Company
New York, Philadelphia, Chicago nd. (c.1900)
xxxi+502pp. Illustrated throughout.
270×200mm

Bufton (John) – Tasmanians In The Transvaal War.
S. G. Loone
Newtown/Hobart 1905
xvi+534pp. Numerous illustrations.
250×185mm
A Record of Tasmanian volunteers in the war drawn from various sources.

Bull (Paul B.) – God And Our Soldiers.
Methuen & Co.
London nd. (1904)
xiv+267pp.
200×125mm
Account of the chaplain to Gen. French's cavalry in South Africa.

Buller (General Sir Redvers) – Evidence Of General The Right Hon. Sir Redvers Buller, VC., G.C.B., G.C.M.G. Taken Before The Royal Commission On The War In South Africa.
Longmans, Green & Co.
London, New York and Bombay 1904
160pp.
210×140mm
Cover dated 1903.

Buller (Gen. Sir R. H.) – Memorandum On South Africa, Etc. See – WO. 1.

(Bumpus) (John & E. Ltd.) (Printers) – A Month On The Modder River With The Coldstream.
John & E. Bumpus Ltd.
London nd. (c.1900)
16pp.
197×163mm
Pamphlet attributed to Lt. Col. Dawnay whose name does not appear in the publication. A fascinating account of a visit to Lord Methuen's headquarters near Modder River in December 1899, including a graphic description of the battle of Magersfontein.

Burdett-Coutts (W.) – The Sick And Wounded In South Africa: What I Saw And Said Of Them And Of The Army Medical System.
Cassell & Company, Limited
London, Paris, New York and Melbourne 1900
x+260pp.
203×142mm

Burdett-Coutts (W.) – The Hospitals Commission. Speech By Mr. Burdett-Coutts, M.P., House Of Commons, March 19, 1901. Supplementary Civil Service Estimates. Vote For The Hospitals Commission, (£8,000).
Cassell & Company, Limited
London 1901
16pp.
8vo.   M

Burdett-Coutts (W.) – The Hospitals Commission. Comments On The Inquiry And Report By Mr. Burdett- Coutts, M.P.
Cassell & Co.
London 1901
62pp.
8vo.   M
Supplementary to – 'The Sick and Wounded In South Africa'.

Burleigh (Bennet) – The Natal Campaign.
Chapman & Hall, Ltd.
London 1900
xi+418pp. Folding maps and plates.
210×150mm
Record of events by the correspondent to the London 'Daily Telegraph'.

Burn (Walter Adam) – Claims Against The Military, Or The Requisitioning Of Supplies, &c., Under Martial Law During The South African War, Considered In Relation To International And Municipal Law And The Customs Of War, To Which Is Added The Full Text Of The Hague Convention Concerning The Laws And Customs Of War On Land.
J. C. Juta & Co.
Cape Town 1903
iv+74pp.
Cr.8vo.   M
THB lists copy Johannesburg 1903.

Burne (Lieut. C.R.N., R.N.) – With The Naval Brigade In Natal 1899–1900. Journal Of Active Service Kept During The Relief Of Ladysmith And Subsequent Operations In Northern Natal And The Transvaal Under General Sir Redvers Buller, V.C., G.C.B.
Edward Arnold
London 1902
xi+156pp. Folding map and plates.
230×147mm   p.52

Burne (Major G.H.P.) – The Leicestershire Militia In South Africa.
Clarke & Satchell
Leicester nd. (c.1902)
vii+116pp. Illustrated.
158×252mm   p.93

Burnett (Major Charles) – The 18th Hussars In South Africa. The Records Of A Cavalry Regiment During The Boer War 1899–1902.
Warren & Son, Publishers
Winchester 1905
x+319pp. Folding maps and plates.
225×143mm

Burnley (Florence) – With 'Tommy' On A Transport To The Cape. Reprinted By Permission From *The Windsor Magazine*.
Allan Brothers & Co./Ward Lock & Co.
Liverpool and London nd. (c.1900)
16pp. Illustrated throughout.
240×159mm

Burn-Murdoch (J. H.) – With Lumsden's Horse Agin The Boers.
Barnicott & Pearce, printers
Taunton 1901
vii+157pp. Illustrated.
225×175mm   p.25

Burns (John) – The New Imperialism. A Speech Delivered In Battersea Park, On May 13th, 1900.
'Stop the War' Committee
London nd. (1900)
7pp.
227×149mm

Burns (Right Hon. John) – The Trail Of The Financial Serpent. South African War. Full Report Of The Speech In The House Of Commons, By John Burns, M.P. To Which Is Added A List Of The Leading Shareholders In The Chartered Company.
Published by the Committee
London 1900
8pp.
8vo.   M
Unnumbered pamphlet published by the 'Stop-The-War'-Committee.

(Burt & Sons) (Printers) – Diary Of Services Of The First Battalion The Royal Scots During The Boer War. South Africa, 1899–1902.
Burt & Sons, Printers
London 1904
84pp. Illustrated.
215×140mm
Edited by Maj. G. Deane. Printed for private circulation.

Butler (Josephine E.) – Native Races And The War.
Gay & Bird/London
Mawson, Swan & Morgan/Newcastle-On-Tyne 1900
ii+154pp.
200×150mm
M lists copy of 133pp.

Butler (Sir William Francis) – Correspondence Initiated By Sir William Butler With The War Office In November 1901.
War Office
London 1903
ii+12pp.
340mm   SABIB
Correspondence in connection with the War in South Africa.

Butler (James) and Richardson (Lawrence) – Friends' South African Relief Fund. Report On Visit To Orange River And Transvaal Colonies, And Relief Work, In Autumn, 1903.
Headley Bros., printers
London (1903?)
10pp.
210mm   SABIB

Buttery (J. A.) – Why Kruger Made War Or Behind The Boer Scenes With Two

Chapters On The Past And Future Of The Rand And The Mining Industry By A. Cooper Key.
William Heinemann
London 1900
viii+298pp.
195×130mm

Buxton (S. C.) – The War, Its Cost, Finance And Legacies. Reprinted By Permission From The *National Review*.
Liberal Publication Department
London 1903
24pp.
8vo.   M

Byron (Capt.) (Editor) – The Grouse. South Africa 1901. A Journal For General Campbell's Flying Column.
Office. The Yellow Wagon
Jan. 14. 1901 np.
32pp. Illustrated.
300×230mm
Reprint edition. Possibly published for private circulation.

C

Cadbury (Richard) – Everyday Life In Cape Colony In Time Of Peace. By X. C. See (X.C.).

Cairnes (W. E.) – An Absent Minded War, Etc. See entry under BRITISH STAFF OFFICER.

Caldwell (Colonel) – The Tactics Of To-Day.
Edinburgh 1900
Pagination not shown.
THB. *Possible reference to following entry.*

Callwell (Sir Charles Edward) – The Tactics Of To-Day.
William Blackwood and Sons
Edinburgh/London 1900
xii+153pp.
190mm   SABIB

Cameron (Major N. G.) (Compiler) – South African War Record Of The 1st Battalion Queen's Own Cameron Highlanders 1900–1–2.
The Northern Counties Printing and Publishing Company, Limited.
Inverness 1903
vii+258pp. Illustrations and folding maps.
245×185mm   p.19
A special edition of 'The 79th News'.

Campbell (A. N.) – Dutch Phrase-Book And Vocabulary. Compiled For The Intelligence Department By Capt. A. N. Campbell, Royal Artillery.
W. A. Richards & Sons, printers
Cape Town (1899?)
ii+158pp.
150mm   SABIB

Campbell (Lieut. Colin) – Eight Months On An Armoured Train. Boer War, 1899–1900–1901. By Lieutenant Colin Campbell, Cape Garrison Artilllery.
W. A. Richards & Sons
Cape Town 1901
31pp.
8vo.   M

Campbell (Lt.-Col. J.) – Western Australia. History Of Western Australian Contingents, Etc.
See – SIMPSON (Fred. Wm.)
(Government Printer.)

Campbell (R. G.) – Neutral Rights And Obligations In The Anglo-Boer War.
John Hopkins Press
Baltimore 1908
149pp.
250mm   H

Campbell-Bannerman (Sir Henry) – The Transvaal Question, Imperialism, And Social Questions. A Speech Delivered At Birmingham, November 24th, 1899.
Liberal Publication Department
London 1899
15pp.
220mm   SABIB

Campbell-Bannerman (Sir Henry) – The Transvaal War, Temperance, And The Housing Question. A Speech Delivered At Manchester, November 15th, 1899.
Liberal Publication Department
London 1899
16pp.
210mm   SABIB

Campbell-Bannerman (Sir Henry) – The South African Settlement. A Speech Delivered At Oxford, March 2nd, 1901.
Liberal Publication Department
London 1901
8pp.
220mm   SABIB

Campbell-Bannerman (Sir Henry) – The Third Year Of The War. A Speech Delivered On October 25th, 1901 At Stirling.
Liberal Publication Department
London 1901
15pp.
220mm

Campbell-Bannerman (Sir Henry) – The Government And The War. A Speech Delivered. . . At Plymouth, On November 19th, 1901.
Liberal Publication Department
London 1901
16pp.
220mm   SABIB
Critical of the British governments' conduct of the war.

Campbell-Bannerman (Sir Henry) – The 'Eighty' Club. The South African Settlement. Speeches Delivered By The Rt. Hon. Sir Henry Campbell-Bannerman, G.C.B., M.P. (President Of The 'Eighty Club'). Mr. E. Wright (President Of The Russell Club), The Hon. Sir John Cockburn, K.C.M.G. And The Right Hon. Lord Battersea (Chairman), At The Town Hall, Oxford, On March 2, 1901.
J. A. Mackay
London nd. (c.1902)
25pp.
Cr.8vo.   M

Cana (Frank R.) – Boers And British. Facts From The Transvaal.
See entry under – ST. JAMES'S GAZETTE.

(Canada/Militia) – The 3rd, 4th, 5th And 6th Regiments Canadian Mounted Rifles And Draft For 2nd Regiment, C.M.R. Organized In Canada For Service In The Field In South Africa.
Roll Of Officers, Non-Commissioned Officers And Men.
Publisher/printer not shown
np. 1902
31pp.
(Ref. WO. Cat./1912) See entries under DAWSON. S. E. (Printer). Possible parliamentary paper printed in Ottawa.

(Canada/Parliamentary Papers) – See entries under DAWSON. S. E. (Printer.)

(Canada) (Dept. of Militia and Defence) –
See – DAWSON. S. E. (Printer.)

(Candlelight Club) (Publisher?) – The
Candlelight Club Twelfth Meeting, Held
At The Windsor Hotel, Thursday,
February 1, 1900. One Hundred Present.
The South African War – Is England's
Position Justifiable And Should She
Succeed.
Publisher/printer not shown
(New York 1900)
39pp.
8vo.   M
*Ref. – BM library. A debate on the South
African War.*

(Cape Colony) Martial Law – Magisterial
Reports. See entry under CAPE TIMES
LIMITED.

(Cape Copper Company, Limited. The)
(Publisher) – The Cape Copper
Company, Limited, Reports And
Accounts To Be Presented At The 15th
Ordinary General Meeting 17th
December, 1902.
Unwin Brothers, Ltd.
London 1902
133pp. Illustrated.
                              M
*Contains a report from the
Superintendent, dated May 14, 1902,
giving particulars of the siege of Ookiep
and of damage done by Boers.*

(Cape Government Railways) (Publisher)
– Return Of Refugees To The Transvaal.
Chief Traffic Manager
Cape Town 1900
7pp.
350mm   SABIB
*Cape Government Railways notice No.
1034. Instructions for guidance of railway
staff concerning arrangements for the
return of war refugees to the Transvaal.*

(Cape Printing) – Distribution List Of All
The Corps In Payment Of The Imperial
And Indian Army Pay Offices In South
Africa, Corrected To May 1901.
Publisher/printer not shown
Cape Town 1901
*Item marked 'Official Print' from War
Office list of publications. WO. ref. – WH
Loc: SA 62.*

(Cape Times) (Printers) – Soldiers Graves
In Cape Colony, Etc. See entry under
(GRAVES).

(Cape Times Limited) (Printers) – Papers
With Regard To The Defence Of
Kimberley, 1899–1900.
Cape Times Limited
Cape Town 1900
39pp.
345×216mm   p.34

(Cape Times Limited) (Printers) – Cape
Of Good Hope, Copies Of Minutes And
Memoranda With Enclosures Which
Passed Between His Excellency The
Governor And The Late Ministry,
Regarding The Compensation To Be
Paid For Losses Sustained During The
War And Rebellion, And The Course To
Be Pursued Towards Those Who Have
Been Engaged In Rebellion, Including
The Final Minute Tendering The
Resignation Of Ministers. Printed By
Order Of Mr. Speaker, July, 1900.
Cape Town 1900
50pp.
330×207mm   CC

(Cape Times Limited) (Printers) – Cape
Of Good Hope, Magisterial Reports
Having Reference To The Occupation By

The Enemy Of, And The Attitude Of
The Population In, The Districts Now Or
Recently Under Martial Law. (Being A
Return To A Resolution Adopted By
The Honourable The House Of
Assembly On The 26th Of July 1900.)
Printed By Order Of Mr. Speaker,
August 1900. (A.5–1900)
Cape Times, Limited
Cape Town 1900
186pp.
330×209mm   CC
*Reports sent from nineteen towns and
districts indicating, in almost every case,
the majority of the Dutch population
joined the enemy or assisted them to a
great extent.*

(Cape Times Ltd. The) (Printers) –
Report Of War Losses Compensation
Commission, Covering Period July, 1900,
To February, 1904.
The Cape Times Ltd.
Cape Town 1904
iii+34pp.
330mm   H

(Cape Times Ltd. The) (Printers) – First
Interim Report Of The War Losses
Compensation Inquiry Commission...
Dated 31st Jan., 1905.
Cape Times Ltd.
Cape Town 1905
Pagination not shown.   H

(Cape Times Limited) (Printers) – Second
Interim Report Of The War Losses
Compensation Inquiry Commission
Appointed Under Act No. 30, 1904,
Dated March 13th, 1906.
Cape Times Limited, Government
Printers
Cape Town 1906
Pagination not shown.
293×187mm   RCSL

(———?) – Final Report Of The War
Losses Compensation Inquiry
Commission.
Printer/publisher not shown
(Cape Town 1907?)
19pp.
293×182mm   H
*Printer/publisher not shown. Possibly
'Cape Times Ltd.'. Entry from collection
of Library of Congress.*

(Cape Times Limited) (Publisher) –
Souvenir Of Cape Town & Suburban
Town Guard, Boer War 1899–1901.
Cape Times Limited
Cape Town nd. (1901)
106pp. Illustrated.
206×282mm
*Souvenir of the corps formed in the
colony during the war, being a roll of the
town guard by companies.*

Carew (Major, 7th Hussars) – Rhodesian
Field Force. Standing Orders 1st Brigade
Australian Bushmen. Notes On Drill,
Detached Duties & Marching In South
Africa.
The Argus Printing and Publishing
Company, Ltd.
Bulawayo 1900
49pp.   RCSL

(Carr-Ellison Family) – Carr-Ellison
Family. Home Coming Of And
Presentations To Major R. H. Carr-
Ellison, Captain H. A. Carr, Mrs. R. H.
Carr-Ellison And Captain M. R. Carr,
Also To H. G. Carr-Ellison Esq., And
R. C. W. Esq., 1902–1903.
Privately printed
Alnwick nd. (1903)
42pp. Illustrated.
250×180mm

Carrington (Sir F.) – Report On The
Delay In Bringing Force From Beira,
Etc. See WO. 5.

Carter (A. C. R.) – The Art Annual, 1900
The Work Of War Artists In South Africa.
'The Art Journal' Office
London 1900
32pp. Illustrated throughout.
332×250mm   p.24
*A title published in cloth cover, paper
cover [338×260mm] and in a special
numbered edition of 250 copies printed on
Japan paper.*

Casgrain (Capt. P. H. Du P.) – Report
On Survey And Mapping Section.
See WO. 97.

(Cassell & Company Limited)
(Publishers) – Cassell's Illustrated
History Of The Boer War.
Cassell & Company Limited
London, Paris, New York, Melbourne
nd. (c.1900)
Parts 1–49. Paper covered.
1560pp. Illustrated.
233×166mm

(Cassell & Company Limited)
(Publishers) – Cassell's Illustrated
History Of The Boer War 1899–1902.
Cassell & Company Limited
London, Paris, New York & Melbourne
nd. (c.1902)
Published in 30 parts. (Illustrated wraps.)
1903pp. Illustrated throughout.
247×186mm   p.16

(Cassell and Company Limited)
(Publishers) – Cassell's History Of The
Boer War 1899–1902. Revised And
Enlarged Edition.
Cassell and Company, Limited
London, Paris, New York & Melbourne
1903
2 vols.
viii+928pp. Illustrated.
viii+975pp. Illustrated.
245×185mm
*See DANES, Richard – Cassell's History
Of The Boer War 1899–1901.*

(Cassell & Co.) (Publishers) – F. W.
Galpin 1866–1900.
Author not shown
187pp.
*Approx: half the volume concerns the
Boer War.*

(Casualties) – List Of Casualties In The
South African War 1899–1902 From 11th
October 1899 To 31st May 1902.
Printer/publisher not shown
(np.) 1900–1902
790pp.
*A list of British forces casualties with
corrigenda and addenda slips. Name,
rank and number are listed with type of
casualty, location, date and remarks. This
set bound in period half calf. See
CASUALTY LISTS/WAR OFFICE for
separate printings.*

(Casualty Lists/War Office) –
Lists of casualties from War Office
library. Publications lack WO. imprint.

List Of Casualties In The South African
Field Force From 11 Oct., 1899 To 20
March, 1900; Prepared By The Casualty
Department, Cape Town.
[Official print] Publisher not shown
(np. 1900?)
ix+115pp.   MOD
*WH Loc: Bd. in SAIA
SABIB lists 'Addenda and corrigenda
supplements to printed list of casualties
from the 11th Oct., 1899 to 20th March,
1900. 1p.+ixpp.*

List Of Casualties In The South African Field Force From 21 March, 1900 To 31 July, 1900; Prepared By The Casualty Department, Cape Town.
[Official print] Publisher not shown
(np. 1900?)
vi+161pp.   MOD
WH Loc: Bd. in SAIA

List Of Casualties In The South African Field Force From 1 Aug. To 31 Dec., 1900; Prepared By The Casualty Department, Cape Town.
[Official print] Publisher not shown
(np. 1901?)
iv+94pp.   MOD
WH Loc: Bd. in SAIA

List Of Casualties In The South African Field Force From 1 Jan. To 30 June 1901; Prepared By The Casualty Department, Cape Town.
[Official print] Publisher not shown
(np. 1901?)
ii+121pp.   MOD
WH Loc: Bd. in SAIA

List Of Casualties In The Army In South Africa From 1 July To 31 Dec. 1901; Prepared By The Casualty Department, Cape Town.
[Official print] Publisher not shown
(np. 1902?)
xvii+111pp.   MOD
WH Loc: Bd. in SAIA

List Of Casualties In The Army In South Africa From 1 Jan. To 31 May 1902; Prepared By The Casualty Department, Cape Town.
[Official print] Publisher not shown
(np. 1902?)
ii+95pp.   MOD
WH Loc: Bd. in SAIA

Report On Casualties; By Col. Ivor Herbert. Nov. 1900.
(WO?) 1902
10pp.   MOD
WH Loc: SA39AA / PRO Loc: WO. 108/264.

Caunter (Major J. E.) – The Campaign In The Free State (To The 13th March, 1900) And Its Lessons.
Gale & Polden, Ltd.
London/Aldershot nd. (1901)
38pp. With 3 maps.
209×138mm

Cauvin (E. C.) and Roberts (H.) – Souvenir Of Deelfontein Hospital.
Dennis Edwards & Co., Printers
Cape Town (1900?)
iv+28pp. Illustrated.
140×220mm   SABIB
Item catalogued from cover. Description of the Imperial Yeomanry Hospital at Deelfontein.

Cave (Henry W.) – Uva And Its Connection With The Great South African War Of 1900.
Cave & Co.
Colombo nd. (1900)
47pp. Illustrated.
140×215mm
A description of the province of Uva in Ceylon with an account of Boer prisoners of war at Diyatalawa camp.

Cave (T. S.) and Tebbutt (L.) – Mobilisation For War. The South African Field Force And Home Defence, 1900.
Gale & Polden, Ltd.
London 1900
40pp.
8vo.   M

Caverhill (T. F. S.) – Self-Aid In War. With Practical Hints For The Cavalry

Wounded In South Africa. 1900
M/ De Bussy's African Catalogue 1900.

C.B. (Capt. C. Battine?) – Some Tactical Considerations Arising From Recent Events In South Africa.
United Service Institution of India.
nd./np.
14pp.
219×149mm   CC
Pamphlet, 'Capt. C. Battine 15th Hussars' written on the cover.

Cecil (Evelyn) – On The Eve Of The War. A Narrative Of Impressions During A Journey In Cape Colony, The Free State, The Transvaal, Natal and Rhodesia September 1899, To January 1900.
John Murray
London 1900
viii+147pp. Folding map and plates.
197×129mm   p.18.

(Censorship) – Rules As To Press Messages.
Publisher/printer not shown.
np./nd.
1p.   MOD
Item from War Office library. WO. ref. – WH Loc: SA58.

(Censorship) – Circular Memorandum: Censoring Of Letters.
Publisher/printer not shown.
———1901?
1p.   MOD
Item from War Office library. 'Official Print'. WO. ref. – WH Loc: SA58.

Chamberlain (Joseph) – Why We Are At War With The Republics. The Right Hon. Joseph Chamberlain's Great Speech On The Transvaal-War.
Grocott and Sherry (Printers)
Grahamstown 1899.
32pp.
220mm   SABIB

Chamberlain (Joseph) – Mr Chamberlain On The Cost Of The War And Who Will Pay The Bill.
McCorquodale
London 1901
4pp.
220mm   SABIB

Chamberlain (Joseph) – Mr. Chamberlain On Pro-Boer Slanders And Continental Animosity.
McCorquodale
London 1902
8pp.
220mm   SABIB

Chamberlain (Joseph) – Mr. Chamberlain's Defence Of The British Troops In South Africa Against The Foreign Slanders. (Reprinted From *The Standard*.)
John Murray
London 1902
15pp.
8vo.   M

Channing (Francis Allston) – The Transvaal War And Democracy. (Four Speeches In East Northamptonshire, November 1899.)
P. S. King and Son.
London 1899
16pp.
250mm   SABIB

Chapman (W.E.) – 'Notes From The Diary Of A Special Service Officer. Relief Of Kimberley'. And Some Comments Thereon.

(No other details.)
1901
23pp.
8vo.
Pamphlet listed in M. attributed to W. E. Chapman. Content relates to events in Kimberley during the siege and to untruthful inference contained in 'Notes on The Boer War from the diary of a Special Officer' by Major W. A. J. O'Meara.

Chiera (Alberto) – Three Letters For The Cessation Of The Anglo-Boer War, 17 January – 20, 28 February. Translated From Italian.
Tipografia Popolare
Rome 1900
16pp. Illustrated.
170mm   SABIB
Without title page. Catalogued from cover.

Chiera (Alberto) – (4th Letter – 24 March 1900). To The Hon. R. P., Deputy In The House Of Commons, London.
The Author
Rome 1900
8pp.
180mm   SABIB
Pages numbered 17–24 in continuation of the third letter.

Childers (Driver Erskine) – In The Ranks Of The C.I.V. A Narrative And Diary Of Personal Experiences With The C.I.V. Battery (Honourable Artillery Company) In South Africa.
Smith, Elder & Co.
London 1900
vii+301pp. With frontispiece.
198×130mm   p.33

Childers (Erskine) – War And The Arme Blanche.
Edward Arnold
London 1910
xvi+379pp.
210×138mm

(Chiswick Press) (Printers) – Capetown Cathedral Memorial Of The South African War, 1899, 1900, 1901, 1902. Exhibition Of The Book (Unbound In Framed Sheets) Containing The Names Of Those Who Died In The War On Behalf Of The Empire, 23rd May And Three Following Weeks, Victoria And Albert Museum, South Kensington.
Chiswick Press, printers
London (1914?)
14pp.
Brochure – A description of the book by the craftsmen who were commissioned to write and decorate it, Graily Hewitt and Allan F. Vigers.

(Christchurch Press Company) (Publisher) – Canterbury's Demonstration On The Departure Of The N.Z. Rough Riders For South Africa Hagley Park Sat. Feb. 17, 1900.
Christchurch Press Company
Christchurch 1900
4pp.
220×140mm   BIM

Church (Sir William) MacCormac (Sir William) and Jameson (Surg.-General J.) – Medical Administration In The South African War Being A Report Of Speeches Delivered By Sir William Church, Bart., President Of The Royal College Of Physicians Of London. Sir William MacCormac, Bart., President Of The Royal College Of Surgeons, England And Surg.-General J. Jameson, C.B. Late Director-General Army Medical Service At A Complimentary Dinner Given To The Latter By The Medical

Profession Of Great Britain And Ireland,
On The 24th July, 1901.
Privately printed.
Printer not shown.
nd./np. (1901)
15pp.
209×135mm   CC
*Essentially a reprint of the speech
delivered by J. Jameson on leaving the
office of Director-General of the Army
Medical Service. Card covered pamphlet.*

Churcher (Bt.-Major D. W.) – With The
Irish Fusiliers From Alexandria To Natal
1899–1900.
J. Read, Printer
Reading nd. (1900)
92pp. Illustrated.
207×142mm
*Cover title – From Alexandria To
Ladysmith With The 87th.*

Churchill (Lady Randolph) (Chairman of
the Executive Committee) – The
American Hospital Ship 'Maine' Fund
For South Africa From October 27th,
1899 To April 30th, 1900.
Printer/publisher not shown
np./nd. (c.1900)
56pp. Illustrated.
266×251mm
*Report by Lady Churchill together with a
list of medical and nursing staff,
subscription list, donations etc. Edition
bound in card cover.*

Churchill (Lady Randolph) (Chairman of
the Executive Committee) – Report Of
The American Hospital Ship 'Maine'.
Wightman Mountain & Andrews Ltd.
(Printers)
London nd. (c.1900)
72+11pp. Illustrated.
289×217mm   p.43

Churchill (Winston Spencer) – London
To Ladysmith Via Pretoria.
Longmans, Green, and Co.
London 1900
xiv+498pp. Maps and plans.
197×130mm   p.2

Churchill (Winston Spencer) – Ian
Hamilton's March Together With
Extracts From The Diary Of Lieutenant
T. H. C. Frankland A Prisoner Of War
At Pretoria.
Longmans, Green, and Co.
London 1900
xiii+409pp. Frontispiece, maps and
plans.
195×130mm

(Church Of England) – Forms Of Prayer
For Public, Domestic, And Private Use
During The War In South Africa
Sanctioned By The Bishops Of London,
Rochester And St. Albans. Published
Under The Direction Of The Tract
Committee, London, Society For
Promoting Christian Knowledge.
E. & J. B. Young & Co.
Brighton, New York, 1900
47pp.
220mm   SABIB

(Church Of England) (Occasional Offices)
– A Form Of Intercession With Almighty
God, On Behalf Of Her Majesty's Naval
And Military Forces Now In South
Africa, To Be Used In All Churches And
Chapels In England and Wales, And In
The Town Of Berwick-Upon-Tweed On
Such Occasions As Each Bishop Shall
Appoint For His Own Diocese. By
Authority.
Eyre and Spottiswoode
London 1900
8pp.
250mm   SABIB

*See entry under EYRE and
SPOTTISWOODE, printers. – A Form of
Intercession, etc.*

(Church Of England) (Occasional Offices)
– Form Of Prayer To Be Used At
Open-Air Services For The Militia, Etc.
(Drawn Up By The Chaplain General,
And Approved By The Archbishop Of
Canterbury. It May Also Be Used In
Garrison Churches As An Extra Service).
Published Under The Direction Of The
Tract Committee.
Society For Promoting Christian
Knowledge.
London nd. (c.1900)
24pp.
130mm   SABIB
*Cover title:- A Form Of Prayer For Open
Air Services. For Army In South Africa.*

(Church Of England) (Occasional Offices)
– A Form Of Prayer And Thanksgiving
To Almighty God For The Restoration
Of Peace In South Africa. Issued Under
The Direction Of His Majesty The King
For Use On Sunday The Eighth Day Of
June 1902. By Authority.
Eyre and Spottiswoode
London 1902
4pp.
240mm   SABIB

**(Church Of The Province Of South Africa
Cape Town Diocese)** – Form Of Service
Put Forth By The Archbishop Of
Capetown On The Day Of Thanksgiving
To Almighty God On The Restoration
Of Peace To South Africa.
S. A. Electric P. and P. Co.,
Capetown 1900
4pp.
200mm   SABIB
*Publication anticipating cessation of
hostilities in South Africa.*

C. J. D. (Translator) – An English
Translation Of All Dutch Official
Telegrams Received In Vryheid, Etc. See
WILTER, Frank. (Publisher.)

Clare (Israel Smith) – British-Boer War.
An Historical And Pictorial Souvenir
History Of South Africa And The
British-Boer War. Illustrations From
Special Photographs And Drawings By
A. J. Hencke, J. P. Robertson, R. J.
Wallace And Others. Complete And
Accurate Maps, Political And Historical.
Sold Only By Subscription.
Geo. F. Cram
Chicago nd. (1900)
190pp. Illustrated throughout.
Page 155–190 Maps
370×290mm
*M records copy of 198pp. SABIB lists
edition published by Souvenir Publishing
Co. 1900.*

Clark (Mrs Cresswell) – Report Of Work
Done In Soldiers Comforts Office For
Receiving And Distributing Gifts During
The Period Of The Anglo-Boer War.
Townshend Taylor & Snashall, Printers
Capetown 1900
23pp.
170×106mm   RCSL

Clark (Gavin Brown) – The Official
Correspondence Between The
Governments Of Great Britain, The South
African Republic, And The Orange Free
State, Which Preceded The War In South
Africa. Compiled From The Blue Books
by Dr. G. B. Clark, M.P.
William Reeves
London 1900
104pp.
215×145mm

Clark (Dr. G. B.) – Speech In The House
Of Commons On Feb. 7, 1900. By Dr.
G. B. Clark, M.P., In Support Of Mr.
Redmond's Amendment.
The Transvaal Committee
Westminster (1900?)
8pp.
8vo.   SABIB
Catalogued from caption title.

Clarke (Sir Edward George) – House Of
Commons – Autumn Session 1899. The
War In The Transvaal. Speech By Sir
Edward Clarke, Q.C., M.P., On
Thursday, 19th October 1899. Reprinted
From The 'Parliamentary Debates'.
(Authorised Ed.)
Wyman & Sons
London 1899
11pp.
230mm   SABIB

Clarke (Sir Edward George) – House Of
Commons – Autumn Session, 1899.
How And Why We Became Involved In
The War Reprinted From The
'Parliamentary Debates' (Authorised Ed.)
Issued By The South African Conciliation
Committee In The Interests Of Truth.
Wyman & Sons, printers
London 1900
11pp.
250mm   SABIB

Clarke (Col. R. F. Noel) – Report On
Army Ordnance Department. See –
WO. 38.

Claverhouse (Pseud:) – Plain Talks To
Little Englanders.
F. E. Coe, Simpkin Marshall/London
John Heywood/Manchester
(1900)
30+iipp. Illustrated.
240mm   SABIB
*A pamphlet addressed to those in England
who disapproved of the war.*

Clay (Philip Stephens) – Lays Of The
Veldt.
Simpkin, Marshall, Hamilton, Kent
& Co./London
James Bell & Son/Nottingham
1900
31pp.
Cr.8vo.   M
Poems on the war.

Cleaver (M. M.) (Editor) – A Young
South African: A Memoir Of Ferrar
Reginald Mostyn Cleaver, Advocate And
Veldcornet.
W. E. Hortor
Johannesburg 1913
xv+200pp. Portrait frontispiece.
196×132mm

(Clements Printing Works Ltd.)
(Publishers?) – Tommy Atkins As A
Journalist, The Pretoria Prisoners' Paper,
Extraordinary Souvenir Of The Boer
War, The Paper Published By The British
Prisoners, Absolute Fac-Simile Of The
'Waterfall Wag' The Most Remarkable
Journal Ever Issued.
Clements Printing Works Ltd.
London nd. (1900)
28pp. (With additional pages of
advertisements.) Illustrated.
247×188mm
*A reprint of the British P.O.W.'s paper
originally published near Pretoria. Two
issues of the magazine and a supplement
are reproduced. Title from cover.*

Cleveland (Frederick A.) – The South
African Conflict – Its Legal And Political
Aspects.
Publications of the American Academy

of Political and Social Science.
Philadelphia 1899
40pp.
8vo.   M
A paper submitted to the American Academy of Political and Social Science. No.265, November 28, 1899.

Clifford (John) – Brotherhood And The War In South Africa.
Parlett. W. Walker
London 1900
24pp.
Cr.8vo.   M

(Clifton College) – Cliftonians Serving In South Africa, Feb. 1900.
E. Austin & Son, (Printers)
Clifton (1900?)
16pp.
120mm   SABIB

(Clifton College) – The Memorial To Old Cliftonians Who Fell In The South African War.
J. W. Arrowsmith (Printer)
Bristol (c.1900)
16pp. Illustrated.
220mm   SABIB

(Clifton College) – Old Cliftonians In South Africa.
Publisher/printer not known
Clifton nd. (1900?)
3pp.
220mm   SABIB

Clinton-Baker (Major) – Trekking With The Royal Irish Rifles Mounted Infantry.
Privately printed
Hertford nd. (c.1905)
77pp.
165×120mm
Cover title – Seventeen months trekking with the R.I.R.M.I.

Cloud (William F.) – Webster Davis On Toast. Facts, Not Fiction. Sense Not Sobs, About The Boer-British War, With Strictures On The Flop.
Publisher/printer not shown
Kansas City 1900
26pp. Portrait.
Cr.8vo.
An attack on Webster Davis' work 'John Bulls Crime'.

Clout (C.) – The Story Of My Adventures. My Bit Of Brag.
Printer/publisher not shown
Privately printed
np./nd. (c.1900)
24pp.
180×120mm
Poem, being the adventures of a trooper in Kitchener's Horse. Paper covered.

Clowes (William) (Printer) – The War In South Africa And The Hague Conventions.
William Clowes, printer
(London 1901?)
7pp.
280mm   SABIB
No title page. Statement addressed to signatory powers of the Hague Conventions by Deputation of the South African Republics.

Clulee (Charles Thomas) – Index to Proclamations And Ordinances For 1900, 1901 And 1902.
Lebbink & Co.
Pretoria (1903?)
32pp.
250mm   SABIB

Cockran (W. B.) – Proceedings Of The Boer Rescue Meeting, Auditorium

Chicago, December 8, 1901, Under The Auspices Of The Chicago Branch Of The American Transvaal League.
Publisher/printer not shown (American Transvaal League?)
np. (Chicago)
nd. (1901)
24pp.   CB

Cohen (Simon) – A Review Of The Work And Correspondence In Connection With The Beth Hamedrash, Lomdi Torah… With Fragmentary Notes Relating To The War In South Africa.
'Jewish Express' Printing works
London 1900
124pp.   H
Volume recorded at Library of Congress.

(Coldstreamer) – Ballads Of The Boer War Selected From The Haversack Of Sergeant J. Smith, By 'Coldstreamer'.
Grant Richards
London 1902
89pp.
178×113mm
Author – Harry Graham. An enlarged edition of 104pp. was published the same year.

Collen (Edwin H.) – Diary And Sketches Of The South African War.
Military Department Press
Calcutta 1901
ii+106pp. Illustrated.
240mm   SABIB
Diary of Lieut. E. H. Collen R.A. from 18 Jan–28 Sept. 1900. The writer was appointed transport officer.

Collingridge (W. H. & L.) (Publishers) – The C.I.V. And The War In South Africa 1900. The City Press Illustrated Souvenir Of The City Of London Imperial Volunteers.
W. H. & L. Collingridge 'City Press' Offices.
London nd. (1900)
Unnumbered (48p.) Illustrated throughout.
290×220mm

Collingridge (W. H. & L.) (Publishers) – No. 2. The C.I.V. And The War In South Africa, A.D. 1900. The City Press Illustrated Souvenir Of The City Of London Imperial Volunteers.
W. H. & L. Collingridge 'City Press' Offices.
London nd. (1900)
32pp. Illustrated throughout.
278×219mm

Collingridge (W. H. & L.) (Publishers) – No. 3. The City Press C.I.V. War Souvenir.
W. H. & L. Collingridge 'City Press' Offices.
London nd. (1900)
32pp. Illustrated throughout.
278×217mm
Issue No. 3. contains The Official Roll of The City Of London Imperial Volunteers.

Collingridge (W. H. & L.) (Publishers) – No. 4. 'City Press' Souvenir Of The C.I.V.
W. H. & L. Collingridge 'City Press' Offices.
London nd. (1900)
32pp. Illustrated throughout.
279×220mm   p.111

Collingridge (W. H. & L.) (Publishers) – The City Of London Imperial Volunteers In South Africa, A.D. 1900. The 'City Press' C.I.V. Souvenir (Complete Edition).
W. H. & L. Collingridge 'City Press' Offices.

London nd. (1900)
285×220mm   p.111
Complete edition of four issues unpaginated except for issue 4. (32pp.) Clothbound.

(Colonial Office) (Publisher?) – Correspondence (4 Oct. 1899 To 31 Dec. 1900) Connected With Claims On Account Of Losses Arising From The War In South Africa. Nov. 1901.
Colonial Office
(London) 1901
xxvi+382pp.   MOD
Item from War Office library. WO. ref. – WH Loc: SA35B.

(Colonial Office) (Publisher?) – Correspondence (9 Oct. 1899 To 31 Mar. 1900) Relating To Contraband Of War Etc. In South Africa. May 1901.
Colonial Office
(London) 1901
lxiii+666pp.   MOD
Item from War Office library. WO. ref. – WH Loc: SA35B.

(Colonial Office) (Publisher?) – Further Correspondence (1 Apr. 1900 To 31 Dec. 1900) Relating To Contraband Of War Etc. In South Africa. Sept. 1901.
Colonial Office
(London) 1901
xxxvi+350pp.   MOD
Item from War Office library. WO. ref. – WH Loc: SA35B.

(Colonial Office) (Publisher?) – Correspondence (4 Mar. 1901 To 14 Feb. 1902) Relating To Refugee Camps In South Africa. July 1902.
Colonial Office
(London) 1902
xxii+252pp.   MOD
Item from War Office library. WO. ref. – WH Loc: SA35B.

(Colonial Office) (Publisher?) – Further Correspondence (1 Jan. 1901 To 31 Dec. 1902) Connected With Claims On Account Of Losses Arising From The War In South Africa. Nov. 1903.
Colonial Office
(London) 1903
xlv+439pp.   MOD
Item from War Office library. WO. ref. – WH Loc: SA35B.

(Colonial Office) (Publisher?) – Further Correspondence (15 Feb. 1902 To 8 Aug. 1903) Relating To Refugee Camps In South Africa. Jan. 1904.
Colonial Office
(London) 1904
xvi+365pp.   MOD
Item from War Office library. WO. ref. – WH Loc: SA35B.

Colvile (Major-General Sir H. E.) – The Work Of The Ninth Division.
Edward Arnold
London 1901
xiii+247pp. Folding maps and plans.
229×247mm   p.43

Colvin (Bt. Lieut.-Colonel F. F.) and Gordon (Captain E. R.) – Diary Of The 9th (Q.R.) Lancers During The South African Campaign, 1899 To 1902.
Cecil Roy
London 1904
xv+304pp. Pocket map and various illustrations.
204×151mm   p.vii

(Commonwealth Of Australia) – Parliamentary and other Official Publications in reference to the South African War 1899–1902, held in the

National Library of Australia and at Australian War Memorial, Canberra. Pagination and size not shown

Conference Of Military Commanders, Victoria Barracks, Melbourne, September, 1899: Proposed United Australia Contingent For The Transvaal (1899).   NL

Courts Martial – Sentences On Officers In South Africa – Despatches From The Commander-In-Chief In South Africa And Extracts From The Proceedings Of The Two General Courts Martial Relating Thereto; Commonwealth Parliament, House Of Representatives. Victoria 1902   NL

Report On The Royal Commission Appointed To Inquire Into And Report Upon The Arrangements Made For The Transport Of Troops Returning From Service In South Africa In The S.S. Drayton Grange And S.S. Norfolk: Commonwealth Parliament, House Of Representatives. Victoria 1902 17pp. Two folding plans.   NL

Parliamentary Papers Relating To Australian Troops In South Africa: South African War, 1899–1902. Commonwealth Parliament, House of Representatives. Melbourne 1902   NL

Supply Of Meat To Troops In South Africa. Commonwealth Parliament c.24 April 1902. Victoria   NL

(New South Wales)

First And Other Contingents To South Africa. Sydney 1902   NL

Imperial Bushmen's Contingent: Amounts Paid To Persons Not Under Military For Work In Connection With; (NSW Legislative Assembly 26 July 1900.)   NL

New South Wales Military Forces: List Of Officers, Non-Commissioned Officers And Men Of New South Wales Military Contingents In The Boer War, 1899–1900. Sydney 1900   NL

New South Wales Military Forces: Nominal Roll Of 2nd Regiment Mounted Rifles Organised For Service In South Africa. 1st Ed. (nd.)   NL

New South Wales Military Forces, Maj. Gen. G. A. French. C.M.G., R.A., Commanding, To The Principal Under Secretary: Giving Details Of Clothing To Contingents For Boer War, NSW Legislative Assembly. Sydney 1900   NL

New South Wales Soudan And South African Contingents 1884–1907: Including Report Of The Royal Commission Of Inquiry Into Claims Of Members Of The NSW Contingents In South Africa, With Copy Of Commission Minutes Of Proceedings And Evidence And Appendix, 26 June 1906. (A second report published in 1907.)   AWM

South African Contingents: Reports Of The Military Authorities Regarding Equipment Of., NSW Legislative Assembly, 2 August 1900. Sydney 1900   AWM

New South Wales Troops In Service In South Africa: Return, Giving Numbers Of Officers And Men And Those Killed Or Died Of Disease, (Maj. Gen. G. A. French, C.M.G. R.A., NSW Military Forces.) NSW Legislative Assembly, 5 December 1901.   NL

Papers Relating To Australian Troops In South Africa, 1900–1902. NSW Legislative Assembly: South African Contingents, 1 August 1900. Sydney 1900   NL

(Queensland)

Approval By Legislative Assembly Of Proposal To Despatch A Force Of Volunteers For Service In South Africa; Queensland Legislative Assembly. 24 October 1899. 1899   NL

Captain Pelham's Appointment As An Officer Of The Transvaal Contingent. 10 November 1899. Brisbane 1899?   NL *Includes list of officers appointed and seniority.*

Correspondence Relating To Despatch Of Seventh Contingent To South Africa (In Continuation Of Parliamentary Paper A16-1901) Queensland Legislative Assembly, 4 September 1901. Brisbane 1901

Despatch Of Details To South Africa Per Transport Britannic: Copy Of Correspondence Respecting. Queensland Legislative Assembly, 7 August 1901. Brisbane 1901   NL

Proposed Despatch Of Additional Australian Troops To South Africa. Brisbane 1899   NL

Queensland Land Forces. The Official Quarterly List Of Officers Of The Queensland Land Forces, Including Permanent Force, Defence Force, Volunteers, Cadets And Rifle Clubs; Also List Of Queensland Land Forces To 31 July 1900. Brisbane 1900   AWM

Queensland Troops For The Transvaal: Further Correspondence; Queensland Legislative Assembly. Brisbane 1899   NL

Returned Soldiers From South Africa Going Back Per RMS 'Britannic'; Queensland Legislative Assembly, 7 August 1901. Brisbane 1901

Testing Of Rifles For The Queensland Transvaal Contingents, 2 November, 1899. Brisbane 1899

(Tasmania)

Deporting Of Boer Prisoners To Tasmania: Copy Of Correspondence Between The Secretary Of State For The Colonies, The Prime Minister And The Premier Of Tasmania, 21 June 1901; Commonwealth Parliament, The Senate. Victoria 1901   NL

Tasmanian Bushmen Contingent: Return Of Horses Purchased; Tasmanian House Of Assembly 20 September 1900. Tasmania 1900   AWM

(Victoria)

Acts/Contingents To South Africa. – Victorian Military Contingent Act, 1899. Vic. Legislative Assembly. Melbourne nd. 1899?

Victorian Military Contingent Act, 1900. Vic. Legislative Assembly. Melbourne nd. 1900?

Victorian Third Military Contingent Act, 1900. Vic. Legislative Assembly. Melbourne nd. 1900?

An Act To Authorize Contributions By Municipal Councils, Banks And Other Bodies Towards Military Contingents For South Africa Or Any Members Thereof Or Their Relatives. Melbourne 1900

Contingents to South Africa:–

First Victorian Contingent For South Africa: Nominal Roll Of Officers, Warrant Officers, Non-Commissioned Officers And Men Of The Victorian Contingent For Service In South Africa. Melbourne 1899

Muster Roll Of Victorian Contingent (Five Companies Of Mounted Rifles) Of Imperial-Australian Regiment. Melbourne 1900

Second Victorian Contingent For South Africa: Two Companies Of Mounted Infantry: Nominal Roll Of Officers, Warrant Officers, Non-Commissioned Officers And Men Who Embarked On SS Euryalus On 13 January 1900 For Service In South Africa. Melbourne 1900

Third (Or Bushmen's) Contingent For Service In South Africa: Two Companies Of Mounted Rifles: Roll Of Officers, Non-Commissioned Officers And Men. Melbourne 1900

Comyns (T. W.) – The War, Britons v. Boers: The Causes Of The War In The Transvaal. Muir? Brisbane 1900 *Pagination not shown.*

Coney (H. T.) – Report On Army Chaplain's Department, Etc. See WO. 59.

Congreve (Celia) – The Transvaal War Alphabet Dedicated To Our Soldiers Children By A Soldier's Wife. George Falkner & Sons Manchester 1900 29pp. 206×164mm   p.36

(Connaught Rangers, The) – Regimental Records Of 1st Battalion The Connaught Rangers The Boer War 1899–1901. Publisher/printer not shown np./nd. 70pp. Four folding maps. 205×167mm   p.41 *Volume bound without title page. Title from cover. The first section of the full history. See entry under RICHARDS, W. A. & SONS.*

(Convalescent Depot Gazette) – Convalescent Depot Gazette Germiston Transvaal. Publisher/printer not shown Germiston 1901 138pp. 205×130mm   DC   p.104 *Six issues (complete run) of a magazine published from June to November 1901.*

Cook (E. T.) – Rights And Wrongs Of The Transvaal War. Edward Arnold London 1901 xi+378pp. 230×145mm

Cooke (John H.) (Compiled by) – 5,000 Miles With The Cheshire Yeomanry In South Africa. A Series Of Articles Compiled From Letters And Diaries Written By Officers, Non-Commissioned Officers And Men Of The 21st And 22nd (Cheshire) Companies Of Imperial Yeomanry, Relating Their Experiences During The South African War In The Years 1900–1901; Also Articles From 'The Times', 'The Times History Of The War', And Other Papers Relating To The Marches, Movements And Operations Of The Two Companies.
Mackie & Co. Ltd./Warrington
Phillipson & Golder/Chester
1913–1914
xxxiii+434pp. Folding map in separate pocket. Numerous illustrations.
252×188mm   p.75
Also published in a superior edition with red half calf binding.

Corelli (Marie) – A Social Note On The War Patriotism Or Self-Advertisement?
Norton & Neal
Birmingham nd. (c.1900)
34pp.
231×180mm
SABIB attributes item to Mary Mackay.

Corner (William) – The Story Of The 34th Company (Middlesex) Imperial Yeomanry From The Point Of View Of Private No. 6243.
T. Fisher Unwin
London 1902
xix+540pp. Folding map and plates.
228×148mm

(Corporal. The) – 'I.Y.' An Imperial Yeoman At War By 'The Corporal'.
Elliot Stock
London 1901
iv+133pp.
190×130mm
Extracts from the diary of a trooper. SABIB lists author – P. Bodington.

(Corrigan W. H.) (Publisher) – Programme Of Imperial Troops Visit To New Zealand With Annotations On The Battles Won.
W. H. Corrigan
Christchurch 1901
32pp. Illustrated.
185mm   BIM
Title from cover.

Cory (Capt. E. J.) – Notes From A Diary In South Africa 1900–1901 By Capt. E. J. Cory, D.S.O. 69th (Sussex) Squadron, Imperial Yeomanry And Who Was Seconded From 1st Cinque Ports Rifle Volunteer Corps For Service In South Africa.
Printer/publisher not shown
Privately printed
np./nd. (c.1900)
iv+80pp. Portrait frontispiece.
184×126mm   CC
A campaign diary. Account relates to events in The Transvaal.

(Cosmos?) (Printer/Publisher) – How The Boers Made War; Comprising Battle Scenes, Generals, Transvaal Republic Official Executive Council, Field Artillery, Commandos, &c. &c.
Cosmos?
Cape Town (c.1900)
12pp. (24 plates)
160×220mm   SABIB
No title page. Catalogued from cover. Text in Afrikaans and English.

(Cossack Post) – The Cossack Post Journal Of B. Squadron Paget's Horse, Etc. See – JUNIOR ARMY AND NAVY STORE LIMITED.

Cotgreave (A.) – The Transvaal And South Africa. A Collection Of References To Books Containing Articles On The Above Subject Which Appear In Cotgreave's 'Contents – Subject Index To General And Periodical Literature' Together With A List Of Special Works Dealing With South African Affairs.
West Ham Public Libraries
London 1900
12pp.
12mo.   M
The catalogue is useful as a reference to magazine articles on the war and the South African question in 1899 and preceding years. The list of books on the Transvaal is incomplete – M.

Cottle (H. C.) (Printer) – South Africa. Correspondence Respecting Terms Of Surrender Of The Boer Forces In The Field.
H. C. Cottle (Acting Government printer, Ceylon.)
Colombo 1902
ii+8pp.
335×213mm   CC   p.122
See entry under HMSO – Cd.1096.

Courtenay (Colonel Arthur Henry) – With The 4th Battalion The Cameronians (Scottish Rifles) In South Africa, 1900–1901.
Printed for the Author by William Brown
Edinburgh 1905
vii+95pp. Sketch map.
192×129mm

Courtney (The Rt. Hon Leonard. Lord) – Great Britain And The Transvaal. An Address Delivered By The Rt. Hon. Leonard Courtney, M.P., Before The South-East Cornwall Liberal Unionist Association, At Liskeard, On January 23rd, 1900.
John Philp
Liskeard 1900
16pp.   M
The author denounces the South African war as an unnecessary war brought on by terrible diplomacy.

Cowie (Lieut. W. R.) – Letters From W. Russell Cowie 2nd Lieut. 2nd Battalion Seaforth Highlanders.
Publisher/printer not shown
nd. (c.1900)
iii+104pp. Frontispiece and two plans.
272×211mm   GC
Cover title – 'From Fort George to Magersfontein' A privately printed volume compiled after Lieut. Cowie's death at Magersfontein. Reproduced directly from typed pages.

Cowper (Pte. W.) – Amateur Atkins On Active Service With The Seaforths' First Volunteer Company In South Africa.
Peter Reid & Coy.
Wick 1902
110pp.
184×123mm   p.66

Craddock (Col. M.) – Diary Of The 2nd New Zealand Mounted Rifles On Active Service In South Africa From 24th Feb. 1900, To 21 March 1901. Also From 1 April 1901–8 May 1901.
Evening Star
Dunedin 1915
50pp. With portrait.
225mm   BIM

Creswicke (Louis) – South Africa And The Transvaal War.
T.C. & E.C. Jack
Edinburgh 1900–1901
Supplementary vols. vii & viii published by The Caxton Publishing Co.
London nd. (c.1902)

Vol.I   – xii+200pp.
Vol.II   – viii+201+iipp.
Vol.III   – viii+200pp.
Vol.IV   – viii+216pp.
Vol.V   – viii+199pp.
Vol.VI   – viii+216pp.
Vol.VII   – xvi+214pp.
Vol.VIII   – viii+199pp.
Illustrated throughout
251×177mm   p.80

Creswicke (Louis) – South Africa And The Transvaal War.
The Caxton Publishing Co.
London nd. (c.1902)
(Pagination as previous entry.)

Creswicke (Louis) – South Africa And The Transvaal War.
The Publishers Syndicate (Limited)
Toronto 1900 &
T. C. & E. C. Jack
Edinburgh 1900
Vols 1–6

Crichton (E. L.) – Songs And Ballads Of The Transvaal War – By E.L.C. And C.E. Nelson New Zealand May 1900.
The Brett Printing Coy.
Auckland 1900
28pp.
180mm   BIM
Cover title – 'Our Boys' Or Ballads Of The Transvaal War.

Crispin (H. T.) – 'Ikona' Sketches. See – H.T.C.

Cronwright-Schreiner (Mr.) – South Africa. Address By Mr Cronwright-Schreiner To The Holmfirth Division Liberal Association At Penistone, On Saturday, April 21st, 1900.
Eli Collins & Company Limited 'Express' Office
Holmfirth 1900
16pp.
214×136mm
Reprinted from the 'Holmfirth Express' – corrected and revised.

Cronwright-Schreiner (S. C.) – The Land Of Free Speech. Record Of A Campaign On Behalf Of Peace In England And Scotland In 1900.
The New Age Press
London 1906
xxxiv+456+1pp. Illustrated.
196×142mm   CC

Crosfield (Sir A. H.) – The True Causes Of, And The False Excuses For, The War In South Africa.
National Reform Union
Manchester (1901)
35pp.
220mm   SABIB

Crosland (T. W. H.) – The Absent Minded Mule, And Other Occasional Verses.
At the sign of the Unicorn VII Cecil Court (Publishers)
London 1899
31pp.
12mo.   M
An amusing skit on Rudyard Kipling's poem 'The Absent-minded Beggar'.

Crowe (George) – The Commission Of H.M.S. 'Terrible' 1898–1902.
George Newnes Limited
London 1903
xvii+370pp. Illustrated.
222×142mm   p.102

Crowe (George) – From Portsmouth To Peking, Etc. See entry under 'HONG KONG DAILY PRESS' OFFICE.

139

(Crowing Cock. A) – Chantic-Learics By A Crowing Cock. Entered under SIMPKIN, MARSHALL, HAMILTON, KENT & CO. LTD.

Crum (Major F. M.) – With The Mounted Infantry In South Africa Being Side-Lights On The Boer Campaign 1899–1902.
Printed for private circulation
Macmillan and Bowes
Cambridge 1903
viii+223pp.
195×130mm
A record of the Mounted Infantry Company 1st. King's Royal Rifles. In 1950 the author published 'Memoirs of a Rifleman Scout. Parts I-IV'. The first section of the volume relates to the South African War.

Cunliffe (F. H. E.) – The History Of The Boer War.
Methuen and Co.
London 1901
Vol.1 – viii+520pp.
Vol.2 – xiii+646pp.
Maps and illustrations throughout.
254×190mm   p.64

(Curlings Standard Printing Works) (Printers) – War Telegrams. Officially Issued By The Late O.F.S. Government Up To The Occupation Of Bloemfontein.
Curling's Standard Printing Works
Bloemfontein 1900
iii+95pp.
210mm   SABIB

(Curtis & Beamish, Ltd.) (Printers) – In Memoriam. J.W.A.C., W.B.K., H.P.P., F.M., R.McK., K-S., C.D.S., F.O.B., J.D.D-H., D.R.Y.
Printed for private circulation
Curtis & Beamish, Ltd.
Coventry nd. (c.1902)
35pp.
165×137mm
Tribute to St. Ninian's boys who died in South Africa 1899–1900.

Cust (A. P. Purey) – The Ethics Of War. A Sermon Preached At York Minster, Sunday After Trinity, November 26th, 1899.
John Sampson
York (1899?)
15pp.
220mm   SABIB

Cuthbert (Captain J. H.) (Editor) – The 1st Battalion Scots Guards In South Africa 1899–1902.
Harrison & Sons
London nd. (c.1902)
x+259 pp. Large pocket map. Numerous illustrations.
248×300mm
An illustrated record with calendar of events, Battalion roll and medal list.

(C.W.P.) – Letters From Ladysmith.
Printed privately
W. Bishop, printer
London nd. (c.1900)
93pp.
182×125mm
Letters to his wife written by Col. Park of the Devonshire Regt.

D

('Daily Graphic') (Publishers) – The 'Daily Graphic' Special C.I.V. Number.
Daily Graphic
London 1900
16pp. Illustrated
Folio   W/L 389
Newspaper dated Oct. 27, 1900. Includes double page coloured portrait of C.I.V. members.

(Daily Graphic, The) (Publisher) – The Ladysmith Lyre. An Exact Facsimile Of The Humorous Illustrated Paper Published In Ladysmith During The Siege.
Issued by 'The Daily Graphic'.
Printed and published for the Proprietors by Alfred Gould Grover
London 1900
16pp. Illustrated.
436×308mm
Vol. 1. Nos. 1–4, 27th Nov–15th Dec. 1899.

(Daily Mail) (Publisher) – The Ghastly Blunders Of The War. A Guide To The Report Of The Royal Commission On The South African War, 1899–1900.
'Daily Mail' offices
London nd. (c.1903)
48pp.
268×186mm   p.11

('Daily News', Military Expert Of) – Notes On The War To The Occupation Of Bloemfontein.
Macmillan
London 1900
Pagination not shown.   THB

(Dan) (Pseudonym) – Paul By Dan. Peregrinations Of Paul, Prophet, Priest, President, Late Of Pretoria.
Jarrold & Sons
London 1901
39pp.
180×120mm

Danes (Richard) – Cassell's History Of The Boer War 1899–1901.
Cassell and Company, Limited
London, Paris, New York & Melbourne 1901
viii+1560pp. Illustrated.
231×164mm   p.16
See entries under CASSELL & COMPANY LIMITED.

(Dangerfield Printing Company, Ltd., The) (Publisher) – Souvenir Programme Of Grand Military And Patriotic Concert Organized By Miss Ellaline Terriss And Mr. C. P. Little In Aid Of The Sick And Wounded, The Widows And Orphans, And The Families Of Our Troops Now Serving In South Africa, On Tuesday, December 5th, 1899.
The Dangerfield Printing Company, Ltd.
London nd. (1899)
Unnumbered (24pp.) Illustrated. Bound with 12 colour plates of uniform.
310×230mm

Daniell (Gordon) Church (Dicky) Brandon (E. E.) and Harris (Owen) (Editors and Publishers) – The 'Mexican' Mercury No. 1 Vol. 1 Week Ending March X, 1900 Kharki Edition. A Quick & Quizical Racy Record And Pleasant Probe Of Our Daily Doings.
Printed on the High Seas crossing the Line 1900
32pp. (including cover)
290×185mm   p.5

Darling (George) – A Volunteers Letters. A Record Of Service (1900–1) In The South African War. By Corporal George Darling. With An Introduction And A Supplementary Narrative.
W. Pomphrey *Press and Advertiser* Office Wishaw 1902
46pp.
Cr.8vo.   M
Letters from a member of staff of the 'Wishaw Press and Advertiser' sent from South Africa.

(Darlington Yeomanry) – Complimentary Banquet To The Darlington Contingent Of Yeomanry And Volunteers On Their Return From South Africa.
Publisher/printer not shown
Darlington 1901
12pp. Illustrated.
166×128mm
A banquet in celebration of Darlington volunteers in the 14th and 15th Companies (Northumberland) I.Y. and the Service Company of the 1st Volunteer Batt. Durham Light Infantry. Card covered.

Davidson (John Morrison) – Why I Am A Pro-Boer (Reprinted From 'Reynolds Newspaper'.)
John Dicks
London (1902)
31pp.
8vo.   M
Cover title – Africa for the Africanders.

Davidson (Major H.) (Editor) – The Seaforth Highlanders South Africa 1899–1902.
W. & A. K. Johnston Limited
Edinburgh and London nd. (c.1904)
vii+86pp. Folding map and two plates.
252×186mm   p.103

Davin (Nicholas F.) – South African War; The Canadian Contingents. A Speech By Nicholas Flood Davin, M.P., Delivered In House Of Commons, Feb. 16, 1900.
Printer/publisher not shown
(Ottawa?) 1900
10pp.
250mm   H

Davin (Nicholas Flood) – Strathcona Horse. Speech By Nicholas Flood Davin At Lansdowne Park, March 7th, AD. 1900. On The Occasion Of The First Parade Of The Strathcona Horse When A Flag From The Town Of Sudbury Was Presented By Her Excellency The Countess Of Minto.
James Hope & Sons
Ottawa 1900
20pp. Illustrated.
168×120mm

Davis (Richard Harding) – With Both Armies In South Africa.
Charles Scribner's Sons
New York 1903
xi+237pp. Illustrated.
200×134mm   p.106
M. lists an edition of 1900.

Davis (Webster) – John Bull's Crime; Or Assaults On Republics.
The Abbey Press
New York 1901
xxvi+225pp. Illustrated.
250×165mm

Davis (Col. J.) Woulds (Sergeant-Major J.) and Harrison (Sergeant H. R.) – Some Notes On The Queen's Royal West Surrey Regiment Together With An Account Of The 2nd And 3rd Battalions In The Late South African Campaign And Guildford's Aid To The Troops During Peace And War.
Frank Lasham
Guildford 1904
94pp. Illustrated.
189×125mm   p.44

Davitt (Michael) – The Boer Fight For Freedom.
Funk & Wagnalls Company
New York and London 1902
xii+603pp. Folding map and illustrations.
225×150mm   p.2

Davitt (M.) – The Boer Fight For Freedom From The Beginning Of Hostilities To The Peace Of Pretoria.
Funk & Wagnalls Company
New York 1902
xii+607pp. Map and illustrations.
225×145mm
Third edition, revised, with variant binding.

Davson (Major H. M.) – The Story Of 'G' Troop Royal Horse Artillery.
Publisher/printer not shown
Woolwich 1914
viii+106pp. Plates and maps.
220×140mm
A history compiled from various sources. Most of the content relates to the war in South Africa.

Dawnay (Hugh Richard) – With General Bruce Hamilton In The Eastern Transvaal, June 1902.
np.
Privately printed 1902
34pp.
220mm   SABIB

Dawnay (Lt. Col.) – A Month On The Modder River With The Coldstream. See BUMPUS, John & E. Ltd. (Printers).

Dawson (Captain E.) – Some Notes On The War In South Africa, With Reference To Indian Volunteers.
United Service Institution of India
nd./np. (Simla 1901?)
10pp.
220×148mm   CC
The paper relates to the Indian volunteer force Lumsden's Horse.

(Dawson, S. E.) (Printer) – Dept. Of Militia And Defence, Canada. Correspondence Relating To The Despatch Of Colonial Military Contingents To South Africa.
Printed By Order Of Parliament
(Canada. Parliament. Sessional Paper No. 20 & 20a.)
S. E. Dawson
Ottawa 1900
51pp.
250mm   SABIB
Two parts, paper No.20a titled – Supplementary Correspondence Respecting The Despatch Of Colonial Military Contingents To South Africa.

(Dawson, S. E.) (Printer) – Dept. Of Militia And Defence, Canada. Return Copies Of Orders In Council, General Orders, Appointments To Office, And Militia Orders Affecting The Contingents, In Connection With The Despatch Of The Colonial Military Force To South Africa.
S. E. Dawson
Ottawa 1900
107pp.
Canada. Parliament. Sessional Paper No. 49, 1900.

(Dawson, S. E.) (Printer) – Canada. Parliament. House Of Commons Select Committee On Emergency Rations. Reports Of The Select Committee Appointed To Enquire Into The Purchase Of Emergency Rations For The Use Of The Canadian Troops In South Africa, Also With Minutes Of Proceedings And Evidence And Exhibits. Printed By Order Of Parliament.
S. E. Dawson, printer
Ottawa 1900
xxxvi+287pp.   H
Parliament. H of C. Journals. Session 1900. Appendix 3.

(Dawson, S. E.) (Printer) – Sessional Paper No. 35A. Department Of Militia And Defence For The Dominion Of Canada. Supplementary Report Organization, Equipment, Despatch And Service Of The Canadian Contingents During The War In South Africa 1899–1900. Printed By Order Of Parliament.
S. E. Dawson, printer
Ottawa 1901
23+192pp. Folding maps and chart.
250mm   SABIB

———— Further Supplementary Report, 1902.
(S. E. Dawson?)
(Ottawa 1903?)
99p. With tables.
250mm   SABIB
Canada. Parliament. Sessional paper, No.35A, 1903.

Dawson (W. H.) – War Songs 1899–1900.
J. Walch & Sons/Hobart 1901
A. W. Birchall & Sons/Launceston 1901
George Robertson & Co. Pty. Ltd.
Melbourne 1901
Pagination not shown   ALH

Deane (Maj. G.) (Editor) – Diary Of Services Of The First Battalion The Royal Scots During The Boer War. Etc., See under – BURT & SONS, Printers.

Deane (M. Milles.) – Saint George And The Transvaal Dragon.
Simpkin, Marshall, Hamilton, Kent & Co.
London (1900)
viii+48pp.
Cr.8vo.   M
M. records British Museum Library copy.

De Bloch (J.) – The Transvaal War And It's Problems.
Horace Marshall & Son
London (1900)
32pp.
236×153mm   CC

De Bloch (J.) – Lord Roberts' Campaign And Its Consequences.
Horace Marshall & Son
London (1900)
47pp. With maps and a profile of the South African Railways.
250mm   SABIB

('Defender') – Sir Charles Warren And Spion Kop A Vindication.
Smith, Elder & Co.
London 1902
xiii+244pp. Frontis. and folding map.
210×140mm

De Kock (Johannes Jacobus) – The Following Is A Full And True Account Of Events Which Occurred To Me Before, During, And After The Boer Occupation Of Belmont. . .
Publisher/printer not shown
np./nd. (1901?)
23pp.
210mm   SABIB
A complaint against the Army by De Kock, a storekeeper at Belmont. Text in English and Dutch. No title page, catalogued from caption.

De La Rey (Mrs. General) – A Woman's Wanderings And Trials During The Anglo-Boer War.
T. Fisher Unwin
London 1903
v+143pp. Illustrated.
190×125mm
Account of Mrs J. E. De La Rey, wife of the Boer General. Translated by Lucy Hotz.

De La Rey (General J. H.) and Smuts (General J. C.) – Official Reports Of General J. H. De La Rey And General J. C. Smuts. Together With Other Documents Relating To The War In South Africa, Recently Received By The Boer Representatives In Europe.
Translated From The Dutch.
The New Age Press
London 1902
30pp.
8vo.   M

De La Warr (The Earl) – Some Reminiscences Of The War In South Africa.
Hurst and Blackett, Limited
London 1900
xvi+120pp.
183×123mm   p.25

Dell (Robert Edward) (Editor) – The Scapegoat: Being A Selection From A Series Of Articles Which Have Appeared In *'The Review Of The Week'* On The Case Of Sir Henry Colvile; With A Preface By The Editor.
Bickers & Son
London 1901
vi+pp.7–77
210mm   SABIB
Articles in reference to Major-General Colvile OC Ninth Division.

Demolins (Edmond) – British Colonial Policy Scientifically Vindicated By A Prominent Frenchman. Boers Or English: Who Are In The Right? Being The English Translation Of 'Boers Et Anglais: Où Est Le Droit?'
The Leadenhall Press, Ltd.
Simpkin Marshall Hamilton, Kent & Co. Ltd.
London 1900
Charles Scribner's Sons
New York (1900?)
42pp.+24pp. Publishers advertisements.
186×125mm

Dennison (C. G.) – A Fight To A Finish.
Longmans, Green & Co.
London 1904
viii+192pp. Illustrated.
196×130mm   p.57
Experiences of a colonial officer, commander of 'Dennison's Scouts'.

(Deportation) – List Of Persons Who Have Been Expelled From Or Given Free Passages From South Africa, 1900.
Pubisher/printer not shown
np./nd.
59pp.   MOD
Item from War Office Library 'Official Print'. WO. ref. – WH Loc: SA38B.

(Deportation) – Minutes Of Evidence Taken Before The South African Deportation By The Military Authorities Compensation Commission.
Publisher/printer not shown [official print]
————1901
1229pp.   MOD
From War Office Library. WO. Ref. – WH Loc: SA38A.

Deratt (V.) – A Brief Account Of The South African Situation Delivered Before The Chicago Teachers' Federation, November 25th, 1899.
Ryan & Hart, printers
Chicago (1899?)
22pp.
220mm   SABIB
Survey of South African history and the events leading to war.

Dersley (G. H.) (Photographer?) – Historic Pictures Of The War In And

Near King William's Town, South Africa, 1900 & 1901.
Printer/publisher not shown
nd./np.
120×155mm CC
48 photographs mounted one per page with descriptive letterpress laid down.

(Despatches) – Schedule Of Despatches And Recommendations For South Africa During The Command Of FM Lord Roberts From 10 Jan. 1900 To 29 Nov. 1900.
Publisher/printer not shown
——1902
67pp. MOD
Item from War Office Library. 'Official Print', WO. Ref. – WH Loc. SA23.

Dewar (Thomas F.) – With The Scottish Yeomanry Being A Reprint Somewhat Altered And Extended, Of Letters Written From South Africa During The War Of 1899–1901.
T. Buncle & Co.
Arbroath 1901
vii+198pp.
190×125mm

De Wet (Christiaan Rudolf) – Three Years War (October 1899–June 1902)
Archibald Constable and Co. Ltd.
Westminster 1902
520pp. Frontispiece and folding map.
230×145mm

De Wet (Christiaan Rudolph) – Three Years War.
Charles Scribner's Sons
New York 1902
x+448pp. Frontispiece, folding map and plans.
220mm SABIB

Diack (William) – Boer And Briton In South Africa. A Historical Sketch.
Twentieth Century Press
London (1900?)
16pp.
210mm SABIB
Pro-Boer pamphlet published during the war.

(Diamond Fields Advertiser) (Publishers) – With Kekewich At Kimberley. Being A Diary Of The Principal Events In And Around Kimberley During The Siege.
'Diamond Fields Advertiser'
Kimberley (1900)
34pp.
170mm SABIB
Covers period Oct. 14, 1899 to Feb. 15, 1900.

(Diamond Fields Advertiser Limited. The) (Publisher) – The Siege Of Kimberley 1899–1900. Special Illustrated Number Of The 'Diamond Fields Advertiser' Kimberley.
The Diamond Fields Advertiser, Limited
Kimberley nd. (1900)
164pp. Illustrated.
250×320mm
Volume containing list of defence forces.

(Diamond Fields Advertiser, Limited. The) (Publisher) – The Siege Of Kimberley 1899–1900. Special Illustrated Number Of The 'Diamond Fields Advertiser' Kimberley.
The Diamond Fields Advertiser, Limited
Kimberley nd. (1900)
80pp. Illustrated.
430×276mm
Content similar to previous item completely reset to larger format.

(Diamond Fields Advertiser Ltd. The) (Publisher) – The Diamond Fields

Advertiser Xmas Number. Sidelights On The War In Griqualand West & Bechuanaland.
The Diamond Fields Advertiser Ltd.
Kimberley, December 1900
32pp. Illustrated.

(Diary) – Diary Of The Anglo-Boer War, 11th October, 1899–31st May, 1902.
Printer/publisher not shown
Johannesburg 1902
Unpaginated
Roy.8vo. M
Journal of events during the war. The volume is interleaved with portraits of generals serving in the British Army.

(Diary) – Diary Of The Siege Of Ladysmith. 1st Battalion Manchester Regiment. 31st Oct. 1899–28th Feb. 1900.
Publisher not shown
nd. (1900?)
12pp
180mm SABIB

Dickson (W. K.-L) – The Biograph In Battle Its Story In The South African War Related With Personal Experiences.
T. Fisher Unwin
London 1901
xx+296pp. Folding panorama and other illustrations.
199×141mm p.101

Dillon (John) – Conduct Of The War In South Africa. Debate On The Kings Speech. Speech By Mr. Dillon, M.P. On Monday, February 25, And Tuesday February 26.
Wyman & Sons
London 1901
23pp.
240mm SABIB
Reprinted from 'The Parliamentary debates'. House of Commons – session 1901. Pro-Boer speeches.

Dimbleby (S.) – The Boers And The War, From The Impartial Foreigners' Point Of View. Etc.
See – S. N. D.

Dinakar (M.) – A Ballad Of The Boer War Written For The Day Of The Coronation Of Their Most Gracious Majesties The King Emperor Edward VII And Queen Alexandra; In Celebration Of The Prowess Of The British Army By M. Dinakar, Of The *Greater Marava*.
Printed at the Lakshimi Vilas Press
Ramnad 1902
23pp.
Cr.8vo. M

(D.I.S.) – The Dead Victors. A Poem Of The South African War, 1900.
Elliot Stock
London 1900
15pp.
12mo. M

(Distinguished Englishmen) – The War In South Africa. Authoritative Sketches Of The Boers.
Publisher/printer not shown
London 1899
Pagination not shown. THB

Dixon (Captain C.M.) – The Leaguer Of Ladysmith.
Eyre and Spottiswoode
London nd. (1900)
39pp. Illustrated.
238×304mm p.7

Docking (A. Shipway) – The Great Boer War 1899–1900.
Greening & Co. Ltd.

London 1902
viii+pp.9–150
197×130mm GC
Poems of the war. Contents include The march from Glencoe, Battle of Colenso, Kimberley relieved, etc.

Doke (J. J.) – M. K. Gandhi An Indian Patriot In South Africa.
The London Indian Chronicle
Ilford 1909
vii+97pp. With portrait.
220×140mm
Reference to Gandhi in the South African conflict.

(Dominion Company, The) (Publisher) – Glimpses Of South Africa In Peace And In War.
The Dominion Company
Chicago 1900
Unpaginated. (18 issues of 16pp., each with limp card cover)
232×307mm CC
A pictorial record of the country and the present war published weekly from Jan. 10–May 9, 1900. Parts 1–18, with descriptive letterpress throughout.

Dooner (Mildred G.) – The Last Post: Being A Roll Of All Officers (Naval, Military Or Colonial) Who Gave Their Lives For Their Queen, King And Country, In The South African War, 1899–1902.
Simpkin, Marshall, Hamilton, Kent & Co., Ltd.
London nd. (1903)
viii+446pp. With frontispiece.
228×147mm p.61

Dorman (George L.) – Letters From South Africa.
William Rapp & Sons, printers
Saltburn-By-The-Sea. nd. (c.1902)
vi+260pp. Illustrated.
229×150mm
Letters written by Lieut. George Dorman during the war. Author died at Kroonstad on 30th March 1901. Illustrations include some hand coloured plates.

Dormer (Francis J.) – Vengeance As A Policy In Afrikanderland A Plea For A New Departure.
James Nisbet & Co. Limited
London 1901
xl+244pp.
230×150mm

Doughty (Charles) – Under Arms 1900.
Army & Navy Co-operative Society, printers
London (c.1900)
30+1pp.
220mm SABIB
Poems regarding British troops in South Africa.

Doyle (Sir Arthur Conan) – The Great Boer War. (Complete Ed. 18th Imp.)
Smith, Elder, & Co.
London 1902
x+769pp. With maps.
210×132mm
A volume published in various editions/ impressions between 1900–1903. Over twenty printings listed in SABIB including Tauchnitz 2 vol. Ed. Leipzig 1900.

Doyle (Sir Arthur Conan) – The War In South Africa Its Cause And Conduct.
Smith, Elder & Co.
London 1902
vii+pp.9–156
213×140mm

Doyle (Sir Arthur Conan) – The War In South Africa Its Cause And Conduct.

McClure, Phillips & Co.
New York 1902
iv+140pp.
215×145mm

Doyle (Sir Arthur Conan) – The War In South Africa Its Cause And Conduct.
Bernhard Tauchnitz
Leipzig 1902
271pp.
160mm   SABIB

Drage (Geoffrey) – The Grievances Of British Subjects In The Transvaal. Speech On The Address To The Throne. By Mr. Drage, M.P. House Of Commons, October 17, 1899.
Imperial South African Association
London 1899
16pp.
Cr.8vo.   M

Drage (G.) – Real Causes Of The War, And Some Of The Elements Of The Final Settlement. Speech At The Drill Hall, Derby, 7th December 1899.
Imperial South African Association
London 1899
16pp.
220mm   SABIB

Drage (G.) – South Africa Speeches In The House Of Commons, October 17th 1899, And At The Drill Hall, Derby, December 7th 1899.
Imperial South African Association
London nd. (1899)
28pp.
215×140mm

Du Cane (Colonel Hubert) (Translator) – The War In South Africa The Advance To Pretoria After Paardeberg, The Upper Tugela Campaign, Etc. Prepared In The Historical Section Of The Great General Staff, Berlin.
John Murray
London 1906
viii+iii+374pp. Folding map and plates.
225×145mm
See also – Waters, Col. W. H. H.

Duff (Beauchamp) – What Is Now Being Done In South Africa, Etc. See – MILWARD (Victor.)

Dulles (Allen Welsh) – The Boer War: A History.
Beresford (Printer)
Washington 1902
31pp.
150mm   SABIB/H
For private circulation (3rd. Ed.). Said to be the work of a boy eight years of age.

Dulles (Allen Welsh) – The Boer War: A History.
John W. Foster
Washington 1902
33pp.
150mm   SABIB
Copy of the 4th Ed.

Dumaresq (Capt.) – Report On Searchlight Equipment. Etc.
See WO. 124.

Du Moulin (Lieut.-Col. E.) – Two Years On Trek Being Some Account Of The Royal Sussex Regiment In South Africa.
Murray And Co.
London 1907
vi+323+xipp. Various maps.
222×145mm
A paper covered edition for N.C.O.'s and men was published without the maps – 215×145mm.

Dunn (Joseph Smith) (Publisher/printer) – (Johannesburg. Military Commissioner Of Police.) Official Handbook For The Guidance Of Civilians Returning To The Rand Under Martial Law. Issued Monthly. October 1900.
Joseph Smith Dunn
Johannesburg 1900
iii+16 leaves. Folding plans.
250mm   SABIB
V.R. Issued by authority. Military occupation of Johannesburg.

E

Earle (W.) – Five Patriot Songs To Be Sold For The Benefit Of The 'Officers Widows, Wives, & Families' Fund.
A. J. Lawrence
Rugby 1900
13pp.
192×135mm   CC

(East Surrey Regt.) – 2nd Battalion. Digest Of Services In South Africa.
Lucknow, nd.
(No other details)
Listed under military histories, records. Etc. in THB.

(Ecclesiasticus Anglicanus) – The War: A Message From The Church. Part Criticism Of A Sermon By The Rev. Canon Newbolt, M.A., Preached In St. Paul's Cathedral, Third Sunday In Advent, 1899.
The Peace Society
London 1900
16pp.
190mm   SABIB

Edmonds (Maj. J. E.) – Military Retrospect Of The War In South Africa, Etc. See WO. 11.

Edmondson (Joseph) – The Judge, The Policeman, And The Soldier.
Simpkin, Marshall, Hamilton, Kent & Co. Ltd./West, Newman & Co.
London 1902
22pp.
8vo.   M
Political comment in reference to the war.

(Edwards. Dennis & Co.) (Publishers) – The Anglo-Boer War. An Album From The Most Authentic Sources, Photographs And Sketches With Brief Descriptions, Diary, Etc. Illustrating The Chief Events, Battlefields, Episodes, Forces, And Salient Features Of The Struggle For British Supremacy In South Africa.
Dennis Edwards & Co.
Cape Town (1900)
192pp. Illustrated.
250×320mm   SABIB
12 parts with original covers.

(Edwards. Dennis & Co.) (Publishers) – The Anglo-Boer War, 1899–1900. An Album Of Upwards Of Three Hundred Photographic Engravings. A Picture Record Of The Movements Of The British, Colonial, And Boer Forces Engaged In The Conflict.
Dennis Edwards & Co.
Cape Town nd. (c.1901)
iv+200+xxi+iiipp. Illustrated throughout.
252×312mm   p.29

(Edwards. Dennis & Co.) (Publishers) – The Anglo-Boer War, October 11th, 1899 –May 31st, 1902. An Album Of Upwards Of Five Hundred Photographic Engravings. A Picture Record Of The Movements Of The British, Colonial,

And Boer Forces Engaged In The Conflict.
Dennis Edwards & Co.
Cape Town nd. (c.1902)
vi+260+xxi+iiipp. Illustrated throughout.
251×311mm   CC

Edwards (Captain E. L. P.) (Compiled by) – A Continuation From 1881 To 1913 Of Lieutenant-Colonel William Starke's Short History Of The East Yorkshire Regiment.
np. (Aldershot 1913)
vii+60pp.
185×125mm

Edwards (Neville Perrin) – The Transvaal In War And Peace.
H. Virtue & Co.
London 1899–1900
384pp. Illustrated.
280mm   SABIB
12 parts in original wraps. Title from cover.

Edwards (Neville) – The Transvaal In War And Peace.
H. Virtue & Co.
London 1900
iv+384pp. Illustrated throughout.
275×220mm

Edwards (Captain R. F.) (Editor) – Professional Papers Of The Corps Of Royal Engineers. Royal Engineers Institute Occasional Papers.
Vol. XXVI. 1900.
W. & J. Mackay & Co., Ltd. (Printers)
Chatham 1900
v+234pp. Folding plates, maps and charts.
220×145mm
*Papers include – 'Siege of Kimberley. Official Report' with 16 folding charts, and 'Lists of Service Ordnance with Guns, Ammunition, Carriages and Slides. Corrected to June 1900.'
See entry under MOORE (Major A. T.) Editor.*

Edwards (Captain R. F.) (Editor) – Professional Papers Of The Corps Of Royal Engineers. Royal Engineers Institute Occasional Papers. Vol. XXVII 1901.
W. & J. Mackay & Co., Ltd. (Printers)
Chatham 1901
vii+233pp. Folding plates and charts.
220×145mm
Papers include – 'The work of The Royal Engineers in Natal'. With 11 folding charts.

Egersdörfer (H.) – Book of Fifty Famous Cartoons, Etc. See – SOUTH AFRICAN REVIEW, The.

Elcum (Charles Cunningham) – 'Richardson, V.C.'.
Printer/Publisher not shown
Liverpool nd. (c.1901)
8pp.
210mm   SABIB
Text, in verse, describes the action in which Sergt. Richardson of Strathcona's Horse won the V.C. Text signed: C.C. Elcum, Liverpool, March 5th, 1901. No title page. Title from caption.

Elliot (J. A. G.) – Campaigning In South Africa 1900–1901. See Entry Under MOUNTED BLACK.

Ellis (John Edward) – Speeches On South African Affairs.
Printer/Publisher not shown
London 1900
41pp. Portrait frontispiece.
220mm   SABIB
Author advocates a policy of appeasement.

Ente (Jacob Smeltzer) – How Ladysmith Was Relieved, By A Member Of The Escort To Lieut.-Gen. Sir Charles Warren. Collated From Letters To His Father.
The Author?
Natal (c.1900)
15pp.
210mm   SABIB
Printed for private circulation only. The author was one of 25 scouts providing a bodyguard to General Warren on the expedition to relieve Ladysmith. The account covers the period Nov. 23, 1899, to March 9, 1900. No title page. Title from caption.

Etchegoyen (Olivier d') – Ten Months In The Field With The Boers, Etc. See – EX-LIEUTENANT.

Evans (W. Sanford) – The Canadian Contingents And Canadian Imperialism. A Story And A Study.
T. Fisher Unwin
London 1901
xii+352pp. Maps and illustrations.
208×138mm   p.39
Canadian edition – The Publishers' Syndicate Ltd. Toronto 1901.
xii+352pp. Illustrated.

Evans-Gordon (Major W.) – The Cabinet And The War.
Archibald Constable & Co., Ltd.
London 1904
vii+216pp.
Cr.8vo.   M
A criticism of the 'Cabinet System' with regard to its control and administration of the forces of the empire. Listed under GORDON in M.

Everett (Marshall) (Editor) – Thrilling Experiences In The War In South Africa. Edited By Marshall Everett, The Greatest Descriptive Writer The World Has Ever Known. Including The Official History Of The British-Boer War, As Told By The Commanders. Thrilling Stories Of Bravery, Exciting Personal Experiences, Wonderful Descriptions Of Desperate Battles. Illustrated With Nearly 500 Half Tone Photographs, Each Picture Graphically Explained By Wymble Flemming, A Native Of Africa. To Which Is Added The Life Of Cecil Rhodes, The Wonderful Career Of Paul Kruger, And A Complete History Of The Transvaal, The History Of South Africa, The Diamond Mines And The Gold Fields. The Cartoons Of The War Explained.
The Educational Company
Chicago, Ill. 1900
404pp. Illustrated.
240×310mm
SABIB names editor as Henry Neil. A copy of 306pp. listed.

Exham (Col. R.) – Experiences Of The British Army Medical Services In The War In South Africa.
Publisher/printer not shown
np. 1903
12pp. Plates.
Item from WO. Cat./1912.

(Exile) (And Others) – Rhodes Triumphant! Englands Future Premier. Notes And Letters On The War.
Publisher not shown
Cape Town (c.1900)
14pp.
240mm   SABIB
For private circulation only. Mainly letters written to the 'South African News' and the 'Cape Argus' on the political situation, critical of Cecil Rhodes. No title page. Catalogued from cover.

(Ex-Lieutenant) – Ten Months In The Field With The Boers By An Ex-Lieutenant Of General de Villebois-Mareuil.
William Heinemann
London 1901
v+248pp. Frontispiece and folding map.
195×130mm   p.23
Author – Olivier d'Etchegoyen.

(Exoriar) – Fatal Imperialism. By Exoriar.
Watts & Co.
London 1902
40pp.
8vo.   M
An attack on imperialism, the British Government of the day, and Sir Alfred Milner.

('Express' Printing Works) (Printers) – Orange Free State. Correspondence Between His Honour The State President And His Exc. The High Commissioner On The Placing Of Troops On The Borders Of The Republics, Etc.
'Express' Printing Works
Bloemfontein nd. (1899)
pp.1–20+1–18
330×205mm
Paper covered document in Dutch (pp.1-20) and English (pp.1-18), being a reproduction of 21 telegrams passed between the representatives of the British Government and The Orange Free State from Sept. 19 to Oct. 9. (1899).

Eyre-Lloyd (Capt. T. H.) – Boer War. Diary Of Captain Eyre Lloyd. Etc. – See entry under LLOYD (T. H. EYRE.)

(Eyre & Spottiswoode) (Printers) – The Border Regiment In South Africa 1899–1902 From Photographs By Officers Of The Regiment.
Eyre & Spottiswoode, printers
London nd. (c.1902)
Unpaginated. (66 printed rectos.)
220×142mm   p.52
Pictorial record of the regiment in South Africa, 128 photographs with captions.

(Eyre & Spottiswoode) (Printers) – A Form Of Intercession With Almighty God, On Behalf Of Her Majesty's Naval And Military Forces Now In South Africa, To Be Used In All Churches And Chapels In England And Wales, And In The Town Of Berwick-Upon-Tweed On Such Occasions As Each Bishop Shall Appoint For His Own Diocese.
Eyre & Spottiswoode, printers
London 1900
32pp.
206×164mm

F

F. (A. W.) – The Present Phase Of The Boer War.
Langley & Sons (printers)
London (c.1900)
12pp.
210mm   SABIB
Pro-Boer pamphlet. No title page. Catalogued from caption.

Fairbairn (John) – Report Of The Cape Of Good Hope Society For Aid To Sick And Wounded In War.
Richards
Cape Town (1902)
Pagination not shown   THB

Fairchild (F. R.) – The Financing Of The South African War.
(King?)
No other information   THB

Fairholme (Maj. W. E.) – Lines Of Communication, Cape Colony. Etc.
See WO. 115.

Farr (H.) – Letters From South Africa 1900–1901. Printed For Private Circulation.
J.W. Moore (Printer)
Chichester nd. (c.1902)
106pp. With a diagram.
185×125mm   HC   p.33

Farrelly (M. J.) – Our Hold On South Africa After The War.
J. J. Keliher & Co.
London (c.1900)
12pp.
250mm   SABIB

Farrelly (M. J.) – The Settlement After The War In South Africa.
Macmillan & Co.
London 1900
xv+321pp.
230×145mm

Farrelly (M. J.) – The Settlement After The War In South Africa.
J. C. Juta
Cape Town 1900
xv+321pp.
220mm   SABIB

Farren (George) – An Address On The Transvaal War, Delivered At Trevor On Tuesday The 5th June 1900.
Tom Litherland (Printer)
Carnarvon 1900
38pp.
12mo.   M

Ferrar (Major M. L.) – With The Green Howards In South Africa 1899–1902.
Eden Fisher & Co., Ltd.
London 1904
v+199pp. Illustrated.
190×128mm
War record of 1st Batt. Alexandra Princess of Wales's Own Yorkshire Regiment.

Ferryman (Lieut-Colonel A. F. Mockler-) (Editor) – The Oxfordshire Light Infantry In South Africa.
See MOCKLER-FERRYMAN.

Fiebeger (Gustave J.) – The British-Boer War, 1899–1902.
Printer/publisher not shown
(West Point, nd.)
18pp. with map.
240mm   H

(Field Intelligence Department)

Notes On The Country To The East And North Of Pretoria Compiled From Local Information.
Field Intelligence Dept.
Pretoria (1900)
20pp.   MOD
WH Loc: Rte Bks.

Appendix To Notes On The Country To The East And North Of Pretoria.
Field Intelligence Dept.
Pretoria (1900)
48pp.   MOD
WH Loc: Rte Bks.
A list of property owners in districts near Pretoria.

Appendix No. 1 To Notes On The Country To The East And North Of Pretoria: List Of Farms And Their Owners Within 10 Miles Of The Railway Lines From Pretoria. Aug. 1900.
Field Intelligence Dept.
Pretoria 1900
46pp.   MOD
WH Loc: Rte Bks.

Appendix No.1(A) To Notes On The Country To The East And North Of Pretoria. List Of Farms And Their Owners (a) Ten Miles On Either Side Of The Machadadorp-Lydenburg-Ohrigstadt Route (b) Carolina District, East Of Machadodorp And Between Railway And The Komati River.
Field Intelligence Dept.
Pretoria 1900
24pp.
210mm   SABIB
Imperial Printing Works/Johannesburg, printed on cover.

Appendix No. 2 To Notes On Country To The North And East Of Pretoria.
(Field Intelligence Dept.?)
(Pretoria 1900)
49pp.
210mm   SABIB
Date from preface signed by Capt. H. Yarde Buller. D.A.A.G. Intelligence, Pretoria. Nov. 30, 1900.
MOD library lists a copy of – Appendix No. 2 To Notes On The Country To The East And North Of Pretoria, nd./15pp. Ref. WH Loc: Rte Bks.

Appendix No. 3 To Notes On The Country To The East And North Of Pretoria. Routes In The Country North And East Of Lydenburg And Pietersburg.
Field Intelligence Dept.
Pretoria 1900
1+1+21pp. (Supplement to Appendix No.3)
210mm   SABIB

Boer Army List. Orange River Colony, Transvaal And Cape Colony, November 20th, 1901.
Field Intelligence Dept.
nd./np. (1901?)
iii+99 leaves.
330mm   SABIB
Lacks title page. Title made up from captions and half titles in text.

Confidential. Boer Army List. Cape Colony District. November 30, 1901.
C. Ross Capt. D.A.A.G. Intelligence.
Capetown 1901
37 numbered rectos + 2pp.
161×103mm   p.3
Blank pages provided for corrections and additions.

Boer Army List. Cape Colony District.
March 31st, 1902.
F.I.D.
Cape Town 1902
xii+152pp. (With some photographs pasted down.)
160mm   SABIB
Cover marked Confidential The volume contains blank pages for corrections and additions.

Districts, Towns, Villages, Railway Stations, Sidings, Post And Telegraph Offices In Cape Colony. Issued By Intelligence Department.
F.I.D.
Cape Town 1901
1+1, xvii+174pp.
140×100mm   SABIB
Cover title – Cape Colony Directory.

Directory Of Districts, Towns, Villages, Railway Stations, Sidings, Post And Telegraph Offices In Cape Colony.
(Compiled and published by Capt. P. H. du P. Casgrain. R.E., D.A.A.G.I. Mapping Section F.I.D. Cape Town.)
F.I.D.
Cape Town 1902
2+1,xv,127pp.+1 leaf.
170×100mm   SABIB
Cover title – Cape Colony Directory.

Dutch Phrase-Book And Vocabulary. Compiled For The Intelligence Department. See CAMPBELL, Capt. A. N.

Farm List, O.R.C., By Districts.
Published By F.I.D. Etc. See – ARGUS P.&P. Co. (Printers)

Intelligence Organisation And Administration (South Africa). Revised Instructions. May, 1901.
Government Printing Works.
Pretoria 1901
1+1,17+12pp. Two folding maps.
210mm   SABIB
No title page. Catalogued from cover.

Intelligence Organisation And Administration (South Africa) Revised Instructions, August 1901.
(Field Intelligence Dept.?)
————1901
43pp. With maps. MOD
WH Loc: 6C4.

List Of Burghers Entitled To Vote For Members Of The First And Second Volksraads.
Government Printing Works
Pretoria 1900
3 vols. listed.
330mm   SABIB
On cover: – Intelligence Dept.
Pretoria ward – Krugersdorp district.
– Zoutpansberg district. Catalogued from cover.

List Of Burghers Entitled To Vote For Members Of The First Volksraad And Also Entitled To Vote In Elections Which Affect The Whole Republic, The Ward, Or The Voting Division.
Government Printing Works
Pretoria 1900
18 vols. listed.
330mm   SABIB
On cover: Intelligence Dept. Pretoria district – Bethal – Bloemhof – Carolina – Ermelo – Lydenburg – Lichtenburg – Marico – Middelburg – Piet Retief – Potchefstroom – Rustenburg – Standerton – Utrecht – Vryheid – Wakkerstroom – Waterberg – Wolmaranstad.
No title page. Catalogued from cover.

List Of Burghers Of The Orange Free State Who Have Taken The 'Oath' To The Transvaal Government...
Government Printing Works
Pretoria 1900
4pp.   SABIB
No title page. Catalogued from cover.

List Of Burghers Who Have Surrendered Their Arms In The Transvaal And Orange Free State.
Government Printing Works
Pretoria 1900
ii+83pp.   SABIB

List Of Farmers And Others In The Colony Of The Cape Of Good Hope Who Have Been Absent From Their Farms, &c., During A Portion, Or The Whole, Of The War, And Who Are Suspected Of Having Joined The Enemy.
Government Printing Works
Pretoria 1901
28pp.
330mm   SABIB
Catalogued from cover.

List Of Farms In The . . . Transvaal, With The Names Of Their Registered Owners.
Government Printing Works
Pretoria 1900–1901
(22 vols. listed, Pagination where shown taken from M.:–
330mm   SABIB
Bethal (1900) – Bloemhof (1901) – Carolina (1900) – Ermelo (1901)(9pp.) – Heidelberg (1900) – Krugersdorp 1900) – Lichtenburg (1901) – Lydenburg (1900) – Mapochs Gronden (1901) – Marico (1901) – Middelburg (1900) – Piet Retief (1901)(8pp.) – Potchefstroom (1900) –

Pretoria (1900) – Rustenburg (1901) – Standerton (1901) – Utrecht (1901)(9pp.) – Vryheid (1901)(16pp.) – Wakkerstroom (1901) – Waterberg (1901) – Wolmaransstad (1900) – Zoutpansberg (1901)
No title page. Catalogued from cover.

List Of Germans, Frenchmen, &c., Other Than British Subjects, Who Have Taken The Oath Of Allegiance To The Transvaal Government.
Government Printing Works
Pretoria 1900
11pp.
180mm   SABIB
Catalogued from cover.

Names Of British Subjects Who Have Taken The 'Oath' To The Transvaal Government Since War Commenced.
Government Printing Works
Pretoria 1900
22pp.
330mm   SABIB
Appendix 1p. Appendix 11, 1p.

Naturalised Burghers Of The South African Republic Who Have Taken Full Burgher Rights Since War Commenced. (Cover title)
Government Printing Works
Pretoria 1900
4pp.
330mm   SABIB

Routes In The Northern Portion Of The Orange River Colony. Compiled In The Field Intelligence Dept. S.A.F.F.
Imperial Printing Works
Johannesburg 1900
ii+41pp.
210mm   SABIB
MOD Library lists copy of above title published Pretoria 1900. 41pp. Ref:– WH Loc: Rte Bks.

South African Almanac, October 1900–September 1901. Compiled In The Field Intelligence Department, Cape Town. Calculations Made At The Royal Observatory, Cape Town.
Argus Printing and Publishing Co.
Cape Town 1900
28pp. Map, tables, diagrams.
150mm   SABIB

South African Almanac, October 1901–September 1902. Compiled In The Field Intelligence Department, Cape Town.
Argus Printing and Publishing Co.
Cape Town 1901
28pp. Illustrated.
150mm   SABIB

Subjects Of European Nations (Other Than British Subjects) Who Have Taken Full Burgher Rights Under The Transvaal Government Since The Commencement Of War Arranged Under Their Different Nationalities.
Government Printing Works
(Pretoria 1900?)
ii+16pp.
330mm   SABIB

List Of Officers Serving With Mounted Infantry In South Africa Pretoria 1901.
Government Printing Works
Pretoria (1901?)
vii+33pp.

List Of Officers Serving With The Mounted Infantry In South Africa.
Military Intelligence Dept.
Pretoria 1902
vii+35pp.   MOD
Item from War Office Library. WO. Ref:– WH Loc: Camps Boer.

Boer Army List, Nov. 1901 [With MSS Amendments.]

Directorate Of Military Intelligence, Army HQ.
Pretoria 1901
99pp.   MOD
WO. Ref:– WH Loc: SA59.

HQ And Command Staff Of The Boer Army, Revised To Jan. 1902.
Intelligence Department?
Newcastle 1902
11pp.

(Fifeshire Advertiser) (Publishers) – The Kirkcaldy War Album Containing Portraits Of Over Two Hundred Fife Men Serving In South Africa And Groups And Views Connected With The War.
Fifeshire Advertiser (Publishers)
Kirkcaldy 1901
64pp. Illustrated.
283×223mm   p.75

Fisher (Sydney G.) – The American Revolution And The Boer War. An Open Letter To Mr. Charles Francis Adams On His Pamphlet *'The Confederacy And The Transvaal'*.
George H. Buchanan. (Printer)
Philadelphia 1902
33pp.
230×150mm
Reprinted from the 'Philadelphia Sunday Times' of January 19, 1902. A copy of the 2nd ed.

Fitzgibbon (Maurice) – Arts Under Arms An University Man In Khaki.
Longmans, Green, And Co.
London 1901
xii+232pp. Illustrated.
195×130mm

Fitzpatrick (J. P.) – The Transvaal From Within A Private Record Of Public Affairs.
William Heinemann
London 1899
xiv+452pp.
230×145mm
Not a war book but an important reference to Transvaal politics in the years preceding war.

Fleischer (F.) – September 15th, A Day Of Tears, Not Only In South Africa.
J. H. Keizer
Noord-Scharwoude 1901
15pp.
220mm   SABIB
Reference to Lord Kitchener's proclamation threatening banishment of Boers who had not surrendered by 15th Sept. 1901. Published on behalf of the International Boer Women and Children's Distress Fund.

Fleming (Major A. D.) – Record Of The First Volunteer Service Company The Royal Warwickshire Regiment In South Africa, 1900–1901.
The Midland Counties Herald Limited
Birmingham 1907
vi+66+iipp. Coloured map and illustrations.
255×181mm   p.77

Fleming (Rev. Canon.) – Weeping For The Slain. Sermon At St. Michael's, Chester Square, On Feb. 11, 1900.
Entered from M. Ref:– De Bussy's African Catalogue, 1900.

Fleming (Mrs. Robert) – 'Following The Drum'.
Soldiers' Home
Pietermaritzburg 1903
22pp. Illustrated.
191×105mm   RCSL

Flemming (Wymble) – Glimpses Of South Africa In Peace And War. Illustrating And Describing, By Camera And Pen, The Entire South African Continent And Transpiring Events Of The British-Boer War From The Cape To The Front.
Publisher/printer not shown
nd. (Chicago 1902?)
Unpaginated (272pp.)
236×305mm
A collection of illustrations of South Africa and the South African War, 1899–1902, reproduced from a variety of sources, with letterpress.

Fletcher-Vane (Francis P.) – Pax Britannica In South Africa.
Archibald Constable & Co. Ltd.
London 1905
xvi+388pp. Map and plates.
230×148mm

Fletcher-Vane (Francis P.) – The War And One Year After. Containing Reports Made By An Imperial Officer To The Colonial Office Respecting Farm Burning, The Arming Of Natives, Martial Law Mal-Administration, And A Reprint Of The *'Contemporary Review'* Article, Called *'The Fruits Of The War'*.
South African Newspaper Co.
Cape Town 1903
44pp.
220mm   SABIB

Flower (Richard Fordham) – Richard Fordham Flower. See under FOX (Edward) Printer.

Fluck (Arthur W.) – Transvaal Crisis. Some Truth About The Transvaal.
Woolridge
London (1899?)
12pp.
220mm   SABIB
Reference to war as imminent.

Ford (R.) – The Supply Park In The Advance From Orange River, Via Jacobsdal, Bloemfontein, Pretoria, To Komati Poort, By Captain R. Ford, A.S.C. (Late Major S.A.F.F.), O.C. Supply Park.
Army Service Corps Printing Office
Aldershot nd. (c.1900)
16pp.
210mm   · SABIB
Relates to the transportation of army supplies by ox-wagons.

Forestier-Walker (Lt. Gen. Frederick) – Report On Lines Of Communication. See WO. 95.

Fortey (William S.) (Publisher?) – The War Songster, Containing A Collection Of Patriotic And Popular Songs.
William S. Fortey
London (1900?)
32pp.
8vo.   M
Ref. BM Library.

Foster (R. Adams) – 'Thankful Tommy'.
Dean & Son
London nd. (c.1900)
16pp. Illustrated.
137×220mm   DC
An illustrated poem, a reply to 'The Absent-Minded Beggar'. Card cover.

Foster (Sir Walter M.P.) – The Care Of The Sick And Wounded In South Africa. A Speech Delivered By Sir Walter Foster, M.P., In The House Of Commons, On February 15th, 1901.
The Liberal Publication Department
London 1901
12pp.
223×136mm

Fourie (Hendrik Willem) – An Afrikander's Appeal To Afrikanders To Assist In Bringing About Peace In South Africa.
'De Kolonist' Office, printers
Cape Town 1902
23pp.
215×140mm

Fowler (Sir Henry) – The Right Hon. Sir Henry Fowler, G.C.S.I., M.P., On The War In South Africa. Report Of A Speech Delivered On February 16th, At The Mayoral Banquet To Service Volunteers For South Africa, At The Town Hall, Wolverhampton.
John Heywood
Manchester and London 1900
15pp.
8vo.   M

Fowler (Henry H.) – Sir Henry H. Fowler On The South African Question: Extracts From A Speech Delivered At Wolverhampton On April 19th, 1900.
Field, Pearson (Printers)
(London 1900?)
8pp.
220mm   SABIB
Imperial Liberal Council, pamphlet no. 3.

(Fox. Edward) Printer) – Richard Fordham Flower.
Edward Fox, printer
Stratford-On-Avon
nd. (c.1900)
iii+43pp. Portraits.
255×140mm   DC
Memoir of Lieut. Flower of the Warwickshire Company I.Y., killed in action at Haman's Kraal, August 20th, 1900.

Frazer (Rev. W. H.) – Lectures On *'Experiences In South Africa During The War'* By Rev. W.H. Frazer D. D., Late Acting-Chaplain To The Forces. Being A Paper Read Before The Victoria Institute.
Publisher/printer not shown
(London 1903)
12pp.
8vo.   M

('Free Briton') – Mr. Chamberlain Against England. A Record Of His Proceedings. By Free Briton.
Watts & Co.
London (1900?)
56pp.
8vo.   M
An attack on Mr. Chamberlain's policy in regard to the Dutch Republics in South Africa.

Fremantle (Francis E.) – Impressions Of A Doctor In Khaki.
John Murray
London 1901
xvi+549pp. Illustrated.
208×135mm   p.89

French (Lt. Gen. J. D. P.) – Report On The Organisation And Equipment Of Cavalry, Etc. See WO. 56.

Freshney (Tpr. Fred A.) – My Experiences In The South African War, 1899–1900.
Gazette and Echo Printing Works
Lincoln nd. (1902)
44pp. Portrait.
184×124mm   p.79

(Friend The) (Edited By The War Correspondents With Lord Roberts' Force) – 'The Friend' a newspaper published for an army in the field. 27 issues were produced at Bloemfontein between March 16 and April 16, 1900, prior to the enterprise being turned over to the proprietors of the 'Johannesburg Star'. The editorial team included Messrs. Julian Ralph. H. A. Gwynne, Perceval Landon And F.W. Buxton. Folio.

Froes (T.) – Expelled From The Randt. Notes Before And After Leaving Johannesburg, With Experiences At Delagoa Bay. Dedicated To The Many Thousands Of Refugees From The Golden City.
Wm. Taylor
Cape Town 1899
32pp.
8vo.   M

Froes (T.) – The Destruction Of Johannesburg, The Revenge Of The Defeated Boer. A Forecast, On The Authority Of Transvaal Officialdom.
The Colonial Publishing Co.
Cape Town 1900
8pp. With cartoon.
8vo.   M

(Frowde. Henry) (Publisher) – The Marked New Testament.
Henry Frowde
London 1900
362pp.
8vo.   W/L 487
Bible for troops serving in South Africa. Red cloth binding blocked in gilt. 'South Africa 1900'.

Furley (Sir John) – In Peace And War (The Red Cross In South Africa.)
Publisher/printer not shown
London 1905
Pagination not shown.
                                    THB
Possible Boer war content?

G

Gage (Captain M. F.) (Editor) – Records Of The Dorset Imperial Yeomanry. 1894–1905.
F. Bennett
Sherborne 1906
v+iv+265pp. Map and illustrations.
225×175mm   p.vi
The volume includes a number of coloured plates of uniform not present in the cheap edition.

Gale (George) – The Exploitation Of The British Flag By Rhodes, Chamberlain, Milner & Co.
J. H. Wigglesworth, printer
Leeds (c.1902)
36pp.
220mm   SABIB
Anti-war pamphlet censuring British policy and the war in South Africa.

(Gale & Polden Ltd.) (Printers) – 2nd Battalion Worcestershire Regiment.
Gale & Polden Ltd.
Aldershot nd. (c.1902)
9pp. (Unnumbered) Illustrated.
104×131mm   DC
Card covered souvenir of the 2nd Batt. Worcestershire Regt. in South Africa from Jan. 1900 to the proclamation of peace in 1902. The letterpress records the campaign in the Orange Free State and Transvaal divided into four periods, with a coloured map present for each section. Three sections open out to a page size of 190×125mm. The publication includes some monochrome vignette illustrations.

(Gale & Polden) (Publishers) – A Handbook Of The Boer War.
Gale And Polden Limited

London and Aldershot 1910
viii+377pp. With maps & plans.
188×128mm

Gallagher (Michael) – Mick Gallagher At The Front.
John Richardson & Sons (Printers) for Mac's Sugar-House Press
Liverpool (1900)
51pp.
234×148mm   CC
Letters written from South Africa by private M. Gallagher, an employee at Macfie and Sons, Sugar-House, Liverpool. The author served in the Fifth (Irish) Volunteer Battalion of The King's Liverpool Regiment during the war. The publication is edited by R. A. Scott Macfie, who wrote the introduction dated Oct. 1900. An edition of 500 copies.

Gallwey (Col. T. J.) – Medical Report, The Campaign In Natal.
See WO. 100.

Galvayne (Sydney) – War Horses Present And Future; Or, Remount Life In South Africa.
R. A. Everett & Co.
London 1902
202pp.
188×126mm   CC   p.55

Garnier (Jules) – England's Enemies: A Warning.
W. R. Russell
London 1900
4+1+118pp.
190mm   SABIB
A pro-British analysis of the causes and events leading up to war.

Garrett (Daisy) – Daisy's Diary. Kimberley. October 15th, 1899–February 15th, 1900. For Private Circulation.
Printer/Publisher not shown
nd. (c.1900)
16pp.
160mm   SABIB
A letter in diary form, describing daily life in besieged Kimberley. No title page. Catalogued from cover.

Garrish (A. G.) – The Records Of 'I' Company. A Brief History Of The East Surrey Volunteers' Service In The South African War.
Walbrook & Co., Limited
London 1901
xvi+103pp. Folding map and illustrations.
222×145mm   p.90

Gaselee (Brig. Gen. Alfred) – Scheme For An Indian Contingent, Etc.
See WO. 34.

Gaskell (H. S.) – With Lord Methuen In South Africa February 1900 To June 1901 Being Some Notes On The War With Extracts From Letters And Diaries.
Henry J. Drane
London 1906
ii+349pp.
185×128mm

Gaskill (W. & Co.) – Boer Version Of The South African War. Comprising: An Authentic Translation Into English Of All The Boer Official Telegrams Issued At Vryheid Throughout The War.
W. Gaskill & Co.
London (1902)
ii+95pp.
221×144mm   CC
Second edition.

(Gentlewoman. The) (Publisher) – The Theatre Of War Described & Illustrated.

Alex J. Warden for 'The Gentlewoman' Ltd.
London (1900?)
64pp. Map and illustrations.
207×291mm   CC

Gilbert (Sharrad H.) – Rhodesia – And After Being The Story Of The 17th And 18th Battalions Of Imperial Yeomanry In South Africa.
Simpkin Marshall, Hamilton, Kent & Co., Ltd.
London 1901
350pp. Mounted frontispiece, folding maps and illustrations.
210×138mm   p.89

Gildea (Col. J.) (Compiled by) – For King And Country Being A Record Of Funds And Philanthropic Work In Connection With The South African War 1899–1902.
Eyre & Spottiswoode
London 1902
xviii+198pp.
314×252mm
A detailed record of funds received by various organizations during the South African War with reference to distribution and expenditure.

Gildea (Colonel Sir James) – For Remembrance And In Honour Of Those Who Lost Their Lives In The South African War 1899–1902 Lest We Forget.
Printed by Eyre and Spottiswoode, Ltd.
London 1911
xv+429pp Illustrated
313×252mm   p.67

Gill (W. H.) – On The Transvaal Border: An Album Of Fifty Fully Described War Pictures From Photographs Taken Mainly On The Boer Side By A Resident In The Orange Free State During The Campaign.
W. H. Gill (Published by?)
London (1900)
25pp.
Small folio   M
50 captioned photographs on 13 plates. No title page. Catalogued from cover. THB lists publishers – Marion & Co. London, 1900.

Gillet (N. J.) (Publisher/Printer?) – With Methuen To Kimberley. The Advance Reviewed By An Eye-Witness. President Steyn's Villany Unmasked By The Boers. Receives £50,000 Blood Money. Afrikander Bond As An Ally. Free Staters Demoralised To The Point Of Mutiny. Confessions Of A C.M.R., A Gunner In The Boer Ranks. The End Of The War At Hand. Deserting *En Masse* By Free State Boers Headed By Their Fighting General. Life In The Boer Camp. Boer General Refuses To Storm Kimberley. Boers Refuse To Believe That Lancers Are Englishmen. Naval Brigade's Perfect Shelling. 2000 Casualties In One Engagement.
N. J. Gillet
Cape Town 1900
16pp.
8vo.   M
The author of the sketch appears to have taken notes from a prisoner who had formerly been in the Cape Mounted Rifles.

Gilson (Captain Charles J. L.) – History Of The 1st Batt. Sherwood Foresters (Notts. And Derby Regt.) In The Boer War, 1899–1902.
Swan Sonnenschein & Co. Ltd.
London 1908
xviii+v+236pp. Two folding maps in separate pocket, other maps, plans and portraits.
221×142mm   p.x

An earlier edition was published without date to title page. Possibly 1907?

Girouard (Lt. Col. Sir E. P. C.) – Military Railways. South Africa. General Report By Lt. Col. Sir E. P. C. Girouard. Vol. 1.
Publisher/printer not shown [official print].
————1902
164pp. Maps and plates.   MOD
War Office library. WO. ref:– WH Loc: SA17B.

Girouard (Lt. Col. E. P. C.) – Report. Telegraph Wires, Etc. See WO. 117.

Girouard (Lieut-Colonel Sir E. P. C.) – History Of The Railways During The War In South Africa, 1899–1902.
Printed for H.M.S.O. by Harrison and Sons.
London 1903
149pp. With plates, tables and map.
327×210mm
First part of a history of railway operations during the war by the Director of Railways S.A. Field Force. See – Royal Engineers Institute – 'Detailed History of the Railways in the South African War, 1899–1902.'

(Glasgow South African War Fund) – 27 Printed Notices Relating To The Glasgow South African War Fund.
c.1900
(Various sizes)   CC

Glover (Lady) (Compiled by) – Lest We Forget Them.
Fine Art Society and Simpkin, Marshall, Hamilton, Kent & Co., Ltd.
London nd. (1900)
64pp. (Unnumbered) Illustrated.
394×285mm
2nd Ed. recorded. Cover title – Lest We Forget Them: Our Sailors And Soldiers, 1899–1900. SABIB.

Gluckstein (S. M.) – Queen Or President? An Indictment Of Paul Kruger.
Grant Richards
London 1900
xi+178pp.
195×130mm

Goffe (Edward) – Notes On The Construction Of 'Long Cecil' A 4.1-Inch Rifled Breechloading Gun, In Kimberley, During The Siege, 1899–1900.
By Edward Goffe, A.M.I.Mech.E.
Excerpt Minutes Of Proceedings Of The Meeting Of The Institution Of Mechanical Engineers In London, 28th June 1900 Sir William H. White, K.C.B., L.L.D., D.Sc., F.R.S., President. By Authority Of The Council.
Published by the Institution
Westminster nd. (1900)
pp.359–374. Photographic plate and drawings.
216×140mm   p.70

Goldmann (Charles Sydney) – With General French And The Cavalry In South Africa.
Macmillan and Co., Limited
London 1902
xix+462pp. Folding maps and plates.
230×148mm   p.105

Goldreich (C.) – The Ultimatum To Paul Kruger. Sep. 1899.
(Johannesburg 1899?)
16pp.
220mm   SABIB
According to M. The BM copy is inscribed by the author – C. Goldreich. A criticism of the social and economic conditions in the Transvaal at that time.

Goltz (Gen. C. V. D.) – The Military Lessons Of The South African War.
The National Review
London 1903
24pp.
215mm   NAM/THB

Gooch (G. P.) – The War And Its Causes.
The Transvaal Committee
(London?) 1900 (Fourth Edition)
35pp.
8vo
Pamphlet on the causes of the war from a pro-Boer standpoint. M lists 3rd ed. of 34pp.

(Good Hope Society) (Publisher?) – Report Of The Good Hope Society For Aid To Sick And Wounded In War. South African War 1899–1902.
W.A. Richards & Sons
Cape Town 1902
68pp. Illustrated.
Quarto   WO. Cat./1912
The society was organised on November 3, 1899, and was the means of alleviating the sufferings of a large number of men during the war. M.

Goodwyn (James Edward) – Unfounded Attacks On British Officers Etc. See – XXX and LIX.

(Goose. Agas H.) (Printer) – The Cloud & Its Silver Lining, By The Sister Of An Officer. 'At The Front'.
Agas H. Goose, printer
Norwich (c.1900)
16pp.
150mm   SABIB
Words of consolation to relatives of soldiers who have embarked for the Cape.

Gordon (A. A.) – A Short Official Account Of The Edinburgh And East Of Scotland Hospital For South Africa, With List Of Subscriptions, &c.
W. Blackwood & Sons
Edinburgh 1900
73pp. Illustrated.   GC
Account of the scheme, list of staff, etc. See – WALLACE & BOYD.

(Gordon and Gotch) (Publishers) – Souvenir Of The Queensland Contingent For Service In South Africa.
Gordon and Gotch
Brisbane 1899
(Pagination not shown.)   ALH

Gore (Lieut.-Colonel St. John) (Edited by) – The Green Horse In Ladysmith.
Printed For Private Circulation
Sampson Low, Marston & Company Limited
London 1901
xi+171pp. Folding map and plates.
190×127mm
Large paper edition of 100 specially bound and numbered copies published the same year – 230×145mm.

Gould (F. Carruthers) – The Westminster Cartoons. Vol. IV. A Pictorial History Of Political Events Connected With South Africa, 1899–1900.
'The Westminster Gazette'
London 1900
47pp. Illustrated.
369×250mm
A collection of forty-three cartoons and sketches, culled from the 'Westminster Gazette', the 'Westminster Budget' and 'Picture Politics', all bearing on present relations between Great Britain and the South African Republics – Illustrated wrap. Also published in an edition of 250 numbered copies signed by the author. This edition has two extra plates. Clothbound 347×242mm.

Gould (F. Carruthers) – The Khaki Campaign Westminster Cartoons General Election, 1900.
'The Westminster Gazette'
London 1900
47pp Illustrated
347×242mm
Sketches and cartoons relating to the general election of 1900. Many of the drawings concern events in South Africa. A special clothbound edition of 250 copies signed by the author. Standard edition bound in illustrated wrap – 370×250mm.

Gould (Mary Ellen) – Tommy And The Boer. An Incident In The War.
(No pagination, place or date.) (1899?)
3pp.
16mo.   M
Entered from BM.

(Government Printer) (Printers) – Government Gazette Extraordinary (Military Government, Publishers?)
Pretoria 1900
618+xxiv pp.
384×255mm
37 issues of the 'Gazette' bound together with index. The paper, printed in English and Dutch is dated June–December 1900. Contents include proclamations and notices concerning commerce, posts, railways, currency, foodstuffs and civil administration. Some general advertising is included.

(Government Printer. Pretoria) (Printed by) – Army Orders Issued By Field Marshal Lord Roberts And Gen. Lord Kitchener Of Khartoum From 10th January 1900 To 23rd June 1902.
Govt. Printer
Pretoria 1900–1902
Unpaginated
334×208mm   CC   p.20
Army orders numbered 1–566 together with notices numbered 1–68. Orders 1–19 published at Cape Town. Nos. 19A–91 and No. 233 published at various locations on line of march. Remainder published at Pretoria.

(Government Printing Office) (Printers) – War Department . . . Adjutant General's Office No. XXXIII. Reports On Military Operations In South Africa And China. July 1901.
Government Printing Office
Washington 1901
600pp. Maps, diagrams.
238×157mm
Extracts from reports of Capt. S. L'. H. Slocum on operations of the British Army in South Africa. Together with extracts from reports of Capt. Carl Reichmann on operations of the Boer Army. With a summary of events in South Africa and China c.1900.

(Government Printing Office) (Printers) – War Department. . . Office Of Chief Of Staff. Second (Military Information) Division. General Staff. No. 4. Selected Translations Pertaining To The Boer War. April 1, 1905.
Government Printing Office
Washington 1905
243pp. With four loose maps.
230×148mm

(Government Printing Office) (Printers) – Register Of Soldiers Graves In The Transvaal. See entry under (GRAVES).

(Government Printing Works) (Printers) – List Of Officers Serving With Mounted Infantry In South Africa.
Government Printing Works
Pretoria 1901
vii+35pp.
197×128mm   GC

(Government Printing Works) (Printers) –
Letter In Dutch From Lord Kitchener To
His Honour Schalk Burger, Dated 22nd
September 1901, Referring To
Negotiations For Peace, And The
Meeting With General Botha.
Government Printing Works
Pretoria 1901
6pp.
Folio   M
*English translation and some Government
notices appended.*

(Government Printing Works) (Printers) –
Transvaal Colony. Proclamations From
1900–1902.
Government Printing Works
Pretoria 1902
ix+729pp.
240mm   SABIB

Graham (E. Maud) – A Canadian Girl In
South Africa.
William Briggs
Toronto 1905
192pp. Illustrated.
199×130mm   p.116

Graham (Harry) – Ballads Of The Boer
War. See – COLDSTREAMER.

Grant (John) – The Story Of The Boer
War. An Original And Complete Record
Of The Campaign.
Lewis's (Publisher)
Manchester (c.1900)
144pp.
183×122mm

Grant (M. H.) – History Of The War In
South Africa, 1899–1902, Etc. See
MAURICE & GRANT.

Grant (M.H.)–Words By An Eyewitness,
Etc. See LINESMAN.

Grant (M. H.) – The Mechanism Of War.
See LINESMAN.

(Graves) – List Of Graves In The
Transvaal.
Publisher/printer not shown
———1904
175pp.   MOD
*Item from War Office Library. 'Official
Print'. WO. ref. WH Loc: SA5C.
Possible HMSO publication.*

(Graves) – List Of Graves In The Orange
River Colony.
Publisher/printer not shown
HMSO 1904
162pp.   MOD
*Item from War Office library 'Official
Print' WO. ref – WH Loc: SA5E.*

(Graves) – Register Of Graves In Natal
Publisher/printer not shown
———1904
261pp.   MOD
*Item from War Office library 'Official
Print'. WO. ref: WH Loc: SA5H.
Possible HMSO publication.*

(Graves) – Register Of Soldiers' Graves
In The Transvaal.
Government Printing Office
Pretoria 1905
88pp. With map.   MOD
*Item from War Office library. WO. ref.
WH Loc: SA5D/PRO Loc: WO.?
108/193.*

(Graves) – Soldiers' Graves In Cape
Colony, Anglo Boer War, 1899–1902.
(Dec. 1907)
Surveyor Generals' Office

Government of Cape.
Cape Town 1907
83pp.   MOD
*Item from War Office library. WO. ref.
WH Loc: SA5B.
SABIB entry gives publication date –1908.*

(Graves) – List Of Graves Of Soldiers
Who Died During The Anglo Boer War,
1899–1902.
Publisher/printer not shown
Bloemfontein nd.   MOD
*Item from War Office library WO. ref.
WH Loc: SA5F.*

Gray (A.) – The Boer War And Other
Papers On Kindred Topics.
Publisher/printer not shown
Illinois 1902
31pp.   CB
*Includes papers on Pro-Boer meeting of
American sympathy, concentration
camps, etc.*

**(Great Yarmouth Printing Co., Ltd.,
The.)** (Publisher) – The South African
War. Photographs Of The Yarmouth
Volunteers In The 1st & 2nd Active
Service Companies And 3rd Draft, And
The P.W.O.
The Great Yarmouth Printing Co., Ltd.
Yarmouth nd. (1900?)
4pp. advertisements & 5 plates.
218×281mm

Green (James) – Causes Of The War In
South Africa. A Paper Read Before The
Worcester Society Of Antiquity.
Printer/Publisher not shown
Worcester Mass. 1900
26pp.
240mm   SABIB

Green (James) – Causes Of The War In
South Africa From The American
Lawyer's Standpoint. A Paper Read
Before The Worcester Society Of
Antiquity. 2nd Ed.
Printer/Publisher not shown
Worcester Mass. 1900
28pp.
Roy.8vo.   M

Green (James) – Causes Of The War In
South Africa From The American
Lawyer's Standpoint.
Imperial S. African Assoc.
London 1901
24pp.
190mm   SABIB
Catalogued from cover.

Green (James) – The Story Of The
Australian Bushmen (Being Notes Of
A Chaplain).
William Brooks & Co., Ltd.
Sydney 1903
ii+xix+230pp. Illustrated.
190×127mm

(Greening & Co.) (Printers) – The Two
Howitzers, Ladysmith.
Greening & Co., printers
Ladysmith nd. (1900)
4pp.
165×108mm   CC
*A short account of guns named 'Castor'
and 'Pollux' and their use in the
Ladysmith siege.*

Greenwood (T. J.) – Fighting The Boers.
Argus Printing and Publishing Co., Ltd.
Bloemfontein 1900
278pp.
12mo.   M
*Narrative of events from the crisis in
Johannesburg to the relief of Ladysmith.*

*Most of the content was first published in
the Cape Argus.*

Greer (Lt.Col. J.) – Report On Military
Postal Service. See WO.109.

Grendon (Robert) – Paul Kruger's
Dream, The Struggle For Supremacy In
South Africa Between Boer And Briton,
Or The Overthrow Of 'Corruption',
'Falsehood', 'Tyranny', 'Wrong', And
The Triumph Of 'Justice', 'Truth',
'Liberty'. 'Right'. A Poem.
Munro Bros. (Printers)
Pietermaritzburg 1902
vii+133pp.
220mm   SABIB

Grey (Edward) – Current Problems – At
Home And Abroad. A Speech Delivered
At Nottingham, March 28th, 1900.
Liberal Publication Dept.
London 1900
14+1pp.
210mm   SABIB
*Electioneering speech on the subject of
Imperial control of South Africa after the
war.*

Grey (Sir Edward) – 'Eighty Club', 'The
War And After'. Speeches Delivered By
Sir Edward Grey, Bt., M.P., J. G.
Shipman, LL.B. M.P., Henry Norman,
M.P., and Sir Robert Reid, G.C. M.G.
K.C. M.P. (Chairman). At The Hotel
Cecil, On February 20, 1901.
J. A. K. Mackay
London (1902?)
29pp.
8vo.   M

Grey (J. G.) – Freedom Of Thought &
Speech In New Zealand. A Serious
Menace To Liberty. Mr. Seddon,
Premier, Mr. J. Grattan Grey, Journalist.
An Interesting Correspondence. No. 1.
Wright & Grenside (Printers)
Wellington 1900
21pp.
210mm   SABIB
*Mr. Grey disapproved of the sending of
contingents from New Zealand to South
Africa during the war. His article in the
'New York Times' led to correspondence
with the Premier.*

Grey (James Grattan) – Freedom Of
Thought & Speech In New Zealand.
A Serious Menace To Liberty. The Story
Of The Boers. Things Worth Knowing.
No. 2.
Wright and Grenside (Printers)
Wellington 1900
80pp.
200mm   SABIB

(Griffith W. P. & Sons Ltd.) (Printers) –
Historical Record Of The 3rd County Of
London (Sharpshooters) Imperial
Yeomanry 1900–1905.
W. P. Griffith & Sons Ltd.
London nd. (c.1905)
72pp. Coloured frontispiece
140×110mm   p.84
*Short record of the 18th, 21st, and 23rd
Battalions I.Y.*

(Grocott & Sherry) (Publishers/printers?)
– Diary Of The Siege Of Kimberley,
During The Transvaal War, October,
1899, To February, 1900, By
A Beaconsfield Resident.
Grocott and Sherry
Grahamstown 1900
89pp.
214×133mm   p.45
Copy of the 2nd edition. Title from cover.

Grout (Rev. Lewis) – The Boer And The Briton In South Africa; Or, The Present War In Its Historical And Moral Bearings. A Paper Read At A Meeting Of The Brattleboro Professional Club, November 14, 1899.
The Phoenix Job Printing Office
Brattleboro 1900
24pp.
8vo.   M

Grout (Rev. Lewis) – A Critique On Bishop Hartzell's Great Lecture In Chicago, May 2, 1900, On 'The Briton And The Boer' By The Rev. Lewis Grout.
The Phoenix Job Printing Office
Brattleboro V.T. 1900
16pp.
228×153mm

Guers (E.) – Prisoners Of War, And How They Fare. With Seventeen Full-Page Illustrations, 1900.
                         M
All shown, M states the volume is bound in khaki. Ref. – De Bussy's African Catalogue, 1900.

Guest (H. M.) (Printed and published by) – The Anglo-Boer War. With Lord Methuen From Belmont To Hartebeestfontein.
H. M. Guest
Klerksdorp 1901 (Second edition)
72pp.
200×134mm   CC

Guest (H. M.) (Printed and published by) – The Anglo-Boer War. Vicissitudes Of A Transvaal Dorp. Klerksdorp.
H. M. Guest 'Mining Record' Office
Klerksdorp 1901
47pp.
201×140mm   p.108

Guest (H. M.) – The Anglo-Boer War. A Prisoner's Experiences.
H. M. Guest
Klerksdorp (c.1901)
8pp.
200mm   SABIB
No title page. Catalogued from cover.

Guest (H. M.) – With Lord Methuen
H. M. Guest
Klerksdorp 1901
4 parts (40pp.)
210mm   SABIB
No title pages. Caption titles. At head of each:- The Anglo-Boer War. Paged continuously. Pt.1. – Belmont, pp.1–12. Pt.2. – Graspan, pp.13–20. Pt.3. – Modder River, pp.21–27. Pt.4. – Magersfontein, pp.29–40.

Guest (H. M.) – With Lord Methuen: From October 1899, To December 1901. (3rd Ed.)
H. M. Guest
Klerksdorp 1901
1+1+95+2pp.
200mm   SABIB
Edition from cover.

Guest (H. M.) – Portfolio Of Klerksdorp Views. 31 Views.
H. M. Guest
Klerksdorp 1902
8vo. oblong   M
The letterpress contains a short history of the town and incidents during the war. The views include scenes of the local campaign.

Guest (H. M.) (Printed and published by) – The Anglo Boer War. Incidents In The Western Transvaal.
H. M. Guest

Klerksdorp, Transvaal 1902
63pp.
204×137mm   p.108

Guest (H. M.) (Printed and published by) – The Anglo Boer War With Lord Methuen And The First Division.
H. M. Guest
Klerksdorp, Transvaal 1902
124pp. Illustrated.
203×134mm

Guillum Scott (Guy H.) and McDonell (Geoffrey L.) – The Record Of The Mounted Infantry Of The City Imperial Volunteers. See entry under SCOTT.

Gwynne (John) – Homer 2nd's Bulliad. A Satire Of The South African Campaign.
Germania Press
Milwaukee, Wisconsin, U.S.A. 1900
16pp.
Cr.8vo.   M
Pro Boer verse holding the British to scorn. SABIB lists author – A. L. Peticolas.

H

Haagner (Sigmund) – The South African War. When Is The End To Be? A Note On The Present Position Of The Refugees.
Argus Printing & Publishing Co. (Printers)
Cape Town (1901?)
7pp.
220mm   SABIB

(H. A. C. a member of) – Twelve Months With General Buller In South Africa. See entry under ROBINSON, PICKERING & HUNT.

Haldane (Capt. Aylmer) – How We Escaped From Pretoria.
William Blackwood and Sons
Edinburgh and London 1900
i+126pp. Illustrated.
200×140mm
Sixth impression. Paper cover.

Haldane (Capt. Aylmer) – How We Escaped From Pretoria.
William Blackwood and Sons
Edinburgh and London 1901
xii+231pp. Folding map and plates.
194×130mm
New edition, revised and enlarged.

Hales (A. G.) – Campaign Pictures Of The War In South Africa (1899–1900) Letters From The Front.
Cassell and Company, Limited
London 1900
xi+303pp. Portrait frontispiece.
195×130mm
Account of the special correspondent of the 'Daily News'. Chapters relate to Australians at the front.

Hall (Robert) – The South African Campaign.
John K. Milne
Aberdeen 1901
vii+285pp. Portrait frontispiece.
188×130mm   p.94

Halstead (Murat) – Briton And Boer In South Africa: The Story Of England's War With The Brave Boers And The Eventful History Of South Africa.
W. E. Scull (Publisher?)
(Philadelphia?) 1900
485pp. Folding map and illustrations.
230×165mm

SABIB records copy published by John C. Winston, Philadelphia (1900?). Publication consists of two parts – *A history of S. Africa to the war of 1899–1900. Part two – The war between England and the Boers. xxiii+1 +pp.25–542. Folding map and illustrations.*

Hamilton (Bernard) – Wanted – A Man! Apply John Bull And Co. (Late Of Dame Europa's School) A War Story For Big Boys. Told By Bernard Hamilton.
Simpkin, Marshall and Co., Limited
London nd. (1900)
31pp.
12mo.   M
A skit on English politicians and the South African War.

Hamilton (F. J.) – Sunbeams Through The War-Cloud: Short Poems On Special Incidents In South Africa.
Elliot Stock
London 1900
63pp.
199×134mm

Hamilton (Lt.Gen. Sir Ian) – Letter Regarding Proposal On Courts Martial, Etc. See WO. 72 & 150.

Hamilton (J. Angus) – The Siege Of Mafeking.
Methuen & Co.
London 1900
xi+332pp. Folding plan and illustrations.
197×132mm

(Hamilton Bros. Ltd.) (Printers) – Roll Of Officers, Non-Commissioned Officers And Men Who Were Killed In Action, Or Who Died Of Wounds Or Disease, Or Other Causes, During The South African Campaign 1899–1902.
Hamilton Bros. Ltd., Printers
London 1906
12pp.
181×123mm   DC
Paper covered. Cover title – Scots Guards. 'This Roll is issued for the information of all who served in the Scots Guards during the War in South Africa, their relations, comrades, and friends.' F. ROMILLY, Colonel, Commanding Scots Guards.

Hammond (J.) (And others) – Three Plain Sermons For The Day Of Intercession (Septuagesima Sunday, February 11, 1900), In Respect Of The War In South Africa By The Rev. Canon Hammond, Rev. H. J. W. Buxton, Rev. S. C. Lowry.
Skeffington & Son
London (1900)
27pp.
8vo.   M

Hammond (J.) (And others) – Three Plain Sermons For The Day Of Thanksgiving In Respect Of The War In South Africa . . . .
Skeffington & Son
London (1900)
27pp.
210mm   SABIB
Published when the first phase of the war ended. BM lists a later publication – 'Three Plain Sermons On Thanksgiving In Respect Of The Conclusion Of The War In South Africa'. (1902?)

Hannah (George) – The Imperial Raid In South Africa.
The DeVinne Press
New York 1901
28pp.
Roy.8vo.   M
Pamphlet opposing British aggression in South Africa.

Harcourt (Sir W. G. G.) – The Government And The War. Two Letters To *'The Times'* Nov. 5th And 13th. Revised By The Author.
National Reform Union
Manchester (1901?)
23pp.
210mm   SABIB

Harding (William) – War In South Africa And The Dark Continent From Savagery To Civilization The Strange Story Of A Weird World From The Earliest Ages To The Present, Including The War With The Boers Embracing The Explorations And Settlements, Wars And Conquests, Peoples And Governments, Resources And Produces, Of This The Least Known, Yet By Nature Endowed As The Richest And Most Wonderful Of Continents, And A Detailed History Of The Causes And Events Of The British-Boer War.
Butler & Alger
New Haven/Conn. nd. (1900)
534pp. Illustrated.
243×178mm   p.9
Various editions recorded. SABIB lists J. S. Ziegler, Chicago (1900). Dominion Co. Chicago (1900) 546pp. Butler & Alger, New Haven/Conn. (1900) 489pp.

Hargrove (Rev. Charles) – Shall We Go To War With Our Brethren? A Question Before God. A Sermon By The Rev. Charles Hargrove, M.A., September 24th, 1899.
Goodall and Suddick, printers
Leeds nd. (1899)
15pp.
182×121mm
A plea to the nation to avoid the imminent conflict in South Africa.

Hargrove (E. T.) – An American View Of The South African Situation: Etc. See (T.).

Harman (N.) – The Clinical And Pathological Characters Of Veld Sore Prevalent Amongst The Troops In South Africa.
(Pathological Society of Great Britain & Ireland)
London 1903
iii+37pp. Plates (some coloured) & tables.
255×160mm
Reprinted from 'Journal of pathology & bacteriology', August 1903.

(Harper Brothers) (Publishers) – Briton And Boer. Both Sides Of The South African Question.
Harper Brothers
New York and London 1900
xi+310pp.
190×129mm
Articles on the political situation by various authors. Reprinted by permission from the 'North American Review'. New and enlarged edition. SABIB lists a New York edition of 1900. vi+251pp. Folding map and plates.

Harris (Frank) – How To Beat The Boer: A Conversation In Hades. Dramatis Personae: Washington, Samuel Johnson, Thomas Carlyle, C. S. Parnell, Lord Randolph Churchill, Aylward – a Fenian.
William Heinemann
London 1900
29pp.
8vo.   M

Harris (John Charles) – Refugees And Relief . . . .
Imperial South African Association
London 1901
32pp.
210mm   SABIB
Pro-British publication relating to concentration camps for Boer women and sufferings of British refugees who had to leave the Boer Republics.

Harrison (Benjamin) – Ex-President Harrison On The Boer War.
'New Age' Press
London (1901?)
16pp.
190mm   SABIB
Reprinted from the 'North American Review' March 15, 1901.

Harrison (F.) & Herbert (A.) – Two Open Letters To Lord Salisbury On The Iniquity Of A War Against The Transvaal. I. Frederic Harrison. II. The Hon. Auberon Herbert.
Alexander & Shepheard (Printers)
London (1899?)
4pp.
210mm   SABIB
Catalogued from caption title.

(Harrison & Sons) (Printers) – The True History Of The War. Being The Official Despatches And Enclosures From The General Commanding-In-Chief The Forces In South Africa.
Harrison & Sons
London nd. (1900)
186pp.
315×194mm   p.115
Five parts published in limp card covers:–
Part I. From Nov. 9th to Dec. 28th 1899. Reprinted from the 'London Gazette' of January 26th, 1900.
Part II. Contents: Victoria Cross and Special Awards. Despatches of Lord Roberts, Lord Methuen, General Gatacre, Admiral Harris, Sir Redvers Buller, Sir C. Warren. List of European deaths in Kimberley District. Synopsis of Part I. Reprinted from the 'London Gazettes' of Feb. 2nd, March 13th, 16th, and 30th, April 6th and 17th, 1900.
Part III. Describing the Military Operations at Colesberg, Kimberley, Paardeberg, Bloemfontein, Kroonstadt, and Pretoria.
Part IV. Enclosing Report on the Siege of Mafeking from Major-General Baden-Powell.
Part V. Enclosing an account of the Defence and Relief of Ladysmith.

Hart (J. J.) – Incidents Of The South African Campaign. Being Chiefly The Personal Experiences Of The Author.
'The Telegraph Press'
St. John N.B. 1901
xi+140pp.
175×115mm
J. J. Hart, late of the Grenadier Guards.

Hart-McHarg (W.) – From Quebec To Pretoria, With The Royal Canadian Regiment.
William Briggs
Toronto 1902
276pp. Illustrated.
195×128mm

Hartzell (Joseph Crane) – Moral Aspects Of The War. South Africa's Future.
South African Vigilance Committee
Cape Town 1902
4pp.
8vo.   M

Harvey (Major C. B.) – Letters Written By Major C. B. Harvey (10th. Royal Hussars) To His Wife During The Months Of November & December, 1899.
(Text type-written by The Women's Institute, London.)
Printer/publisher not shown
np. nd. (London c.1900)
84pp. (Printed rectos only) Portrait frontispiece laid down.
244×186mm
Letters and campaign diary of Maj. Harvey, killed in action during the advance on Colesberg. The volume contains newspaper notices and extracts from letters of other correspondents. A record published by the family from a typescript copy.

Hassall (John) – An Active Army Alphabet.
Sands & Co.
London 1899
53pp. Illustrated.
298×240mm   p.42

Hassell (John A.) – The Boer Concentration Camps Of Bermuda.
John A. Hassell
New York (1902?)
16pp. Illustrated.
218×147mm   CC
Anti British account written by an American officer in the Boer army.

Hawdon (Mrs. A. J.) – New Zealanders & The Boer War, Etc. See – NEW ZEALANDER.

Hay (Col. G. J.) – An Epitomised History Of The Militia (The 'Constitutional Force') Together With The Origin, Periods Of Embodied Service, And Special Services (Including South Africa, 1899–1902) Of Militia Units Existing October 31, 1905.
'United Service Gazette'
London 1906
444pp.
Roy.8vo.   M
Much information is given respecting services of militia regiments during the South African War.

Hay (R. Paterson) – Diary Of An Edinburgh Trooper Being A Series Of Letters Written During The South African Campaign 1901–2.
Bishop & Sons (Printed for private circulation)
Edinburgh 1903
vi+137pp. Illustrated.
191×124mm   p.68

Hayes (M. H.) – Horses On Board Ship: A Guide To Their Management.
Hurst and Blackett
London 1902
viii+iv+271pp. Illustrated
200mm   SABIB
Reference to remounts shipped to South Africa during the war.

Heath (Maj. G. M.) – Remarks On Lt. Blakeney's Report, Etc. See WO. 53.

Henderson (Lt.Col. David) – Boer Forces In The Field, Etc. See WO. 19.

Henderson (Lt.Col. David) – Report On Field Intelligence. Etc. See WO. 92.

Henderson (Lt.Col. G. F. R.) – Rules For Guidance Of Press Censors; By Lt.Col. G. F. R. Henderson.
Publisher/printer not shown
np./nd.
1p.   MOD
Item from War Office library. 'Official Print'. WO. Ref. – WH Loc: SA58.

Henderson (Lt.Col. G. F. R.) – Rules For Guidance Of Censors; By Lt.Col. G. F. R. Henderson.
Publisher/printer not shown
Cape Town, Jan. 1900
1p.   MOD
Item from War Office library 'Official Print'. WO. Ref. – WH Loc: SA58.

Henderson (James) (Publisher) – The Transvaal War Of 1881, And All About The Boers Up To The Present Situation Of Peace Or War! 'Weekly Budget' Special.
James Henderson
London nd. (c.1899)
16pp. Illustrated.
276×202mm
Title from cover. Cheaply produced 'Special'. Paper covered.

Henderson (James) (Publisher) – The Transvaal War Of 1881 And All About The Boers Up To The Latest Situation Of The Present War, With Particulars Of The British Forces In South Africa. 'Weekly Budget' Special.
James Henderson
London nd. (c.1899)
16pp. Illustrated.
Fourth edition. Title from cover.

Henderson (James) (Publisher) – The Transvaal War Illustrated & The Transvaal War Pictorial.
James Henderson
London nd. (1899–1900)
Each issue 16pp. Illustrated.
291×200mm
30 issues of a publication relating to the present war in South Africa and to the earlier conflict of 1881. (See first two HENDERSON entries.) The issues are bound in contemporary buckram (298×202mm) with the original wraps removed. 14 issues are titled 'The Transvaal War Illustrated' and 14 others have the title 'The Transvaal War Pictorial'. The magazine is similar in style to 'Black and White Budget' and 'Under the Union Jack'. The titles are drawn from page 1 of each issue.,

Henderson (Mark) – War Diary, 1899–1900 . . . . 5th Ed., Containing The Most Complete Diary Of The Siege Of Kimberley, Every Item Of Interest Dating From September 21st, 1899, To End of March, 1900. Graphic Accounts Of Bombardments And Engagements, With Complete List Of Killed And Wounded. Lord Roberts' Movements, Etc., Etc.
Diamond Market Printing Works, Kimberley (1900)
98pp.
120mm   SABIB

(Henderson) – Henderson's Monthly Diary Containing Diary Of The Siege Of Kimberley And Principal Events Of The War To Date.
Diamond Market Printing Works
Kimberley 1899–1900
3 vols.
110mm   SABIB
Vol 1: Dec. 1899, Siege Ed. 97+1p.
Vol. 2: Jan. 1900. Henderson's war diary: being a special siege edition of Henderson's monthly diary, railway and postal guide.
98pp.

Henderson (Mark) – Mark Henderson's War Diary, February, 1900. Special Siege Edition Of Henderson's Monthly Diary, Railway And Postal Guide, Containing A Complete Diary Of The Siege Of Kimberley, Every Item Of Interest Dating From September 21st, 1899, To

End Of January, 1900. Graphic Accounts Of Bombardments And Engagements, With Complete List Of Killed And Wounded.
Diamond Market Printing Works
Kimberley 1900
98pp. (Including numerous advertisements.)
111×76mm   CC   p.70
Item listed as vol. 3, Henderson's Monthly Diary, in SABIB. Title from cover.

Henderson (Lieutenant W.) (Compiler) – The New South Wales Contingents To South Africa, From October, 1899, To March, 1900, With A 'Roll Call Of Honour', Being The Names Of Our Officers And Men At The Front. Compiled From Official And Other Sources By Lieutenant W. Henderson, (National Guard Of New South Wales), With Photographic Portraits And Scenes.
Turner & Henderson
Sydney 1900
ii+50pp. Illustrated.
135×217mm   CC
A second enlarged edition of 60pp. was published the same year listing contingents departed from October 1899 to June 1900.

Henley (William Ernest) – For England's Sake: Verses And Songs In Time Of War . . . .
David Nutt
London 1900
xi+24pp.
200mm   SABIB
Patriotic verses written during the war.

(Herald Office) (Printers) – The Family Camp, Race Course, Port Elizabeth. When We Were Refugees. How We Managed Our Camp. A Memoir Of The Britishers' Exile From The Transvaal And Orange Free State During The Boer War, 1899–1900.
Herald Office (Printers)
Port Elizabeth (1900?)
11+1p.
250mm   SABIB
An account of the organization and activities of the relief settlement established at the Port Elizabeth Race Course in succession to the previous settlement at the Agricultural Society's Show yard, for refugees from the Transvaal and Orange Free State. Printer listed in SABIB – 'E. P. Herald' Office.

(Herald Publishing Co. The) (Publisher) – Canadians In Khaki South Africa, 1899–1900 Nominal Rolls Of The Officers, Non-Commissioned Officers & Men Of The Canadian Contingents And Strathcona's Horse With Casualties To Date And Also R. M. C. Graduates With The Army In South Africa.
The Herald Publishing Co.
Montreal 1900
127pp. Illustrated.
221×146mm   CC   p.35

Herbert (Col. Ivor) – Report On Casualties. See under CASUALTY LISTS WAR OFFICE.

Hewlett (Lionel Mowbray) (Compiler) – Old Harrovians Serving In South Africa.
F. W. Provost, Printer
Harrow 1900
16pp.
230mm   SABIB
Issued as supplement to 'The Harrovian', February 24th, 1900.

Heyer (A.) – A Brief History Of The Transvaal Secret Service System From Its Inception To The Present Time; Its Objects, Its Agents, The Disposal Of Its

Funds, And The Result As Seen Today – War Against Great Britain.
Wm. Taylor
Cape Town 1899
1+1+31pp.
210mm
2nd Ed. 1899
3rd Ed. 1899
ii+31pp.
210mm
4th Ed. 1899
4th Ed. (Revised) 1900
ii+28pp.
200mm   SABIB

(Heywood. John) (Publisher) – Report Of The Great Trial Of Bull v. Burgher. Speeches Of The Advocate-In-Chief And Sir Ernest Tresfort. Evidence Of Mr. Porcelain And Mr. Rouger. Summing-Up Of The Lord High Justice. Verdict.
John Heywood
Manchester (1900?)
23pp.
8vo.   M
Amusing skit on the war.

(Higginbotham & Co.) (Printer/Publisher?) – The War In South Africa, In The Light Of Facts And History.
Higginbotham & Co.
Madras 1900
103pp.
8vo.   M
A defence of the war and Imperial policy.

Higgins (Henry Bournes) – Speech By Mr. H. B. Higgins, M.P., On The South African War.
Robt. S. Brain Govt. Printer
Melbourne 1902
11pp.
250mm   SABIB
Reprinted from the 'Parliamentary debates' of the Commonwealth of Australia, 14th Jan. 1902. Catalogued from caption title.

Highton (E. Gilbert) – The Siege Of Mafeking. A Patriotic Poem.
Harrison and Sons
London 1900
14pp.
8vo.   M

Hiley (Alan R. I.) and Hassell (John A.) – The Mobile Boer Being The Record Of The Observations Of Two Burgher Officers.
The Grafton Press
New York nd. (1902)
xvii+277pp. Folding map and illustrations.
192×129mm   p.96

Hill (William) – Who Shall Inherit The Goldfields? A Pressing Problem. A Casual Contribution To A People's Programme.
(Printer not shown) Victoria House?
London nd. (1900)
11pp.
8vo.   M
A suggestion that the gold and diamond mining industries should be heavily taxed and the proceeds used to pay for the war and to benefit the Empire.

Hillegas (Howard C.) – The Boers In War. The Story Of The British-Boer War Of 1899–1900, As Seen From The Boer Side, With A Description Of The Men And Methods Of The Republican Armies.
D. Appleton & Company
New York 1900
xii+300pp. Folding map and illustrations.
195×130mm

Hillegas (Howard C.) – With The Boer Forces.
Methuen & Co.
London 1900
318pp. Illustrated.
192×128mm
An assessment of the republican military organization. M lists 2nd. ed. 1901. SABIB records 3rd ed. 1901.

Hippisley (Lieut.Col. R. L.) – History Of The Telegraph Operations During The War In South Africa 1899–1902.
His Majesty's Stationery Office
London 1903
85pp. With 100 charts
332×208mm   p.119

Hippisley (Lt.Col. R. L.) & Girouard (Lt.Col. E. P. C.) – Report. Telegraph Wires, Etc. See WO. 117.

(Hippophagist) – A Siege Experience: Kimberley, 1899–1900.
J. Bain & Sons, printers
Edinburgh 1901
59pp. Illustrated.
220mm   SABIB
Author – Samuel Tait.

Hirst (H. D.) – The 3rd Battalion 'The Buffs' In South Africa.
H. J. Goulden
Canterbury 1908
59pp.
190×125mm

Hitchcock (Michelmore) – Briton Versus Boer; Or, The Sermon On The Mount Up To Date.
National Reform Union
Manchester (1900?)
iv+16pp.
180mm   SABIB
See National Reform Union Publications.

(H. K.) (Editor) – Chaplains In Khaki: Methodist Soldiers In Camp, On The Field, And On The March.
Charles H. Kelly.
London 1900
viii+344pp. Portrait & Map.
188×123mm

(H.M.R. & S.L.; E. H. Francis) (Printers) – Field Marshal Lord Roberts' Farewell Address To The Troops In South Africa, 29th Nov. 1900.
A Souvenir Of The Anglo-Boer War. 1899–1900.
H.M.R. & S.L.; E. H. Francis
Pretoria (1900?)
4pp.
140mm   SABIB
No title page. Catalogued from cover.

(HMSO) – British Official Publications issued from His/Her Majesty's Stationery Office. Publications include House of Lords Papers and Bills (HL), House of Commons Reports and Papers (HC), Acts, Command Papers (C) & (Cd.) and Non-Parliamentary Publications. The following entries are listed in the order shown above. Some titles are separately listed under author.

General size 330×210mm

HL. – Publications are listed in date order. The numbering sequence starts anew each year.

(67) – Campaign In South Africa (Members Of Either House Of Parliament On Active Service) – Return Of The Names Of Members Of Either House Of Parliament At Present Serving, Or Under Orders To Serve, Her Majesty In South Africa, The Capacity In Which They Serve, And The Dates At Which

They Sailed Or Are Under Orders To Sail.
1900   BOPP

(149) – Army – Return Of The Strength, & C., Of The Cavalry Regiments In The First And Second Brigades Of The First Army Corps On The 1st July 1899, The Number Of Officers, Men, And Horses Embarked With Each Cavalry Regiment In Those Brigades Sent To South Africa When Placed On The War Establishment, Officers, Men And Horses Borne On The Strength Of Each Regiment Previously; From What Sources The Three Effective Squadrons Were Brought Up To Proper Strength; The Strength And Establishment Of The Regiments Forming The Third Brigade Sent From India On The 1st July; And The Numbers Of Their War Establishment When Landed In South Africa.
1900   BOPP

(230) War Office Contracts – Report From The Select Committee [Of The House Of Commons]; With Proceedings, Evidence, And Appendix.
1900   BOPP

(230-Ind.) Ditto – Ditto: Index And Digest Of Evidence To The.
1900   BOPP

(231) – South African Republic And Orange Free State. Return To An Address Of The House Of Lords, Dated 8th March 1900, For Return With Reference To Each Of The Railways In The Orange Free State And In The South African Republic Respectively, Showing Whether Such Railways Belong To The State Or To Private Companies; And Also Giving The Cost Or Capital Value Of The Same.
London 1900
3pp.

(30) – South African Campaign. Return To An Address Of The House Of Lords, Dated 21st February 1901, For Return Stating The Number Of Sailors And Soldiers, Giving Their Names And Description, Who Have Been Invalided Home Since The Commencement Of The South African Campaign, And Have Died From Wounds Or Diseases.
London 1901
11pp.

(175) Army (Volunteers) – Proposed Amendment Of Scheme Relative To The Efficiency Of.
1901   BOPP

(180) – Charitable Agencies For Relief Of Widows And Orphans Of Soldiers And Sailors – Report From Joint Select Committee.
1901   BOPP

(180) Ditto – Ditto; With Proceedings, Evidence, Appendix, And Index.
1901   BOPP

HC. – Publications are listed in date order. The numbering sequence starts anew each year.

63. Army – Estimates For 1899–1900.
1899   BOPP

36. Army – Supplementary Estimate, 1899–1900. Further Provision For The War In South Africa.
1900
5pp.   BOPP

110. Army Supplementary Estimates, 1899–1900 – Subheads (War In South Africa).
1900
5pp.   BOPP

115. Imperial Yeomanry – Return Showing The Number Of Companies Of, That Have Been Formed, The Names Of The Regiments And Of The Counties From Which Each Company Has Been Raised, The Number That Have Embarked With Horses, And The Number That Have Left Either Wholly Or Partially Without Horses.
1900   BOPP

158. Army (Members Of Either House Of Parliament Serving In South Africa) – Return Showing The Names Of Members At Present Serving, Or Under Orders To Serve, Her Majesty In South Africa, The Capacity In Which They Serve, And The Dates At Which They Sailed Or Are Under Orders To Sail.
1900
3pp.   BOPP

184. – South Africa (Transports). Return Showing The Name, Tonnage, And Speed Of Each Vessel Employed To Convey Troops To South Africa Since The 1st Day Of July Last, The Date And Port Of Her Departure From These Shores, And Arrival At Cape Town, Durban, Or Elsewhere, Respectively, Including Arrival At And Departure From Intermediate Port Of Call; The Number Of Troops And Horses Or Mules Carried On Each Occasion, The Number Of Horses Or Mules Lost On Voyage, Vessels Provided With New Pattern Fittings, Vessels Provided With Old Pattern Fittings, Vessels Provided With Slings For Each Horse Or Mule, Vessels Not So Provided; And The Time Occupied By Each Vessel In Making The Voyage, In The Following Form:-
London 22 May 1900.
16pp.

268. South Africa (Unwounded Soldiers Dead Or Invalided Home) Return To An Address Of The Honourable The House Of Commons, Dated 28 May 1900; – For, 'Return Of The Number Of Officers And Men Who Since The Commencement Of The Present War Have Died Or Been Invalided Home From Causes Other Than Wounds Received In Action'.
London 1900
3pp.   CC

279. Medical And Sanitary Arrangements At The Cape. Return To An Address Of The Honourable The House Of Commons, Dated 10 July 1900; – For, 'Return Of Correspondence Between The Honourable Member for Ilkeston And The War Department In Relation To Medical And Sanitary Arrangements At The Cape.' War Office 14 July 1900.
George Wyndham.
London 1900
3pp.   CC

290. Army – Supplementary Estimate, 1900–01 [Chiefly War In South Africa And Affairs In China].
1900   BOPP

310. Natal Correspondence.
'Return Of Correspondence, Recently Published In The 'Natal Witness', Containing Minutes From The Prime Minister And Governor Of Natal And Generals Buller And Murray, Respecting The Censorship In That Colony Of Letters And Telegrams.'
London 1900
3pp.

378. Army – Second Supplementary Estimate, 1900–01. [War In South Africa And Affairs In China].
1900
6pp.   BOPP

142. South Africa (Naval Brigade). 'Copies Of Despatches In Regard To The

Naval Brigade In South Africa, Which Were Published In The 'London Gazette' Of The 12th Instant.'
London 1901
58pp.

150. Wars In South Africa And China – Return Of Estimated Cost Of, Showing How The Expenditure Is Best To Be Met.
1901
4pp.   BOPP

289. Charitable Agencies For Relief Of Widows And Orphans Of Soldiers And Sailors – Report From The Joint Select Committee.
1901   BOPP

289. Ditto – Ditto, With Proceedings.
1901   BOPP

289. Ditto – Ditto, Evidence, Appendix, And Index.
1901   BOPP

293. South Africa Telegraphs – Copy Of Agreement And Treasury Minute, July 1901.
1901
25pp.   BOPP

374. South Africa (Transports) Return Showing The Name, Tonnage And Speed Of Each Vessel Employed To Convey Troops To South Africa Since The 1st Day Of July 1899, The Date And Port Of Her Departure From These Shores, And Arrival At Cape Town, Durban, Or Elsewhere, The Number Of Troops And Horses Or Mules Carried On Each Occasion, The Number Of Horses Or Mules Lost On Voyage, Vessels Provided With New And With Old Pattern Fittings, Vessels Provided Or Not With Slings For Each Horse Or Mule, And The Time Occupied By Each Vessel In Making The Voyage.
1901   BOPP

30. Army – Supplementary Estimate, 1901–02, To Meet Additional Expenditure Due To The War In South Africa.
1902   BOPP

155. Wars In South Africa And China (Cost And Expenditure). Return 'Showing (1) The Estimated Amount Of War Charges In South Africa And China, Which Will Be Incurred Up To 31st March 1903; (2) How These Charges Have Been Or Will Be Met; And (3) How The Money Borrowed Has Been Raised.'
London 1902
5pp.

360. South Africa (Transports) Return Showing The Name, Tonnage, And Speed Of Each Vessel Employed To Convey Troops To South Africa Since The 1st Day Of April 1901, And Up To And Ending 31st Day Of March 1902, The Date And Port Of Her Departure From These Shores And Arrival At Cape Town, Durban, Or Elsewhere, Respectively, Including Arrival At And Departure From Intermediate Port Of Call; The Number Of Troops And Horses Or Mules Carried On Each Occasion, The Number Of Horses Or Mules Lost On Voyage, Vessels Provided With New Pattern Fittings, Vessels Provided With Old Pattern Fittings, Vessels Provided With Slings For Each Horse Or Mule, Vessels Not So Provided; And The Time Occupied By Each Vessel In Making The Voyage, In The Following Form:-
London 21 October 1902
14pp.

43. Army Estimates Of Effective And Non-Effective Services For 1903–4. (Including South African Compensation Claims) With Statements Of The Variations Of Numbers Of H.M. British Forces, &C.
1903   BOPP

43-I. Army Estimates, 1903–4 – Appendices 18 And 19 Restated.
1903   BOPP

130. Wars In South Africa And China – Return Showing Estimated Amount Of War Charges Incurred Up To 31st March, 1903; How These Charges Have Been Met; And How The Money Borrowed Has Been Raised.
1903
6pp.   BOPP

153. Army (Commissions) – Return As To Number Of Commissions Granted During Each Of The Years 1899 To 1902.
1903   BOPP

189. Aliens (Naturalization: Transvaal And Orange River Colony) – Ordinances Containing Rules And Regulations Respecting.
1903   BOPP

354. Transports (South African War). Return 'Giving The Names Of All The Transports Hired For The Conveyance Of Troops, Stores, And Material To South Africa In 1899, 1900, 1901 And 1902. And Giving In A Tabular Form The Following Particulars:- (1) Name Of Vessel; (2) Owner; (3) Broker, If Any, Through Whom The Vessel Was Chartered; (4) Tonnage; (5) Speed; (6) Rate Per Ton Per Month; (7) Minimum Time For Which Engaged; (8) Date Of Agreement; (9) Date At Which Pay Commenced; (10) Date At Which Pay Ceased; And (11) Total Sum Paid By Government For Hire And Other Charges'.
London, 13 August 1903
57pp.

172. Militia (Service Outside United Kingdom) – Return Showing The Number Of Officers And Men Serving In The Militia On 1st Jan., 1900; And The Number Who Served Outside The United Kingdom Between Oct., 1899, And June, 1902.
1905   BOPP

228. Army (Sales And Refunds) (South Africa) – Correspondence Relative To The Disposal Of Surplus Stores In South Africa.
1905   BOPP

Acts.

War Loan Act. 1900. c.2./Ref: (32) 114.

Supplemental War Loan Act. 1900. c.61./Ref: HC 318.

Electoral Disabilities (Military Service) Removal Act. 1900. c.8.

South African Loan And War Contribution Act. 1903. c.27./Ref: HL (203.) HC 189.

War Stores (Commission) Act. 1905. c.7./Ref: HL (123) HC 257.

Papers by Command.

(C.9345.) – South African Republic. Papers Relating To The Complaints Of British Subjects In The South African Republic.
London 1899
243pp.
Proposals for a Conference at Bloemfontein.

(C.9404.) – South African Republic. Correspondence Relating To The Bloemfontein Conference, 1899.
London 1899
iii+66pp.

(C.9530.) – South African Republic. Further Correspondence Relating To The Political Affairs Of The South African Republic.
(In continuation of [C.9521] September, 1899.)
London 1899
viii+70pp.
Text of Boer ultimatum.

(C.9531.) Army, 1899–1900 – Memorandum Showing The Principal Heads Of Expenditure Provided For In The Army Supplementary Estimate In Consequence Of The Military Situation In South Africa.
1899   BOPP

(Cd.18.) – South Africa. Correspondence Relating To The Despatch Of Colonial Military Contingents To South Africa.
London 1899
x+28pp.

(Cd.33.) Africa. No. 1 (1900) – Correspondence Respecting The Action Of Her Majesty's Naval Authorities With Regard To Certain Foreign Vessels.
1900
iv+28pp.   BOPP
Correspondence in respect of foreign vessels including the German mail steamers 'Bundesrath' and 'Herzog' suspected of conveying war material to the Boer Republics.

(Cd.34.) Miscellaneous. No. 1 (1900) – Correspondence Respecting The Seizure Of The British Vessels 'Springbok' And 'Peterhof' By United States Cruisers In 1863.
1900   BOPP
Document having reference to events in the South African War.

(Cd.35.) – Africa. No. 2 (1900) Correspondence With The Presidents Of The South African Republic And Of The Orange Free State Respecting The War.
London 1900
3pp.

(Cd.43.) South Africa. Further Correspondence Relating To Affairs In South Africa. (In Continuation of [C.9530], October, 1899.)
London 1900
xiii+253pp.
Reference to commencement of hostilities, martial law, etc.

(Cd.44.) Natal. Correspondence Relating To The Defence Of Natal.
London 1900
iv+26pp.

(Cd.53.) South Africa – Notice Issued By The High Commissioner For South Africa, On 26th January 1900, Relative To Forfeitures, &c. Of Property Situated In The South African Republic Or In The Orange Free State, Declared Subsequently To 10th October 1899.
1900
Folded sheet.   BOPP

(Cd.122.) – South African War. Telegrams From Field-Marshal Lord Roberts To The Secretary Of State For War Reporting (1) A Telegram Addressed By Him To The State Presidents Of The Orange Free State And South African Republic, In Reference To The Abuse Of The White Flag, And (2) The Reply Of The President Of The Orange Free State.
London 1900
Folded sheet.

(Cd.128.) – South Africa. Proclamation Issued By The High Commissioner For South Africa, On 19th March, 1900, Relating To Alienations Of Property By the Governments Of The South African Republic Or Orange Free State. Made Subsequently To The Date Of The Proclamation.
(In continuation of Cd.53.)
London 1900
Folded sheet.

(Cd.155.) – Army. (War In South Africa). Telegrams Relating To The Publication Of Despatches.
London 1900
3pp.
Concerning Gen. Buller's despatches on Spion Kop operations.

[Cd.196.] War Relief Fund Committee – Treasury Minute, Dated 17th February 1900, Relative To The Appointment Of A Committee To Consider, With The Assistance Of The Managers Of The Various Charitable Funds Available For The Relief Of Persons Who Have Served Or Are Serving In The Field, Or Of The Families Of Such Persons, How These Funds May Be Distributed With The Least Waste And To The Best Advantage Of Those For Whom They Were Intended; Together With A Copy Of The Report Of The Committee, Dated 28th May 1900.
1900   BOPP

(Cd.230.) – Telegrams Respecting Hospital Arrangements For The Troops in South Africa.
London 1900
4pp.

(Cd.248.) War Relief Funds Committee – Minutes Of Evidence, Appendices, And Index.
1900   BOPP

(Cd.261.) – South Africa. Further Correspondence Relating To Affairs In South Africa. (In continuation of [Cd.43.] January, 1900).
London 1900
xi+193pp.
Events from Jan. to June 1900.
Annexation of Orange Free State May 24th, 1900.

(Cd.264.) Cape Colony. Correspondence Relating To Affairs Of The Cape Colony.
London 1900
iv+44pp.
Treatment of Cape rebels. Resignation of Schreiner ministry.

(Cd.279.) Army – Statement Of Stores Transferred From Navy To Land Service For South Africa Up To 31st December 1899.
1900
Folded sheet.

(Cd.369.) South Africa. Correspondence Relating To The Recent Political Situation In South Africa.
London 1900
iii+19pp.

(Cd.420.) South Africa – Further Correspondence Relating To Affairs In South Africa. (In continuation of [Cd.261 and Cd.264.]).
1900
v+122pp.
Reference to Cape rebels and martial law.

(Cd.421.) – Army. Return Of Military Forces In South Africa, 1899–1900.
London 1900
Folded sheet.

(Cd.426.) Army. Proclamations Issued By Field-Marshal Lord Roberts In South Africa.
London 1900
23pp.

(Cd.453.) – Royal Commission On South African Hospitals. Report Of The Royal Commission Appointed To Consider And Report Upon The Care And Treatment Of The Sick And Wounded During The South African Campaign.
London 1901
vi+71pp.
Detailed investigation of medical services during the war. The enquiry embraced both military and private establishments including field hospitals, hospital ships and hospital trains. The equipment staffing and function of these units is examined and suggestions submitted for improvement of medical services generally.

(Cd.454.) – Royal Commission On South African Hospitals. Minutes Of Evidence Taken Before The Royal Commission Appointed To Consider And Report Upon The Care And Treatment Of The Sick And Wounded During The South African Campaign.
London 1901
lii+ii+565pp.

(Cd.455.) – Royal Commission On South African Hospitals. Appendix To Minutes Of Evidence Taken Before The Royal Commission Appointed To Consider And Report Upon The Care And Treatment Of The Sick And Wounded During The South African Campaign.
London 1901
ii+368pp.

(Cd.457.) – South Africa Despatches. Vol.I.
London 1901
140pp.
Lord Roberts' Despatches.

(Cd.458.) – South Africa Despatches. Vol.II. Natal Field Army.
London 1901
138pp.
Cd.457./458. are Despatches from Generals in the field to the Secretary of State for War.

(Cd.461.) – Army. Correspondence Between Field-Marshal Lord Roberts, Commanding-In-Chief South African Field Force, And Acting Commandant-General Louis Botha, Dated 12th, 13th, 14th, And 15th June, 1900.
London 1901
3pp.

(Cd.462.) Army. Return Of Military Forces In South Africa, 1899–1901.
London 1901
Folded sheet.

(Cd.463.) – South Africa Despatches. Supplementary.
London 1901
8pp.
See Cd.457. & Cd.458.

(Cd.464.) Reported Outrage On Esau At Calvinia – Telegram From Sir A. Milner To Secretary Of State For War Relating To.
1901
Folded sheet.   BOPP

(Cd.467.) – Army. Correspondence Relative To The Recall Of Major-General Sir H. E. Colvile, K.C.M.G., C.B.
London 1901
6pp.

(Cd.469.) – Army. Return Of Military Forces In South Africa. Oversea Colonial Contingents.
London 1901
Folded sheet.

(Cd.470.) – Army. Finding Of A Court Of Enquiry Held At Barberton On 25th September, 1900, To Investigate The Circumstances Under Which Lieutenant-Colonel B. E. Spragge, D.S.O., XIIIth Bn. Imperial Yeomanry, And Others, Became Prisoners Of War.
London 1901
Folded sheet.

(Cd.520.) – Army. Report By Lieut.-General Sir H. E. Colvile, K.C.M.G., C.B., On The Operations Of The Ninth Division At Paardeberg.
London 1901
10pp.

(Cd.522.) – South Africa Despatches. Despatch By General Lord Kitchener, Dated 8th March, 1901, Relative To Military Operations In South Africa.
London 1901
16pp.

(Cd.524.) – South Africa. Return Of Buildings Burnt In Each Month From June, 1900, To January, 1901, Including Farm Buildings, Mills, Cottages And Hovels.
London nd. (1901)
19pp.

(Cd.528.) – South Africa. Papers Relating To Negotiations Between Commandant Louis Botha And Lord Kitchener.
London, March 1901
7pp.

(Cd.546.) – South Africa. Letter From Commandant Louis Botha To Lord Kitchener, Dated 13th February, 1901.
London 1901
Folded sheet.

(Cd.547.) – South Africa. Further Correspondence Relating To Affairs In South Africa. (In continuation of [Cd.420.], December, 1900.)
London 1901
viii+77pp.
Reference to Colonial contingents, martial law, etc.

(Cd.578.) – Army. Return Of Military Forces In South Africa, 1899–1901. (In continuation of [Cd.462.].)
London 1901
Folded sheet.

(Cd.582.) – South Africa. Correspondence, &c., Between The Commander-In-Chief In South Africa And The Boer Commanders So Far As It Affects The Destruction Of Property.
London 1901
13pp.

(Cd.605.) – South Africa Despatches. Despatch By General Lord Kitchener, Dated 8th May, 1901, Relative To Military Operations In South Africa.
(In continuation of [Cd.522.].)
London 1901
36pp.

(Cd.608.) – South Africa. Return Of Numbers Of Persons In The Concentration Camps In South Africa, June 1901.
London 1901
Folded sheet.

(Cd.610.) – Army. Strength Of Volunteer Service Companies And Drafts

Embarked For South Africa In 1900.
London 1901
Folded sheet.

(Cd.623.) – South Africa. Report Of The Transvaal Concessions Commission, Dated 19th April 1901.
London 1901
161pp. With map.

(Cd.624.) – South Africa. Report Of The Transvaal Concessions Commission, Dated 19th April 1901. Part II. Minutes Of Evidence.
London 1901
iv+268pp.

(Cd.625.) – South Africa. Report Of The Transvaal Concessions Commission, Dated 19th April 1901. Part III. Appendix Of Documents.
London 1901
315pp.

(Cd.626.) – South Africa. Report Of The Lands Settlement Commission, South Africa. Dated 28th November 1900.
London 1901
24pp.

(Cd.627.) – South Africa. Report Of The Lands Settlement Commission, South Africa. Dated 28th November 1900. Part II. Documents, Evidence, &c.
London 1901
364pp.
Settlement of soldiers in South Africa.

(Cd.628.) – South Africa. Report By Sir David Barbour, K.C.S.I., K.C.M.G., On The Finances Of The Transvaal And The Orange River Colony, Dated March 29, 1901.
London 1901
i+30pp.

(Cd.663.) – South Africa. Further Papers Relating To Negotiations Between Commandant Louis Botha And Lord Kitchener. (In continuation of [Cd.528.] March 1901, and [Cd.546.] April, 1901.)
London 1901
18pp.

(Cd.693.) – South Africa. Report From Brigadier-General Dixon On The Operations At Vlakfontein On 29th May, 1901.
London 1901
4pp.

(Cd.694.) – South Africa. Further Return Of Numbers Of Persons In The Camps Of Refuge In South Africa, July, 1901. (In continuation of [Cd.608.].)
London 1901
Folded sheet.

(Cd.695.) – South Africa Despatches. Despatch By General Lord Kitchener, Dated 8th July, 1901, Relative To Military Operations In South Africa. (In continuation of [Cd.605.].)
London 1901
42pp.

(Cd.714.) – South Africa. Papers Relating To Certain Legislation Of The Late South African Republic Affecting Natives.
London 1901
124pp.

(Cd.732.) – South Africa. Correspondence Relating To The Prolongation Of Hostilities In South Africa.
London 1901
7pp.

(Cd.781.) – South Africa. Proclamation Issued By Lord Kitchener, As Administrator Of The Transvaal, On 1st

July, 1901, Respecting Payments Under Contracts To Purchase Or Lease Land Or Mining Rights, &c., Entered Into Prior To The War.
London 1901
4pp.

(Cd.789.) – South Africa. Further Return Of Numbers Of Persons In The Camps Of Refuge In South Africa, August, 1901. (In continuation of [Cd.694.].)
London 1901
Folded sheet.

(Cd.793.) – South Africa. Return Of Numbers Of Persons In The Concentration Camps In South Africa, September, 1901.
London 1901
Folded sheet.

(Cd.803.) – Imperial Yeomanry. Report Of The Deputy Adjutant-General Of The Force Regarding Its Home Organisation, Inspection Of The Constitution Of Its Base And Advanced Depots, And Distribution Of Stores In South Africa, And Proposals For Future Organisation. Called For By The Secretary Of State For War, 1st June, 1900, And Submitted 15th May, 1901.
London (1901)
255pp.

(Cd.819.) – Reports, &c., On The Working Of The Refugee Camps In The Transvaal, Orange River Colony, Cape Colony, And Natal.
London 1901
387pp.

(Cd.820.) – South Africa Despatches. Despatches By General Lord Kitchener, Dated 8th August, 8th September And 8th October, 1901, Relative To Military Operations In South Africa, Including A Supplementary Despatch, Dated 18th October, On The Actions At Itala Mount, Fort Prospect, And Moedwill. (In continuation of [Cd.695.].)
London 1901
68pp.

(Cd.821.) – South Africa. Correspondence Relative To The Treatment Of Natives By The Boers.
London 1901
6pp.

(Cd.822.) – South Africa. Further Correspondence Relative To The Treatment Of Natives By The Boers.
London 1901
4pp.

(Cd.823.) – South Africa Despatches. Despatch By General Lord Kitchener, Dated 8th November, 1901, Relative To Military Operations In South Africa. (In continuation of [Cd.820.].)
London 1902
11pp.

(Cd.824.) – South Africa Despatches. Despatch By General Lord Kitchener, Dated 8th December, 1901, Relative To Military Operations In South Africa. (In continuation of [Cd.823.].)
London 1902
23pp.

(Cd.853.) – South Africa. Further Papers Relating To The Working Of The Refugee Camps In The Transvaal, Orange River Colony, Cape Colony, And Natal. (In continuation of [Cd.819.] November, 1901.)
London 1901
viii+131pp.

(Cd.884.) – Army. Return Of The Numbers Of Troops And Horses That

Have Embarked For South Africa From 1st January, 1900, To 31st December, 1901.
London 1902
3pp.

(Cd.885.) – Army Expenditure, 1902–3; (South African War). Statement Showing Approximately Under Principal Subheads The Sums Still Required To Be Expended On The Army In South Africa In 1902–3.
London 1902
Folded sheet.

(Cd.888.) – South Africa. Further Correspondence Relative To The Treatment Of Natives By The Boers.
London 1902
10pp.

(Cd.890.) – South Africa Despatches. Despatch By General Lord Kitchener, Dated 8th January, 1902, Relative To Military Operations In South Africa. (In continuation of [Cd.824.].)
London 1902
12pp.

(Cd.892.) – Army. Return Of Military Forces In South Africa, 1899–1902. Strength Of Garrison On 1st August, 1899. Reinforcements And Casualties, &c., Since That Date, And Strength On 1st January, 1902. (In continuation of [Cd.578.].)
London 1902
Folded sheet.

(Cd.892*.) – To be Substituted for (Cd.892.) Already Issued.
Army. Return Of Military Forces In South Africa, 1899–1902. Strength Of Garrison On 1st August, 1899. Reinforcements And Casualties, &c., Since That Date, And Strength On 1st January, 1902. (In continuation of [Cd.578.].)
London 1902
Folded sheet.

(Cd.893.) – Concentration Camps Commission. Report On The Concentration Camps In South Africa, By The Committee Of Ladies Appointed By The Secretary Of State For War; Containing Reports On The Camps In Natal, The Orange River Colony, And The Transvaal.
London 1902
i+208pp.   p.109

(Cd.902.) – South Africa. Further Papers Relating To The Working Of The Refugee Camps In South Africa. (In continuation of [Cd.853.], December, 1901.)
London 1902
iv+134pp.

(Cd.903.) – South Africa. Further Correspondence Relating To Affairs In South Africa. (In continuation of [Cd.547.], April, 1901.)
London 1902
x+202pp.
Peace efforts, situation in Cape Colony and civil administration in Transvaal.

(Cd.904.) – Transvaal. Papers Relating To Legislation Affecting Natives In The Transvaal. (In continuation of [Cd.714.], July, 1901.)
London 1902
v+46pp.

(Cd.906.) – Africa. No.1 (1902). Correspondence With The Netherland Government Regarding The War In South Africa.
London 1902
i+3pp.

(Cd.921.) – South Africa. Petition From Boer Prisoners Of War At Bermuda.
London 1902
2pp. (Folded sheet.)

(Cd.933.) – South Africa. Letter From Assistant-General Tobias Smuts To Commandant-General L. P. Botha.
London 1902
4pp.

(Cd.934.) – South Africa. Further Papers Relating To The Working Of The Refugee Camps In South Africa.
(In continuation of [Cd.902.], January, 1902.)
London 1902
v+103pp.

(Cd.936.) – South Africa. Further Papers Relating To The Working Of The Refugee Camps In South Africa.
(In continuation of [Cd.934.], February, 1902.)
London 1902
ii+32pp.

(Cd.939.) – South Africa. Statistics Of The Refugee Camps In South Africa.
(The last previous figures will be found in [Cd.936.], March, 1902.)
London 1902
7pp.

(Cd.941.) – South Africa. Correspondence Relating To Proposed Additions Of Territory To Natal.
London 1902
12pp.

(Cd.942.) – South Africa. Statistics Of The Refugee Camps In South Africa.
(In continuation of [Cd.939.], April, 1902.)
London 1902
5pp.

(Cd.961.) – Army.
I. – Tender Of M. Bergl. & Co., Dated 6th January, 1902, For Supply Of Meat To Troops In South Africa.
II. – Letter Of Undertaking, Dated 27th January, 1902, As To Source Of Supply Of Meat.
III. – Letter Of Acceptance, Signed By Director Of Army Contracts, Dated 27th January, 1902.
London 1902
7pp.

(Cd.963.) – Army (Remounts).
Reports, Statistical Tables And Telegrams Received From South Africa. June, 1899, To January 22nd, 1902.
London 1902
56pp.
Report by Lt.-Col. W. H. Birkbeck Assistant Inspector of Remounts.

(Cd.964.) – Army.
I. – Tender Of The Imperial Cold Storage And Supply Company, Limited, Dated 4th March, 1902, For Supply Of Meat To Troops In South Africa.
II. – Letter Of Undertaking, Dated 4th March, 1902, As To Source Of Supply Of Meat.
III. – Letter Of Acceptance, Signed By Director Of Army Contracts, Dated 12th March, 1902.
London 1902
7pp.

(Cd.965.) – South Africa Despatches. Despatch By General Lord Kitchener, Dated 8th February, 1902, Relative To Military Operations In South Africa.
(In continuation of [Cd.890.].)
London 1902
12pp.

(Cd.967.) – South Africa. Report From Lieut.-General Lord Methuen On The

Action That Took Place Near Tweebosch On 7th March, 1902
London 1902
6pp.

(Cd.968.) – South Africa. The Spion Kop Despatches.
London 1902
48pp.

(Cd.970.) – South Africa Despatches. Despatch By General Lord Kitchener, Dated 8th March, 1902, Relative To Military Operations In South Africa.
(In continuation of [Cd.965.].)
London 1902
24pp.

(Cd.979.) – South Africa. Returns Of Farm Buildings, &c., In Cape Colony And Natal, Destroyed By The Boers.
London 1902
6pp.

(Cd.981.) – Papers Relating To The Administration Of Martial Law In South Africa.
London 1902
297pp.
See [Cd.1423.].

(Cd.984.) – South Africa Despatches. Despatch By General Lord Kitchener, Dated 8th April, 1902, Relative To Military Operations In South Africa.
(In continuation of [Cd.970.].)
London 1902
14pp.

(Cd.986.) – South Africa Despatches. Despatch By General Lord Kitchener, Dated 1st June, 1902, Relative To Military Operations In South Africa.
(In continuation of [Cd.984.].)
London 1902
23pp.

(Cd.987.) – South Africa. Telegrams Concerning The Siege Of Ladysmith.
London 1902
4pp.

(Cd.988.) – South Africa Despatches. Despatch By General Lord Kitchener, Dated 23rd June, 1902, Relative To Military Operations In South Africa.
(In continuation of [Cd.986.].)
London 1902
41pp.

(Cd.990.) – Army. Return Of Military Forces In South Africa, 1899–1902. Strength Of Garrison On 1st August, 1899. Reinforcements And Casualties, &c., Between 1st August, 1899, And 31st May, 1902. (In continuation of [Cd.892.*].)
London 1902
Folded sheet.

(Cd.993.) – Army Remount Department – Report Of A Court Of Enquiry On The Administration Of The Army Remount Department Since Jan. 1899, By Order Of The Commander-In-Chief Dated 20th Feb. 1902.
1902
iv+34pp.   BOPP

(Cd.994.) – Army Remount Department – Minutes Of Evidence, With Appendices.
1902
viii+369pp.   BOPP
Enquiry into the administration of the Army Remount Department. With Appendices.

(Cd.995.) – Reports By Officers Appointed By The Commander-In-Chief To Inquire Into The Working Of The

Remount Department Abroad.
London 1902
88pp.
Reports on remount operations in the United States and Canada by General Sir R. Stewart and Lieut-Colonel E. Holland. Remount operations in Austro-Hungary by Lieut-General Sir M. G. Gerard. Remount operations in South Africa, Australia and New Zealand by Major-General Viscount Downe.

(Cd.996.) – Army Expenditure, 1902–03. (South African War.) Statement Showing Approximately The Revised Amounts Now Required Under The Various Votes In View Of The Conclusion Of Peace As Compared With The Provision Made In The Estimates Submitted To Parliament, With Explanations Of The Differences.
London 1902
3pp.

(Cd.1096.) – South Africa. Correspondence Respecting Terms Of Surrender Of The Boer Forces In The Field.
London 1902
13pp.

(Cd.1161.) – South Africa. Statistics Of The Refugee Camps In South Africa.
(In continuation of [Cd.942.], May, 1902.)
London 1902
5pp.

(Cd.1162.) – Petition For The Temporary Suspension Of The Cape Constitution And Reply Of His Majesty's Government.
London 1902
9pp.

(Cd.1163.) – South Africa. Further Correspondence Relating To Affairs In South Africa. (In continuation of [Cd.903.] January, 1902.)
London 1902
viii+178pp. With charts.
Reference to slanders against British troops.

(Cd.1284.) – South Africa. Papers Relating To An Interview Between The Secretary Of State For The Colonies And Generals Botha, De Wet, And De La Rey, On September 5th, 1902.
London 1902
24pp.

(Cd.1329.) – South Africa. Correspondence Relating To The Appeal Of The Boer Generals To The Civilized World.
London 1902
11pp.
Reference to destruction of Boer farms, etc.

(Cd.1364.) – South Africa, 1902. Report Of The Royal Commission Appointed To Enquire Into Sentences Passed Under Martial Law.
London 1902
v+63pp.
List of those sentenced with recommendations of the Commission.

(Cd.1423.) – Papers Relating To The Administration Of Martial Law In South Africa. (In continuation of [Cd.981.])
London 1903
156pp.

(Cd.1498.) – Report Of The Commission On The Nature, Pathology, Causation And Prevention Of Dysentery And Its Relationship To Enteric Fever.
Appointed By The Secretary Of State For War, August, 1900.
London 1903
147pp. Illustrated. (Some colour plates.)
Reference to cases treated during the war.

(Cd.1499.) – Army. Letter From General Officer Commanding The Forces In South Africa Transmitting The Proceedings Of A Board Of Officers Assembled To Report Upon Certain Supplies Of 'Meat And Vegetable' Rations At Pretoria Considered To Be Unfit For Issue.
London 1903
7pp.

(Cd.1551.) – South Africa. Papers Relating To The Progress Of Administration In The Transvaal And Orange River Colony. (In continuation of [Cd.1463.], February, 1903.)
London 1903
ii+202pp. With maps.
Contains reports from Sir A. Milner and a report on the South African Constabulary by Major-General Baden-Powell.

(Cd.1552.) – South Africa. Papers Relating To The Finances Of The Transvaal And Orange River Colony.
London 1903
iv+115pp. With map.

(Cd.1553.) – South Africa. Further Papers Relating To The Progress Of Administration In The Transvaal. (In continuation of [Cd.1551.], April, 1903.)
London 1903
45pp.
Pages 3–19 relate to Transvaal Burgher Camps, Burgher land settlement and general statistics concerning repatriation in the Transvaal.

(Cd.1789.) – Report Of His Majesty's Commissioners Appointed To Inquire Into The Military Preparations And Other Matters Connected With The War In South Africa.
London 1903
viii+316pp.   p.8

(Cd.1790.) – Royal Commission On The War In South Africa. Minutes Of Evidence Taken Before The Royal Commission On The War In South Africa. (Volume I.)
London 1903
xii+534pp.

(Cd.1791.) – Royal Commission On The War In South Africa. Minutes Of Evidence Taken Before The Royal Commission On The War In South Africa. (Volume II.)
London 1903
x+720pp.

(Cd.1792.) – Royal Commission On The War In South Africa. Appendices To The Minutes Of Evidence Taken Before The Royal Commission On The War In South Africa.
London 1903
ii+445pp.

(Cd.2433.) – Army – Return Of Stores And Supplies Despatched To South Africa During The Period 1899–1901, Destroyed Locally.
1905
5pp.   BOPP

(Cd.2435.) – Sales And Refunds To Contractors In South Africa – Committee Appointed To Consider The Question Of. Report; With Appendices.
1905
43pp.   BOPP

(Cd.2436.) – Sales And Refunds To Contractors In South Africa – Committee Appointed To Consider The Question Of. Minutes Of Evidence.
1905
iv+531pp.   BOPP

(Cd.2440.) – Army. Abstract Of Recommendations Of The Royal Commission On The Care And Treatment Of The Sick And Wounded During The South African Campaign, Together With The Action Taken.
London 1905

(Cd.3127.) – The Royal Commission On War Stores In South Africa. Report Of The Royal Commission On War Stores In South Africa, Together With Appendices.
London 1906
vi+68+xxv pp.

(Cd.3128.) – Royal Commission On War Stores In South Africa – Minutes Of Evidence. Vol. I.
1906
xvi+532pp.

(Cd.3129.) – Royal Commission On War Stores In South Africa – Minutes Of Evidence. Vol. II.
1906
xiii+466pp.

(Cd.3130.) – Royal Commission On War Stores In South Africa – Report With Appendices, Of Messrs. Annan, Kirby, Dexter & Co., Chartered Accountants. Vol. III.
1906
22pp.

(Cd.3131.) – Royal Commission On War Stores In South Africa – Reports On South African Contractors, With Appendices, By Messrs. Deloitte, Dever, Griffiths, Annan & Co., Chartered Accountants. Vol. IV.
1906
207pp.

Non-Parliamentary Publications.

(HMSO) – Report By The Central British Red Cross Committee On Voluntary Organisations In Aid Of The Sick And Wounded During The South African War.
London 1902
vi+209pp. Plates & various folding plans.
Among organisations noted in the report are the National Aid Society, St. John Ambulance Asssociation and St. John Ambulance Brigade, the Army Nursing Service Reserve and Foreign Red Cross Societies. Sections relate to Hospital Ships and Hospital Trains.

Railways During The War In South Africa, 1899–1902. History Of. By Lt.-Col. Sir E. P. C. Girouard, K.C.M.G., D.S.O., R.E.
1903   BOPP
See under GIROUARD Sir E. P. C.

Telegraph Operations During The War In South Africa 1899–1902. History Of. By Lt.-Col. R. L. Hippisley, C.B., R.E.
1903   BOPP
See entry under HIPPISLEY Lt.-Col. R. L.

(HMSO) – Special Report On Organisation And Equipment Of The Engineer Arm In South Africa.
HMSO
London 1900
89pp. Illustrated.
*Document marked Confidential $\frac{079}{3305}$.
Contents include reports on Engineer units and auxiliary forces. Reports on equipment with appendices. Reports of the Directors of Railways and Telegraphs, with appendices. Supplementary reports of Engineer-In-Chief. Title similar to that of a report attributed to Maj.-Gen. Elliott Wood. [See WO.73]. Possibly the same document?*

(HMSO) – Conditions Of Service Of South African And Over-Sea Contingents

Employed In The South African War, 1899–1902.
London 1904
348pp.
Attestation or contract of engagement, discharge certificates and rates of pay of Australasian and of South African Irregular forces, Cape Colony and Natal.

(HMSO) – South African War. Medical Arrangements. Report. See under WILSON Sir W. D.
                                 BOPP

(HMSO) – South African War, 1899–1902. Surgical Cases Noted In The. Report On. 1905. See STEVENSON (Surgeon-General W.F.)
                                 BOPP

(HMSO) – South Africa. War Stores In. Royal Commission On. 8th And 9th Days' Evidence. *1st to 7th days' Evidence not put on Sale.*
1905   BOPP

Hobhouse (C. E.) – Report And Evidence Of the War Commission Collated And Arranged By C. E. Hobhouse, M.P.
J. W. Arrowsmith
Bristol 1904
143pp.
8vo.   M

Hobhouse (Emily) – The Concentration Camps. Official Facts.
'The Morning Leader'
London 1901
2pp.
Quarto   M
Statistics regarding the mortality rate in concentration camps.

Hobhouse (Emily) – To The Committee Of The South African Distress Fund. Report Of A Visit To The Camps Of Women And Children In The Cape And Orange River Colonies.
Friars Printing Association, Limited
London nd. (c.1901)
39pp.
244×163mm   p.71

Hobhouse (Emily) – A Letter To The Committee Of The South African Women And Children's Distress Fund.
The Argus Printing Co., Ltd.
London (1901)
11pp.
12mo.   M

Hobhouse (Emily) – Christmas In Cape Colony. A.D. 1901.
Taylor, Garnett, Evans & Co.
Manchester (1902?)
16pp.
220mm   SABIB
Reprinted from the 'Manchester Guardian'.

Hobhouse (Emily) – The Brunt Of The War And Where It Fell.
Methuen & Company
London 1902
xvi+356pp. Map and illustrations.
197×128mm   p.109

Hobson (J. A.) – Capitalism And Imperialism In South Africa.
The Tucker Pub. Co.
New York nd. (1900)
30pp.
200×136mm

Hobson (J. A.) – The War In South Africa: Its Causes And Effects.

James Nisbet & Co.
London 1900
viii+324pp.
225×150mm
*Copy published by Macmillan & Co.,
London 1900; listed in SABIB.*

Hofmeyr (Rev. A.) – The Story Of My
Captivity During The Transvaal War,
1899–1900.
Edward Arnold
London 1900
xii+302pp. Illustrated.
200×132mm

Holdsworth (A.) – Lines On The
Transvaal. 'Neath Freedom's Flag. By
A. Holdsworth (Irene Gordon), Great
Horton.
William Forster, printer
Bradford (1900?)
12pp.
Cr.8vo.   M
Entered from BM collection.

(Hollandia) – Special Transvaal Number.
See entry under SIMONS. L. (editor).

**(Hollandsche Stoomdrukkerij En
Uitgeversmaatschappij)** (Publisher?) –
The People Of Holland To The People
Of Great-Britain And The Civilised
World.
Hollandsche Stoomdrukkerij en
Uitgeversmaatschappij
Amsterdam 1900
12pp.
Roy.8vo.   M
*An attack on the British army's conduct in
South Africa.*

Home (Lieut. W.) – With The Border
Volunteers To Pretoria.
W. & J. Kennedy
Hawick 1901
viii+203pp. Folding map and plates.
189×126mm   p.3

('Hongkong Daily Press' Office)
(Publisher) – From Portsmouth To
Peking Via Ladysmith With A Naval
Brigade.
'Hongkong Daily Press' Office
Hongkong 1901
viii+151pp. With two maps.
233×167mm   p.4
*The name of the author, George Crowe,
does not appear on the title page. See
CROWE – The Commission of H.M.S.
'Terrible' 1898–1902.*

(Honourable Artillery Company) – List
Of The Chiefs, Officers, Court Of
Assistants, &c., &c., &c., See entry
under MERRITT & HATCHER Ltd.

Hooker (Le Roy) – The Africanders
A Century Of Dutch-English Feud In
South Africa.
Rand, McNally & Co.
Chicago and New York 1900
279pp. Folding map and plates.
190×130mm
Prelude to the war of 1899–1902.

Hopkins (J. Castell) and Halstead (Murat)
– South Africa And The Boer-British
War. Comprising An Authentic History
Of The Dark Continent From The
Earliest Discoveries – Its People – Their
Government And Progress – The Wealth
And Development Of The World's
Richest Diamond And Gold Fields –
Causes Of The Present Conflict –
Greatest Battles In History – Leading
Generals.
J. L. Nichols & Co.

Toronto/Canada nd. (1902)
Vol. 1 – 448pp.
Vol. 2 – vi+525–858+63pp.+36pp.
Both vols. illustrated throughout.
Complete set despite erratic pagination.
226×160mm
*Various editions recorded. Some editions
include a 63pp. section on the Life of
Cecil John Rhodes and a 36pp. appendix
concerning Australians in the war. Also
published in one vol. under J. L. Nichols
imprint. (xxvi+542pp. Illustrated.) SABIB
lists ed. with imprint of The Bradley-
Garretson Company, Limited. Brantford/
Canada and Linscott Publishing
Company, London, to vol.2.*

Hopkins (J. Castell) and Halstead (Murat)
– South Africa And The Boer-British
War Comprising A History Of South
Africa And Its People, Including The
War Of 1899, 1900, 1901 And 1902.
J. L. Nichols & Co.
War Book Publishing Co.
Toronto/Canada nd. (c.1902)
2 vols.
858pp. Illustrated.

(Horace Marshall & Son) (Publishers) –
The Story Of H.M.S. Powerful, From
The Diary Of A Powerful Man.
Dedicated By Permission To Capt.
Hedworth Lambton, R.N.
Horace Marshall & Son
London 1900
92pp.
Cr.8vo.   M
*An account of the Naval Brigade in the
South African War.*

Horne (Maj. H. S.) – Reminiscences Of
The South African War.
Privately printed
np./nd. (c.1900)
50pp.
210×140mm
*Diary of Maj. Horne, RHA, from Jan.
–Sept. 1900.*

Horton (R. F.) – 'Peace On Earth':
A Lecture Delivered At Lyndhurst Road
Congregational Church, Hampstead, On
Sunday Evening, December 6th, 1903.
Hampstead Peace And Arbitration
Society
Hampstead (c.1903)
15pp.
180mm   SABIB
*An examination of the principles which
led to the South African War.*

(Howden. Alexr. & Company)
(Publishers) 1899–1900 List Of
Transports From UK Ports To South
Africa (Compiled From Best Available
Sources.)
Alexr. Howden & Company
London 1900
i+8pp. (Printed rectos)
373×276mm   p.35
Title from cover.

Howe (The Countess) (Editor) – The
Imperial Yeomanry Hospitals In South
Africa 1900–1902.
Arthur L. Humphreys
London 1902
Vol. 1 – viii+194pp.
Vol. 2 – xv+266pp.
Vol. 3 – xi+274pp.
Illustrated throughout with folding plans,
photographs and maps.
283×218mm   p.6
Single vol. ed. 283×218mm.

Howe (George) & Howe (Martha Storr) –
Field Work In South Africa During The
Campaign Of 1899–1902.

np./nd. (c.1902?)
34pp. Illustrated.
170×210mm   SABIB
*Administration of soldiers homes in
various British military camps, providing
comforts for troops and opportunity for
christian worship.*

Howland (Frederick Hoppin) – The Chase
Of De Wet And Other Later Phases Of
The Boer War As Seen By An American
Correspondent.
Preston and Rounds Company
Providence 1901
vii+203pp. Plate and map.
210×134mm

(H & S) (Printers) – List Of Persons Who
Have Been Expelled From, Or Given
Free Passages From, South Africa, 1900.
H & S printers
(London 1902?)
59pp.
330mm   SABIB
*No title page. Catalogued from cover.
Page 1. – Confidential. Office of the
Commissioner of Police, Johannesburg.*

(H. S.) (Compiler) – A Souvenir Of
Sympathy Compiled By H. S., Banff.
Aberdeen Journal Office
Aberdeen 1900
199pp. Illustrated.
224×145mm
*A volume published during the war to
raise money for the 'Those Left Behind'
Fund. Contents include a portrait of
General Hector Macdonald and Poems of
the War, together with many articles of
general Scottish interest.*

(H. T. C.) – 'Ikona' Sketches.
Printed at St. George's Press
Dover nd. (c.1902)
32pp. Illustrated.
214×282mm   p.38

Hubly (Russell C.) – 'G' Company, Or
Every-Day Life Of The R. C. R. Being
A Descriptive Account Of Typical Events
In The Life Of The First Canadian
Contingent In South Africa.
The Witness Printing House
Montreal 1902
x+pp.11–111. With portrait of the
author.
185×130mm
*Variant bindings. Green cloth and pink
card covers recorded.*

Hudleston (W.) (Compiler) – The War In
South Africa, 1899–1900.
Harrison and Sons (Printers)
London 1900
402pp. Tables.
220mm   SABIB
*Newspaper extracts with commentary,
dealing with events from Oct. 1899–Sept.
1900.*

Hughes (C. E.) and Begbie (E. H.) –
Gulliver Joe, Etc. See – QUICK
(Jonathan).

Hume (Lt.-Col. C. V.) – Report On
Intelligence Department. See – WO.90.

Hundermark (F. C.) (Printer) – The War
Between Great Britain And The
Republics. The Boer Side. A Record Of
All Telegrams Issued For Public
Information By The O.F.S. Information
Commission, From The Commencement
Of Hostilities Up To The Occupation Of
Bloemfontein By The British, And Some
Other Interesting Extracts.
F. C. Hundermark, Printer

Jagersfontein 1900
116pp.
180×120mm
SABIB lists an edition by F. C.
Hundermark, printer. Jagersfontein
O.R.C. 1900? 95pp.

Hunt (Lieutenant Meynell) – With The
Warwickshire Yeomanry In South Africa
. . . . From February 1900 To June 1901.
Cornish Brothers
Birmingham 1902
iv+173pp. Illustrated.
232×150mm

Hunter (A. A.) – The Old Cheltonian
South African War Memorials: Memorial
Cross, Reredos In College Chapel,
Kneeling Desk.
Norman, Sawyer and company
Cheltenham 1904
83pp. Illustrated.
283×224mm

Hutcheson (R.) – The Truth About The
South African Question.
Adams' News Depot
Washington 1900
16pp.
230mm   SABIB
No title page. Catalogued from cover. An
edition of 31pp. (150mm) listed in SABIB,
attributed to 'British-American
Association'. Tract No.1. Published
Washington DC, 1900.

(Hutchings & Crowsley) (Printers) –
Souvenir Of The Kensington, Brompton,
Knightsbridge And Belgravia Carnival
Held On Wednesday & Thursday, 10th &
11th October, 1900 In Aid Of The 'Daily
Telegraph' Fund For The Widows And
Orphans Of Those Of Her Majesty's
Forces Who Fell In The Boer War,
1899–1900.
Hutchings & Crowsley, printers
London 1900
61pp. Illustrated throughout.
248×186mm
With additional pages of advertisements.

Hutton (Lt.-Gen. Sir E. T. H.) –
Operations Of General Hutton's Force:
South African Campaign 1900.
Publisher/printer not shown
nd. (c.1901)
270×200mm
Uncommon item. The 5 maps and 11
plans were printed as illustrations to Gen.
Hutton's letters from South Africa, March
20–October 17 1900. (unpublished.)
These appear to be extra copies privately
bound by the author.

Huyshe (Wentworth) – The Graphic
History Of The South African War 1899
–1900 Complete Narrative Of The
Campaign By Wentworth Huyshe With
Special Chapters. The Siege Of
Ladysmith. By Lieut. M. F. McTaggart,
5th Lancers, who took part in the
Defence. The Siege Of Kimberley. By
G. M. C. Luard, Reuter's Correspondent
during the Investment. The Siege Of
Mafeking. By Major F. D. Baillie,
Correspondent of the 'Morning Post'
during the Investment. With Roberts To
Bloemfontein. By G. D. Giles, Special
Artist-Correspondent of 'The Graphic'.
The Volunteers In The Campaign. By
Colonel Sir Howard Vincent, K.C.M.G.,
C.B., M.P. The Care Of The Wounded
In The Field. By Sir William
MacCormac, Bart., K.C.V.O., P.R.C.S.
Illustrated by sketches and photographs
from W. T. Maud, C. E. Fripp, G. D.
Giles, and R. Thiele, Special Artists of
'The Graphic' and from Officers at the
Front.

The Graphic Office
London 1900
108pp. Illustrated throughout.
417×308mm   p.13

Hyndman (H. M.) – The Transvaal War
And The Degradation Of England.
Twentieth Century Press
London 1899
16pp.
220mm   SABIB
Reprinted from 'Justice', expressing
opinions on the Transvaal question.

I

(I.C.W.C.) – President Kruger's
Oversight And Its Results.
Publisher/printer not shown
Truro (1902)
Pagination not shown
8vo.   THB

('Ignotus') – A Tract For The Times.
Reprinted From The *South African News*
Of January 18 And 27, 1900. How To
Stop The War: A Call To The People Of
God.
South African Newspaper Co.
Cape Town (1900?)
12pp.
210mm   SABIB
Title from cover.

Illingworth (Clafton) – With Lord
Methuen's Column.
The Scarborough Post Co., Ltd.
Scarborough 1901
32pp.
207×161mm
Letters from South Africa relating to
Imperial Yeomanry attached to Lord
Methuen's force, March–December 1900.

(Illustrated London News) (Publishers) –
Fugitives From Pretoria, The Adventures
Of Captain F. N. Le Mesurier And
Captain Haldane, Who Escaped From
Pretoria To Lorenzo Marques.
Supplement To The Illustrated London
News, June 30, 1900.
Illustrated London News
London 1900
8pp. Illustrated.   CB

**(Illustrated London News And Sketch,
Limited)** (Publishers) – The Illustrated
London News Record Of The Transvaal
War, 1899–1900. The Achievements Of
The Home And Colonial Forces In The
Great Conflict With The Boer Republics.
The Illustrated London News and Sketch,
Limited.
London nd. (c.1900)
84pp. Illustrated throughout.
414×305mm   p.85
A superior numbered edition signed by
various contributors was published the
same year.

(Imperial Liberal Council) (Publisher) –
The War; Its Causes And Objects.
A Brief Survey For Liberal Leaders.
Imperial Liberal Council
London (1900?)
15pp.
8vo.   M

(Imperial South African Association)
(Published by) – Leaflets published in
London from 1896–1908. Some in
reference to the South African war listed
below. SABIB and M include extensive
lists.
SABIB – Vol.2 pp.637–639. M – Vol.2
pp.375–376. Other ISAA publications are
catalogued under author.
211×137mm

The Treatment Of The Cape Boers By
The English Government And The
Treatment Of The English By The Boer
Government (1899?)
2pp.

The British Case Against The Boer
Republics. (1900) (No.26)
36pp.

Mr. John Morley And The Pro-Boers.
(1900?) (No.33)
4pp.

The Plain Issue. Sir Henry Fowler On
The War. (1900?) (No.35)
2pp.

The New Pro-Boer Delegates. Who Are
They? Why Are They Here? (1901)
(No.36)
8pp.

Conduct Of British Soldiers In South
Africa. (1901)
2pp.

The South African War And The Franco-
German War. (1901) (No.40)
4pp.

The Concentration Camps. Sir Neville
Chamberlain's Mistake. (1901) (No.41)
4pp.

Slanders On Our Troops In South Africa.
[Letter By] Mr. And Mrs. Osborn Howe.
(1901?) (No.42)
2pp.

The Refugee Camps. A Boer Woman's
Testimony To Their Comfort. (1901?)
(No.43)
2pp.

The Pro-Boer Meeting. [Queen's Hall]
(1901?)
2pp.

Liberal Leaders On The War And The
Settlement In South Africa. (1902)
(No.44)
16pp.

Canada's Reply To Pro-Boer Slanders.
(1902) (No.46)
4pp.

The Concentration Camps. The Truth
About Their Condition, By A Minister
On The Spot. (Rev. F. J. Williams)
(1902) (No.47)
2pp.

The Responsibility For The
Concentration Camps. Boer
Commandant-General's 'Mercy', Lord
Kitchener's Exposé. (1902) (No.48)
2pp.

Pro-Boer Speeches And The War.
'Methods Of Barbarism – An Echo From
The Veldt.' (1902) (No.50)
2pp.

Methods Of Humanity. Tribute To Our
Troops By General Count Huebner.
(1902) (No.51)
1p.

Boer General [Tobias Smuts] On Farm-
Burning And Concentration Camps.
(1902) (No.52)
1p.

The Terms Of Peace. (1902) (No.53)
2pp.

Liberal Leaders On The Peace. (1902)
(No.54)
2pp.

The Future Of South Africa. Essentials
Of Settlement.
(1902?)
1p.   SABIB

(Imperial South African Association)
(Publisher) – Handy Notes On S. Africa.
For The Use Of Speakers And Others.
Fourth Edition – Revised.
Imperial South African Association
London 1901
113pp.
8vo.   M
*This edition contains much useful
information respecting the South African
War.*

(Imperial Yeomanry) – Imperial
Yeomanry Orders. Jan. 1900 – Feb. 1903.
[Part Typescript].
Publisher/Printer not shown
——— 1900 – 03
(Var. pag.)   MOD
*Item drawn from War Office list of
publications. WO. ref. – WH Loc: SA48.*

(Imperial Yeomanry) – Imperial
Yeomanry Orders. Jan. 1900 – Apr. 1900,
Mar. 1902.
Publisher/Printer not shown
——— 1900 – 02
(Var. pag.)   MOD
*Item drawn from War Office list of
publications. WO. ref. – WH Loc:
SA48A.*

(Imperial Yeomanry) – Imperial
Yeomanry: Proceedings Of The HQ Staff
Committee From 15 Jan. 1900 To 15 May
1900.
Publisher/Printer not shown
——— 1900
60pp.   MOD
*Item drawn from War Office list of
publications. WO. ref. – WH Loc:
Cttee. Rpts.*

(Incorporated Law Society) – South
African War. Official Report Of The
Banquet, Etc. See entry under
SPOTTISWOODE & CO. LTD.

('Independent' Press) (Printers) – Boer
Prisoners In Ceylon: Report Of
A Cricket Match Between An XI,
Selected From The Prisoners-Of-War
At Diyatalawa And The Colombo Colts,
Played On The Ground Of The
Nondescript Cricket Club, Victoria Park,
On Friday & Saturday, July 5th & 6th,
1901; Group Photograph Of Teams By
A. W. Andree.
'Independent' Press
——— (1901?)
18pp. Frontispiece.
210mm   SABIB
Reprinted from 'The Ceylon Independent'.

Inder (W. S.) – On Active Service With
The S.J.A.B. South African War, 1899 –
1902. A Diary Of Life And Events In
The War Hospitals At Wynberg, Nourse
Deep, Johannesburg, And Other Places,
By The Late W. S. Inder, Orderly, And
2nd Class Supernumerary Officer,
Kendal Division, No.4 District, St. John
Ambulance Brigade, Attached To The
Royal Army Medical Corps.
Atkinson and Pollitt, printers
Kendal 1903
ix+318+iii pp. Illustrated.
220×139mm   p.v

Inder (W. S.) – On Active Service With
The St. John Ambulance Brigade (South
African War, 1899 – 1900).
Dale, Reynolds & Co., Ltd.
London 1905
321pp. Illustrated.
8vo.   M

Inglis (Alice St. Clair) – A Souvenir Of
The First New Zealand Contingent To
South Africa 1899 – 1901.
Arthur Cleave & Co.
Auckland 1902
63pp. Illustrated.
245mm   BIM

Ingram (Percy T.) – Songs Of The
Transvaal War.
Palmer & Son
Grantham 1900
31pp. Vignette illustrations
Cr.8vo.   M
*A book of verse on the South African
War. Poems include 'French's march to
Kimberley' and 'Cronje's last stand.'*

(Intelligence Dept.) – See entries under
FIELD INTELLIGENCE DEPT.

(Intelligence Officer. The) – On The
Heels Of De Wet.
William Blackwood & Sons
Edinburgh/London 1902
vii+346pp.
198×128mm   p.91
Name of author – Lionel James.

(International Arbitration League)
(Publisher?) – 'Now Tell Us All About
The War, And What They Killed Each
Other For.'
The League
London (1900?)
4pp.
210mm   SABIB
*Also published with slight differences, by
the 'Morning Leader' under title –
'Labour Leaders and the War'.*

Ireland (Alleyne) – The Anglo-Boer
Conflict: Its History And Causes.
Small, Maynard & Company
Boston 1900
ix+141pp.
162×106mm   CC

Ireland (Alleyne) – The Anglo-Boer
Conflict. Its History And Causes.
Sands & Company
London 1900
128pp.
Cr.8vo.   M

Ives (Herbert) – Britons And Boers.
John Lane
London/New York nd. (1900?)
46pp. Illustrated.
140×190mm
*Verse relating to the war illustrated by
Scotson Clark.*

Iwan-Muller (E. B.) – Lord Milner And
South Africa.
William Heinemann
London 1902
xxxii+751pp. With two portraits.
230×147mm
*Lord Milner's work in South Africa to the
outbreak of war.*

J

Jackson (Mrs. C. N.) – Shot Or Patrol.
A True Incident Of The Present War,
Etc. See – SKEFFINGTON & SON,
publishers.

Jackson (E. L.) – A Pictorial And
Descriptive Souvenir Of Saint Helena.
Publisher/printer not shown
St. Helena (1902?)
34pp. Map and illustrations.
167×231mm
*Souvenir booklet issued in the 400th year
of the discovery of St. Helena.*

*Illustrations include views of Boer
prisoners and prison camps. CC lists an
extended edition of 46pp. Map and
illustrations.*

Jackson (George) – Christianity And The
War: A Sermon Preached In The Synod
Hall, Edinburgh . . . . With Letters From
Rev. T. G. Selby, Rev. Jas. Hope
Moulton, Mr. W. M. Crook . . . . Rev.
W. Kingscote Greenland, Rev. T. Wynne
Jones, Rev. G. Talalun Newton, Dr.
H. S. Lunn.
Horace Marshall & Son
London 1900
16pp.
220mm   SABIB
*A sermon denouncing the war in South
Africa, with letters expressing similar
views from various ministers and laymen.*

**Jackson (Bvt.Lt.-Col. H. M.) & Casgrain
(Capt. P. H. Du P.)** – Report On Survey
And Mapping Section. See WO. 97.

Jackson (Murray Cosby) – A Soldier's
Diary South Africa 1899 – 1901.
Max Goschen Limited
London 1913
xii+366pp. Illustrated.
205×130mm
*Campaign experiences of an NCO in the
7th Battn. Mounted Infantry. The writer
took part in the advance from
Bloemfontein to Pretoria. Copies recorded
bound in light brown cloth and purple
cloth, the latter of larger format –
229×146mm.*

Jackson (T.) (Photographer/Publisher?)
– Pictorial Views Of St. Helena And
Illustrations Of The Military Camps And
Boer Prisoners Of War.
(Title from cover)
Published by T. Jackson?
np./nd. (c.1902) St. Helena?
16pp. (Photographs with captions.)
150×190mm
*Views of the island including
Broadbottom and Deadwood prison
camps, Cronje and his officers, etc.*

('Jack The Sniper') – 'A Peep Over The
Barleycorn' In The Firing Line With The
P.W.O., 2nd West Yorkshire Regiment,
Through The Relief Of Ladysmith.
John T. Drought (Printer)
Dublin 1911
214pp. Illustrated.
190×124mm   p.63
Author – Charles James O'Mahony.

**(Jacob and Johnson 'Hampshire
Chronicle' Office)** (Printers) – The Happy
Warrior A Short Account Of The Life Of
David, 9th Earl Of Airlie.
Jacob and Johnson 'Hampshire
Chronicle' Office
Printed for private circulation only
Winchester 1901
iv+168pp. Illustrated.
220×175mm
*Memoir of David William Stanley,
Lieut.-Col. 12th Lancers. Killed at
Diamond Hill, June 1900.*

Jacson (Col. M.) – The Record Of
A Regiment Of The Line Being
A Regimental History Of The 1st
Battalion Devonshire Regiment During
The Boer War 1899 – 1902.
Hutchinson & Co.
London 1908
xv+226pp. Folding map and plates.
193×130mm

James (Lionel) – On The Heels Of De
Wet. See – INTELLIGENCE OFFICER.

Jameson (J.) – Medical Administration In The South African War, Etc. See – CHURCH, MACCORMAC and JAMESON.

Jasper (G.) – With General French To Pretoria.
np./nd. (c.1900?)
ii+20pp.
230×120mm   SABIB
Narrative poem. No title page, preface signed G. Jasper.

(J. A. W.) – The British-Boer War 1899–1902.
Publisher/printer not shown
New York nd. (1902)
18pp. With folding map.
230×150mm
Pamphlet signed J. A. W. Paper covered.

Jeans (T. T.) (Editor) – Naval Brigades In The South African War 1899–1900 Written By Officers Attached To The Various Brigades.
Sampson Low, Marston & Company (Limited)
London 1901
xx+307pp. Folding map and plates.
190×124mm

(J. G. D.) (Compiler) – Soldiers Of Banffshire 1899–1900, Etc. See – BANFFSHIRE JOURNAL OFFICE.

Joe (Dennison) – Nicholson's Nek! Townshend, Taylor & Snashall, printers for Eastern Press
Cape Town (1899)
ii+pp.11–18. Illustrated.
210mm   SABIB
Poems for the period No. 2. For No. 1. see WALLACE Edgar.

(John Lewis & Company, The Selkirk Press) (Publishers?) – Souvenir Of The Siege Of Mafeking. Being Fac-Simile Reproductions Of The Most Interesting General Orders Issued To The Garrison Of Mafeking By General Baden-Powell During The Siege. With Introduction By Chas. E. Hands, War Correspondent For The 'Daily Mail'.
John Lewis & Company, The Selkirk Press
London nd. (1900)
Unpaginated (34pp.) With two illustrations.
263×209mm   p.97
Also published by The Smith Premier Typewriter Co. In some copies their imprint appears on the title page above that of John Lewis & Compy.

Johnson (Henry) – With Our Soldiers At The Front; Or, Conflict And Victory In South Africa.
The Religious Tract Society
London (1900?)
192pp. Illustrated.
202×135mm

Johnson (L. H.) – The Duke Of Lancaster's Own Yeomanry Cavalry, 23rd Co., I.Y.: A Record Of Incidents Connected With The Services Of The First Contingent Of The D.L.O.Y.C. In The South African Campaign Of 1899–1900–1901–1902; Of Interest Also To The Westmorland And Cumberland Yeomanry, 24th Co., I.Y., Who Were Our Partners And Comrades-In-Arms.
Published by the author
Bolton nd. (1902)
158pp. Folding map and illustrations, some coloured.
223×150mm   p.94
Copy recorded in SABIB published by Tillotson Press, London 1902.

Jolley (Robert) (Printer?) – Souvenir Of The Victorian And Tasmanian Contingents. 1899.
Robert Jolley
Melbourne nd. (1899)
Unpaginated (28pp.) Illustrated.
111×151mm
Photographs of colonial troops departing for South Africa. 12 printed rectos and 16 blanks. Title from cover.

Jones (Capt. H. S.) – Remarks On Recommendations. Balloon Section, Etc. See – WO. 52.

Josling (Harold) – The Autobiography Of A Military Great Coat Being A Story Of The 1st Norfolk Volunteer Active Service Company 1900–1.
Jarrold & Sons
London nd. (1907)
425pp. Illustrated.
190×130mm
Author – Harold Josling Bryant.

Joubert (General P. J.) – An Ernest Representation And Historical Reminder To Her Majesty Queen Victoria, Of Great Britain And Ireland, Empress Of India, &c., &c., In View Of The Prevailing Crisis.
'Land én Volk' Office
Pretoria 1899
18pp.
8vo.   M
An open letter from the Boer Commander-in-Chief to Queen Victoria in reference to unscrupulous capitalists seeking to undermine the peaceable government of the Transvaal.

Joy (Samuel) – A Service Of Godspeed To The West Kent Company Of The Imperial Yeomanry, In The Parish Church – All Saints, Maidstone, On Friday, January 26th, 1900. The Sermon Preached By The Rev. Canon Joy.
W. Hobbs, printers
Maidstone 1900
8pp.
220mm   SABIB

(J. R.) – Thrilling Experiences Of The First British Woman Relieved By Lord Roberts.
Printed at the Aberdeen Journal Office
Aberdeen 1900
40pp.
185×126mm   CC
A diary of the war recording experiences of a resident of Jacobsdal, Orange Free State, over a period of four and a half months. During this time the battles of Belmont, Graspan, Modder River and Magersfontein were fought nearby. Author – Mrs. J. Robb.

(Junior Army and Navy Stores, Limited) (Publishers) – The Cossack Post Journal Of B Squadron, Paget's Horse, De La Rey's Farm, Lichtenberg, Transvaal, February To May, 1901.
Junior Army and Navy Stores, Limited
London 1901
iv+189pp. Illustrated.
220×143mm

K

Kaler (J. O.) – Fighting For The Empire: The Story Of The War In South Africa. See – OTIS (James).

Kane (Thomas R.) – Stenographic Report Of The Pro-Boer Mass-Meeting Held At The People's Church, January 6, 1900. Thomas R. Kane's Brilliant Address:

History Of The South African Republics. From The 'Daily Volkszeitung', January 10, 1900.
St. Paul, Minn. (U.S.A.) 1900
61pp.
Narrow 16mo.   M
Item held in the Library Of Congress, Washington. Described as 'a most violent diatribe'.

Kaspary (Joachim) – The Humanitarian View Of The British-Boer War, Of The Chinese Question, And Of The Restoration And Maintenance Of Peace.
The Humanitarian Publishing Association
London 1901
48pp.
8vo.   M

Kaspary (Joachim) – An Addition To The Humanitarian View Of The British-Boer War And Of The Restoration And Maintenance Of Peace.
The Humanitarian Publishing Association
London 1901
14pp.
8vo.   M

Kearsey (A. H. C.) – War Record Of The York And Lancaster Regiment 1900–1902. From Regimental And Private Sources.
George Bell & Sons
London 1903
x+277pp. Folding map and plates.
215×140mm

(Keliher. J. J.) (Printers) – The Household Brigade Magazine 1899–1900–1901–1902.
Printed by J. J. Keliher
London (1899–1902?)
xiii+860pp. Plans and illustrations
xx+822pp. Illustrated.
xii+848pp. Illustrated.
xv+844pp. Illustrated.
222×140mm   L/W 291–294
Four vols. of the Household Brigade Magazine. Limited Boer War content.

(Keliher. J. J. & Co., Limited) (Publisher/Printer?) – The Official Records Of The Guards Brigade In South Africa.
J. J. Keliher & Co., Limited
London nd. (1904)
344pp. Illustrated.
224×144mm
Preface by Major H. Ruggles-Brise, Grenadier Guards – 1904. Printed for confidential circulation among the officers of the Brigade of Guards.

Kelly (Maj.Gen. W. F.) – Report On Adjutant General's Department, Etc. See WO. 25.

Kemp (Colour-Sergt. R. E.) (Compiled by) – 'My Colleagues In South Africa. Ubique.' A List Of Telegraphists Withdrawn From Various Postal Telegraph Offices In Great Britain, Who Are Members Of The 'L' Company 24th Middlesex (P.O.) Rifle Volunteers (Royal Engineer Reserves) On Active Service.
Printer not shown
London 1900
Unnumbered. 12pp. (including covers)
147×109mm   CC
Statistics in reference to telegraphists serving in South Africa and a list of transports employed. A copy of the 4th ed. July 2nd, 1900. Title from cover.

Kemp (R. E.) (Editor) – 'Khaki Letters' From My Colleagues In South Africa. Correspondence From The Post Office Telegraphists Of The 24th Middlesex

(P.O.) Rifle Volunteers (Royal Engineer Reserves) On Active Service.
Published for the Postal Telegraph Service
London 1901
424pp. Illustrated.
213×140mm
Complete set of 21 issues. The original issues were published from 1900–1901 in paper covers. Bound sets have original wraps removed. Various cloth bindings recorded. Also found in publishers half calf.

Kenyon (Captain L. R.) – The Boer War, 1899–1900.
Royal Artillery Institution
Woolwich nd. (c.1901)
206pp.
247×155mm   p.40
Reprinted from 'Proceedings' R.A.I. Vols. xxvii & xxviii.

Kestell (J. D.) – Through Shot And Flame The Adventures And Experiences Of J. D. Kestell, Chaplain To President Steyn And General Christian De Wet.
Methuen & Co.
London 1903
x+347pp.
198×128mm

Kestell (J. D.) & Van Velden (D. E.) – The Peace Negotiations Between The Governments Of The South African Republic And The Orange Free State, And The Representatives Of The British Government, Which Terminated In The Peace Concluded At Vereeniging On The 31st May, 1902.
Richard Clay & Sons, Ltd.
London 1912
xix+212pp. Illustrated.
240×160mm

Key (W. S.) – The Boer Prisoners At Bermuda.
(Publisher/printer not shown)
New York 1902
4pp.
240mm   SABIB
Report on the Boer camps at Bermuda by an English clergyman in the service of the Lend-a-Hand Society of Boston.

Kidd (Dudley) – Echoes From The Battlefields Of South Africa.
Marshall Brothers
London 1900
xvi+192pp. Illustrated.
198×128mm   p.48
Edition of 1902 – xvi+174pp. Illustrated. 200×130mm

(Kimberley) – Martial Law In The Kimberley District.
Publisher/printer not shown
Kimberley 1902
61pp.
210mm   SABIB

Kinahan (J.) – From The Front. Pages From The Diary Of One Of Miss Sandes' Soldiers' Home Workers In South Africa During The War.
Marshall Brothers
London 1900
x+62pp.
8vo.   M

King (Capt. Bastien) – The Diary Of A Dug-Out, Or The Experiences Of A Reserve Officer.
Sands & Co.
London 1901
66pp.
12mo.   M
The author was called out as a reservist officer during the war but does not appear to have served at the front.

(King. P. S. & Son) (Publisher) – Light On Dark South Africa.
P. S. King & Son
London 1900
20pp.
Cr.8vo.   M
Pamphlet in reference to the war.

(King. P. S. & Son) (Publisher) – The Fight For Piet's Farm.
Westminster nd. (c.1902)
20pp.
12mo.   M
Allegory on the Anglo-Boer question expressing sympathy with the Boers.

(King. R. E. Limited) (Publisher) – The Boer War, 1899–1900. From The Ultimatum To The Occupation Of Bloemfontein. Compiled From Authentic Sources.
R. E. King, Limited
London 1900
ii+316pp. Illustrated.
242×180mm   p.67

(King. R. E. Limited) (Publisher) – The Boer War, 1899–1900. Complete And Fully Illustrated.
R. E. King, Limited
London 1900
344pp. Illustrated.
230mm   SABIB
An edition with additional chapters: The relief of Mafeking; and, The fall of Pretoria.

(King. The) – The King's Handbook Of The War, Etc. – See entry under NEWNES (George Ltd.)

Kingwill (Annie E.) – Siege Of Kimberley, 15th October To 16th February.
C. Sandford, printer
Graaf Reinet (c.1900)
25pp.
160×105mm

Kinnear (Alfred) – To Modder River With Methuen, Briton, Boer and Battle.
J. W. Arrowsmith/Bristol
Simpkin, Marshall Hamilton, Kent & Co., Limited/London.
nd. (c.1900)
vi+173pp.
188×122mm

Kipling (Rudyard) – The Absent-Minded Beggar.
Daily Mail Publishing Co.
London (c.1900)
Foldout chart of three panels with the poem reproduced together with a portrait of the author and 'A gentleman in kharki'. Printed on silk and paper. Silk – 290×578mm opened.

Kipling (Rudyard) – The Absent Minded Beggar.
The Printing Arts Company L'd
London nd. (c.1900)
16pp. (including covers) Illustrated.
146×205mm   CC
Limp card cover. Illustrations in colour and monochrome.

Kipling (Rudyard) – The Absent-Minded Beggar.
Brentano's (Publisher)
New York 1900
16pp.
8vo.   M

Kipling (Rudyard) – The Science Of Rebellion, A Tract For The Times. Specially Written For The Imperial South African Association.

Vacher and Sons (Printers)
London 1901
10pp.
8vo.   M
Pamphlet relating to passive sedition indulged in by many of the Cape Dutch population during the conflict.

Kisch (A.) – Boer War; Photographs By A. Kisch, No.1
A. Kisch (Publisher?)
nd. (c.1900?)
10 Plates.
190×246mm   CC
Item catalogued from cover.

Kisch (A.) – Boer War; Photographs By A. Kisch, No.2
A. Kisch (Publisher?)
nd. (c.1900?)
12 Plates.
190×246mm   CC
No title page. Catalogued from cover.

Kisch (Henry) & Tugman (H. St. J.) – The Siege Of Ladysmith In 120 Pictures.
George Newnes Limited
London 1900
xxviii+117pp. Illustrated.
254×316mm
Copies recorded in cloth binding, full morocco and full calf.

Kisch (Henry) & Tugman (H. St. J.) – The Siege Of Ladysmith. Described In 64 Pictures From The Only Complete Set Of Photographs Taken During The Siege By A Resident Photographer (Henry Kisch). The First Photographs Brought To England After The Relief Of The Town, With Descriptions By An Eye-Witness (H. St. J. Tugman.)
George Newnes Limited
London nd. (1900)
64pp. Illustrated.
230×237mm
Card covered edition. Title from cover.

Kitchener (Gen. H. H.) – Letter In Dutch From Lord Kitchener, Etc.
See entry under GOVERNMENT PRINTING WORKS, Pretoria.

Kitchin (George William) – Overcome Evil With Good. A Sermon Preached In Durham Cathedral On Sunday, January 21st, 1900.
Thos. Caldcleugh (Printer)
Durham 1900
9pp.
210mm
A sermon against the war in South Africa.

Knight (E. F.) – South Africa After The War A Narrative Of Recent Travel.
Longmans, Green & Co.
London, New York, Bombay 1903
xi+356pp. Illustrated.
219×144mm
Travel in the new colonies in the period following hostilities.

Knollys (Col. W. W.) – Our Volunteers Described By Col. W. W. Knollys, Late Commanding 93rd Sutherland Highlanders.
Raphael Tuck & Son Ltd.
London/Paris/New York
nd. (1900)
14pp. Illustrated.
Oblong 4to.   CB

Knox (Lieut. E. Blake) – Buller's Campaign With The Natal Field Force Of 1900.
R. Brimley Johnson
London 1902
xx+336pp. Map, plans and other illustrations.
228×150mm

(Kosmos – Veritas – Americus) – Illustrations Submitted, In View Of The Proximity Of The General Election In Both England And The United States Of America, To Those Most Concerned As Regards The Burning, All-Absorbing Question Of Anti-Boer's Might As Contrasted With Pro-Boer's Right. In The Garb Of A Pasquinade (Satira En Excelsior), Entitled The English Canaille. In Juxta-Position To Its Prototype Or Parallel, The French Canaille.
(Publisher not shown)
nd. (c.1900)
32pp.
8vo.   M

(K.O.Y.L.I.) – 1st V.B. King's Own Yorkshire Light Infantry. Souvenir. See entry under ANON.

Kritzinger (P. H.) and McDonald (R. D.) – In The Shadow Of Death.
Printed for private circulation by William Clowes and Sons
London 1904
v+178pp. Illustrated.
220×140mm
A narrative of personal experiences during the war.

Kruger (S. J. P.) – The Memoirs Of Paul Kruger Four Times President Of The South African Republic.
T. Fisher Unwin
London 1902
Two vols.
xi+235pp. Portrait frontispiece.
ix+pp.239–543. Portrait frontispiece.
228×150mm
Biography of the South African President brought down to the end of the war. Also published in an edition of 50 copies bound in vellum.

Kuyper (Prof. A.) – The South-African Crisis. Translated And Prefaced By A. E. Fletcher.
Stop The War Committee
London nd. (1900)
81pp.
227×141mm
Reprinted from the 'Revue Des Deux Mondes' for February 1900.

L

Labat (Gaston P.) – Le Livre D'Or (The Golden Book) Of The Canadian Contingents In South Africa With An Appendix On Canadian Loyalty Containing Letters, Documents, Photographs.
Publisher/printer not shown
Montreal 1901
xii+178pp. & xii+200pp. & 66pp.
Various illustrations.
230×156mm   p.51

Labistour (G. A. De Roquefeuil) – The Constitutional Settlement Of The Orange River Colony And The Transvaal.
F. W. Potter & Co.
London 1901
22pp.
8vo.   M

Labouchere (Henry du Pré.) – Our South African War. Letter Of H. Labouchere, M.P., To The Northampton Trades Council.
Love & Wyman (Printers)
London (1900?)
23+1pp.
220mm   SABIB
Anti war statement with historical sketch of events leading to the present situation.

(Ladysmith Lyre. The) – The Ladysmith Lyre. Vol.1. Nos.1–4.
Published Ladysmith 1899
4 issues together with supplements
No.1. – 27th November, 1899. Single sheet 378×253mm with cartoon supplement. 200×323mm
No.2. – 30th November, 1899. Single sheet 379×252mm with cartoon supplement. 322×221mm
No.3. – 5th December, 1899. Single sheet 379×255mm with cartoon supplement. 322×204mm
No.4. – 15th December, 1899. Single sheet 353×221mm with cartoon supplement. 219×340mm
See entry under DAILY GRAPHIC.

(Lancashire Fusiliers) – A Militia Unit In The Field. See entry under WOODFALL & KINDER.

Langfier (Louis)/Polden (E. Russell) & Coke (Arthur J.) (Compilers) – The National Bazaar Under Royal And Distinguished Patronage Held At Royal Palace Hotel, The Empress Rooms And Adjoining Grounds Kensington, W. On May 24th, 25th & 26th 1900. Souvenir & Official Programme.
Langfier (Publisher?)
London 1900
184pp. Illustrated.
276×216mm
Edition of 158pp.? (quarto) listed in M.

Langlois (Hippolyte) – Lessons From Two Recent Wars. (The Russo-Turkish And South African Wars) Translated For The General Staff, War Office, From The French.
Printed by Mackie and Co., For H.M.S.O.
London 1909
viii+145pp. Folding maps.
202×133mm

Lasham (Frank) (Publisher) – Some Notes On The Queen's Royal West Surrey Regiment, Etc. See entry under – DAVIS (Col. J.) WOULDS (J.) and HARRISON (H. R.)

Laurence (E. C.) – A Nurse's Life In War And Peace.
Smith, Elder & Co.
London 1912
xi+311pp.
192×125mm   p.68

Laurence (E. C.) – A Nurse's Life In War And Peace.
G. Bell & Sons
London 1912
xi+311pp.
190mm   SABIB
Bell's Indian and colonial library.

Laurence (Sir P. M.) – On Circuit In Kafirland And Other Sketches And Studies.
Macmillan & Co., Limited/London
J. C. Juta & Co./Cape Town
1903
vi+335pp.
Cr.8vo.   M
Limited Boer War content. Reference to court held in Cape Colony in 1901 and to the Hague peace conference and the war.

Layriz (Lt.-Col. O.) – Mechanical Traction In War For Road Transport, With Notes On Automobiles Generally. Translated By R. B. Marston.
Sampson Low, Marston & Co.
London 1900
xii+102pp. Illustrated. (41 plates.)
254×160mm

Limited reference to mechanical transport in the war.

Lazenby (C. W.) – With The Second Battalion East Yorkshire Regt. In South Africa, 1900–1901–1902.
Gale & Polden Ltd.
Aldershot 1902
41pp.
7in   W

(Leadenhall Press. The) (Printers) – Fifty-Six Portraits Of Our Heroes' Orphans. Children Of Fathers Who Lost Their Lives In The South African War, 1899–1900.
The Leadenhall Press, Ltd.
London nd. (1900)
32pp. Illustrated.
102×160mm   p.29
Portraits of orphans being fed gratis by the generosity of the proprietors of Mellin's Food. The Introduction is signed W. L. N.

(League Against Aggression and Militarism) – Pamphlets relating to the Transvaal question and the war. Two groups are listed in SABIB (Vol.3. p.67), numbered 1–4 and 1–7. Most of the pamphlets are 2 or 4pp. The titles shown are from the second group printed in London 1900 by Spottiswoode & Co. and National Press Agency, printers.
212×125mm

2. Towards A Practical Settlement. 4pp.

5. Peace – National And Industrial. Address By Mr. J. P. Thomasson. 4pp.

6. The Cost Of Chamberlainism. 4pp.

(League Against Aggression and Militarism) (Publisher) – Report Of The Proceedings Of The Conference Of Liberals On Foreign & Colonial Policy, Held At The Westminster Palace Hotel, London, On February 14th, 1900.
League against Aggression and Militarism.
(London 1900?)
40pp.
220mm   SABIB
Against the South African War.

Leather-Culley (Mrs. J. D.) – On The War Path A Lady's Letters From The Front.
John Long
London 1901
vii+133pp. Illustrated.
198×126mm   p.87

Lecky (W. E. H.) – Moral Aspects Of The South African War.
W. L. U. Association
London (1900)
8pp.
210mm   SABIB

Leech (H. Brougham) – The South African Republics: Their History And International Position. Three Lectures Delivered In The Law School, During Hilary Term, 1901.
W. McGee
Dublin 1901
Simpkin, Marshall, Hamilton, Kent & Co.
London 1901
56pp.
216×140mm

Lees (Capt. Sir Elliott) – Order Book Of The 26th (Dorset) Company I.Y. For About A Year In South Africa. Compiled From What Remains Of The Company's Order Books, For Private

Circulation Among The Members Of The Company.
Henry Ling
(Dorchester 1903)
xvi+224pp. Folding map and illustrations.
223×141mm   p.34

Lees (Nursing sister) – The Last Message To Mother From A Hero Of Ladysmith. Dedicated To The Red Cross Sisters.
John and E. Bumpus
London 1900
8pp.
230mm   SABIB
A poem signed at end:- Nursing sister Lees, Military Camp, Ladysmith.

Lees (Nursing sister) – The Last Message From A Hero Of Ladysmith. Dedicated To The Red Cross Sisters.
Privately published by E. S. Dahl, Esq.
nd. (1900?)
8pp.
8vo.   M
M reference – British Museum Library.

Leggett (T. C.) (Printer/Publisher?) – The Hospital Scandals In South Africa.
T. C. Leggett
(Ipswich 1900?)
4pp.
210mm   SABIB
Pre-election pamphlet, condemning the treatment of the sick under a Conservative government during the war.

(Leng. John & Co.) (Printers) – Letters From The Front By A Black Watch Volunteer On Active Service In South Africa, 1900–1901.
John Leng & Co.
Dundee 1901
36pp. Frontispiece and folding map.
211×168mm   p.110

Lennox (E. Gordon) – Diary Of The Hon. E. Gordon Lennox, Scots Guards, A.D.C. To Major-Gen. B. Campbell, M.V.O., Commanding The 16th Brigade, 8th Division. From April 14th, 1900, To February 20th, 1901.
Publisher/printer not shown
Privately printed
np. (c.1901)
103pp.
12mo.   M
Author was present at the battle of Biddulphs Berg and particularly active in farm burning operations.

Lewis (Caroline) (Pseud:) – Clara In Blunderland.
William Heinemann
London 1902
xvi+150pp. Illustrated.
190×115mm
Political parody of Lewis Carroll's 'Alice's adventure in Wonderland' with reference to the South African war. Attributed to M. H. Temple and Harold Begbie.

Lewis (Caroline) – The Coronation Nonsense-Book. In The Style Of The Old 'Book Of Nonsense' By The Late Edward Lear. By The Poet And Painter Of 'Clara In Blunderland'.
William Heinemann
London 1902
(Unnumbered) Twenty cartoons.
Oblong 8vo.   M
Several cartoons refer to the South African War.

Lewis (Mrs. H. R. Stakesby) – See entries under STAKESBY-LEWIS.

(Lewis. John & Compy.) (The Selkirk Press) (Publishers) – Souvenir Of The Siege Of Mafeking. Etc. See entry under JOHN LEWIS & COMPANY.

Lewis (Major R. C.) – On The Veldt A Plain Narrative Of Service Afield In South Africa.
J. Walch and Sons (Printers)
Hobart 1902
xv+159pp. Folding map.
194×133mm
Account of the 1st Tasmanian Imperial Bushmen in South Africa written by the officer commanding assisted by Frank Morton, journalist.

(Liberal Imperialist) – John Bull's Guinea-Pigs; Or The World And The War. By A True Liberal Imperialist.
C. W. Bradley & Co.
London (1900?)
51pp.
8vo.   M
Attitude of rival powers to Great Britain during the war together with remarks on the future of the British Empire.

(Liberal Publication Department) – Pamphlets published London 1899–1908, many in reference to the war. Some entered below, others listed under author. For comprehensive list see SABIB Vol.3 pp.113 & 114.

The General Election: How The Tories Won, Why The Liberals Lost.
Liberal Publication Department
London 1900
28pp. Including 8 facsimiles.
210mm
Title from cover. Reprinted from the Liberal magazine, Nov. 1900. Analysis of the British general election results of 1900, which were significantly affected by the South African War.

Leaflets, nos. 1805–1908. Published 1899–1900. –

1805. – Sir Henry Campbell-Bannerman On Great Britain And The Transvaal. (From A Speech At Ilford, June 17th, 1899.) 4pp.

1822. – Sir Edward Clark On The War In South Africa. 1p.

1829. – The Strange Story Of The Spion Kop Despatches. (8pp.?)

1836. – The Government And The Soldiers. 2pp.

1846. – Ask Your Wife To Tell You What The War And Tory Doles Mean. 1p.

1851. – Hustling It On. What A Khaki Election Means. 2pp.

1852. – Hiding Behind Bobs. Folding sheet.

1855. – The Absent Minded Ministry. 2pp.

1879. – The War. Always Over But Never Ended. 1p.

1880. – The Tory Government And The War. By A Tory M.P. (Thomas Gibson Bowles.) 4pp.

1881. – The South African War. Liberal Leaders On The Main Lines Of Settlement. 4pp.

1908. – War! The Record Of The Tory Government Is Everywhere A Record Of War. 1p.
220mm   SABIB

The South African War Commission Its Report And Evidence Summarised And Analysed.
Liberal Publication Department, in connection with the National Liberal Federation and the Liberal Central Association
London 1903
31pp.
220mm   SABIB
Review of the findings of the Royal Commission on the War in South Africa.

The Well-Conducted War. Interesting Facts, Figures, And Opinions.
Liberal Publication Department
Westminster (1900)
15pp. Illustrated.
210mm   SABIB
Propaganda leaflet of the Liberal Party in reference to the war.

Limpus (Sir Arthur Henry) – Mountings Of The Naval Guns, Etc. See entry under SCOTT, P.

Lines (G. W.) – The Ladysmith Bombshell.
G. W. Lines
Ladysmith 1899–1900
8 issues. Illustrated.
Eight issues of a magazine produced at Ladysmith during the siege. Each number has a cover cartoon by Earl Robert.

No. 1. – 18/11/99. Six sheets (printed rectos.) 312×292mm

No. 2. – Nov. 24/99. Six sheets (printed rectos.) 382×257mm

No. 3. – Nov. 99. (manuscript date 2/12/99) Six sheets (printed rectos, Sepia on ledger paper) 332×204mm

No. 4. – Dec. 9/99. Six sheets (printed rectos.) 381×253mm

No. 5. – 16 Dec. 1899. Six sheets (printed rectos.) 380×255mm

No. 6. – Dec. 23, 1899. The Christmas number. Seven sheets (printed rectos. Purple on orange, blue and white paper. Some illustrations in the text.)
447×287mm

No. 7. – Jan. 1st 1900. Six sheets (printed rectos.) 447×291mm

No. 8. – 8th Jan. 1900. Five sheets with single sheet supplement. (printed rectos.)
325×205mm   CC

Lines (G. W.) – The Ladysmith Siege 2nd Nov. 1899–1st March, 1900. Record Containing: Regiments Defending The Besieged Borough. Lists Giving Names Of Local Volunteer Defence Force. Statistics. The Residents: Including Women And Children. Copies Of Various Military And Municipal Notices. And A Complete Copy Of The 'Ladysmith Bombshell' Published During The Siege.
Wilson's Music and General Printing Co. Ltd.
London nd. (c.1900)
96pp. Cartoon sketches.
201×136mm   p.114
Back cover has imprint of Budge & Co., printers, Ladysmith.

Lines (G. W.) – The Ladysmith Siege, 2nd Nov. 1899 To 1st March, 1900. Record Containing Regiments Defending The Besieged Borough; Lists Giving Names Of Local Volunteer Defence Force; The Residents, Including Women And Children; Short Particulars As To Intombi Camp; Copies Of Various Military And Municipal Notices; And A Complete Copy Of The 'Ladysmith

Bombshell', With Cartoons And Other Illustrations Published Therewith.
P. Davis & Sons
Maritzburg 1900
31pp. advertisements+27pp.+8 issues of *Ladysmith Bombshell* unpaginated.
Cartoon illustrations.
302×238mm   p.114
Cover title – The Ladysmith Siege, 2nd November 1899 to 1st March 1900.

(Linesman) – Words By An Eyewitness: The Struggle In Natal.
William Blackwood & Sons
Edinburgh/London 1902
xi+343pp.
195×134mm
SABIB records twelve printings 1901–1902.

(Linesman) – The Mechanism Of War.
William Blackwood & Sons
Edinburgh/London 1902
viii+183pp.
190×130mm
Much of the content is reproduced from the 'Spectator'.

Linklater (Joseph) – On Active Service In South Africa With 'The Silent Sixth'. Being A Record Of Events, Compiled By The Writer, From The Time Of The Formation Of The Regiment In New Zealand Until Its Return From South Africa.
McKee & Co., printers
Wellington nd. (1902)
102pp. Illustrated.
189×128mm   CC   p.78
Campaign diary of Joseph Linklater, B. Squadron, 6th N.Z. Mounted Rifles.

Livingston (F. J.) – My Escape From The Boers The Exciting Experiences Of A Canadian Medical Missionary.
William Briggs
Toronto nd. (1900)
35pp.
216×144mm   RCSL

Lloyd (J. Barclay) – One Thousand Miles With The C.I.V.
Methuen & Co.
London 1901
xii+288pp. Folding map and frontispiece.
196×132mm

Lloyd (T. H. Eyre) – Boer War. Diary Of Captain Eyre Lloyd, 2nd Coldstream Guards, Assistant Staff Officer, Colonel Benson's Column, Killed At Brakenlaagte, 30th October, 1901.
Army and Navy Co-operative Society, Limited.
London 1905
300pp. Illustrated.
203×131mm   p.44
Printed for private circulation amongst the family.

Lloyd-George (The Rt. Hon. David) – Mr. Lloyd-George, M.P. At Llanelly. Great Peace Making. A Reprint Of The Leader And Verbatim Report (By Mr. Rowland Thomas, Silver Medallist) From The 'Llanelly Mercury' Thursday, October 10th, 1901.
('Llanelly Mercury')?
Llanelly 1901
11pp.
8vo.   M
Speech by Lloyd-George asserting the government 'Knows neither how to conduct a successful war nor to conclude an honourable peace'.

Lloyd (Brigadier-General F.) & Russell (Brevet-Major Hon. A.) (Compiled by) – First Or Grenadier Guards In South Africa, 1899–1902. Records Of The

Second Battalion Compiled By Brigadier-General F. Lloyd, C.B., D.S.O. Records Of The Third Battalion Compiled By Brevet-Major Hon. A. Russell.
J. J. Keliher & Co., Limited
London 1907
114pp.+138pp. Folding charts and map.
217×140mm   p.83

(L. N.) – Letters Home. 1900 By L. N.
Printed for private circulation
F. Calder Turner
London (1900)
147pp.
190mm   SABIB
The letters describe experiences with the Imperial Yeomanry in South Africa to June 1900.

('London Letter. The' Publishing Co.) – The Nonsense Blue-Book ('The London Letter Learics'.) Second Edition. The Pictures And Verses In This Book Are Reprinted From A Series Of Topical Cartoons In 'The London Letter' In The Style Of The Old 'Book Of Nonsense' By The Late Edward Lear.
'The London Letter' Publishing Co., Ltd.
London 1899
20pp.
Oblong 8vo.   M
A collection of cartoons relating to the situation in South Africa at the commencement of war, 1899–1902.

('Long Tom') – How Thady Maloney Bate The Boers.
Publisher/printer not shown
np./nd.
12pp.
8vo.   M
Skit on PaulᐟKruger and the Transvaal. Entered in M under 'South African War'.

Looney (J. C.) (Printer) – A Pottery Man's Journal Of The Siege Of Kimberley.
J. C. Looney, Printer
Kimberley 1900
62pp.
180×125mm
Authors name – J. Bradley. M records an edition printed by Townshend, Taylor & Snashall at Cape Town 1900. 63pp.

Lowry (Rev. E. P.) – With The Guards' Brigade From Bloemfontein To Koomati Poort And Back.
Horace Marshall & Son
London 1902
xii+277pp. Illustrated.
208×137mm   p.62

Lucas (Col. A. G.) – Report, Imperial Yeomanry. See WO. 33.

Lückhoff (A. D.) – Woman's Endurance.
See – A. D. L.

Lunn (H. S.) – Empire And Nationality: The Transvaal War In The Light Of Scripture And History. A Sermon Of Henry S. Lunn M.D.
Horace Marshall & Son
London (1900)
16pp.
8vo.   M
The author asserts that war was waged in favour of capitalists.

Luther (E. W.) – Diary Of E. W. L. Of 201st Regiment Of New York Volunteers And Of Blake's Irish Brigade, Who Was Wounded In Action Near Weltevreden On Sunday, 9th September, And Died In The Hospital, Machadodorp, On The 11th September, 1900.

Intelligence Dept.
South Africa 1900
52pp.
Item listed in WO. Cat./1912.

Luttman-Johnson (Colonel F.) – Record Of Services Of The 3rd. Battn. The Prince Of Wales's Leinster Regiment (Royal Canadians) In The South African War, 1900, 1901, 1902.
Army and Navy Co-operative Society, Limited.
London 1913
148pp. Maps and plates.
221×142mm   p.95

Lyell (Lt. David) – Report: Siege Railway Plant. See WO. 118.

Lygon (E. H.) – The Diary Of The Hon. E. H. Lygon, Lieut. And Adjt. 3rd Batt. Grenadier Guards. Oct. 26th 1899 To March 21st 1900.
Privately printed
Angus & Robertson
Sydney 1900
iii+iii+45pp.
289×200mm   p.121

Lyttle (R.) – Origin Of The Fight With The Boers. Sketch Of South African History. The Whole Case Stated. Misrepresentations Exposed. 3rd. Ed. With New Chapter.
Wm. Brown & Sons (Printers)
Belfast 1899
31pp.
220mm   SABIB

Lyttle (Rev. Richard) – Origin Of The Fight With The Boers.
Wm. Brown & Sons, Printers
(Belfast 1900?)
25pp.
215×140mm
Sixth edition with additional chapters.

M

Macdonald (D.) – How We Kept The Flag Flying The Story Of The Siege Of Ladysmith.
Ward, Lock & Co., Limited
London nd. (1900)
xi+pp.13–303. Illustrated.
197×130mm

Macdonald (D.) – How We Kept The Flag Flying: The Siege Of Ladysmith Through Australian Eyes.
Ward Lock
London 1900
xi+pp.13–303. Plates and map.
190mm   SABIB

Macdonald (J. M.) – Briton Versus Boer. The Struggle For The Flag In South Africa.
Publisher/printer not shown
(Education Society's Steam Press?)
Bombay 1900
88pp. Illustrated.
Square 16mo.   RCSL

Macdonald (J. Ramsay) – What I Saw In South Africa, September And October, 1902.
'The Echo'
London nd. (1902)
135pp. Illustrated.
187×124mm

Macdonald (Maj. Gen. H. A.) & Seddon (R. J.) – In Memory Of New Zealands Sons Fallen In South Africa.

New Zealand Times office (printers)
Wellington 1902
16pp.
200mm BIM
A list of men who died with cause of death.

Macduff (John Ross) – The Soldier's Text Book Or Confidence In Time Of War. Issued By The Presbyterian Church Of Otago And Southland New Zealand.
N.Z. Bible Tract And Book Society (Dunedin?) 1900
62pp.
105mm BIM

Macfie (R. A. Scott) (Editor) – Mick Gallagher At The Front. See entry under GALLAGHER, Michael.

Mackarness (F. C.) – Martial Law In The Cape Colony During 1901.
National Press Agency
London 1902
32pp.
212×139mm CC

Mackarness (F.) – Lifting The Veil In Cape Colony, Being Some Further Facts About Martial Law.
National Press Agency Ltd.
London (1902)
36pp.
212×139mm CC

Mackay (Mary) – A Social Note On The War, Etc. See – CORELLI. (Marie).

Mackenzie (W. D.) & Stead (A.) – South Africa Its History, Heroes And Wars.
American Literary and Musical Association
Chicago nd. (1900)
3–663pp. Illustrated.
248×180mm
Numerous editions listed in SABIB – Monarch Book Co. Chicago/Philadelphia 1900. – Reeve Publishing Co. Chicago 1900. – Sunset Publishing Co., San Francisco 1900. – Horace Marshall & Son. London (1900?) – J. M. MacGregor Publishing Co. Vancouver B.C. (1900). Pagination varies in editions. Also – The Chas. B. Ayer Company, Chicago, Ill. nd. (c.1900)

Mackern (H. F.) – Side-Lights On The March The Experiences Of An American Journalist In South Africa.
John Murray
London 1901
xv+256pp. Illustrated.
210×140mm

(Mackie) (Publisher?) – The South Lancashire Regiment In The South African War 1899–1902.
Mackie?
Warrenton nd.
20pp. Illustrated.
7¾in W

Mackinnon (H. V.) – War Sketches, Reminiscences Of The Boer War.
Publisher/printer not shown
Charlottetown 1900
73pp.
8vo. RCSL

Mackinnon (Maj.-Gen. W. H.) – The Journal Of The C.I.V. In South Africa.
John Murray
London 1901
xii+252pp. Maps and illustrations.
207×140mm
Superior edition – Grey paper cover, wide borders – 272×226mm.

Maclean (A. H. H.) – Public Schools And The War In South Africa, 1899–1902.

Some Facts, Figures, And Comparisons, With A List Of Specially Distinguished Officers.
Edward Stanford
London 1903
99pp.
8vo. M

Macleod (Mrs. E. S.) – For The Flag Or Lays And Incidents Of The South African War.
Archibald Irwin (Printer)
Charlottetown, Prince Edward Island 1901
viii+185pp. Illustrated.
222×145mm p.14

Macpherson (Lt.-Col. W. G.) – General Reports On Sanitary Conditions, Etc. See WO. 102 & 103.

Macvane (S. M.) – The South African Question As It Appears In The Official Correspondence.
Victorian Club
Boston 1900 (Preface)
36pp.
250mm SABIB

Maddison (F.) – The Transvaal. Great Liberal Meeting In The Burngreave Vestry Hall, On November 21st, 1899. Important Speech By Mr F. Maddison, M.P. (Full Report).
Parrer Bros. (Printers)
Sheffield 1899
24pp.
210mm SABIB
Speech against war with the South African Republic.

Madill (James) – With The Silent Sixth.
Printer/publisher not shown
(Auckland 1901?)
3pp.
220mm BIM
Cover title – To My Comrades of The 6th Contingent – With The Compliments Of James Madill Tuakau Auckland New Zealand.

(Mafeking) – Particulars Of The Siege Defences Of Mafeking.
Printed at the *'Mail'* Office for Mafeking Municipality
Mafeking (1900)
9pp. Folding map.
170×210mm SABIB
No title page. Item catalogued from cover. Details of British forts, town defences. Boer forts and laagers in vicinity of Mafeking during the siege of 1899–1900.

('Mafeking Mail' The) – See entry under TOWNSHEND & SON.

Mahan (Capt. A. T.) – The Story Of The War In South Africa 1899–1900.
Sampson Low, Marston and Company Ltd.
London 1900
vi+322pp. Map and frontispiece
204×140mm
M lists copy published 1901.

Mahan (Capt. A. T.) – The War In South Africa A Narrative Of The Anglo-Boer War From The Beginning Of Hostilities To The Fall Of Pretoria.
Peter Fenelon Collier & Son
New York 1901
viii+208pp. Colour plates, and other illustrations.
290×434mm
M. lists copy viii+216pp. published 1902. SABIB lists copy published 1900.

('Maine' Hospital Ship) – Report Of The American Hospital Ship 'Maine'. See CHURCHILL, Lady Randolph.

Makins (Lieut.-Col. E.) (Editor) – The Royals In South Africa (1899–1902). Published by the Editor of *'The Eagle'* (Potchefstroom) 1914
xii+199pp. Illustrated.
220×145mm
An edition was published the same year at Secunderabad, India, printed by B.V.R. Balreddy & Co. v+150pp. Without illustrations.

Makins (G. H.) – Surgical Experiences In South Africa, 1899–1900. Being Mainly A Clinical Study Of The Nature And Effects Of Injuries Produced By Bullets Of Small Calibre.
Smith, Elder & Co.
London 1901
xvi+493pp. Illustrated.
229×150mm
Edition published Philadelphia 1901 by P. Blakiston's Son & Co. xvi+493pp. Illustrated. 227×150mm Edition published London 1913 by Henry Frowde/Hodder & Stoughton. xvi+504pp. Illustrated.

Malcolm (Sergt. K. G.) – The Seventh New Zealand Contingent Its Record In The Field, Second South African Boer War, 1901–1902.
Deslandes & Lewis
Wellington 1903
vi+44pp. Illustrated.
7×4¼in ROTE
Brief record of service in OFS and Transvaal between April 1901 and Feb. 1902.

Malley (James) – The Truth About The Transvaal; Who And What Caused The War.
Pite and Thynne
London 1900
ii+44pp. With map.
190mm SABIB

(Manchester Evening Mail) – War Cartoons.
Manchester Evening Mail
Manchester (1901?)
280mm
Five volumes noted in SABIB. Reprinted from the newspaper, 1899–1900.

(Manchester Regiment) – Diary Of Siege Of Ladysmith. 1st Battalion, Manchester Regiment, 31st October 1899– 28th February, 1900.
(No Imprint)
12pp.
7in WO. Cat./1912. W

(Manchester Transvaal Committee) (Publisher) – Leaflets printed at Manchester, W. Hough, 1899. 1–4pp. Sixteen titles listed in SABIB Vol.3 p.244. Most relate to the war. Some of the pamphlets were also issued by the National Reform Union.

1. What War With The Transvaal Would Mean. Mr Chamberlain's View. 1p.

2. What Are We Going To Fight About? 2pp.

5. The Franchise: What Was Asked, And What The Boers Offered. 2pp.

6. Our Right Of Interference In The Transvaal. 4pp.

7. The Suzerainty Question. 4pp.

10. A Conservative View Of The Transvaal Crisis. 2pp.

14. A Diplomatic Muddle. 4pp.

16. Unionists Against War. 2pp.

220mm SABIB

(Manchester Transvaal Peace Committee) (Publisher) – Leaflets printed at Manchester, Wm. Hough, 1899–1900. 1–8pp. Eleven titles listed in SABIB Vol.3 pp.244–245. Some of the pamphlets were also issued by the National Reform Union.

1. How War Was Brought About. 8pp.

3. Mr. F. Selous On The War. 7pp.

4. 'I Do Not Think It Was Worth A War'. (Mr. Chamberlain, In The House Of Commons, October 25th, On The Differences Between Mr. Kruger And Himself.) 2pp.

7. The Blessings Of War, From The Financier's Point Of View. 3pp.

8. Why Did The Boers Arm? (Excerpt From A Letter By Mr. J. B. Robinson To The 'Daily News' Of Jan. 16th, 1900.) 4pp.

10. The Government's South African Policy, By Sir Robert Reid (A Speech In The House Of Commons, Jan. 31st, 1900.) Robert Aikman, printer, Manchester. 8pp.

11. The Reasons For The War, And Why They Are Bad Reasons. 8pp.

220mm   SABIB

Mann (A. M.) – Songs For The Front (Nos. 1, 2, 3, all published.) Townshend, Taylor and Snashall (Printers) Cape Town (1900) Each number 8pp. 8vo.   M

Marais (J. L.) – South Africa, Martial Law. Marais And Van Reenen Cases (Privy Council) Publisher/printer not shown 1901–04? 6pp. *Ref. WO. Cat./1912.*

Marden (Maj. A. W.) & Newbigging (Capt. W. P. E.) (Compiled by) – Rough Diary Of The Doings Of The 1st Battn. Manchester Regt. During The South African War, 1899 To 1902. John Heywood Manchester nd. (c.1903) 151pp. Folding maps. 188×126mm   p.11

Marks (Alfred) – Bullets, Expansive, Explosive, And Poisoned. Reprinted from the '*Westminster Review*' (London) 1902 19pp. With diagrams. 237×160mm   CC   p.32

Marks (Alfred) – The Churches And The South African War. '*New Age*' Office London 1905 40pp. 12mo.   M

Marling (Maj. P. S.) – Extracts From Diary And Letter Of Major P. S. Marling, V.C., XVIII Hussars, Ladysmith, October 20th, 1899– March 1st, 1900. Privately printed (Printer not shown) np. (1900?) 32pp. 160mm   SABIB *Title page marked – 'Not for publication'.*

Marquis (T. G.) – Canada's Sons On Kopje And Veldt. A Historical Account Of The Canadian Contingents Based On The Official Despatches Of Lieutenant-Colonel W. D. Otter And The Other Commanding Officers At The Front; On The Letters And Despatches Of Such War Correspondents As C. Frederick Hamilton, S. C. Simonski, Stanley McKeown Brown, John Ewan And W. Richmond Smith. The Canada's Sons Publishing Co. Toronto, Guelph, Brantford nd. (1900) xviii+490pp. Illustrated. 215×140mm *A volume found in various bindings including full morocco gilt.*

Marriott (Sir William) – The War And Its Cost. Who Should Pay? Letters From South Africa. Argus Printing Company, Limited. London 1901 iii+105pp. Cr.8vo.   M *Reprinted from 'The Financial News'.*

Marshall (A.) – Photos Of Boer Commandos. Percy Lund Humphries (Printers) Bradford/London nd. (c.1900) 4pp.+27 illustrations. 200×270mm   SABIB

(Marshall. Horace & Son) (Publisher/Printer?) – The Story Of H.M.S. *Powerful*, From The Diary Of A *Powerful* Man. Dedicated By Permission To Capt. Hedworth Lambton, R.N. Horace Marshall & Son London 1900 92pp. Cr.8vo.   M *Account of the Naval Brigade in South Africa and of Powerful's cruises.*

(Marshall. John) (Printer) – British Statesmanship And South Africa, 1895–1900. A Study For Electors. Printed And Published For The Proprietor By John Marshall At The Offices Of '*The Westminster Gazette*'. John Marshall London 1900 24pp. Illustrated. Folio   M

(Martial Law) – Martial Law In The Cape Colony. Publisher/printer not shown nd./np. (c.1902) 22pp. 205×140mm   CC *Title from page 1. A document in reference to British oppression of Dutch people in Cape Colony during the period of Martial Law. Pink wraps without title or imprint.*

Martin (E. E.) – The Transport Of Horses By Sea. Thacker Spink Calcutta 1901 vi+49pp. Folding plan. 170mm   SABIB *As veterinary Officer of the Remount Depot, Calcutta, the author was concerned with transport of horses to the army in South Africa during the war.*

Mason (William Ernest) – The War In South African Republics.... Speech Of Hon. Wm. E. Mason, Of Illinois, In The Senate.... December 11, 1899. Government Printing Office Washington 1899 31pp. 8vo.   GR

(Mathew. James P.) (Printers) – Boers Wha Hae Wi' Botha Bled.... James P. Mathew, printers Dundee (1901?) 8pp. 130mm   SABIB *No title-page. Catalogued from cover. A pro-Boer pamphlet. Author – W. Walsh.*

Matthews (Vet. Col. I. A.) – Report On Army Veterinary Dept. See – WO.162.

Mattison (Sergt. John Todd) – 'Spectemur Agendo'. (By Our Deeds We Are Known.) Privately printed Printer not shown np./December 1900 18pp. 129×101mm   CC *Memoranda of events, in ragged rhyme, of the experiences in South Africa of the 1st Royal Dragoons. – Preface.*

Maude (A.) – War And Patriotism Grant Richards London 1900 35pp. 8vo.   M *A reply to John Bellow's pamphlet 'The Truth About The Transvaal War And The Truth About War'. SABIB lists edition published by A. Bonner, London 1900. 35pp.*

Maurice (Major-General Sir Frederick) & Grant (Capt. M. H.) – History Of The War In South Africa 1899–1902 Compiled By Direction Of His Majesty's Government. Hurst and Blackett Limited London 1906–1910 Four vols. text and four cases of folding maps. Vol. 1. (1906) xvii+i+526pp. Vol. 2. (1907) xvi+701pp. Vol. 3. (1908) xiii+609pp. Vol. 4. (1910) xv+767pp. 1 plate. Vol. 1. (Maps) South Africa general map and maps 1–17. With 6 freehand sketches. Vol. 2. (Maps) No.18–No.37. With 6 freehand sketches. Vol. 3. (Maps) No.38–No.55. With 11 freehand sketches. Vol. 4. (Maps) No.56–No.64. 244×177mm   Frontis: *The Official history of the South African War. Vols. 1 & 2 compiled by Sir F. Maurice. Vol. 3 by other officers. Vol. 4. by M. H. Grant.*

(May & Co.) (Printers) – XIII Hussars South African War. October, 1899–October 1902. Compiled by Capt. J. H. Tremayne May & Co. Aldershot nd. (c.1905) ii+202pp. 188×127mm   p.58 *Author's name does not appear on title page.*

May (Lt.-Col. E. S.) – A Retrospect On The South African War. Sampson Low, Marston & Company, Limited. London 1901 viii+216pp. 213×139mm

Maydon (J. G.) – French's Cavalry Campaign. C. Arthur Pearson, Ltd. London 1901 xxix+pp.31–198. Illustrated. 191×127mm   p.66

(McArthur & Co. Colin) (Publishers) – The Imperial Idea.

Colin McArthur & Co. Incorporated
Montreal nd. (c.1900)
24pp. Illustrated.
215×250mm   WS
*Patriotic souvenir in reference to colonial
aid to Britain. 24 printed rectos including
5 colour plates. Item published by a
wallpaper manufacturing company.*

M'Caw (R.) – Outposts And Convoys
With The Ayrshire Volunteers In
South Africa.
Dunlop & Drennan
Kilmarnock 1901
ix+150pp. Two plates.
192×127mm   p.93
*An account of the Volunteer Service
Company of the Royal Scots Fusiliers in
South Africa. Paper covered ed. –
184×124mm.*

McCombie (R. B.) – Briton Or Boer:
Which Should Rule In South Africa?
Effingham Wilson
London 1902
31pp.
8vo.   M
*Critical of A. M. S. Methuen's 'Peace Or
War In South Africa'.*

McCulloch (C.) – The Boers As I Know
Them. A Paper Read At A Private
Meeting Of The South Africa
Conciliation Committee Liverpool,
30th April, 1900.
South Africa Conciliation Committee
(Liverpool Branch) 1900
12pp.
220mm   SABIB
*Enquiry as to the rights and wrongs of the
circumstances which have led Great
Britain into war with the South African
Republics.*

McDonell (G. L.) – See SCOTT. G.H.G.
and McDONELL.

**McElligott (Quarter-Master-Sergeant
James)** (Compiled by) – Royal Scots
Greys. South Africa, 1899–1901.
Banks & Co. (printers)
Edinburgh nd. (1901?)
32pp.
185×120mm
*Regimental record with list of casualties
and nominal roll.*

McHugh (R. J.) – The Siege Of
Ladysmith.
Chapman & Hall, Ld.
London 1900
viii+213pp. Illustrated.
194×132mm   p.26
*SABIB lists copy published by George Bell
& Sons, London 1900.*

(McKee & Co.) (Printers) – Souvenir Of
The N.Z. 2nd Contingent For The
Transvaal January 1900.
McKee & Co.
Wellington 1900
23pp. Illustrated.
145×270mm   BIM

McKenzie Rew (Capt. H. G.) – Records
Of The Rough Riders (XXth Battalion
Imperial Yeomanry). See entry under
REW (Capt. H. G. McKenzie.)

McLean (W.) And Shackleton (E. H.) –
'Troopin, Troopin, Troopin To The Sea'
'O.H.M.S.' An Illustrated Record Of
The Voyage Of S.S. 'Tintagel Castle'
Conveying Twelve Hundred Soldiers
From Southampton To Cape Town
March 1900.

Simpkin Marshall, Hamilton, Kent &
Co., Limited
London 1900
59pp. Illustrated.
287×195mm   p.69

M'Clelland (R.) – Heroes And
Gentlemen. An Army Chaplain's
Experiences In South Africa.
J. & R. Parlane/Paisley
John Menzies and Co./Edinburgh
and Glasgow
Houlston and Sons/London
1902
159pp. Frontispiece and map.
188×126mm   p.82

Mead (E. D.) – The Two Englands And
Their Lessons For America.
Printer/publisher not shown
Boston 1900
24pp.
240mm   SABIB
*Material in reference to the war. The
author, in sympathy with the Boer cause,
condemns the England of greed and
oppression and the wars which are their
fruit.*

Melladew (B. N.) – 'Bona-Fide
Negotiations?', A Reply To A Question
Of The Chairman Of The Commission
On The War In South Africa.
Swan Sonnenschein and Co., Ltd.
London 1903
37pp.
220×134mm   RCSL

(Mellin's Foods) (Publisher) – Fifty-Six
Portraits Of Our Heroes' Orphans, Etc.
See entry under LEADENHALL PRESS.

Mellish (Annie Elizabeth) – Our Boys
Under Fire Or Maritime Volunteers In
South Africa.
Printed at the Examiner Office
Charlottetown 1900
120pp. Illustrated.
220×145mm

('Men At The Front') – Pen Pictures Of
The War By Men At The Front. Volume
1. The Campaign In Natal To The Battle
Of Colenso.
Horace Marshall & Son
London 1900
vii+343pp. Illustrated.
193×131mm   p.113
One volume only published.

**Mends (Col. H. R.) Campbell (Maj. Sir
Guy) Wortley (Capt. R. M. Stuart)**
(Compilers) – The King's Royal Rifle
Corps Chronicle 1901.
Warren and Son
Winchester 1902
viii+190pp. Illustrated.
224×141mm
Significant Boer War content.

**Mends (Col. H. R.) Campbell (Sir Guy)
Wortley (Capt. The Hon. R. M. Stuart)**
(Compilers) – The King's Royal Rifle
Corps Chronicle 1902.
Warren and Son
Winchester 1903
viii+147pp. Illustrated.
224×141mm
South African war content.

Menpes (Mortimer) – War Impressions.
Being A Record In Colour By Mortimer
Menpes. Transcribed By Dorothy
Menpes.
Adam & Charles Black
London nd. (1901) (Reprinted 1903)

xiv+254pp. Folding chart and plates,
most in colour.
227×162mm
*Also edition de luxe of 350 large paper
copies, 1901. 276×212mm*

Mercer (A.) – 'At Modder River' A Few
Incidents Of Mission Work Amongst
Soldiers Whilst Under Fire In South
Africa, Culled From Articles Written For
The South African Pioneer By Mr
Dudley Kidd, Mr Percy Huskisson And
Mr Darroll.
Marshall Bros;
South Africa General Mission
London nd. (1900)
36pp. Illustrated.
180mm   SABIB

Mercer (A.) – 'With General Buller's
Force In Natal'.
South Africa General Mission
(London 1900?)
35+5pp.? Illustrated.
90×120mm   SABIB

Mercer (A.) – Taking The Gospel From
Block-house To Block-house.
South Africa General Mission
(London 1901?)
32+4pp. Illustrated.
90×120mm   SABIB

Mercer (A.) – 'At Ladysmith': Being An
Account Of Evangelistic Work Done
Amongst Soldiers By Mr Ion Smyth and
Mr James Taylor, During The Siege Of
Ladysmith.
South Africa General Mission
London (1900?)
28+4pp.
90×120mm

Mercer (A.) – 'The Surrounding Of
Cronje'. Being A Sequel To 'At Modder
River' Culled From Information Supplied
By Mr Dudley Kidd and Mr Percy
Huskisson.
South Africa General Mission
London (1903?)
24pp.
90×120mm

Merriman (J. X.) – The South African
Settlement, A Speech By Mr. J. X.
Merriman, Delivered In The Birmingham
Town Hall, April 17th, 1901.
Printer not shown
np. (1901?)
12pp.
200mm   SABIB
*Pamphlet without title page. Reprinted
from the 'Manchester Guardian', April
18th, and revised by the author.*

Merritt (Maj. Wm. Hamilton) – The
Work Of The Colonial Division Under
Brabant And Dalgety. A Summary Of
The Work Of The Division, By Major
Wm. Hamilton Merritt, Governor
General's Body Guard, Canada; Late
Extra A.D.C. To General Brabant, And
Galloper To Colonel Dalgety.
Offices of 'South Africa'
London nd. (1901?) &
J. C. Juta & Co.
Cape Town/Port Elizabeth
nd. (1901?)
28pp. Illustrated.
Sq.16mo.   M
Reprinted from 'South Africa'.

(Merritt & Hatcher, Ltd.) (Printers) –
List Of The Chiefs, Officers, Court Of
Assistants, &c., &c., &c., Of The
Honourable Artillery Company, For The
Year 1901.
Merritt & Hatcher Ltd.
London 1901

113pp. With three plates.
216×140mm
With Annual Report of the Court of Assistants, and list of the members on the roll on the 31st December, 1900. Together with a report of military proceedings during the past year with names of members of H.A.C. who proceeded to South Africa.

Methuen (A. M. S.) – Peace Or War In South Africa.
Methuen & Co.
London 1901
vii+224pp. With two maps.
188×128mm
Various editions published up to 1902. Pagination varies. SABIB lists an American edition by Charles D. Pierce, New York, 1901 – 250mm. A cheap paper covered edition of 128pp. was published in 1901.

Methuen (A. M. S.) – The Tragedy Of South Africa.
Methuen & Co.
London nd. (1905)
168pp.
197×130mm
A revised edition of 'Peace Or War In South Africa'.

Meysey-Thompson (Sir Henry, Bart.) – The Transvaal Crisis. Remarks On The Present Condition Of Affairs. Together With A Reprint Of An Article By Him, In The 'Nineteenth Century Review' On The 'Real Grievances Of The Uitlanders'.
Sampson Low, Marston & Company Limited.
London 1899
30pp.
Roy.8vo.   M

Middlemiss (Sergt. G.) – With The Northumberland Volunteers In South Africa 1900–1901.
'Alnwick and County Gazette' and Steam Printing Company Limited.
Alnwick 1902
iv+88pp. Illustrated.
190×127mm

Miller (J.) – Chants For The Boer.
Whitaker & Ray Co.
San Francisco 1900
28pp.   M
Listed from De Bussy's African catalogue 1900. – Chants For The Boer, A Series Of Stirring War Poems, Written On Behalf Of The Boers.

Miller (James M.) – South Africa. Scenes From The 'Dark Continent' And The British-Boer War.
Stereopticon & Film Exchange
Chicago 1900
16pp.
240mm   H
Lecture illustrated by fifty-five lantern slides.

Milne (James) – The Epistles Of Atkins. Being Some Of The Lights, On Human Nature In The Ordeal Of War, Which Illumine The Letters Of The Common Soldier, Written From South Africa To His People At Home; And So An Answer To The Question, 'How Does It Feel To Be In Battle?'.
T. Fisher Unwin
London 1902
vii+227pp. Illustrated.
198×134mm
SABIB lists Unwin's Colonial Library edition and an edition published by J. M. Dent, London 1914.

Milner (A.) – The Nation And The Empire Being A Collection Of Speeches And Addresses: With An Introduction.
Constable & Co.
London 1913
xlix+515pp.
8vo.   W/L 608
Approximately 100 pages relate to speeches made during the war.

Milward (Victor) – 'What Is Now Being Done In South Africa'. A Reply.
Vacher & Sons, Printers
Westminster (London) 1900
14pp.
8vo.   M
An answer to one of W. T. Stead's broadsheets on the South African War. Listed in SABIB under DUFF.

Mitchell (Arthur) – In Memoriam. The Empires Dead. British Slain In South Africa, A Memorial Address Given In The Wesleyan Church Coromandel, On Sunday, Sept. 23, 1900.
The Brett Printing & Publishing Coy. Ltd.
Auckland 1900
4pp.
220mm   BIM
Title from cover.

Mitchell (Chas. J.) (Publisher?) – Souvenir British-Boer War. The Empire's Commanders.
Chas. J. Mitchell
Charlottetown (Prince Edward Island) (1900?)
16mo.   M
Small album consisting of twelve mounted photographs of commanders in South Africa. Without letterpress.

M'Kerrell (Thomas) – The Truth About The South African War, By An Outlander (Tom M'Kerrell.)
Printer/publisher not shown
———— 1901
16pp. Portrait.
190mm   SABIB

Mockler-Ferryman (Maj. A. F.) (Editor) – The Oxfordshire Light Infantry Chronicle 1899–1900–1901–1902.
Eyre and Spottiswoode (Printers)
London 1900–1903
viii+284pp. Illustrated.
xii+319pp. Illustrated.
ix+279pp. Illustrated.
viii+270pp. Illustrated.
218×140mm   CC
Four vols. of the O.L.I. Chronicle. Boer War content throughout.

Mockler-Ferryman (Lieut.-Colonel A. F.) (Editor) – The Oxfordshire Light Infantry In South Africa. A Narrative Of The Boer War From The Letters And Journals Of Officers Of The Regiment, And From Other Sources.
Eyre and Spottiswoode
London 1901
314pp. Maps and illustrations.
218×141mm   p.98

Moeller (Lieutenant B.) – Two Years At The Front With The Mounted Infantry Being The Diary Of Lieutenant B. Moeller. With A Memoir By Lieut.-Colonel L. R. C. Boyle, H.A.C.
Grant Richards
London 1903
xxi+296pp. Illustrated.
198×131mm

Moffett (Private E. C.) – With The Eighth Division: A Souvenir Of The South African Campaign. (Revised by Sergt. F. J. B. Lee.)

Knapp, Drewett & Sons Ltd.
Kingston-On-Thames and Westminster 1903
xiv+222+ii+xlvii.pp. Folding map and plates.
192×128mm   p.61

Monk (Dr. Henry G. H.) – The Fourth Report Upon The Health And Sanitary Conditions Of Kimberley, For The Year 1901 By Henry G. H. Monk, M.R.C.S., D.P.H. (Lond.), &c., Medical Officer Of Health (Kimberley).
Publisher/printer not shown
np. (1902)
43pp.
Roy.8vo.   M
Report addressed to the Chairman and members of the Board of Health in reference to heavy mortality at the refugee camp due to measles.

('Montreal Witness') (Publisher?) – Canada's Contingents And Canada's Future....
Daily Witness Print
Montreal 1902
7pp.
181×94mm   RCSL
Articles reprinted from the 'Montreal Witness' and other sources.

Moodie (J. W.) – Seventy Days With The Troops From Southampton To Ladysmith.
John Thomlinson, Stanley Works/Partick John Menzies & Co./Glasgow and Edinburgh.
1900
71pp. Illustrated.
182×122mm   p.117

Moore (Major A. T.) (Editor) – Professional Papers Of The Corps Of Royal Engineers. Royal Engineers Institute Occasional Papers. Vol. XXX 1904.
W. & J. Mackay & Co., Ltd. (Printers)
Chatham 1905
viii+294pp. Folding plates, maps and charts.
220×145mm
Papers include – 'Pieters Hill: a tactical study', and 'The Blockhouse System in the South African War'. Both papers illustrated. Folding plates, maps and plans. See entries under EDWARDS (Captain R. F.) Editor.

Moore (James G. Harle) – With The Fourth New Zealand Rough Riders.
The Otago Daily Times And Witness Newspapers Co., Limited
Dunedin 1906
200pp. Illustrated.
215×141mm

Moores (Lt.-Col. S.) & Rose (Capt. J. Markham) – Summary Of Tactics For Examination, With Lessons Of The South African War.
Publisher/printer not shown
Portsmouth (1903)
Pagination not shown.   THB

Morley (John) – Mr. John Morley On The Crisis.
Manchester Transvaal Committee
(Manchester 1899?)
15pp.
220mm   SABIB
Reprint of a speech against the war at Arbroath Sept. 5th 1899. See – Manchester Transvaal Committee.

Morley (John) – Two Years Of War – And After. Two Speeches At Arbroath, On October 31st, 1901, And At Forfar, On November 4th, 1901.

Liberal Publication Department
London 1901
24pp.
220mm   SABIB
Criticism of the British government in
connection with the war. See – Liberal
Publication Department.

Morley (W.) – South African War Stamps
1899–1900–1901.
Publisher/printer not shown
London nd. (1902)
12pp.
165×105mm
Stamp dealers revised price list.

(Morning Leader) (Publisher) – Leaflets
numbered 1–8 relating to the war and
events leading to war. Titles listed below
are of 4pp.
No. 1 – When And Why The Boers
         Armed.
No. 4 – The Uitlander Grievances.
No. 5 – The Real Motive For The War.
No. 6 – Mr Chamberlain And The Raid.
No. 7 – The Hawksley Dossier.
'Morning Leader'
London 1899–1900
210×128mm
SABIB lists 9 leaflets in above series
together with other 'Morning Leader'
pamphlets. See Vol.3, pp.378–379.

(Morning Leader) (Publisher) – Why We
Are At War.
'Morning Leader'
London (1900)
20pp.
215×130mm
Also published by the Birmingham
Auxiliary of the South African
Conciliation League.

(Morning Leader) (Publisher) – Muddling
Into War. Chapter And Verse Of The
Astounding Revelations Of The War
Commission.
'Morning Leader' Publication
Department
London 1903
40pp.
8vo.   M

Morris (Col. Charles C.) – Is Invasion
Possible? How To Defend Ourselves
A Lesson From The Boer War.
Evening Star Co. Ltd.
Dunedin 1900
14pp.
220mm   BIM

Morrison (Lieutenant E. W. B.) – With
The Guns In South Africa.
Spectator Printing Company, Limited
Hamilton 1901
307pp. Illustrated.
195×133mm
Author served in D Battery Royal
Canadian Artillery.

Morrison (Lt. E. W. B.) – The Horrors
Of The War. The Full Text Of Lt. M's
Letter.
South Africa Conciliation Committee
London 1901
16pp.
210mm
See entry SACC.67.

Morrow (R.) – Uniondale, 1901.
(A Memento Of The Anglo-Boer War.)
Economic Printing Works (Printers)
Cape Town nd. (c.1900)
18pp.
210mm   SABIB
A doctor's experiences during the war.

Morton (J. W.) – 8th (King's Royal Irish)
Hussars Diary Of The South African

War, 1900–1902.
Gale & Polden Ltd.
Aldershot 1905
xv+159pp. Illustrated.
220×140mm   p.121

**(Morton & Burt) (In association with Burt
& Sons)** (Publishers) – Borough Of
Paddington. Complimentary Banquet To
The Paddington Contingent Of The
C.I.V. 'King's Hall', Holborn
Restaurant, 19th November, 1900.
Morton & Burt together with
Burt & Sons
London 1900
24pp. Illustrated.
150×235mm   DC
Souvenir produced for the guests of the
Banquet Committee. A menu, list of
entertainments and a brief record of the
C.I.V. in South Africa are included.

(Mounted Black) – Campaigning In South
Africa 1900–1901 By A Mounted Black.
Printed for private circulation
Edinburgh Press
Edinburgh (1901)
vi+240pp.
207×147mm
Possible author – J. A. G. Elliot.

(Mowbray House) (Publisher) – The War
In South Africa, 1899–19—?
'Methods Of Barbarism'. 'War Is War' –
Mr. Brodrick, And 'War Is Hell' –
General Sherman. The Case For
Intervention By W. T. Stead . . . .
Mowbray House
London 1901
96pp.
240mm   SABIB
See entries under STEAD, W. T.

(M. R.) – Letters And Articles Relating
To The War Between Great Britain And
The South African Republics.
The South African Newspaper Company
Limited
Cape Town 1900
23pp.
212×141mm
Articles reprinted from the 'South African
News' in opposition to the war. M records
two parts. Part 1 – 22pp.? Part 2 – 46pp.
1900–1.

Muller (The Right Hon. F. Max.) – The
Question Of Right Between England
And The Transvaal. Letters By The
Right Hon. F. Max Müller. With
Rejoinders By Professor Theodore
Mommsen.
Issued by the Imperial South African
Association
London 1900
44pp.
8vo.   M
The pamphlet consists of two letters from
Professor Müller and two rejoinders by
Professor Mommsen, together with notes
by the former. Content includes reference
to the Jameson Raid and to direct causes
of the present war.

Murray (C.) (Editor) – Alasdair Murray,
1900. A Few Words And Letters
Privately Offered To Those Who, At
Lochcarron And Elsewhere, Knew Him
Well.
Spottiswoode & Co., Printers
London 1901
xvii+122pp. Illustrated.
195×130mm
Tribute to 2nd Lieut. Murray of the 2nd
Batt. Grenadier Guards died of wounds
received at the battle of Biddulphsberg,
May 29, 1900.

(Murray, John) (Publishers) – Report Of
The Committee Of The Portland

Hospital. Printed For Private
Distribution Among The Subscribers
Only.
John Murray
London 1901
176pp. Illustrated.
255×180mm
A record of operations from Jan–July
1900. The hospital was set up at
Rondebosch and removed to
Bloemfontein after three months.
Appendices contain lists of equipment and
patients treated.

(Murray, John) (Publisher) – Letters
From An Uitlander 1899–1902.
John Murray
London 1903
v+167pp.
205×135mm
Letters addressed to Sir Bartle Frere from
June 1899 to November 1902 relative to
affairs in South Africa.

Murray (Mary) – The Salvation Army At
Work In The Boer War By Adjutant
Mary Murray. With A Prefatory Note By
W. Bramwell Booth.
International Headquarters/Trade
Headquarters.
London 1900
viii+112pp. Illustrated.
190×116mm

Murray (Lieut.-Colonel P. L.) (Editor) –
Official Records Of The Australian
Military Contingents To The War In
South Africa. Compiled And Edited For
The Department Of Defence By Lieut.-
Colonel P. L. Murray, R.A.A. (Ret.)
Albert J. Mullett, Government Printer.
Melbourne nd. (1911)
iii+607pp.
248×188mm   p.120
A statistical register and reference of
Australian military contingents to South
Africa 1899–1902.

Musgrave (G. C.) – In South Africa With
Buller.
Little, Brown, and Company
Boston 1900
xviii+364pp. Map and illustrations.
210×135mm
English edition – Gay & Bird, London
1900. xv+364pp. M.

N

Nalder (Marshall) – Battle-Smoke
Ballads, Or Rhymes Of The Transvaal
War.
Lyttleton Times Co. Ltd. (printers)
Christchurch 1902
39pp.
185mm   BIM

Nash (J. Eveleigh) (Editor) – The
Ladysmith Treasury.
Sands & Company
London 1900
344pp.
Cr.8vo.
Collection of stories by various authors.
Volume published for the benefit of the
distressed people of Ladysmith following
the siege. Minimal war interest.

(Natal) – Natal Volunteer Record. Anglo
Boer War. See entry under ROBINSON &
Co.

(Natal. Colony of) – Police Criminal
Investigation Dept. Names Of British
Subjects In Natal Who Are Suspected Of
Disloyalty.

(Prepared by C.I.D. Natal Police)
Printer/publisher not shown
――― (1900?)
67pp.
330mm   SABIB

Nathan (Manfred) – The Legal Effects Of
War On Contracts And Other Liabilities.
J. C. Juta & Co.
Cape Town 1900
37pp.
8vo.   M

(National Press Agency, Ltd.) (Printers) –
The Dutch Reformed Church And
The Boers.
National Press Agency, Ltd.
London nd. (1899?)
24pp.
212×136mm
*A protest against war by ministers of the
Dutch Reformed Church. Paper covered.*

(National Press Agency) (Publishers) –
The War In South Africa, Some
Authoritative Sketches Of The Boers By
Distinguished Englishmen.
(Issued By Friends Of South Africa In
The Interests Of Truth.)
National Press Agency, Ltd.
London 1899
8pp.
8vo.   M

(National Press Agency, Ltd.) (Printers) –
The Pan-Africander Conspiracy.
A Refutation By An Africander Member
Of The Cape Parliament.
National Press Agency, Ltd.
London nd. (c.1900)
16pp.
210mm   SABIB

(National Reform Union) – Various
pamphlets published Manchester 1899–
1901. Printed by Wm. Hough, Taylor,
Garnett, Evans. Most relating to the war
are of 1–4pp. Some of the pamphlets
were also issued by the *Manchester
Transvaal Committee* and the *Manchester
Transvaal Peace Committee*. SABIB
listings – Vol.3 p.468.

141. – 'The Country's Affection' For The
Services: A Dear Luxury. 4pp.

150. – The Transvaal Question. What
Are We Going To Fight About. 2pp.

151. – The Transvaal Question. The
Present Position. 2pp.

152. – The Transvaal Question. Liberals
And The Franchise. 2pp.

153. – The Transvaal Question. The
Franchise: What Was Asked And What
The Boers Offered. 2pp.

154. – The Transvaal Question. Our
Right Of Interference In The Transvaal.
2pp.

156. – The Transvaal Question. The
Suzerainty Question. 4pp.

157. – The Transvaal Question. Canon
Hicks On The Duty Of England. 4pp.

158. – The Transvaal Question. The
Story Of The Boers. 4pp.

159. – The Transvaal Question.
A Conservative View Of The Transvaal
Crisis. 2pp.

161. – The Transvaal Question. 'I Do Not
Think It Was Worth A War.' 2pp.

162. – Who's To Pay? 4pp.

164. – Working Men, Read This! What
We Are Fighting For. 2pp.

172. – Sheltering Behind The Soldiers,
By H. J. Ogden. 1p.

173. – The War In South Africa. 2pp.

174. – The Boer Armaments. 1p.

176. – Gains And Losses Of The War.
2pp.

194. – Mr Goldwin Smith On The War.
2pp.

210–220mm   SABIB

(National Reform Union) (Publisher) –
The Transvaal Question. How War Was
Brought About.
National Reform Union
Manchester (1899?)
7+1pp.
210mm   SABIB
*Also published as leaflet no.1 of the
Manchester Transvaal Peace Committee.*

(National Reform Union) (Publisher) –
The Transvaal Question. Mr F. Selous
On The War.
National Reform Union
Manchester (1899)
7pp.
8vo.   M

**(National Union Of Conservative And
Constitutional Associations)** – Various
pamphlets published by the Conservative
Publication Dept., in connection with the
Conservative Central Office and the
National Union. Some relate to the war
of 1899–1902.
SABIB listings Vol.3 pp.469–470.

C.C.O. – Oct. 1899: No.90. Why This
War? 2pp.

N.U. – Oct. 1899: No.91. The Transvaal
War. Justification Of The Unionist Policy
By Radical Ex-Ministers And Radical
Members Of Parliament. 4pp.

N.U. – Nov. 1899: No.93. Disloyal Irish
Nationalists. The Utterances Of Some Of
The Irish Members On The Transvaal
Question. 4pp.

N.U. – Nov. 1899: No.94. The Transvaal
War. The Patriotism Of Our Colonies.
Little Englanders Put To Shame. 2pp.

N.U. – Sept. 1900: No.53. The
Government And Mounted Troops.
What Really Happened. (Mr George
Wyndham's Speech.) 4pp.

N.U. – Sept. 1900: No.80. The War
Office And The Despatch Of Troops To
South Africa (Mr George Wyndham's
Speech.) 4pp.

C.C.O. – Sept. 1900: No.85. The Boers
In South Africa. 2pp.

C.C.O. – Jan. 1900: No.86. 'Suzerainty'.
Have We Ever Given Up Our
'Suzerainty' Over The Transvaal? 2pp.

C.C.O. – Jan. 1900: No.87. How The
Gentle Boers Treated The Unarmed
British Refugee. 2pp.

C.C.O. – Jan. 1900: No.88. What Are
We Fighting About? 4pp.

C.C.O. – Apr. 1900: No.95. The South
African Question. Opinions Of Ministers
Of Religion. 12pp.

N.U. – Sept. 1900: No.100. Why We Are
At War And Who Is Responsible.
A Short History Of The Negotiations
With The Late South African Republic.
8pp.

N.U. – Sept. 1900: No.101. Local Forces
In South Africa (Mr George Wyndham's
Speech.) 2pp.

N.U. – Sept. 1900: No.106. Radical
Advice To The Enemy. Extract From
Letter From Dr. G. B. Clark, The
Unworthy Radical M.P. For Caithness,
To President Kruger. 1p.

N.U. – Sept. 1900: No.107. Radical
Correspondence With The Enemy. The
Following Letter From Dr. G. B. Clark,
Radical M.P. For Caithness, Has Been
Found In The State Papers At Pretoria.
1p.

N.U. – Sept. 1900: No.108. Letter Found
In State Papers, Bloemfontein. Liberals
Will Lower The Flag. Mr Melius de
Villiers . . . . To Mr Abraham Fischer. 1p.

N.U. – Sept. 1900: No.109. Radical
Enemies Of Their Country. Any Stick
Good Enough To Beat The British
Government With! This Is Apparently
The Motto Of Mr John Ellis. 1p.

N.U. – Aug. 1900: No.110. The
Transvaal War. The Attitude Of The
Disloyal Nationalists Since The Outbreak
Of War. 4pp.

N.U. – Aug. 1900: No.111. The
Transvaal War. Sir 'Facing-Both-Ways'
Campbell-Bannerman, M.P., And Our
Military Preparations. 4pp.

N.U. – Sept. 1900: No.112. Let There Be
No Mistake! This Is The Character Of Mr
Kruger And The Dutch As Portrayed By
Two Of Their Most Enthusiastic
Supporters In This Country. (Quotes
W. T. Stead and L. Courtney.) 2pp.

N.U. – Sept. 1900: No.113. The Simple-
Minded Farmer's Method Of War. 4pp.

N.U. – Sept. 1900: No.114. The
Uitlanders' Grievances. 2pp.

N.U. – Sept. 1900: No.115. The Gentle
Boer And His Brutal Bullet. 2pp.

N.U. – Sept. 1900: No.116. How The
Boers Treat Their Political Prisoners. 2pp.

N.U. – Sept. 1900: No.117. Leading
English Non-Conformists Justify The
Action Of The Government In Their
Transvaal Policy. 4pp.

N.U. – Sept. 1900: No.118. Boer
Government. What It Ought To Have
Been, And What It Was Before The
War. 4pp.

N.U. – Sept. 1900: No.119. Cape
Statesmen Tell The Truth About
President Kruger. 4pp.

N.U. – Sept. 1900: No.121. Lord
Rosebery Upon The Little England Party
And The Duty Of The Democracy To
The Empire. 2pp.

N.U. – Sept. 1900: No.123. Radical
M.P.'s Advising The Enemy. (Quotations
From Letters By Henry Labouchere.) 4pp.

C.C.O. – Jun. 1901: No.15. Boer
Prisoners At Ahmednagar. 1p.

C.C.O. – Jun. 1901: No.16. The Road To
Majuba. 4pp.

C.C.O. – Jul. 1901: No.17. What Our Pro-Boers Do For England. (Quotation From Letter By Sir E. J. Reed.) 1p.

220mm   SABIB

(National Union Of Conservative And Constitutional Associations) (Publisher) – Notes For Speakers On The South African Question.
McCorquodale & Co.
London 1900
26pp.
210mm   SABIB
Notes for speakers correcting misrepresentations of British friends of the Boers.

Naville (Edouard Henri) – The Transvaal Question From A Foreign Point Of View; Translated From The French By M. Vetch.
W. Blackwood & Sons
London 1900
64pp.
Cr.8vo.   M

Neethling (E.) – Should We Forget?
Holl.-Af. Publishing Co.
Cape Town (1903?)
x+128pp. Illustrated.
198×131mm
Experiences of Boer women and children in the concentration camps during the war.

Neil (C. Lang.) (Editor) – South Africa In Peace & War.
Miles & Miles
London nd. (c.1900)
192pp. Illustrated.
280×340mm
General interest publication including reference to the second Boer War.

Neil (Henry) (Editor) – See EVERETT (Marshall) – Thrilling Experiences etc.

Neilly (J. Emerson) – Besieged With B.-P. A Full And Complete Record Of The Siege Of Mafeking.
C. Arthur Pearson Ltd.
London 1900
iii+296pp. Frontispiece.
180×120mm
SABIB lists a third ed. 1900, v+296pp.

Neligan (T.) – Boer War, 1899–1900. From Lancashire To Ladysmith With The 1st Battalion South Lancashire Regiment, (Famous Fighting Fortieth) Giving A Detailed Account Of The Forced March From Estcourt To Springfield, And A Graphic Description Of The Battles Of Spion Kop, Potgieter's Drift, And Pieter's Hill, The Sad Death Of Col. O'Leary, And The Entry Of The Relieving Force Into Ladysmith, Where, For Four Months, British Soldiers Had Upheld The Honour Of Great Britain By One Of The Regiment.
Messrs. Neligan and Carter
Preston 1900
48pp. With frontispiece.
176×120mm   p.106

Neligan (T.) – Boer War, 1899–1900. From Preston To Ladysmith With The 1st Battalion, South Lancashire Regiment, Etc. By One Of The Regiment.
J. & H. Platt (Printers)
Preston 1900
48pp. (With frontispiece.)
12mo.   M

(Nelson. T. & Sons) (Publisher) – Transvaal War Atlas.
T. Nelson & Sons

np./nd. (London c.1900)
40pp. (including covers.) Illustrated.
281×220mm   p.viii

Neville (John Ormond) – Boer And Britisher In South Africa: A History Of The Boer-British War And The Wars For United South Africa Together With Biographies Of The Great Men Who Made The History Of South Africa.
Thompson & Thomas
Chicago nd. (1900)
489pp. Illustrated.
230×155mm
SABIB lists copy published by 'United Subscription Book Publishers of America', Chicago (c.1900). xiii+pp.21–310. Illustrated.

Nevinson (H. W.) – Ladysmith The Diary Of A Siege.
Methuen & Co.
London 1900
viii+310pp. Maps and illustrations. (This edition with the folding chart – Statistics relating to the siege of Ladysmith.)
198×130mm
SABIB lists copy of second edition. Also issued by 'Methuen's Colonial Library'.

Nevinson (Henry W.) – 'Daily Chronicle' Extra. A Review Of The South African War. By Henry W. Nevinson (War Correspondent Of 'The Daily Chronicle'). The Dutch Invasion. The Days Of Disaster. The Days Of Relief. The Days Of Advance. Effective Occupation. Record Of The C.I.V. With Maps And A Diary Of The Principal Events From Day To Day.
Edward Lloyd, Limited, at the 'Daily Chronicle' Office.
London 1900
16pp. With a map.
330×246mm
Title from cover.

(New Age. The) (Publisher) – President Steyn And Lord Kitchener.... Reply To The Proclamation. No Peace Acceptable Without Independence.
A. Bonner for the New Age Press
London (1901)
Pagination not shown.
                          SABIB
Supplement to 'The New Age', November 7th, 1901.

(New Age. The) (Publisher) – The Churches And The South African War 'Lest We Forget'.
The New Age?
np. 1905
40+ii pp.   CB

(New Age Press) (Publishers) – Songs Of The Veld, And Other Poems. Reprinted From 'The New Age'.
New Age Press
London 1902
136pp.
Cr.8vo.   M
Pro Boer poems relating to the war.

Newbigging (Thomas) – Personal Experiences In South Africa With Some Reflections Appropriate To The Present Crisis.
R. S. Chrystal
Manchester 1900
68pp.
Cr.8vo.   M
Narrative of travel in the Transvaal in 1888–9, with an account of the country in 1900.

Newbolt (W. C. E.) – Endurance: A Message From The War; A Sermon Preached At St. Paul's On The Third

Sunday In Advent, 1899. Published By Request.
Office Of 'The Church Times'
London 1900
16pp.
210mm   SABIB

Newbolt (W. C. E.) – The Fruits Of War; A Sermon Preached At Westminster Abbey On Septuagesima Sunday, 1900, Being The Day Set Apart By Authority For Intercession In Behalf Of Our Army Engaged In South Africa.
Office Of 'The Church Times'
London 1900
15pp.
210mm   SABIB

Newland-Pedley (F.) (Editor) – The Devil's Fountain Or Deelfontein Gazette. See entry under PEDLEY (F. Newland-).

(Newnes. George Ltd.) (Publishers) – B.P. The Hero Of Mafeking.
George Newnes Ltd.
London nd. (c.1900)
80pp. Illustrated.
236×155mm
Volume containing account of the Mafeking siege.

(Newnes. George) (Publishers) – The King's Handbook Of The War: A Concise Collection Of Valuable And Interesting Facts About The People And Places In The Present Conflict, Together With A Mass Of Readable And Topical Matter, Easy Of Reference For General Use.
Newnes Publishers
London (1900)
36pp. Maps.
250mm   SABIB
A handbook on the war to be given away with the first number of the illustrated paper 'The King'.

(Newnes. George Ltd.) (Publishers) – Under The Union Jack. Descriptive And Illustrative Of The Campaign In South Africa. The Second Boer War.
George Newnes Ltd.
(London 1900)
2 vols. – viii+432pp. & viii+pp.433–856. Illustrated throughout.
294×230mm   p.53

(Newnes. George Ltd.) (Publishers) – Under The Union Jack.
Vol.1. No.1–18. Vol.2. Nos.19–36.
George Newnes Ltd.
London 1899–1900.
856pp. Illustrated.
300×233mm
Complete set of 36 parts, each with illustrated wrap. Cover of Nos.1 & 2 (Vol.1) are included in pagination.

(Newnes. George Limited) (Publishers) – Khaki In South Africa. An Album Of Pictures And Photographs Illustrating The Chief Events Of The War Under Lord Roberts. With A Chronological History.
George Newnes Limited
London 1900
iv+140pp. Illustrated.
275×346mm   p.39
Also published in 6 parts with paper covers.

(Newnes. George) (Publishers) – Our Heroes Of The South African War, 1899–1900.
George Newnes
London (1900?)
Parts I–IV. Portfolios of portraits, each containing 16 loose plates of Officers

serving in South Africa, with biographical detail.
243×177mm
SABIB states the work was to be completed in about 12 parts. It appears only 4 were issued. L/W 612, lists item – 4 parts in 3. M lists item – 66pp. Illustrated.

(Newnes. George Ltd.) (Publisher) – The C.I.V. Being The Story Of The City Imperial Volunteers And Volunteer Regiments Of The City Of London, 1300–1900. The Inception, Organisation And Fighting Record Of The Corps. With An Historical Introduction.
George Newnes, Ltd.
London nd. (c.1900)
ii+44pp. Illustrated.
354×257mm
Special edition. No.25 of 500 copies.

(New South Wales Bookstall Co. The) (Publisher) – The New South Wales Contingents For South Africa Being A Pictorial Record Of The Organisation Of The Colonies Forces For Active Service, And The Scenes Of Unparalleled Enthusiasm Marking Their Departure For The Front. From Blocks Kindly Lent By *The Sydney Mail* And *The Australian Field* And From New Matter.
The New South Wales Bookstall Co.
Sydney 1900
24pp. Illustrated.
280×219mm   GC
CC includes an edition of 32pp. Limp card cover 280×220mm. Cover title – 'Transvaal War Souvenir.' 'Bushmen's Contingent Souvenir.' A pictorial record of the departure of the First and Second Contingents, including 'A' Battery, Royal Australian Artillery.

Newton (Sir Alfred J.) – Official. Reports On The Raising, Organising, Equipping And Despatching The City Of London Imperial Volunteers To South Africa. Published By Order Of The Right Hon. The Lord Mayor.
Blades, East & Blades, printers
London 1900
v+80pp.
269×210mm
Standard ed. Khaki cloth over bevelled boards.

Newton (Sir Alfred J.) – Official. Reports On The Raising, Organising, Equipping And Despatching The City Of London Imperial Volunteers To South Africa. Published By Order Of The Right Hon. The Lord Mayor.
Blades, East & Blades, printers
London 1900
v+61pp.
286×229mm   p.31
Special edition bound in full morocco, printed on Whatman paper. Presentation copy from the Lord Mayor Sir Alfred Newton to C. W. Bartholomew Esq.

(New Zealander. A) – New Zealanders And The Boer War Or Soldiers From The Land Of The Moa (By A New Zealander.)
Gordon and Gotch
Christchurch nd. (c.1910)
xi+287pp. With two plates.
189×128mm   p.40
Author – Mrs Hawdon? Paper covered edition – 183×124mm.

Nicholl (Captain H. I.) – A South African Journal, 1900.
Printed for private circulation
The Beds. Times Publishing Co., Ltd. (Printers)
Bedford nd. (c.1902)
47pp. Map and illustrations.
220×142mm   p.54

Nicholls (Horace W.) – Uitlanders And Colonists Who Fought For The Flag 1899. 1900. A Series Of 110 First-Class Collotype Photographs, Illustrating Life With The Imperial Light Horse And Other South African Volunteer Regiments.
H. W. Nicholls/The Goch Studio
Johannesburg nd. (c.1900)
Unpaginated. Illustrated throughout.
218×285mm   p.92

Nicholson (Gen. W. G.) – Report On Transport Services. See WO.161.

(9176 I.Y.) – The Fifes In South Africa. See – STURROCK (J. P.)

(Noronha & Co.) (Printers) – South African War Record Of The 1st Battalion Sherwood Foresters, Derbyshire Regiment, 1899–1902.
Noronha & Co., Govt. Printer
Hongkong 1904
iv+195pp.
230mm   W

Norris (F.) (Compiler) – The Roll Call. A Record Of The Part Rhodesia Took In The Transvaal War – 1899, 1900, 1901.
Printed for F. Norris Bulawayo
By T., T., and S., Cape Town. 1901
30pp. Illustrated.
371×251mm   CC
Catalogued from cover.

Norris (F.) (Compiler) – Rhodesians At The Front. Being Part II Of The Roll Call. A Record Of Rhodesia's Share In The South African War. Part I, Oct. 1899 To Jan. 1901. Part II, Jan. 1901 To 1902.
Printed for F. Norris Bulawayo
By T., T., and S., Cape Town. (1902)
32pp. Illustrated.
Folio.   M
Catalogued from cover.

Norris (Major S. L.) – The South African War 1899–1900 A Military Retrospect Up To The Relief Of Ladysmith.
John Murray
London 1900
xi+309pp. With maps.
207×140mm

(North. Charles) (Printer) – The Experiences Of An Artillery Officer During The Boer War, October, 1899 – February 1902.
Charles North
London 1902
ix+109pp. With maps.
230mm   SABIB
Printed for private circulation. Author's name, A. R. G. Begbie, taken from page iii of text. The above item is listed in THB under the cover title – 'Letters On The Boer War, 1899–1902'.

(North American Review Publishing Company) (Publisher) – Britain And The Boers. Both Sides Of The South African Question.
North American Review Publishing Company
New York nd. (1899)
45pp. Folding map.
Roy.8vo.   M
Three articles on the Anglo-Boer question by S. Brooks, Dr F. V. Engelenburg and 'A Diplomat'. See entry under HARPER BROTHERS – Briton and Boer: Both Sides of the South African Question.

Norton (Smedley) – Bramcote Ballads With A Brief Diary Of The Late Conflict In South Africa And The Subsequent Visit Of The Colonial Secretary.
A. Sutton & Co.

Bournemouth 1903
xiv+96pp.
210×140mm
Poems in reference to the campaign with a diary of the war appended.

Norton (Smedley) – Bramcote Ballads, With A Brief Diary Of The Late Conflict In South Africa.
S. H. Monckton & Co.
London nd. (1904)
xiv+96pp. Frontispiece.
210×140mm

Norton (Smedley) – 'Sergeant, Call The Roll'. Poems. Also A Chronological History Of The Principal Events In The South African War, With 13 Full-Page Illustrations By Tom Merry.
Elliot Stock
London 1902
Unpaginated. (26pp.)
Quarto   M

Notcutt (H. Clement) – How Kimberley Was Held For England. The Story Of A Four Month's Siege.
By H. Clement Notcutt, BA., Head Master of the Boy's Public School, Kimberley (nd.) (All shown on title-page.)
35pp.?
150×124mm

Notcutt (H. Clement) – How Kimberley Was Held For England The Story Of A Four Month's Siege. Reprinted, With Alterations And Additions, From The 'Cape Times'. By H. Clement Notcutt, BA. Head Master Of The Boy's Public School, Kimberley.
The S.A. 'Electric' Printing and Publishing Company
(Capetown) nd. (1900)
35pp.
150×125mm
SABIB lists 2nd Ed. (1900) – iv+35+3pp.

('Novocastrian') – Pro Patria. Stories Of Service In South Africa, 1899–1902. See entry under STEVENSON and DRYDEN.

O

O'Connell (Jim) – Transvaal War, 1899–1900. Campaigning With The Durban Light Infantry. Reprinted From The 'Natal Mercury'.
Robinson & Co.
Durban 1900
61pp.
8vo.   M

O'Connor (T. P.) – Who Ought To Win, Etc. See 'RANDOLPH Spencer'.

Ogden (H. J.) – The War Against The Dutch Republics In South Africa Its Origin, Progress, And Results, Annotated With Extracts From Books, Newspapers, Pamphlets, And Speeches By Members Of Parliament And Other Leaders Of Public Opinion.
Taylor, Garnett, Evans & Co., Ltd (Printers) For National Reform Union
Manchester nd. (1901)
344pp.
252×176mm   p.47

O'Leary (Lt.Col. T. E.) – Report On Signalling. See WO.126.

O'Mahony (C. J.) – 'A Peep Over The Barleycorn'. See JACK THE SNIPER.

O'Meara (Major M. A. J.) – Defence Of Kimberley. Notes On The Boer War,

From The Diary Of A Special Service
Officer.
Imperial Government Printing Work
Johannesburg 1901
49pp.
Folio.   M
*A brochure published privately and
anonymously but attributed to Major
O'Meara R. E., the chief intelligence
officer under Major Kekewich. The
author severely criticises the attitude
adopted by Mr Rhodes towards the
military authorities. M indicates the
publication is reproduced from typewritten
copy.*

Omond (G. W. T.) – The Boers In
Europe A Sidelight On History.
Adam & Charles Black
London 1903
iii+276pp.
195×130mm
*Political intrigue attending the Boer
mission to Europe following the war.*

O'Moore (M.) – The Romance Of The
Boer War, Humours And Chivalry Of
The Campaign.
Elliot Stock
London 1901
93pp.
8vo.   M
*Anecdotes and sketches in reference to the
war.*

(One Who Was In It) – Kruger's Secret
Service.
John Macqueen
London 1900
221pp.
190mm

Oppenheim (L.) – Thornycroft's Mounted
Infantry On Spion Kop.
Publisher/printer not shown
np. 1901
18pp.   WO. Cat./1912

(Oriel) – Ballads Of Battle.
Publisher/printer not shown
Melbourne nd. (1900)
35pp. With plate.
8vo.   CB
*Verses in reference to Australian troops in
the war. Author – John Sandes.*

Orr (Trooper A. S.) – Scottish Yeomanry
In South Africa, 1900–1901. A Record
Of The Work And Experiences Of The
Glasgow And Ayrshire Companies.
James Hedderwick & Sons
Glasgow 1901
vii+160pp. Illustrated.
227×180mm

(Orr, Pollock & Co.) (Printers) – List Of
Patients On Board Hospital Ship S.Y.
'Rhouma' Cape Town, 1900.
Orr, Pollock & Co., Printers
Greenock nd. (c.1900)
36pp. Illustrated.
125×188mm   SNH   p.107

Osboldstone (G. A.) (Publisher) – In
Memory Of The Gallant Officers And
Men Of Victoria, Who Died In Defence
Of Our Empire In Transvaal War,
1899–1900.
G. A. Osboldstone
Melbourne 1900
26pp. Illustrated.
230mm
*Album of photographs with short
biographies.*

(Otago Daily Times) (Publisher) – The
Visit Of The Imperial Troops To
Dunedin New Zealand Feb. 1901.

Otago Daily Times
Dunedin 1901
77pp. Illustrated.
140×220mm   BIM

Otis (James) – Fighting For The Empire
The Story Of The War In South Africa.
Dana Estes & Company
Boston nd. (1900)
xxi+pp.11–466. Map and illustrations.
203×142mm   p.78

(Outpost) – Anglo Boer War, 1899–1902.
And St. Kilda's Share Therein.
F. G. Dixon, printer
St. Kilda (c.1905)
iii+52pp. Illustrated.
210mm   SABIB
*Brief history of the war and of Australian
contingents that took part.*

P

Packer (J. W.) (Publisher) – The 'Leader'
Souvenir Of The Departure Of The
Victorian Contingent To The Transvaal,
Oct. 28th 1899.
J. W. Packer for David Syme
(carrying on business as David Syme
and Co.) at The Age Office
Melbourne 1899
16pp. Illustrated.
295×210mm
*Notes on British and Boer commanders
with nominal roll and portraits of the
Victorian Contingent Infantry Unit and
Mounted Rifles. Title from cover.*

Page (Jesse) – Christians In Khaki.
Cameos Of Christian Work Among The
Soldiers, Fresh From The Front.
Marshall Brothers
London 1900
100pp. Illustrated.
192×124mm

Paget (F.) – Redemption Of War.
Sermons In The Cathedral Church Of
Christ.
(No other information)
*M – Ref. De Bussy's African catalogue
1900. SABIB gives title – The redemption
of war, etc. Longmans & Co., London
1900.*

Park (Lt.-Col. C. W.) – Letters From
Ladysmith. See – (C.W.P.)

Parker (F.) (Editor) – Arbitration Or
War? A View Of The Transvaal
Question. See entry under STORY (R.
Douglas).

(Patriotic Association. The) (Publishers) –
Grievances Of The Transvaal Uitlanders.
Boer Tyranny And Misgovernment.
Petition To The Queen. Debate In House
Of Commons. Mr Chamberlain's
Statement.
Vacher, printers for The Association
Westminster (1899?)
16pp.
210mm   SABIB

(Patriotic Association. The) (Publishers) –
The Truth About The Conduct Of The
Boer War. Concentration Camps.
Extracts From The Blue Book. The
British Soldier As He Is.
Published by the Patriotic Association
and Messrs. Simpkin, Marshall,
Hamilton, Kent & Co., Ltd.
London (1901)
32pp.
8vo.   M

(Patriotic Band Festival) – Programme:
Patriotic Band Festival, Royal Albert
Hall.
1900 (No other information)
14pp.
Quarto   M
*Programme of concert held at the time of
military disasters in Dec. 1899.*

Pearse (H. H. S.) – Four Months
Besieged The Story Of Ladysmith Being
Unpublished Letters From H. H. S.
Pearse The 'Daily News' Special
Correspondent.
Macmillan and Co., Limited
London 1900
xiv+244pp. Maps and illustrations.
203×132mm   p.37
*SABIB – 'Macmillan's Colonial Library
edition', London 1900.*

Pearse (Henry H. S.) (Editor) – The
History Of Lumsden's Horse A Complete
Record Of The Corps From Its
Formation To Its Disbandment.
Longmans, Green, And Co.
London/New York and Bombay 1903
xii+506pp. Folding map and numerous
illustrations.
257×185mm   p.37

(Pearson. C. Arthur Ltd.) (Publisher) –
War Pictures.
C. Arthur Pearson Ltd.
London 1900
512pp. Illustrated throughout.
245×185mm   p.17
*16 issues published from Feb. 10–May 26,
1900. Each issue 32pp. Bound volume of
512pp. issued without the pictorial covers.*

Pease (Sir A. E.) – A Private Memoir Of
Sir Thomas Fowler, Bart. Born August
12, 1868, Killed In Action, April 20,
1902.
William Clowes and Sons Limited,
printers
London nd. (1906?)
vii+194pp. Colour plates and other
illustrations. Maps.
226×150mm
*Privately printed memoir of Captain T.
Fowler, 1st Wiltshire I.Y. killed in action
at Moolman's Spruit, 1902.*

Pease (A. E.) – South Africa. Imperial
Justice.
National Press Agency
London 1900
24pp. With tables.
210mm   SABIB
*Author queries reasons put forward as
justification for war in South Africa.*

Pedley (F. Newland-) (Editor) – The
Devils' Fountain Or Deelfontein Gazette.
Printed and published for the Imperial
Yeomanry Hospital.
Deelfontein Hospital 1900
20pp. (9 printed rectos, 1 blank.)
330×202mm   GC
*Issue 1. News and notices of camp life.
Press censor Colonel Sloggett.*

Peel (Hon. Sidney) – Trooper 8008 I.Y.
Edward Arnold
London 1902 (6th Impression)
xi+168pp. Map and illustrations.
230×148mm
*Experiences of a volunteer in the 40th
(Oxfordshire) Co. Imperial Yeomanry.
Impressions 1–5 published 1901.*

(Penny Illustrated Newspaper Co. The)
(Publisher) – Illustrated War Special.
The Penny Illustrated Newspaper Co.
London 1899–1900
356pp. Illustrated. (Including double
page colour spreads.)
417×307mm   p.iv

Bound issues of the War Special. Vol.1. includes Nos.1–26. dated Nov. 21st, 1899–May 16, 1900. Vol. 2. includes Nos.27 & 28 of May 23 and May 30, 1900. DC set includes No.29 of June 6, 1900.

Perkins (W. O.) – The War In South Africa, Or Boer And Briton . . . . Delivered Before The Parker Memorial Science Class; In The Fraternity Lecture Course, Boston; And At Lexington, Mass.
T. J. Southwell
Boston, Mass. (1900)
32pp.
Cr.8vo.   M

Perris (G. H.) (Editor) – A History Of The Peace Conference At The Hague (Concord Extras No.1) Edited By G. H. Perris. With Impressions By Felix Moscheles And W. T. Stead.
International Arbitration Association
London 1899
102pp.
8vo.   M
A contribution by Stead relates to Dum-Dum bullets. He implies that millions of rounds were sent to South Africa for use against the Boers.

Perris (G. H.) – Blood And Gold In South Africa; An Answer To Dr. Conan Doyle. Being An Examination Of His Account Of The 'Cause And Conduct' Of The South African War.
International Arbitration Association
London 1902
79pp.
209×136mm   CC

Perry (Allan) – A Medical History Of Prisoners Of War In Ceylon. 1900–1903.
George J. A. Skeen (Government Printer)
Colombo 1904
36pp. Plan and illustrations.
214×135mm   RCSL
The author was Principal Civil Medical Officer and Inspector-General of Hospitals, Ceylon, responsible for medical care of prisoners of war.

Pétavel (E.) – The Rights Of England In The South African War. Translated By The Rev. Canon St. John.
William Blackwood & Sons
Edinburgh and London 1900
62pp.
190×124mm   RCSL

Peticolas (A. L.) – Homer 2nd's Bulliad, etc. See GWYNNE John.

Pettigrew (R. F.) – The South African Republic. Speech Of Hon. R. F. Pettigrew, Of South Dakota, In The Senate Of The United States, Saturday, April 14th, 1900.
Publisher not shown
Washington 1900
27pp.
Roy.8vo.   M
Violent anti-British speech.

(Pewtress & Co.) (Publisher?) – A Short Criticism Of Mrs Josephine E. Butler's Book 'Native Races And The War', By Another Abolitionist.
Pewtress & Co.
London 1900
27pp.
220mm   SABIB
No title page. Catalogued from cover.

Phelan (T.) – The Siege Of Kimberley Its Humorous And Social Side Anglo-Boer

War (1899–1902) Eighteen Weeks In Eighteen Chapters.
M. H. Gill & Son, Ltd.
Dublin 1913
251pp.
190×125mm

Phillipps (L. March.) – With Rimington.
Edward Arnold
London 1901
x+219pp. 1 plan.
229×148mm
Second – fourth impressions dated 1902.

Phillipps-Wolley (Clive) – In Memory Of Our Dead. At Modder River, Feb. 21, 1900.
Publisher/printer not shown
Victoria, B.C. nd. (1900)
6pp.
230×130mm   RCSL

Phillips (Thomas) – The South African Question: A Lecture On The Transvaal And Its System Of Government, With Some Of The Abuses Of Power Which Have Led To The Present War In South Africa.
Press of the *'Philadelphia Journal'*
Philadelphia, Pa. 1900
22pp.
Cr.8vo.   M

Pienaar (Philip) – With Steyn And De Wet.
Methuen & Co.
London 1902
vi+173pp.
198×129mm
Methuen's Colonial Library edition listed in SABIB. M lists Methuen ed. published 1900?

Pierce (Charles D.) – The South African Republics, Etc. – See (BOER RELIEF FUND).

Pilcher (Col. T. D.) – Some Lessons From The Boer War 1899–1902.
Isbister & Company Limited
London 1903
141pp.
190×130mm

(Pilgrim) – An Open Letter To The Archbishop Of Canterbury.
Friars Printing Association, for the Author
(London 1901?)
14pp.
220mm   SABIB
Writer accuses the archbishop of not having opposed the unjust war in South Africa.

(Pocket War Guide. The) – The Pocket War Guide.
Publisher/printer not shown
(Port Elizabeth 1900?)
(56pp.?)
130mm   SABIB
Copy lacks cover and title page. Catalogued from running title. Includes diary of the war from Oct. 11, 1899 to Feb. 28, 1900. Pagination includes advertisements mainly in reference to Port Elizabeth firms.

Pollock (Major A. W. A.) – With Seven Generals In The Boer War A Personal Narrative.
Skeffington & Son
London 1900
viii+292pp. Maps and illustrations.
193×130mm   p.62

Poole (Bertram W. H.) – South African War Provisionals. A Complete History Of The Famous V.R.I. Provisionals Of

The Orange River Colony And Transvaal, Mafeking Siege Stamps, And Other Local Issues Created By The Exigencies Of The Present War Between Boer and Briton In South Africa.
R. T. Morgan & Co.
London 1901
56pp. Illustrated.
179×119mm

Poore (Maj. R. M.) – Report On Office Of Provost Marshal. See WO.69.

Poore (R. M.) (Compiler?) – Provost Marshal's Orders.
Printer/publisher not shown
nd. (c.1901)
iv+58pp.
210mm   SABIB
Recorded at Merensky library, Pretoria University. Title page removed. Orders signed by Major R. M. Poore, Provost Marshal, Army Headquarters, S.A. Field Force, Pretoria, 15th June, 1901.

(Portland Hospital) – Report Of The Committee, Etc. See entry under MURRAY John.

Pott (Capt. H. Bertram) – With The 36th West Kent Squadron Imperial Yeomanry In South Africa, Jan. 9th 1900–July 19th 1901.
Publisher/printer not shown
np. 1901
Pagination not shown. Illustrated.
4to.   W

(Pottery Man. A.) – A Pottery Man's Journal Of The Siege Of Kimberley. See entry under LOONEY, J. C. printer.

Powell (Rev. F. H.) – Soldier And Padre, The Experiences Of A Chaplain At The Front, By Rev. F. H. Powell, A.K.C. Dist.Org.; Sec.A.C.S., Sometime Chaplain With The South African Field Force.
H. H. Ashworth & Co.
Manchester 1902
152pp. Illustrated.
180mm   SABIB

Pratt (A. G.) – The 1st Battalion Essex Regiment In South Africa, 1899–1902.
(Regimental Press)
Thayetmo/Burma 1908
38+viii pp. Map and tables.
8vo.   W

Pratt Yule (G.) – Refugee Camps – Mortality Statistics.
Printer/publisher not shown
Bloemfontein 1902
44pp. Tables (some folding).
330mm   SABIB
Catalogued from captions – no title page. A report signed by Pratt Yule, Medical Officer of Health, O.R.C.

(Pretoria Friend) – Pretoria Friend. The Authorised Medium For Official News. Volume 1. Nos.1–17.
Publisher/printer not shown
Pretoria 1900
Each issue 4pp.
410×264mm
'Newspaper' established by Lord Stanley at Pretoria during British occupation. Contents include military government notices, proclamations, advertisements and items of news. Publication commenced on Tuesday, 26th June, 1900 and ceased after the issue of Saturday, 14th July, 1900.

Price (Captain Frank Denton) – The Great Boer War 1899–1901. Letters. See REID Andrew & Company, Limited.

(Prisoners Of War) – A List Of Prisoners-Of-War from No.1–No.19430. The lists, consisting of numerous parts, are bound in a single volume marked Green Point Track. The majority of parts have separate title pages. With the exception of one list, printer/publisher is not shown.

1–206. List Of Prisoners-Of-War In Natal.

(206–479. Numbers unused?)

480–2579. List Of Transvaal Prisoners-Of-War.

2580–3019. Second List Of Transvaal Prisoners-Of-War. All At Simon's Town Except Those Marked Ceylon. 3020–3271.

3272–3499. Transvaal List.

3500–4396. List Of Prisoners-Of-War At St. Helena. 4397–4405.

(4406–4499. Numbers unused?)

5000–7101. Free State Prisoners. List Of Free State Prisoners 14th May 1900 With Their Descriptions.
Above paper printed by – Argus Printing and Publishing Co., Bloemfontein 1900.

7102–7328. Green Point Track.

7329–7404. Free State List.
To this point pages are numbered 1–192 including title pages. The remaining sections are numbered separately.

7405–11931. (pp.1–108. No title page.)

11932–12384. Prisoners-Of-War Received At Cape Town From 1st September To 21st September.
(10pp.)

12385–12840. Prisoners-Of-War Received At Cape Town From 23rd September To 7th October.
(10pp.)

12841–13676. Prisoners-Of-War Received At Cape Town From 9th October To 23rd October.
(17pp.)

13677–14201. Prisoners-Of-War Sent To Natal To 5th October.
(11pp.)

14202–15033. Prisoners-Of-War Received At Cape Town From 27th October To 10th November.
(17pp.)

15034–15644. Prisoners-Of-War Received At Cape Town From 13th November To 29th November.
(13pp.)

15645–16481. Prisoners-Of-War Arriving In Cape Town From December 3rd 1900 Until January 2nd 1901.
(17pp.)

16482–16830. Prisoners-Of-War Arriving In Natal To December 28th 1900.
(8pp.)

16831–17475. List Of Prisoners-Of-War Arriving At Cape Town From 4th January 1901 – 14th March 1901.
(14pp.)

17476–17693. List Of Prisoners-Of-War Who Have Arrived At Natal To February 23rd 1901.
(—pp.)

17694–19430. *Lists of 15pp. and 21pp. Untitled.*

212×340mm   DC

(Prisoners Of War) – Documents Relating To Prisoners-Of-War From SABIB Catalogue. Publisher/printer not shown.

List Of Prisoners-Of-War (1901?)
Set of 4 vols. recorded at Merensky Library, Pretoria.
Vol.1. – 192pp. Vol.2. – 108pp.
Vol.3. – 10+10+17+11+17+13pp.
Vol.4. – 14+6pp.
210×330mm
Each part of vols. 3 & 4 with separate title-page.

List Of Prisoners-Of-War Arriving At Cape Town From 4th January, 1901 To 14th March, 1901. Nos.16831 To 17475. Who Have Arrived At Natal To February 23, 1901. Nos.17476 To 17693.
np./nd. (1901)
1+1+14+1+6pp.
210×340mm
Catalogued from cover. Separate title-pages for each section.

Prisoners-Of-War Received At Cape Town From Sept. 1, 1900, To Nov. 29th, 1900. Nos. 11932 To 15644.
Various paging?
230×350mm

Prisoners-Of-War Received At Cape Town From 1st Sept. To 21st Sept. Nos. 11932 To 12384.
1+1+10pp.

Prisoners-Of-War Received At Cape Town From 23rd Sept. To 7th Oct. Nos. 12385 To 12840.
1+1+10pp.

Prisoners-Of-War Received At Cape Town From 9th Oct. To 23rd Oct. Nos. 12841 To 13676.
1+1+17pp.

Prisoners-Of-War Sent To Natal To 5th Oct. Nos. 13677 To 14201.
1+1+11pp.

Prisoners-Of-War Received At Cape Town From 27th Oct. To 10th Nov. Nos. 14202 To 15033.
1+1+17pp.

Prisoners-Of-War Received At Cape Town From 13th Nov. To 29th Nov. Nos. 15034 To 15644.
1+1+13pp.

Prisoners-Of-War Arriving In Cape Town Till January 12, 1902, And Natal Till December 18, 1901. Nos. 25442 To 26689.
np. (1902?)
1+1+25pp.
210×340mm

Prisoners-Of-War Arriving In Cape Town And Natal Till 14th February, 1902. Nos. 27706 To 28664.
np. (1902?)
19pp.
210×340mm
No title-page. Catalogued from cover.

Prisoners-Of-War Arriving In Natal Till 7th March, 1902. Nos. 29423 To 30457.
np. (1902?)
21pp.
210×340mm
No title-page. Catalogued from cover.

Prisoners-Of-War Arriving In Cape Town And Natal Till 17th April, 1902. Nos.

30458 To 31354.
np. (1902?)
18pp.
210×340mm
No title-page. Catalogued from cover.

(Professional Staff. By The) – A Civilian War Hospital Being An Account Of The Work Of The Portland Hospital, And Of Experience Of Wounds And Sickness In South Africa, 1900 With A Description Of The Equipment, Cost, And Management Of A Civilian Base Hospital In Time Of War.
John Murray
London 1901
xii+343pp. Illustrated.
212×150mm
The Professional Staff included A. A. Bowlby, Howard H. Tooth, Cuthbert Wallace, John E. Calverley and Surgeon-Major Kilkelly.

(Pro Patria) – The War. An Appeal To The Patriotism Of Members Of Parliament Against Brutality And Cowardice.
Publisher/printer not shown
——— 1900
7pp.
210mm   SABIB
An appeal to stop the war. The author quotes press accounts of brutal acts by British soldiers in South Africa.

(Pro Patria) – The War. An Appeal To The Patriotism Of Members Of Parliament Against The Brutal And Cowardly Policy Of The Government.
Transvaal Committee
Westminster (1900)
7pp.
210mm   SABIB
As previous entry, with variant title-page.

('P. S.') – A Boer On Boer Designs. Letter From 'P. S.' A Cape-Dutch Correspondent. Reprinted From *The Times*.
George Edward Wright, *'The Times'* Office
London 1901
20pp.
214×138mm

Q

(Quarter Master General. Office of/India) – Report On The Arrangements, Etc., Of Boer Prisoners-Of-War. See – BOER PRISONERS-OF-WAR.

(Quick. Jonathan) (Pseud:) – Gulliver Joe, By Jonathan Quick, Dean Of St. Rattrick's.
Isbister & Company Ltd.
London 1903
108pp. Illustrated.
190mm   SABIB
Satire on 'Joe' Chamberlain's handling of the war. SABIB lists authors names – C. E. Hughes and E. H. Begbie.

Quin (Malcolm) – The Patriot Boers A Sermon Preached In The Positivist Church, Newcastle-On-Tyne, On Sunday, July 6th, 1902, At A Requiem For The Citizens Of The Transvaal Republic And Orange Free State, Who Died Defending Their Country Against British Aggression.
Church of Humanity
Newcastle-On-Tyne 1902
19pp.
200mm   SABIB

R

Rabinowitz (M.) – Letters And Articles Relating To The War, Etc. See – M. R.

(Rae.) (Publisher?) – How Westralia's Sons Served The Empire In South Africa, A.D.1900: An Historical Memento Of An Epoch-Making Period.
Rae?
Melbourne 1900
(Pagination not shown.)
ALH

Railton (G. S.) – The History Of Our South African War.
Salvation Army Book Dept.
London (1902?)
vi+129pp. With map and plan.
140mm   SABIB
Second edition recorded.

(Railways) – Detailed History Of The Railways In The South African War, 1899–1902. (2 vols.) See – ROYAL ENGINEERS INSTITUTE.

Ralph (Julian) – Towards Pretoria A Record Of The War Between Briton And Boer To The Hoisting Of The British Flag At Bloemfontein. With Historical Foreword Appendices And Map.
C. Arthur Pearson Ltd.
London 1900
lvi+pp.57–381. Folding map.
200×132mm
SABIB records 'Pearson's Colonial Library' ed. 1901.

Ralph (Julian) – Towards Pretoria: A Record Of The War Between Briton And Boer To The Relief Of Kimberley. With A Summary Of Subsequent Events To The Hoisting Of The British Flag At Bloemfontein. With Historical Foreword, Appendices And Map.
Frederick A. Stokes
New York (1900)
viii+328pp. Folding map.
193×127mm

Ralph (Julian) – At Pretoria The Capture Of The Boer Capitals And The Hoisting Of The Flag At Pretoria A Companion Volume To 'Towards Pretoria'.
C. Arthur Pearson Ltd.
London 1901
viii+377pp. With frontispiece.
200×130mm

Ralph (Julian) – An American With Lord Roberts.
Frederick A. Stokes Company
New York nd. (1901)
viii+314pp.
187×122mm

Ralph (Julian) – War's Brighter Side The Story Of 'The Friend' Newspaper Edited By The Correspondents With Lord Roberts's Forces, March–April, 1900.
D. Appleton and Company
New York 1901
xvii+471pp. Illustrated.
194×126mm   p.46
English edition published by C. Arthur Pearson, Ltd. London 1901. xv+421pp. Illustrated. 212×140mm.

Ralph (Julian) – War's Brighter Side, Etc.
Pearson's Colonial Library – Four printings listed in SABIB.

(Rand Regiments Memorial Committee) – Johannesburg Public Monument To Rand Regiments. South African War, 1899–1902.
Publisher/printer not shown
(Johannesburg 1905?)
5pp.
330mm   SABIB
Report of negotiations between Johannesburg Town Council and a Committee of representative citizens concerning the erection of a memorial.

(Rand Regiments Memorial Committee) – Johannesburg Public Monument To Rand Regiments. (Including All Transvaal Men Who Fell On The British Side.) South African War, 1899–1902.
Rand Public Monument Committee
(Johannesburg 1909)
8pp.
340mm   SABIB
Paper includes a progress report and a list of donors.

Randolph (Spencer) – Who Ought To Win? Oom Paul Or Queen Victoria? A History Of The Dutch-English Settlement In South Africa From Its Origin To The Present Day With Letters Graphically Describing The Wonderful Bravery Of The Boer And British Armies.
Laird & Lee publishers
Chicago nd. (1900)
287pp. Folding map and illustrations.
198×140mm

Rankin (Reginald) – A Subaltern's Letters To His Wife.
Longmans, Green, And Co.
London 1902
viii+228pp.
197×130mm
A copy of the second edition, eighth impression. Impressions 1–7 are dated 1901.

Rattigan (Sir W. H.) – The Netherlands South African Railway Question From The Point Of View Of International Law.
Wildy and Sons
London 1901
54pp.
215×135mm

Rawnsley (H. D.) – Ballads Of The War.
J. M. Dent & Co.
London 1900
viii+96pp.
192×134mm

Rawnsley (H. D.) – Ballads Of The War.
J. M. Dent & Co.
London 1901
xiv+219pp. Illustrated.
193×134mm   p.71
Poetry relating to the war. The extended edition.

(Raymond. H. A. & Wright. J. & Co.) (Publishers) – The War. A Warning – A Soldiers' Confession – Soldiers' Friends – Peace.
H. A. Raymond/London
John Wright & Co./Bristol
nd. (c.1900)
16pp.
137×91mm
Religious pamphlet for distribution amongst soldiers in South Africa.

(R.C.M.) – Notes On Reconnoitring In South Africa. Boer War, 1899–1900.
Cape Times
Cape Town 1900
24pp.
170mm   SABIB

(R.C.M.) – Notes On Reconnoitring In South Africa. Boer War, 1899–1902.

Longmans, Green & Co.
London 1901
35pp.
140×110mm

Reade (R. E.) – Natal, 12th To 31st October, 1899. A Journal Of R. Ernest Reade, Second Lieutenant, (60th) King's Royal Rifle Corps.
R. Carswell & Son, printers
Belfast 1899
30pp. With map.
180mm   SABIB
'For private circulation only'. No title page. Item catalogued from cover.

Reade (R. E.) – In Memoriam, R. Ernest Reade, D.S.O., Lieutenant, King's Royal Rifle Corps (60th).
Kegan Paul, Trench, Trübner
London 1902
viii+111pp. Folding plan and illustrations.
270mm   SABIB
Lieut. Reade was killed in action near Middelburg, Transvaal. The volume includes a memoir and extracts from his letters and journal.

Reay (Major W. T.) – Australians In War. With The Australian Regiment. From Melbourne To Bloemfontein.
A. H. Massina & Co.
Melbourne 1900
xv+pp.9–382
190×124mm   p.118

(Red Cross) – Report By The Central British Red Cross Committee, Etc. See HMSO Non-Parliamentary Publications.

Redmond (W. H. K.) – Transvaal War. Four Speeches Against It In House Of Commons . . . . Together With Two Letters From Dr. Leyds On The Catholic Question.
C. P. Redmond & Co., printers
Waterford 1901
34pp.
180mm   SABIB

(Rees. Hugh) (Printer) – A Short Account Of The Work Done By The 2nd Battalion Coldstream Guards In South Africa. Nov. 1899, To Sept. 1902.
Hugh Rees, printer
London (1902?)
22pp.
180mm   SABIB
For private circulation.

(Reid. Andrew & Company, Limited) (Printers) – The Great Boer War 1899–1901, Letters.
(Captain Frank Denton Price)
For private circulation
Andrew Reid & Company, Limited
Newcastle-upon-Tyne 1901
v+150pp. Illustrated.
187×128mm   p.100
Authors name does not appear on title page. Letters from Capt. Price, 1st Durham R.E. (Volunteers). Some copies are bound without the campaign diary – v+110pp. Illustrated.

Reid (Sir R. T.) – The War And After. Speech, February 20, 1901.
Eighty Club (1902)
No other information.
THB

Reitz (F. W.) – A Century Of Wrong.
'Review of Reviews' Office
London nd. (1900)
xxiii+152pp.
225×150mm
A review of 'oppression and persecution' endured by the Boers as a result of British policy in South Africa.

Reitz (F. W.) – A Century Of Wrong The Boer-British Case Stated.
'Review of Reviews' Office
London nd. (Preface dated Dec. 1899)
56pp.
*CC includes an American edition of 56pp.
np./nd. Paper covered, 233×149mm.*

Renar (F.) – Bushman And Buccaneer. Harry Morant: His 'Ventures And Verses, With Many Illustrations, And A Map Showing The Bushveldt Carbineers' Operations.
H. T. Dunn
Sydney 1902
63pp. Map, illustrations
210mm   SABIB
Biography of Harry Morant, court-martialled and condemned to death for shooting Boers. Together with some of his poems.

('Review Of Reviews' Office) (Publishers) – How Britain Goes To War A Digest And An Analysis Of Evidence Taken By The Royal Commission On The War In South Africa Compiled From The Blue Books For The Information Of The Public.
'Review of Reviews' Office
London 1903
viii+256pp.
254×155mm

Rew (Capt. H. G. McKenzie) – Records Of The Rough Riders (XXth Battalion Imperial Yeomanry) Boer War, 1899–1902.
Brown & Wilson
Bedford 1907
xiv+289pp. Folding map and illustrations.
220×140mm
*Also published in full calf binding.
220×140mm.*

Rhodes (Right Hon. C. J.) – Mr Rhodes On The Situation.
Imperial South African Association
London 1900
4pp.
8vo.   M
Association publication No.25.

Ricarde-Seaver (F. I.) – An Address On The Transvaal, Past And Future, Delivered At The Junior Constitutional Club, Piccadilly, On Thursday, February 8th, 1900. Mr H. R. Graham, M.P., In The Chair.
McCorquodale and Co.
London 1900
25pp.
210mm   SABIB
Outline of Transvaal history and background to the current conflict between the British and the Boers.

Ricarde-Seaver (F. I.) – Address On The Transvaal Past & Future, Delivered To The Members Of The Junior Constitutional Club, Piccadilly, At The Invitation Of The Political Committee, On Thursday, February 8th, 1900. A Short Biographical Sketch Is Appended.
Publisher/printer not shown
(London 1900?)
12pp. With portrait.
250mm   SABIB
Reproduced from 'South London Chronicle' February 10, 1900.

(Richards. W.A. & Sons) (Printers) – Organisation And Details Of Transport. South African Field Force. Cape Town, 1899.

W.A. Richards and Sons, printers
Cape Town 1899
76pp. Tables.
200mm   SABIB
No title page. Catalogued from cover.

(Richards. W.A. & Sons) (Government Printers) – Cape Of Good Hope. Proclamations And Government Notices Issued During The Period October, 1899, To June, 1900, Having Reference To And Consequent On The Outbreak Of Hostilities In South Africa.
W.A. Richards and Sons
Cape Town 1900
v+23pp.
330×202mm   CC   p.26

(Richards. W.A. & Sons) (Publisher) – The Anglo-Boer War Of 1899–1900. (Parts 1–7)
W.A. Richards and Sons
Cape Town nd. (1900)
Part 1. – 24pp.
Part 2. – pp.25–48
Part 3. – pp.49–72
Part 4. – pp.73–96
Part 5. – pp.97–120
Part 6. – pp.123–144
Part 7. – pp.145–168
Illustrated throughout.
217×284mm   CC
An illustrated record of the campaign in South Africa up to March 1900. Limp card covers. Part 7 contains a coloured facsimile of 'The Queen's Chocolate Box'.

(Richards. W.A. & Sons) (Printers) – The Connaught Rangers Regimental Records 1899–1902.
W.A. Richards and Sons
Cape Town 1902
137pp. Various folding maps.
202×164mm   p.41
See entry under CONNAUGHT RANGERS.

(Richards. W.A. & Sons) (Printers) – Report Of The Good Hope Society, For Aid To Sick And Wounded In War. South African War, 1899–1902.
W.A. Richards & Sons, printers
Cape Town 1902
68pp. Illustrated.
278×206mm   RCSL

Richardson (A. W.) – A Quaker View Of The War.
Headley Brothers
London (1900)
16pp.
8vo.   M

Richardson (Sir Wodehouse) – With The Army Service Corps In South Africa. By Sir Wodehouse Richardson, K.C.B., Colonel (Late Army Service Corps), Deputy Adjutant-General For Supplies And Transport In South Africa, 1899–1900.
Richardson & Co.
London 1903
161pp.
213×140mm   CC   p.56

Richmond (A. H.) – The Siege Of Ladysmith.
S. W. Partridge and Co.
London 1900
12pp.
Oblong 12mo.   M

Ridpath (J. C.) and Ellis (E. S.) – The Story Of South Africa. An Account Of The Historical Transformation Of The Dark Continent By The European Powers And The Culminating Contest Between Great Britain And The South African Republic In The Transvaal War.
Elliott Publishing Co.

Philadelphia 1900
652pp. Illustrated throughout.
252×195mm

Various editions published including –
New England Co.
New York/Chicago (1900?)
641pp. Illustrated.
250×190mm

C. W. Stanton
Chicago (1900?)
692pp. Illustrated.
250mm   SABIB

C. B. Burrows
Bombay and London (1900?)
ii+698+6pp. Illustrated.
230mm   SABIB

C. B. Burrows, c/o William Watson & Co.
Bombay/London (1901?)
ii+712+6pp. Illustrated.
250mm   SABIB

Oceanic Publishing Co.
Sydney, N.S.W. (1901?)
ii+xiii+15–688pp. Illustrated.
240mm   SABIB

World Publishing Co.
Guelph, Ont. (c.1902)
ii+xviii+pp.17–1016. Illustrated.
254×190mm   CC

Ritchie (Captain A. B.) – The Record Of The 4th Battalion West Yorkshire Regiment (Prince Of Wales' Own) During The Boer War, 1899–1902.
John Sampson
York 1903
iv+63pp.
180×125mm

Robb (Col. F. S.) – Memorandum On Cavalry, Artillery And Infantry Drafts, Etc. See – WO.21.

Robb (Mrs J.) – Thrilling Experiences Of The First British Woman Relieved By Lord Roberts. See entry under J. R.

Robert (Earl) (Publisher) – The Ladysmith Bombshell A Souvenir Of The Siege Of Ladysmith.
Published by Earl Robert
Bennett & Davis (printers)
Durban nd. (1900)
Unpaginated (50 printed rectos)
Illustrated.
337×238mm   p.21
Title from cover. The Ladysmith Bombshell was published by George Lines between 18 Nov. 1899 and 8 Jan. 1900. The original eight cyclostyled issues displayed covers and other drawings by Robert. The artist published the above facsimile in 1900 and Lines reproduced all eight issues in his volume. 'The Ladysmith Siege' also published in 1900. See entry under LINES, G.W.

Roberts (Bryn) – The Transvaal War. Speeches.
'Herald' Steam Printing Works
Carnarvon (1900?)
24pp.
210mm   SABIB
Speeches against the South African War.

Roberts (Field Marshal) – Field Marshal Lord Roberts Farewell Address To The Troops In South Africa, 29th November 1900, A Souvenir Of The Anglo Boer War 1899–1900.
Publisher/printer not shown
np./nd. (Johannesburg 1900)
8pp.
140×110mm   CB
Decorative paper cover.

Roberts (F.M. Lord) – South Africa War, 1899–1900. Correspondence, Etc. See WO.12, 13, 14.

Roberts (F.M. Lord) – Memorandum. Court Martial, Etc. See WO.71.

Roberts (F.M. Lord) – Telegrams And Letters, Etc. See WO.150, 153–158.

Robertson (John M.) – Wrecking The Empire.
Grant Richards
London 1901
xlvi+313pp.
204×135mm
Comprehensive account of alleged misdeeds of the British during the war.

Robertson (John M.) – The Truth About The War. An Open Letter To Dr. A. Conan Doyle.
The New Age Press
London 1902
48pp.
8vo.   M

Robertson (John M.) – The Boer War: Open Letter To Dr. Conan Doyle, By John M. Robertson; With, Official Despatches From Generals De La Rey, Smuts And Others.
George H. Buchanan And Company
Philadelphia (c.1900)
94pp.
230×150mm

Robins (William) – The Truth About The Transvaal, Gathered From The Despatches Between The British And Boer Governments And The Official Report Of The Bloemfontein Conference. An Address Delivered, By Request, At Windsor, Ontario, Canada, February 6th, 1900 By William Robins. And Printed For The Benefit Of 'The Soldiers Of The Queen Relief Fund'.
Hiram Walker & Sons
London 1900
iv+43pp. (Third edition.)
255×168mm
Various editions recorded. SABIB lists copy of 9th ed. – 1900.

Robinson (C. N.) (Editor) – Celebrities Of The Army.
George Newnes
London 1900
144pp. Illustrated.
375×275mm
18 numbered parts bound in limp card covers, each part 8pp.

Robinson (C. N.) (Editor) – Celebrities Of The Army.
George Newnes
London 1900
iii+144pp. Illustrated.
358×268mm   p.117
Colour portraits of British Officers with brief career details.

Robinson (C. N.) (Editor) – Celebrities Of The Army.
The Publisher's Syndicate, Limited
Toronto 1900
iii+144pp. Illustrated.
290×270mm   WS

Robinson (C. N.) (Editor) – The Transvaal War Album The British Forces In South Africa. An Album Wherein The Various Regiments And Other Principal Units Of The Forces Engaged In The Boer Campaign Of 1899–1900, Are Illustrated. Portraits Are Also Given Of The Generals Who Have Conducted The Operations, And The Staff And Regimental Officers Who Have

Organized And Lead The British And Colonial Forces.
Geo. Newnes, Ltd.
London nd. (1900)
4+268pp. Illustrated throughout.
370×250mm

Robinson (Commander C. N.) (Editor) – A Pictorial History Of South Africa And The Transvaal.
Geo. Newnes, Limited
London (1900)
122pp. Illustrated.
244×168mm

Robinson (Chas. N.) (Editor) – With Roberts To The Transvaal Being A Pictorial History Of South Africa And The Transvaal.
James Askew and Son
Preston nd. (c.1900)
128+122pp. Maps and illustrations.
242×165mm

Robinson (Chas. N.) (Editor) – With Roberts To The Transvaal. Being The Second Part Of A Pictorial History Of South Africa And The Transvaal.
Geo. Newnes, Limited
London nd. (1900?)
122+128pp. Numerous maps and illustrations.
244×168mm

Robinson (Commander Chas. N.) (Editor) – With Roberts To The Transvaal Being The Second Part Of A Pictorial History Of South Africa And The Transvaal.
Geo. Newnes, Limited
London nd. (1900)
viii+pp.9–128. Illustrations and maps.
Card covered edition.

(Robinson & Co.) (Publisher?) – Natal Volunteer Record: Annals And Rolls Of Service In The Anglo-Boer War, 1899–1900.
Robinson & Co.
Durban 1900
xii+204pp.
12mo.   M

(Robinson & Co.) (Publisher?) – Twelve Months Of War. The Work Of The Natal Government Railways. Transport Of Men And Munitions. Boer War, 1899–1901.
Robinson & Co.
Durban 1902
8pp. Tables.
250mm   SABIB
Reprinted from the 'Natal Mercury', Oct. 27, 1900 and the 'Natal Advertiser', Sept. 6, 1900.

(Robinson F. E. & Co.) (Printers?) – The Army And The Press In 1900. A Study By A British Field Officer.
F. E. Robinson & Co.
London 1901
44pp.
8vo.   M

Robinson (J. A.) – Holy Ground: Three Sermons On The War In South Africa Preached In Westminster Abbey.
Macmillan
London 1900
39pp.
220mm   SABIB

(Robinson W. H.) (Printer?) – The Editor Edited, Etc. See – WAKINSHAW. J. W.

(Robinson, Pickering & Hunt) (Printer/Publisher) – Twelve Months With General Buller In South Africa.

Robinson, Pickering & Hunt
London nd. (c.1900)
80pp. One illustration.
200×128mm   GC
Campaign diary by a member of the South African Light Horse. The record extends from Nov. 12, 1899–Oct. 24, 1900.

Roddy (John W.) – And Britain's Blest With Righteousness? And, The Fate Of Dullstroom.
Grafton Press
New York 1901
51pp.
160mm   SABIB
Two pro-Boer poems.

Rodwell (Major E. H.) – Reflections On The Boer War, Being Three Tactical Lectures Delivered Originally At Meerut And Afterwards At Fort William, Calcutta, In December, 1900, And January, 1901.
Printed at the 'Civil and Military Gazette' Press.
Lahore 1901
39pp.
8vo.   M

Rogers (J. R.) – Only A Man In Khaki And What He's Left Behind. A Pathetic Souvenir Of The Transvaal War.
James Sears
London 1899
16pp. Illustrated.
180×125mm
Tragic ballad of the war.

Rolleston (Sir Lancelot) – Yeomanry Cavalry: Or Mounted Infantry?
Smith, Elder & Co.
London 1901
35pp.
227×145mm

Rolleston (The Lady Maud) – Yeoman Service Being The Diary Of The Wife Of An Imperial Yeomanry Officer During The Boer War.
Smith, Elder & Co.
London 1901
x+310pp. With two illustrations.
210×138mm

Rolleston (T. W.) – Ireland, The Empire And The War.
Sealy, Bryers and Walker
Dublin 1900
23pp.
210×140mm
Pamphlet in support of Britain in the war.

Romer (Major C. F.) & Mainwaring (Major A. E.) – The Second Battalion Royal Dublin Fusiliers In The South African War With A Description Of The Operations In The Aden Hinterland.
A. L. Humphreys
London 1908
xiv+271pp. Illustrated.
224×145mm

Rompel (Frederik) – Heroes Of The Boer War, By Frederik Rompel (Late Parliamentary And War Correspondent Of The *Volkstem*, Pretoria) With An Introduction By Major-General Albert Pfister And A Preface By W. T. Stead.
'Review Of Reviews' Office/London The 'Nederland' Publishing Co./The Hague and Pretoria
1903
xxviii+196pp. Maps and illustrations.
244×170mm   p.27

Rose (E. B.) – The Truth About The Transvaal. A Record Of Facts Based Upon Twelve Years' Residence In The Country.

'Morning Leader' Publication
Department
London 1902
vii+358pp.
Cr.8vo.   M
*An account of the Anglo-Boer dispute
presented from the pro-Boer standpoint.*

Rosebery (The Right Hon. Lord) –
National Policy. A Speech Delivered At
Chesterfield, Dec. 16th, 1901, By Lord
Rosebery. Authorised Edition With
Prefatory Note.
Arthur L. Humphreys
London 1902
39pp.
8vo.   M
Criticism in respect of the present war.

Rose-Innes (Cosmo) – With Paget's Horse
To The Front.
John Macqueen
London 1901
v+180pp. With frontispiece.
200×132mm   p.95

Ross (E. J.) – Siege Views Of Mafeking
From Original Photographs By E. J.
Ross, Oct. 1899–May 1900.
Eyre & Spottiswoode
London nd. (1900)
32+2pp. Illustrated.
184×246mm

Ross (G.) – The South African All-
Absorbing Sham And A Remedy. By
A Refugee.
(No other information)
1901?
114pp.
210mm   SABIB
*Name of author from SABIB. Possible
Boer War interest.*

Ross (Capt. John) – The Boers And The
Cause Of The War In South Africa; By
Capt. John Ross, Late Of Her Majesty's
Border Regiment.
Imrie, Graham & Co.
Toronto 1900
32pp.
8vo.   M

Ross (Malcolm) – A Souvenir Of New
Zealand's Response To The Empire's
Call.
McKee & Co.
Wellington nd. (1900)
32pp. (Including covers.) Illustrated.
185×215mm
*An illustrated souvenir published soon
after departure of the Second Contingent
for South Africa. Title from cover.*

Ross (P. T.) – A Yeoman's Letters.
Simpkin, Marshall, Hamilton, Kent &
Co., Limited
London 1901
xii+186pp. Illustrated.
225×142mm

Rosslyn (Earl of) – The Gram A Social
Magazine Founded By British Prisoners
Of War In Pretoria.
Eyre & Spottiswoode
London nd. (c.1900)
114pp. Illustrated.
267×210mm   p.100
*Facsimile edition of 500 copies reproduced
from 3 original issues printed at Pretoria.
Many copies numbered and signed by the
author.*

Rosslyn (Earl of) – Twice Captured
A Record Of Adventure During The
Boer War.
William Blackwood and Sons

Edinburgh and London 1900
(3rd Edition)
xvi+477pp. Illustrated.
207×137mm   p.107

Routh (Robert S.) – Lines On The War.
J. C. Holmes
Andover (1900?)
27pp.
(Size not shown.)   M

Rowat (G.) – Extracts From A Christian
Soldier's Diary. For Private Circulation.
Printed at the Santal Mission Press
Pokhuria, Gobindpur, Manbhoom
(1901?)
78pp.
8vo.   M
*Account of the Natal campaign by a
sergeant of the 1st Batt. King's Royal
Rifles.*

Rowat (G.) – A Soldier Who Did His
Duty. The Record Of Sergeant-Major
Rowat While On Active Service For
Twelve Years In India And South Africa.
Drummond's Tract Depot
Stirling nd. (1911) &
S. W. Partridge & Co., Ltd.
London nd. (1911)
128pp. Illustrated.
189×126mm
*Most of the volume concerns the war in
South Africa.*

(Royal Artillery) – Record Of Service Of
5th Eastern Division R.G.A. In South
Africa, 1900–1.
Clifford?
Bermuda nd.
*Entered under military histories, records,
etc. in THB.*

(Royal Artillery) – Record Of The
History Of 'U' Battery, Including South
African War, 1899–1902.
(No other details)
*Entered under military histories, records,
etc. in THB.*

(Royal Engineers Institute) (Publisher) –
Detailed History Of The Railways In The
South African War, 1899–1902.
Royal Engineers Institute
Agents: W. and J. Mackay and Co., Ltd.
Chatham 1904
Vol. 1. – Letterpress. xxvi+275+xxvii–
xli pp. With map and folding charts.
Vol. 2. – Illustrations. viii+61pp.
photographs. Together with 93 plates and
a map.
340×218mm   p.74

Ruggles-Brise (H.) – The Official Records
Of The Guards Brigade In South Africa.
See – KELIHER. (J. J. & CO.) Limited.

Russell (Bt.-Major The Hon. A.V.F.V.) –
Letters From South Africa During The
Boer War Of 1899–1902.
J. J. Keliher & Co., Limited
London 1909
228pp.
220×142mm
For private circulation only.

Russell (Brevet-Major Hon. A.)
(Compiler) – First Or Grenadier Guards
In South Africa 1899–1902. Records Of
The Third Battalion. See – LLOYD. F. &
RUSSELL. A.

Ryerson (Lieut.-Colonel G. Sterling) –
Medical And Surgical Experiences In The
South African War. Being Addresses To
The Toronto Clinical Society And
Canadian Medical Association.
(1900?)

(No other information)
16pp.
208×158mm   RCSL
*Address by Col. Ryerson, M.D., lately
British and Canadian Red Cross
Commissioner with Lord Roberts'
Headquarters in South Africa. Reprinted
from 'Canada Lancet' of Nov. 1900 and
'Canadian Practitioner and Review' of
Oct. 1900.*

S

Sackville (G. G. R.) – Some
Reminiscences Of The War In South
Africa. See – DE LA WARR.

Salmond (J. B.) (Editor) – The Muster-
Roll Of Angus. South African War 1899–
1900. A Record And A Tribute.
Published Under The Direction Of Agnes
Lindsay-Carnegie And Jane C. C.
Macdonald.
Brodie & Salmond
Arbroath 1900
238pp. Illustrated.
253×190mm
*2nd Ed. published in 1903, edited by
J. Brodie. Volume is of larger format and
extends to 299pp. Illustrated. 285×220mm.*

Salt (Lieut. G. E. S.) – Letters And Diary
Of Lieutenant G. E. S. Salt During The
War In South Africa, 1899–1900.
John Murray
London 1902
vii+119pp. Map and two illustrations.
221×176mm   p.27
Printed for private circulation.

Samson (Louis) – The Pembrokeshire
South African War Memorial. See –
SMITH (W. H. & SON.)

Sanderson (Edgar) – The Fight For The
Flag In South Africa A History Of The
War From The Boer Ultimatum To The
Advance Of Lord Roberts.
Hutchinson & Co.
London 1900
136pp. Maps and illustrations.
250×170mm

Sanderson (Edgar) – The War In South
Africa 1899–1901.
Printed for private circulation
(Printer/publisher not shown)
nd. (c.1901)
pp.302–416+pp.1–190. Various plates.
266×183mm
*A special edition. Material extracted from
vols. 4 and 5 of the author's – 'Our
Empire At Home And Abroad'. 6 vols.*

Sandford (C.) (Publisher?) – The Trial Of
Scheepers, The Notorious Boer
Commandant.
C. Sandford 'Graaff Reinet Advertiser'
Graaff Reinet (1902?)
37pp.
250mm   SABIB

Saunderson (Capt. L.) – Notes On
Mounted Infantrymen.
Gale & Polden
np. (1903)
Pagination not shown.   THB
Possible Boer war interest?

Savage (Lt.-Col. C. Heyworth) – The
Western Boer Army Under Assistant
Commandant General Jacobus Hercules
de la Rey; Prepared By Lt.-Col.
C. Heyworth Savage, Apr. 1902.
HQ. S.W. District
Klerksdorp, Transvaal 1902
108pp.
WO. ref. – WH Loc: Camps Boer.

Scaife – System Historical Charts. Chart Of The History Of The Boer War, 1899–1902.
Publisher/printer not shown
np. 1902
Ref. WO. Cat./1912.

Scaife (A. H.) – The War To Date (March 1, 1900.)
T. Fisher Unwin
London 1900
xii+372pp. Illustrated.
192×125mm   p.50

Scholfield (Major G. P.) (R. E.) – Report On Steam Road Transport In South Africa.
HMSO
London 1903
42pp.? Plates and tables.
336×206mm
MOD lists same title – 59pp. Maps and diagrams. SCHOFIELD – WO ref. – WH Loc: SA16: Bd. A Papers.

Schooling (Frederick) & Rusher (Edward A.) – The Mortality Experience Of The Imperial Forces During The War In South Africa, 11 October 1899 To 31 May 1902. Read Before The Institute Of Actuaries, 30 March 1903.
Charles and Edwin Layton
London 1903
ii+83pp. With plates.
222×145mm
Statistical study of death rates among British forces during the war by actuaries on the staff of the Prudential Assurance Company.

Schreiner (Olive) – Address By Olive Schreiner Over The Anglo-Boer War. At Somerset East On October 12th, 1900.
Ons Vaderland
Pretoria (1914?)
(7pp.?)
230mm   SABIB
No title page, catalogued from cover. Text in English and Dutch. Possible 7pp. to each section.

Schreiner (Olive) – An English-South African's View Of The Situation. Words In Season.
Hodder & Stoughton
London (1899)
96pp.
Cr.8vo.   M
Appeal against a war in South Africa.

Schreiner (Olive) – The South African Question. By An English South African (Olive Schreiner). Reprint From The *South African News*.
South African Newspaper Company, Ltd.
Cape Town (1899?)
24pp.
Roy.8vo.   M

Schreiner (O. E. A.) – The South African Question, By An English South African (Olive Schreiner).
Charles H. Sergel Co.
Chicago 1899
123pp.
190mm   SABIB

Schreiner (T. L.) – Some Letters On The South African Question, By Theophilus Lyndall Schreiner; And, A Prayer For Peace, By Mrs H. R. Stakesby-Lewis (née Schreiner) 1899–1901.
Vacher & Sons, printers
London (1901?)
16pp.
210mm   SABIB
No title page. Catalogued from cover.

Schreiner (T. L.) – The Afrikander Bond And Other Causes Of The War. Issued By The Imperial South African Association.
Spottiswoode & Co., Ltd.
London 1901
52pp.
Cr.8vo.   M
SABIB lists edition published by Simpkin, Marshall, Hamilton, Kent, London 1901.

Schreiner (T. L.) – 'The Causes Of The War In South Africa'. An Address Delivered At The Junior Constitutional Club, Piccadilly, By Mr Theophilus Lyndall Schreiner, On Thursday, February 7th 1901. Mr. H. Crouch Batchelor In The Chair.
McCorquodale and Co., Ltd. Printers
London 1901
32pp.
8vo.   M

Schreiner (T. L.) – Mr Theo. Schreiner's Report. Reprinted from *Cape Times* Nov. 13th, 1901.
(Cape Times?)
(Cape Town 1901)
9pp.
16mo.   M
Report in reference to the political and military situation in South Africa.

Schreiner (The Hon. W. P.) – The Last Appeal Before The Outbreak Of War, Made In The Cape Parliament By Mr Schreiner (Cape Prime Minister). Reprinted By Permission From The *Daily Chronicle*. Published In The Interests Of Truth By Some Friends Of South Africa.
The National Press Agency, Ltd.
London 1899
7pp.
8vo.   M

Scott (E. D.) – Some Letters From South Africa 1894–1902.
Sherratt & Hughes
Manchester & London 1903
iv+183pp.
200×130mm
Considerable South African War content.

Scott (F. G.) – The Empire And The Colours Of The Flag. A Sermon Addressed To The Canadian Volunteers For The War.
Christian Knowledge Society
London (1900?)
8pp.
8vo.   M

Scott (Guy H. Guillum) and McDonell (Geoffrey L.) (Editors) – The Record Of The Mounted Infantry Of The City Imperial Volunteers.
E. & F. N. Spon Limited
London 1902
xvi+227pp. Folding map.
190×125mm

Scott (James) – Souvenir Of The Siege Of Ladysmith: Being A Diary Of The Events During The Siege, November 2nd, 1899, To February 28th, 1900.
S. W. Leake
Maritzburg 1900
viii+86pp.
201×133mm   CC
A local auctioneers account of the siege.

Scott (Capt. Percy) and Limpus (Capt. A. H.) – Mountings Of The Naval Guns And Their Subsequent Use With The Ladysmith Relief Column Being A Lecture By Captain Percy Scott And Captain A. H. Limpus (Of H.M.S. 'Terrible') Delivered In Hongkong, June 13th, 1900.

'Hongkong Daily Press'
Hongkong 1900
23pp. Various illustrations.
243×170mm

Scratchley (Philip A.) (Compiler) – Old Salopians In The South African War, 1899–1902. A List, With An Obituary.
Harrison & Sons (Printers)
London 1903
50pp.
213×138mm   p.105

(Scripture Gift Mission) (Publisher) – The New Testament Of Our Lord And Saviour Jesus Christ; With Engravings From Drawings Made In Bible Lands By H. A. Harper And J. Clark.
Scripture Gift Mission
London (1901?)
400pp. Illustrated.
120mm   SABIB
Cover title: Soldier's New Testament: South Africa 1900–1901.

Seed (William) – Report Of The Local Auditor Of Army Stores Accounts, South African War 1899–1902; By William Seed July 1903.
Publisher/printer not shown [official print]
———— 1904
117pp.   MOD
War Office library. WO ref: – WH Loc: SA28.

Sellers (W. E.) – From Aldershot To Pretoria A Story Of Christian Work Among Our Troops In South Africa.
The Religious Tract Society
London nd. (c.1900)
ii+224pp. Illustrated.
202×140mm

Selmer (Louis) – Boer War Lyrics.
The Abbey Press
New York nd. (1903)
vii+105pp.
220×140mm

Selous (Frederick Courteney) – Mr F. Selous On The War.
See entry under NATIONAL REFORM UNION.

Sessions (F.) and Grubb (E.) – Some Comments On John Bellows's Apology For The War In South Africa, By Two Members Of The Society Of Friends.
Wellington & Co. Printers
Gloucester (1900?)
14pp.
190mm   SABIB

Sessions (H.) – Two Years With Remount Commissions.
Chapman and Hall
London 1903
304pp. Illustrated.
209×150mm   CC

Seton-Karr (Henry) – The Call To Arms 1900–1901 Or A Review Of The Imperial Yeomanry Movement And Some Subjects Connected Therewith.
Longmans, Green and Co.
London 1902
xviii+329pp. With frontispiece.
198×132mm
Primarily concerned with 'The Sharpshooters', 18th Batt. I.Y.

Settrington (Lady Hilda) – Eleven Months Of My Life.
(Privately printed. No title page, imprint, etc.)
1903
46pp.
Cr.8vo.   M

A curious memento of the war for the perusal of the author's most intimate friends.

Shafroth (J. F.) – The Boer War And The Duty Of The United States Relative To The Same. Speeches Of Hon. John F. Shafroth, Of Colorado, In The House Of Representatives, February 1st And 7th, 1900.
Printer/publisher not shown
Washington 1900
16pp.
8vo.   M

Shaw (Dr. John) – The 'Festering Sore' In South Africa, As Viewed By A Surgeon; And The 'Cry Of The Children', As He Hears It.
John Bale, Sons, & Danielsson, Ltd.
London 1901 (Second Edition)
59pp.
8vo.   M
An appeal for an end to the war.

Shaw (Thomas) – Farm Burning. Speech By Mr Thomas Shaw, M.P. On Tuesday, 2nd April, 1901.
South Africa Conciliation Committee?
London (1901?)
7pp.
250mm   SABIB
No title page. Catalogued from caption. Reprinted from 'The Parliamentary debates'.

(Sheffield Independent Press, Limited. The) (Publishers) – Sheffield At The Front.
The Sheffield Independent Press, Limited
Sheffield nd. (1900)
144pp. (printed rectos) Illustrated.
218×295mm
A souvenir of local men serving in South Africa. Originally issued in parts with limp card covers. Various bindings are recorded including full calf embossed in blind and the standard cover of maroon cloth, front blocked in gold and blind.

Shiell (A. G.) – The Transvaal. An Uninserted Letter To The Editor Of The 'Daily News'.
William J. Smith
Brighton 1899
6pp.
8vo.   M

(Shiell) (A. G.) – The Crisis In South Africa. Some Answers (From Authentic Sources) To Sir A. Milner's Reflections Upon Colonial Loyalty. (Issued By Friends Of South Africa In The Interests Of Truth.)
National Press Agency
London (1899?)
11pp.
8vo.   M
Statements concerning Dutch loyalty at the Cape. Pamphlet attributed to A. G. Shiell.

Shiell (A. G.) – Dum-Dums In The Transvaal, An Expostulatory Epistle To John Bull.
W. J. Smith
Brighton 1899
14pp.
8vo.   M
An attack upon British foreign policy with reference to the Transvaal war.

Shiell (A. G.) – Pro-Boer Lyrics.
King, Thorne & Stace Printers
Brighton (1902?) (Fourth edition enlarged)
55pp.
240mm   SABIB

Shiell (A. G.) – 'Camps Of Refuge', An Uninserted Letter To

'The Brighton Herald'.
W. H. Attwick
Brighton (1901)
8pp.
8vo.   M

Shiell (A. G.) – Briton *Versus* Boer. A Letter To The Clergy Of The Evangelical Church Of Switzerland In Reply To The Bishop Of Liverpool.
W. J. Smith
Brighton 1902
35pp.
8vo.   RCSL

Shipman (J. C.) – The War And After. Speech Feb. 20th, 1901.
Eighty Club
np. (1902)
Pagination not shown.   THB

(Shurey's Illustrated) (Publishers) – Shurey's Pictorial History Of The War (Shurey's Pictorial Budget).
Shurey's Illustrated, Publisher
np./nd. (London 1900?)
12 Parts
Each issue 26pp. Illustrated throughout.
265×180mm   p.14
War illustrated published in 12 parts. Title incorporated with 'Shurey's Illustrated' after part 12.

Sidney-Wilmot (P. C.) and Harris (O.) – Irregular Lines And Moanings From The Veldt, By Sergeants Sidney-Wilmot & Owen Harris, 2nd Battalion Sharpshooters, 21st Battalion Imperial Yeomanry.
Published by the authors?
Ermelo 1902?
iii+19pp.
174×124mm
Verses on soldiering with the Imperial Yeomanry during the war.

Sim (G. H.) – The Relief Of Ladysmith. Outline Of Operations From 16th January To 3rd Of March.
P. Davis & Sons, Printers
Maritzburg 190–?
13pp.
120×180mm   SABIB
Chronology of events, January 16–March 3, 1900. 'By Lt.-Col. G. H. Sim, R.E.'

Simons (L.) (Editor) – Hollandia: A Weekly Paper For Dutchmen Abroad. Special Transvaal Number.
Uitgevers-Maatschappij. 'Nederland'
The Hague 1899
16pp.
Quarto   M
An extra number printed in English for the 'English Reader', devoted to the Transvaal case.

Simons (L.) – Hollandia: A Weekly Paper For The Dutch-Speaking World At Large. Special American-South African Number. Written In English By L. Simons.
Uitgevers-Maatschappij 'Nederland'
The Hague 1900
16pp.
Quarto   M
The writer appeals to the American people to assist the cause of the Boers.

(Simpkin, Marshall) (Publishers) – The Boer Plan Of Campaign. A Forecast. By An Officer On The Active List. 2nd Ed.
Simpkin, Marshall
London (1899?)
8pp. Folding map.
230mm   SABIB
No title page. Catalogued from cover. See – BERESFORD, publisher, for earlier edition.

(Simpkin, Marshall, Hamilton, Kent.) (Publishers) – Boer Version Of The Transvaal War, Or, An English Translation Of All Dutch Official Telegrams Received At Vryheid During The Boer War Up To The Time When British Troops Occupied Vryheid.
Simpkin, Marshall, Hamilton, Kent
London 1901
95pp.
210mm   SABIB

(Simpkin, Marshall, Hamilton, Kent & Co.) (Publishers) – The Fight At Dame Africa's School, Shewing How The Little Boy Stuck Up To The Big Boy And What A Useful Lesson He Taught Him.
Simpkin, Marshall, Hamilton, Kent & Co./London
Henry S. Eland/Exeter
(c.1900)
34pp.
Cr.8vo.   M
Skit on the political situation in South Africa. Ref. BM library.

(Simpkin, Marshall, Hamilton, Kent & Co., Ltd.) (Publishers) – Chantic-Learics By A Crowing Cock.
Simpkin, Marshall, Hamilton, Kent & Co., Ltd.
London 1900
12pp. Illustrated.
299×253mm

(Simpkin, Marshall, Hamilton, Kent & Co., Ltd.) (Publishers) – How To Become A Pro-Boer. A Vade-Mecum For Little-Englanders. By One Of Them. With Introduction By Sir A. D. Windbag Bunkum.
Simpkin, Marshall, Hamilton, Kent & Co., Ltd.
London 1902
23pp.
Quarto   M
Listed in SABIB as – How To Become A Pro-Bore: etc.

Simpson (Fred. Wm.) (Government Printer) – Western Australia. History Of Western Australian Contingents Serving In South Africa During The Boer War (1899–1902).
By Authority
Fred. Wm. Simpson, Government Printer
Perth 1910
68pp.
210×135mm
Compiled by Lt.-Col. J. Campbell. Paper covers. Author's name omitted from title page.

Simpson (Robert J. S.) – The Medical History Of The War In South Africa, An Epidemiological Essay.
J. Bale, Sons & Danielsson, Ltd.
London 1911
viii+236pp. Tables, diagrams.
250mm   H
Reprinted from the journal of the Royal Army Medical Corps.

Singleton (John) (Compiler) – The Battle-Fields Of Natal Re-Visited.
Compiled, illustrated and published by John Singleton
Durban nd. (1900?)
55pp. Folding map, diagram and illustrations.
194×255mm

(Sister X) – The Tragedy And Comedy Of War Hospitals.
John Murray
London 1906
xiv+185pp. Illustrated.
210×150mm
Campaign experiences of a nurse in the RAMC.

(Skeffington & Son) (Publishers?) – Shot Or Patrol. A True Incident Of The Present War. By The Author Of Gordon League Ballads.
Skeffington & Son
London 1900
8pp.
Cr.8vo.   M
British Museum Library lists author's name – Mrs Clement Nugent Jackson.

Skey (William) – Patriotic Rhymes Dedicated By Kind Permission To The Rt. Hon. R. J. Seddon On The Occasion Of The Departure Of The Rough Riders Contingent For South Africa.
Whitcombe & Tombs
Wellington 1900
31pp. Illustrated.
180mm   BIM
Limited edition of 600 copies.

Skirving (R. Scot.) – Our Army In South Africa.
Angus and Robertson
Sydney/Melbourne 1901
v+43pp.
190mm   SABIB
Account based on the diary of the author, consulting surgeon to the Australian contingents.

Sleeper (J. F.) – The South African Republics vs Great Britain. A Last Appeal For A Suffering People By A True American.
Printer/publisher not shown
New York 1900
11pp.
190×170mm   SABIB
See entry under 'True American'.

Sleeper (J. F.) – Cronje's Glory; Koodoosrand.
Sherwood Press
Elizabeth, N.J. 1901
v+9pp.?
270mm   SABIB
Poem in praise of Gen. Piet Cronje's stand at Paardeberg, Feb. 1900. A limited edition of 200 copies.

Sleeper (J. F.) – The Marion Of The Free State.
Sherwood Press
Elizabeth, N.J. 1901
vi+17pp.?
280mm   SABIB
Poem in praise of Gen. De Wet's exploits in the war. A limited edition of 200 copies.

Slocum (Capt. S. L.' H.) & Reichmann (Capt. C.) – Reports On Military Operations In South Africa And China, Etc. See entry under GOVERNMENT PRINTING OFFICE.

Smart (H.) – The South African Light Horse. In Camp And On The Warpath.
No other information
Printed (c.1900)
48 plates.
140mm   SABIB
Catalogued from cover. Scenes from the war connected with the S.A. Light Horse.

(Smith. A. N.) (Publisher?) – The Boers And The British. A History Of The Events Leading To The Hostilities In South Africa.
A. N. Smith
Melbourne 1899
iii+139pp. Folding map.
200mm   SABIB

Smith (C. W.) – The South African War, And The 'Bear' Operator. A Financial Revolution.

P. S. King and Son
London 1902
viii+127pp.
8vo.   M

Smith (Major-General F.) – A Veterinary History Of The War In South Africa 1899–1902.
H. & W. Brown
London nd. (1919)
viii+321pp. Illustrations, folding maps and diagrams.
276×218mm   p.86
Originally issued with 'The Veterinary Record', 1912–1914.

Smith (Godfrey H.) – With The Scottish Rifle Volunteers At The Front.
William Hodge & Company
Glasgow and Edinburgh 1901
xvi+139pp. Illustrated.
188×128mm   p.49

Smith (Goldwin) – In The Court Of History. An Apology For Canadians Who Were Opposed To The South African War.
William Tyrrell & Company
Toronto 1902
71pp.
183×123mm

(Smith Premier Typewriter Co.) (Publisher) – Souvenir Of The Siege Of Mafeking, Etc. See entry under JOHN LEWIS & Compy. The Selkirk Press.

(Smith. W. H. & Son) (Publishers) – The Pembrokeshire South African War Memorial.
W. H. Smith & Son
London nd. (1908)
27pp. Illustrated.
205×140mm   DC
A record of the War Memorial erected to Pembrokeshire men who died in South Africa during the war. A compilation attributed to Louis Samson.

Smuts (J. C.) – Official Reports Etc. See – DE LA REY.

Smyth (Major B.) – A History Of The Lancashire Fusiliers (Formerly XX Regiment).
Volume I. 1688–1821
Volume II. 1822–1903
The Sackville Press
Dublin 1903/1904
Vol. I. – xiv+390pp. Maps, colour plates and other illustrations.
Vol. II. – xiv+ii+504pp. Maps, colour plates and other illustrations.
219×140mm
A record of the 2nd Battalion in South Africa (Vol. II.). Various appendices relate to Mounted Infantry Sections and Volunteer Active Service Companies.

(S. N. D.) (Translator) – The Boers And The War, From The Impartial Foreigners' Point Of View. A History In Brief (1652–1902) Containing Chapters On The Cause And Commencement Of The War; The Gold Discovery And The Consequences It Entailed; Question Of Intervention; Possible Peace Terms; The Women And Children And The Concentration Camps, Tent Life, &c.; Enemies To Peace. With Further Notes; Atrocity Charges Dealt With; Terms Of Peace; Surrender Agreement, &c. Compiled Principally From The Writings Of Eminent Swiss And Other European Publicists. Collated, Translated, And Arranged By S. N. D. With Confirmatory Note By Sir Frederick R. St. John, K.C.M.G., Late British Minister To Switzerland.

Simpkin, Marshall, Hamilton, Kent & Co., Limited. London
Charpentier & Co. Portsmouth
1902
xx+120pp.
185×125mm

Snell (Rev. Bernard) – Sermons On The Boer War (1899–1901) Preached At Brixton Independent Church, London, S.W.
James Clarke & Co.
London 1902
102pp.
8vo.   M

Soames (H. G.) – 'What Is Truth?' By 'Africanus' Revised (With Notes And Statistics.) Seven Essays By 'Africanus', Published In The South African And Home Press, During The Anglo-Boer-War, 1899–1901.
Published by the author, H. G. Soames
Printed by Kenneth B. Dickson
Johannesburg nd. (1902)
28pp.
Cr.8vo.   M

('South Africa') (Publisher?) – Pictures Of The War. The South African Campaign: An Illustrated Record Of The Boer War, Pt. I & II.
'South Africa' Publisher?
London (1899?)
ii+24pp. & ii+pp.25–48. Maps and illustrations.
310mm   SABIB
No title-page. Catalogued from cover.

(South Africa Conciliation Committee. The) – Publications issued by the Committee. Some unnumbered, others listed under author.
National Press Agency Ltd. (printers)
London nd. (1899–1902)
Average size 212×138mm

[1] The South African Crisis. A Plain Statement Of Facts By Percy A. Molteno, M.A. (Son Of The First Premier Of Cape Colony)   7pp.

[2] The Crisis In South Africa. Some Answers (From Authoritative Sources) To Sir A. Milner's Reflections Upon Colonial Loyalty.   11pp.

[3] The War In South Africa. Some Authoritative Sketches Of The Boers By Distinguished Englishmen.   8pp.

[4] The War In South Africa. Letters Contributed To The 'Times' By Mr. F. C. Selous, The Well-Known Traveller And Sportsman (Reprinted By Special Permission Of The 'Times').   8pp.

[5] The Last Appeal Before The Outbreak Of War Made In The Cape Parliament By Mr. Schreiner (The Cape Prime Minister) (Reprinted By Permission From The 'Daily Chronicle').   7pp.

[6] Sir Alfred Milner On The Real Object Of The War. Being An Interview Between The High Commissioner Of South Africa And Mr James Molteno, The Representative Of The Ministerialists In The Cape Parliament, Five Days Before The Outbreak Of War.
          SABIB   8pp.

[9] Extract From Letter From Mr. Courtney, M.P. . . . November 29th, 1899.   1p.

[10] The Boers The White Flag, And The Wounded.   4pp.

185

[74] The Imprisonment Of Mr. Cartwright.
SABIB   16pp.

[75] Fiction And Fable Which Have
Fanned The Flame.   8pp.
SABIB

[77] The Mortality In The Concentration
Camps.   1p.
SABIB

[78] The War, Farm Burning, And
Concentration Camps. (Letter) From
Field-Marshal Sir Neville Chamberlain.
SABIB   2pp.

[79] An English Ex-Minister Of The Cape
On The State Of The Cape Colony.
(Signed) John X. Merriman.
(Pagination not shown)
SABIB

[80] Mr. Bryce On The Boer Rights Of
Belligerency Under The Law Of Nations.
SABIB   4pp.

[81] Sir William Harcourt On The Laws
Of War.   8pp.
SABIB

[82] Field-Marshal Sir Neville
Chamberlain On The Conduct Of The
War. Three Letters Taken From The
'Manchester Guardian' Of August 5th,
August 29th, And September 20th,
1901.   8pp.
SABIB

[83] The Exposure Of Non-Combatants
On Military Trains. (Signed) Frederic
Mackarness.   4pp.
SABIB

[84] Olive Schreiner. Her Treatment
Under Martial Law. Breakdown And
Recovery.   2pp.
SABIB

[85] The Concentration Camps. (Signed)
J. S. Haldane.   1p.
SABIB

[86] Appeal Of Miss Hobhouse To Mr.
Brodrick.   2pp.
SABIB

[87] A Law-Lord On The Imprisonment
And Deportation Of Miss Emily
Hobhouse. (Signed) Hobhouse.   2pp.
SABIB

[88] 'Pro-Boers' Vindicated By Edmund
Burke.   4pp.
SABIB

[89] Salient Facts From The Blue-Books.
The Official Report On The
Concentration Camps.   20pp.
SABIB

[90] Sufferings Under Martial Law.   4pp.
SABIB

[91] A Great Lawyer On The Liberty Of
The Subject. (Signed) Hobhouse.   2pp.
SABIB

[92] The State Of Siege. By Frederic
Harrison.   8pp.
SABIB

[93] Some Comments On The Report Of
The Ladies' Commission On The
Concentration Camps.   16pp.
SABIB

[94] A Pastor And A Doctor Imprisoned
And Exiled Under Martial Law.   4pp.
SABIB

[95] Lord Spencer On Martial Law In The
Cape Colony. A Speech Delivered In

The House Of Lords, On March 17th,
1902.   8pp.
SABIB

[96] The True Facts Of The Cartwright
Case.   2pp.
SABIB

(S.A.C.C.) – Appeal To Lord Salisbury
Against Annexation.
National Press Agency, printers
London nd. (1900)
2pp.
220mm   SABIB
Catalogued from caption title. Statement
signed by Leonard Courtney, F. C. Selous
and Frederic Mackarness urging Lord
Salisbury to stop the war. Also issued as
No.30 of the Committee's pamphlets.

(S.A.C.C.) – List Of Members, Dated
February 10th, 1900.   15pp.
List Of Members, Dated March 17th,
1900.   18pp.
List Of Members, Dated June 27th,
1900.   28pp.
210mm   SABIB

(S.A.C.C.) – The Purpose Of Conquest.
An Appeal To The Nation.
National Press Agency, printers
London 1900
11pp.
210mm   SABIB
An appeal for autonomy in the Transvaal
and Orange Free State at the conclusion of
war. Signed by C. F. Aked and 18 others.
Three printings of above title listed in
SABIB.

SABIB states S.A.C.C. pamphlets were
issued separately and together in 3 vols.
First series – Nos. 1–43 and 2
unnumbered. Second series – Nos. 44–67
and 1 unnumbered. Third series – Nos.
68–96 and 5 unnumbered. Together 104
pamphlets.

(South Africa Conciliation Committee)
(Sheffield Branch) – Leaflets Nos. 1–6.
Published by the Committee, Sheffield
Branch (c.1900)

[1] Dr. Jameson On Boer Armaments At
The Time Of The Raid. Important
Admission.   1p.

[2] The Boer Armaments. Were They
The Cause Of The Jameson Raid Or Its
Effect?   4pp.

[3] The Treatment Of The Cape Dutch.
A Lesson From The Canadian Rebellion.
(By Libertas)   4pp.

[4] An Appeal Against The Suppression
Of Free Government In The Republics.
(By L. Courtney)   2pp.

[5] What We Are Fighting For. High
Dividends: Cheap Labour.   4pp.

[6] How The Press Was Worked Before
The War. Abridged From Mr. J. A.
Hobson's Notable Book, 'The War In
South Africa'.   4pp.

210mm   SABIB

(South Africa General Mission)
(Publishers) – See entries under MERCER
(A.)

('South Africa' Offices Of) – 'South
Africa' Handbooks – No.27. Battles And
Sieges, Ninth Series. General French's
Drive, The Battle Of Stormberg, The
Battle Of Talana Hill. The Battles Of
Belmont And Graspan. The Battles Of
Tweebosch And Hartebeestefontein.

[Reprinted From 'South Africa'.]
The Offices Of 'South Africa'
London nd. (c.1904)
27+i.pp. (advertisement)
152×124mm   CC
Paper covered pamphlet, part of a series
of South African Battles reprinted from
the newspaper 'South Africa'. Title from
cover. Accounts of various battles of the
Second Boer War appear in Series 1–8,
(Nos. 19–26). These issues include
accounts of battles from other South
African wars.

(South African Boer War Exhibition
Company) (Published By) – The South
African Boer War Exhibition. The
Greatest And Most Realistic Military
Spectacle Known In The History Of The
World. Produced Under The Direction
Of Frank E. Fillis The Famous South
African Showman And Organizer Of
Savage South Africa In Greater Britain
Exhibition, Earls Court, London, Etc.,
Etc.
South African Boer War Exhibition Co.
St. Louis 1904
24pp. Illustrated.
240×171mm   p.122
Details of tableaux, brief biographies of
some Boer generals, notes on the battles of
Colenso and Paardeberg, and a
description of the South African Exhibit at
the St. Louis World's Fair.

(South African Field Force) –
Composition Of The South African Field
Force Bloemfontein 29th April 1900.
Printer/publisher not shown
(Bloemfontein 1900)
25pp.
Folio   WL/237
A list of Divisions, Staff, and other
officers serving in the S.A.F.F.

(South African Review. The) (Publisher) –
The South African Review Book Of 50
Famous Cartoons A Unique Souvenir Of
The Anglo-Boer War, 1899–1900.
W. A. Richards & Sons (printers)
Cape Town nd. (1900)
102pp.
178×242mm
Cartoons by Egersdörfer from July 29th,
1897 to June 29th, 1900 with an
introduction by the editor, Alfred Palmer.

(South African Vigilance Committee)
(Publisher) – Papers published c.1900.
Some in reference to the war listed
below. A list of SAVC publications is
included in SABIB, Vol. 4 pp.344–346.

The Voice Of The Churches. The South
African Churches Declare For
Annexation.
SAVC
(Cape Town 1900?)
26pp.
8vo.   M
Vigilance Papers, No. 1.

Speech By The Honourable J. Rose-
Innes, Q.C., M.L.A. (Attorney-General
Of The Cape Of Good Hope, 1890–3) At
The Municipal Hall, Claremont, Cape
Colony, 30th March, 1900.
SAVC
Cape Town 1900
11pp.
8vo.   M
Vigilance Papers, No. 2.

'Liberty!' Versus Liberty. Some Remarks
On A South African Petition.
By R. R. Brydone.
SAVC
Cape Town 1900
8pp.
220mm   SABIB
Vigilance Papers, No. 4.

Never Again. Sir Alfred Milner's Reply
To Ministers' Address.
SAVC
Cape Town 1900
8pp.
8vo.
Vigilance Papers, No. 5.

The Anti-British Crusade In South
Africa. By An Ex-Official Of The
Transvaal.
SAVC
Cape Town 1900
20pp.
8vo.
Vigilance Papers, No. 7.

The Black Man And The War. By The
Rev. J. S. Moffat.
SAVC
Cape Town 1900
11pp.
8vo.
Vigilance Papers, No. 8.

Bishop Hartzell. Moral Aspects Of The
War. South Africa's Future. Powerful
Sermon.
Vacher & Sons, printers for SAVC
Westminster 1902
4pp.
220mm   SABIB

(South African War) – Some Poetry.
Published In England And The United
States.
(No other information)
No date
159+3pp.
230mm   SABIB
*Poems in reference to the war collected in
England and America. Anti-British bias.*

(South African Women And Children
Distress Fund) (Published By?) – South
African Women And Children's Distress
Fund.
The Fund
London 1901
7pp.
220mm   SABIB
*Gives brief news from Miss Hobhouse in
Bloemfontein.*

(South African Women And Children
Distress Fund) (Publisher?) – South
African Women And Children's Distress
Fund.
The Fund
London (1901?)
6pp.
220mm   SABIB
*An appeal for contributions to the fund.
No title page, catalogued from caption.*

(South African Women And Children
Distress Fund) (Publisher?) – Extracts
From Recent Letters From South Africa.
National Press Agency (printed by)
(London 1903?)
12pp.
220mm   SABIB
*Letters from Nov. 1902–Feb. 1903
concerning the progress of repatriation.*

(Southland Returned Troopers Assoc:)
(Publisher) – Souvenir – Photos Copied
By R. Massey Invercargill.
Craig & Company, printers
(Invercargill 1908?)
12pp. Illustrated.
185×220mm   BIM
Title from cover.

(Souvenir) – Souvenir Of The Boer War.
nd./np. (c.1900)
10 Mounted photographs on folding strip
with printed captions pasted below.
130×180mm   SABIB

(Souvenir Syndicate) (Publisher) – The
Transvaal Coronation & Peace Souvenir.
An Illustrated Historical Review. Wealth
And Growth.
Souvenir Syndicate
Johannesburg 1902
188pp. Illustrated.
250mm   SABIB

Spence (Col. J.) & St. Aubyn (Capt. G.) –
A Talk With The 3 Coys. Mounted Infy.
Proceeding From Malta To South Africa
31st December 1900.
Printer/publisher not shown
Malta 1900
i+10pp.
210×154mm   CC

Spex – Mr. Kruger In Peace And War:
5 Illustrations.
Suckling & Co.
(London 1899?)
180×210mm   SABIB
*5 plates in folding strip. Anti-Boer
cartoons issued during the war.
Catalogued from cover.*

(Sphere. The) – The Sphere An
Illustrated Newspaper For The Home.
Jan. 27th, 1900–March 30th, 1901.
Printer/publisher not shown
London 1900–1901
1,872pp. Illustrated.
425×311mm   CC
*Boer War content throughout. Numerous
folding illustrations.*

Spicer (A. R. W.) – Letters From The
Transvaal 1899–1901.
Cole & Co., printers
London nd. (c.1902)
94pp.
180×118mm
*An account of the campaign in Natal and
later episodes in the Transvaal by Lieut.
Spicer of the 3rd Batt. The King's Royal
Rifle Corps. The author died of enteric
fever in May 1901.*

(Spottiswoode & Co. Ltd.) (Printers) –
South African War. Official Report Of
The Banquet Given On The 18th
December, 1902, By The Incorporated
Law Society To The Survivors Of The
Solicitors And Articled Clerks Who
Served In The South African Campaign
1899 To 1902, With A Record Of The
Services Of The Officers And Men So
Engaged.
Spottiswoode & Co. Ltd. Printers
London nd. (1902)
64pp. With illustrations.
270×201mm   DC
*Complete nominal roll with details of
service of 176 officers and men.*

Sprigg (Sir Gordon) – The Situation
(A Speech Delivered By Sir Gordon
Sprigg) Reprinted From 'Cape Times',
July 16, 1901.
(Cape Times?)
(Cape Town 1901?)
32pp.
16mo.   M

Spurgin (Karl B.) – On Active Service
With The Northumberland And Durham
Yeomen, Under Lord Methuen.
(South Africa, 1900–1901.)
Printed for the author by
The Walter Scott Publishing Co., Ltd.
London and Newcastle-On-Tyne
nd. (c.1902)
xx+323pp. Illustrated.
188×126mm   p.30

Stakesby-Lewis (H. R.) – The War.
A Voice From South Africa. A Message
To The Christian People Of Great
Britain. From Mrs. Lewis, Sister Of Mr.

Schreiner, Prime Minister Of Cape
Colony.
Bemrose & Sons, Limited
London (1899?)
8pp.
8vo.   M

Stakesby-Lewis (H. R.) – A New Aspect
Of The Present War. (Being Revised
Reprint Of Article In '*Methodist Times*',
London, January 4, 1900.), Entitled –
A Voice From South Africa: A Message
To The Christian People Of Great
Britain.
Townshend, Taylor and Snashall, printers
Cape Town (1900?)
8pp.
220mm   SABIB

Staniforth (J. M.) – Cartoons Of The
Boer War. Reprinted From The 'Western
Mail'.
Western Mail, Limited
Cardiff 1900/1902
Vol. 1. – 112pp.
Vol. 2. – 104pp. With folding plate.
277×210mm
*Each vol. with 'Introduction' and 'Diary
of the War'. M lists a third and fifth
edition.*

Stanley (Col. Lord) – Report On Press
Censorship; By Col. Lord Stanley.
July 1900.
(War Office 1902?)
4pp.   MOD
*War Office library. WO. ref. – WH Loc:
SA39X/PRO Loc: WO. 108/262.*

(Star Litho Works) (Printers) – New
Zealand Rough Riders Grand Military
Display Auckland Saturday, Feb.
24th 1900.
Star Litho Works
np./nd. (Auckland 1900)
12pp. Illustrated.
185×221mm
*Programme of the military display held at
the Auckland Cricket Ground. The
publication includes various photographs
of members of the 1st and 2nd
Contingents N.Z. Rough Riders and lyrics
to a number of popular songs. The title is
drawn from the cover.*

(Star Litho Works) (Printers) – New
Zealand Army Rough Riders Contingent
Grand Military Display, Auckland
Saturday Mar. 3rd 1900.
Star Litho Works
12pp.
185×220mm   BIM
Title from cover.

Stark (J.) – Among Our Soldiers.
Durban, Colenso, Ladysmith,
Standerton. 1899–1900–1901.
Robinson & Co. printers
Durban nd. (1901?)
15pp.
130mm   SABIB
*Author's name from introductory
paragraph. Brief sketch of work carried
on among troops by Mr. A. C. Playfair,
of Durban, and his friends.*

Stark (J. H.) – The British And Dutch In
South Africa. A Paper Read Before The
Trinity Club Of Trinity Church, The
Dorchester Historical Society, And The
Victorian Club Of Boston, By James
H. Stark. Being A Collection Of Facts
Obtained From The Most Authentic
Sources, Giving A True Account Of
What Caused The Present War In South
Africa, And What Its Effect Will Be On
The Future Of The British Empire.
Published At The Request Of The
Victorian Club By James H. Stark.

Published by the author?
Boston 1900
32pp.
179×120mm   M

Statham (Sister A. K.) – A Nurse's
Album During The Boer War.
1899 To 1902.
Wertheimer, Lea & Co. (Printers)
London nd. (c.1902)
48pp. Portrait frontispiece.
183×123mm

Statham (F. Reginald) – South Africa
And The Transvaal. The Story Of
A Conspiracy. Being A Lecture
Delivered In The Temperance Hall,
Newport, Monmouthshire, On The 25th
September 1899.
The Transvaal Committee
London 1900
16pp.
8vo.   M
*SABIB lists edition published Westminster
1899.*

St. Clair-Erskine (J. F. H.) – The Gram.
See – ROSSLYN, Earl of.

St. Clair-Erskine (J. F. H.) – Twice
Captured, Etc. See – ROSSLYN, Earl of.

Stead (W. T.) – Shall I Slay My Brother
Boer? An Appeal To The Conscience Of
Britain.
'Review Of Reviews' Office
London 1899
64pp.
246×170mm
*Pamphlet issued before the outbreak of
war setting out the case for, and against
armed conflict. The author appeals to all
parties to avoid war.*

Stead (W. T.) – Are We In The Right?
An Appeal To Honest Men.
'Review Of Reviews' Office
London 1899
96pp.
246×156mm   CC
M lists copy – London 1899, 76pp.

Stead (W. T.) – War Against War In
South Africa.
Horace Marshall & Son
London (1899–1900)
448+4pp. Illustrated.
285×221mm
*Twenty eight issues of a pro-Boer
publication issued from Oct. 20th, 1899–
June 1, 1900. M lists two extra numbers,
possibly the start of a second vol. An
index (4pp.) is included in the bound
volume.*

Stead (W. T.) – National Protest Against
The South African War. Supplement To
'War Against War In South Africa'.
Printed by W. Speaight & Sons for
W. T. Stead
London 1900
4pp.
Folio   M

Stead (W. T.) – The Candidates Of Cain.
A Catechism For The Constituencies.
The General Election, 1900.
Stop-the-War Committee
London 1900
128pp.
Roy.8vo.   M

Stead (W. T.) – The War In South Africa,
1899–19—? How Not To Make Peace.
Evidence As To Homestead Burning
Collected And Examined.
Stop-the-War Committee
London 1900
104pp.
Roy.8vo.   M

Stead (W. T.) (Editor) – How Britain
Goes To War. A Digest And An
Analysis Of Evidence Taken By The
Royal Commission On The War In South
Africa. Compiled From The Blue Books
For The Information Of The Public.
'Review Of Reviews' Office
London 1903
256pp. Illustrated.
251×158mm

Stead (W. T.) (Editor?) – In Peril! The
Heart Of The Empire In Danger:
Speeches By The Marquis Of Salisbury
And Earl Of Rosebery. With Articles,
Maps, Etc.
'Review Of Reviews' Office
London (1900)
48pp. Illustrated.
180mm   SABIB
*Speeches by lords Salisbury and Rosebery
etc. References to the war throughout.*

Stead (W. T.) – The Truth About
The War.
'Review Of Reviews' Office
London (1900)
63pp.
180×120mm

Stead (W. T.) – The Truth About The
War In South Africa.
W. & J. Mackay (Printer)
Chatham (1900?)
63pp.
180mm   SABIB

Stead (W. T.) – (See 'MOWBRAY
HOUSE' (Publisher) – The War In South
Africa 1899–19—? The publication is
divided into various chapters concerning
the war. The first, – A Case For
Intervention', is by Stead.)

Steele (Chas.) (Publisher?) –
5th Australian Infantry Regiment –
Souvenir Of 1st Battalion – South
Africa, 1899–1902.
Chas. Steele
Melbourne 1912
(Pagination not shown)
      ALH

Steevens (G. W.) – From Capetown To
Ladysmith An Unfinished Record Of The
South African War. Edited By Vernon
Blackburn.
William Blackwood and Sons
Edinburgh and London 1900
ix+180pp. With two maps, one folding.
196×130mm
*SABIB records the following editions –
Blackwood's colonial library (1900?)
Copp Clark Co./Toronto (1900?)
Dodd, Mead & Co./New York 1900.
iii+198pp. With portrait and folding map.
195×130mm
Bernhard Tauchnitz/Leipzig 1900.
247pp.*

(Stephen Austin & Sons) (Printers) – The
Queenslanders At Elands River August
1900. For Private Circulation Only.
Stephen Austin & Sons
Hertford (1901?)
32pp.
8vo.   M
*Extracts from newspaper articles and
letters in reference to the Elands River
Siege, August 4–16, 1900.*

Sternberg (Count) – My Experiences
Of The Boer War. Translated From
The German With An Introduction By
Lieut.-Colonel G. F. R. Henderson.
Longmans, Green, and Co.
London 1901
xliii+268pp.
201×133mm   p.60

Stevens (F.) – Complete History Of The
South African War, In 1899–1900.
W. Nicholson
London (1901?)
386pp.
190mm   SABIB
Events up to April 1901.

Stevens (F. T.) – Complete History Of
The South African War In 1899–1902.
W. Nicholson
London nd. (c.1903)
400pp. With frontispiece.
190×124mm
*This ed: includes an appendix – The
Guerilla Campaign.*

Stevenson (Rennie) – Through Rhodesia
With The Sharpshooters.
John Macqueen
London 1901
199pp.
199×133mm   p.59

Stevenson (Surg. Gen. W. F.) – Report,
Medical Units. See WO. 101.

Stevenson (Surgeon-General W. F.)
(Editor) – Report On The Surgical
Cases Noted In The South African War,
1899–1902.
Harrison & Sons for H.M.S.O.
London 1905
308pp. Illustrated.
Folio   M
*Report by the late Principal Medical
Officer, Headquarters Staff, South Africa.*

(Stevenson and Dryden) (Printers) – Pro
Patriâ. Stories Of Service In South
Africa, 1899–1902. Told By Old Boys Of
The Royal Grammar School, Newcastle-
Upon-Tyne. First 'Special' Number Of
The 'Novocastrian'.
Stevenson and Dryden, printers
Newcastle-upon-Tyne nd. (1902)
88pp. Illustrated.
219×141mm   p.113

Stewart (R. S.) M.D. – The Mental And
Moral Effects Of The South African War
On The British People.
Adlard & Son
London (1904)
Pagination not shown
Pamphlet listed in THB.

**Stewart-Murray (K. M.) (Duchess Of
Atholl)** (Editor) – A Military History Of
Perthshire 1899–1902, Etc. (See –
TULLIBARDINE, Marchioness of.)

Stickney (A.) – The Transvaal Outlook.
Dodd, Mead & Co.
New York 1900
139pp. Folding maps and plans.
241×152mm
*An assessment of the military situation in
South Africa with reference to the
problems of transport and supply.*

Stirling (J.) – Our Regiments In South
Africa 1899–1902 Their Record, Based
On The Despatches.
William Blackwood and Sons
Edinburgh and London 1903
xiv+532pp.
230×145mm   p.112

Stirling (J.) – The Colonials In South
Africa 1899–1902 Their Record, Based
On The Despatches.
William Blackwood and Sons
Edinburgh and London 1907
xii+497pp.
230×147mm   p.112

(St. James' Church, Sydney) – Form Of Service, For The Unveiling, By His Excellency The Governor, Of The Memorial Window Erected By The Officers, Non Commissioned Officers, And Men Of The 2nd (N.S.W.) Mounted Rifles, To The Glory Of God And In Memory Of Those Of Their Comrades Who Were Killed In Action, Or Lost Their Lives In The South African War, 1901–1902, November 8th, 1903, 22nd Sunday After Trinity.
Publisher/printer not shown
Sydney 1903
15pp.
180×120mm   CB
Contains a roll of officers and men of the Second N.S.W. Mounted Rifles who lost their lives in the war.

(St. James's Gazette. The) (Published By) – Boers And British. Facts From The Transvaal.
St. James's Gazette
London 1899
36pp. With map.
244×158mm
Copy of the sixth edition, revised and enlarged. An historical account of the Dutch in the Transvaal and the case for the Uitlanders with comment on the Bloemfontein Conference and subsequent negotiations. The pamphlet was first published in June 1899. The fifth and sixth editions were published after the outbreak of hostilities.

St. Leger (Captain S. E.) – War Sketches In Colour.
Adam & Charles Black
London nd. (1903)
xiii+274pp. Illustrated.
230×166mm   p.22
De luxe edition of 250 signed copies published the same year.
276×215mm

(Stop-The-War Committee) (Published by) – Pamphlets published London 1899–1901. List extracted from M and SABIB. General size 224×142mm

[1] Did The Boers Begin The War? The Truth About The Ultimatum.   2pp.

[2] More Lies Nailed To The Counter. The Peace Party And The War. (And – Mr. Montagu White's Evidence.)   2pp.

[3] 'Afraid Of God!' Why W. T. Stead Opposes The War.   2pp.

[4] Naboth's Vineyard In South Africa.   2pp.

[5] Jockeyed Into War! The Story Of The Nine-Tenths Acceptance. What Sir Edward Clarke Said.   2pp.

[6] Mr. Chamberlain And The Raid. The Scandal Of The South African Committee. 'Lies, Lies, Lies!'   2pp.

[7] 'Morituri Te Salutant!' Dying For The Dividends Of Dives.   2pp.Illus.

[8] Is This A Stock-Jobber's War? Some Significant Admissions (And – The Bold Buccaneer. By The Late Grant Allen.)   2pp.

[9] The Decisive Question! Is This War Just, Righteous, Inevitable? If Not, Stop It At Once! (And – Dr. Clifford's Counsel.)   2pp.

[10] Will The French Raid London? Our National Peril!   2pp.

[11] Our English Liberties, A.D.1900: The Right Of Free Speech, Free Thought, And Public Meeting.   2pp.

[12] A Fillip To Revolution! The War And The House Of Lords. Sauce For The Boer Goose! Good For The British Gander!   2pp.

[13] The War Blight On Social Reforms.   2pp.

[14] The Swindle Of Suzerainty. The Fraud That Forced On War!   2pp.

[15] Westralia And Its Outlanders. A Sriking Parallel To The Transvaal. 2pp.

[16] How Kruger Begged For Arbitration And Mr. Chamberlain Refused.   2pp.

[17] Death To The Republics! Death! The New War And Its War Cry!   2pp.

[18] The Strange Story Of The Rev. Hugh Price Hughes. A Case Of Dr. Jekyl And Mr. Hyde.   2pp.

[19] Say! Say! Say! To The Absent-Minded Public (After Rudyard Kipling, By W. Macdonald.)   2pp.

[20] More Victims For Moloch. The Demand For Reinforcements.   2pp.

[21] Why See It Through? A Protest By Sir Wilfred Lawson.   2pp.

[22] How Majuba Was Avenged. The Story Of The State And The Sponge. 2pp.

[23] The Raid And The War! Mr. Chamberlain's Complicity. President Kruger's Opinion.   2pp.

[24] Recessional, By Rudyard Kipling; (And – Processional, By State Secretary Reitz.)   2pp.

[25] How We Have Been Befooled. Falsehoods Bred By The 'Land Of Lies'.   2pp.

[26] Our 'Moloch Priests'. The Churches And The War.   2pp.

[27] Stabbing The Heart Of The British Empire. A Letter From Olive Schreiner.   2pp.

[28] The Great African Conspiracy. Briton Or Boer? Secret Despatches Seized At Dundee.   2pp.

[29] The Judgement Of Our Neighbours: What Germans Think Of The War! Professor Mommsen And W. Liebknecht.   2pp.

[30] The Judgement Of Our Neighbours – II. A Dutchman's Appeal (Charles Boissevain)   2pp.

[31] The Men We Are Slaying. A Graveside Memory At Ladysmith. 2pp.

[32] The Transvaal Before The War. 'The Finest Country In The World For The Working Man'.   2pp.

[33] The Men We Are Fighting For. (And – The Men We Are Fighting Against.)   2pp.

[34] Diplomacy Or Highway Robbery? The Story Of Mr. Chamberlain's Methods.   2pp.

[35] President Kruger's Concessions. A Reply To Mr. Chamberlain.   2pp.

[36] The Besetting Sin Of Empires! Nebuchadnezzar's Pride And Punishment. By The Rev. Canon Scott-Holland.   2pp.

[37] The Meteor Flag Of England Up-To-Date. (Illus. Of Flag With Quotation From Mr. Morley's Speech Underneath.)   1p.

[38] Vengeance Or Rebellion! The Natal Loyalists' Threats! The Exceeding Patience Of The Dutch.   2pp.

[39] ———.

[40] Expanding Bullets: Who Use Them? Britons Or Boers? A Curious Chronicle Of Inconsistency.   2pp.

[41] That Petition! How It Was Got Up. Testimony Of Working Men.   2pp.

[42] Our Brave Brother Boer. The Verdict Of Tommy Atkins!   2pp.

[43] Ministers Of Religion And The War. Mr. Chamberlain On Their Responsibilities.   2pp.

[44] How To Win Love And Loyalty. The New Imperialism In Action.   2pp.

[45] An Artists View Of The South African War. (Cartoon By Henry Holiday.)   2pp.

[46] After Seven Months' War.... A Little Sum In Profit And Loss.   2pp.

[47] Some Quotations Worth Remembering.   2pp.

[48] Christ Or Moloch? Mr. Gladstone Versus Lord Rosebery! The Magnanimity Of Majuba!   2pp.

[unnumbered] Stop The War! Ten Good Reasons For Stopping The War. (Cartoon) (Chatham 1900.)   4pp.

[unnumbered] The New War In South Africa, And How It Is Being Carried On. Letter From An Officer In The Field.   19pp.

[unnumbered] Notice! To All Friends Of Peace.   2pp.
No title page, catalogued from caption.

[unnumbered] President Steyn And Lord Kitchener. Reply To The Proclamation. (See entry under NEW AGE, The.)

[unnumbered] Stop The War! An Appeal To The People. (Chatham 1900.)   1p.

[unnumbered] Stop The War! An Appeal To Women. (Chatham 1900.)   1p.

[unnumbered] The Trail Of The Financial Serpent. (See entry under BURNS. J.)

[unnumbered] What Is Now Being Done In South Africa. The Testimony Of British Soldiers At The Front.   4pp.

[A second leaflet marked No. 3.] The Men We Are Fighting And How We Are Fighting Them: An Army Chaplain's Report To Sir Charles Warren.   4pp.
No title page, catalogued from caption.

(Stop-The-War Committee/Blackpool) (Publisher) – Points To Ponder About The War. Pay! Pay! Pay!   4pp.

Story (A. T.) – Golden Deeds Of The War.
George Newnes
London 1900
xii+315pp. Illustrated.
189×124mm   p.73

Story (R. Douglas) (And Others) – Arbitration Or War? A View Of The

Transvaal Question, With A Glance Also At Arbitration In Politics Generally. Printed and published for F. Parker by Harrison & Sons
London 1899
90+i.pp.
8vo.
Analysis of the Transvaal question. The publisher supports a policy of arbitration rather than war in which opinion he is backed by members of the Transvaal Committee. The greatest part of the pamphlet was written by Mr. Story, a newspaper editor. Title from cover.

Stott (Clement H.) – The Boer Invasion Of Natal Being An Account Of Natal's Share Of The Boer War Of 1899–1900, As Viewed By A Natal Colonist.
S. W. Partridge & Co.
London 1900
224pp. Maps, illustrations.
190×130mm

Straus (Bertram S.) – Lecture By Mr. Bertram S. Straus, L.C.C., On 'The Relationship Between The Present War In South Africa And The Jameson Raid', Delivered At The Paddington Radical Club, On Monday, 26th February, 1900.
(Printer/publisher not shown)
London? 1900
15pp.
8vo.   M

Strong (Daniel B.) – Why The Boer Cause Should Command Our Sympathy And An Appeal For Arbitration.
Publisher/printer not shown
New York 1900
4pp.
Narrow Roy.8vo.   M

Stuart (John) – Pictures Of War.
Archibald Constable & Co. Ltd.
Westminster 1901
iv+414pp. With maps.
198×128mm

Sturrock (J. P.) (9176 I.Y.) – The Fifes In South Africa Being A History Of The Fife And Forfar Yeomanry In The South African War, 1900–1901.
A. Westwood & Son
Cupar-Fife 1903
xii+197pp. With map and illustrations.
225×148mm   p.ix
Author's name does not appear on title-page.

Sulzer (William) – The South African Republic. Speech Of Hon. William Sulzer, Of New York, In The House. . . . Mar. 27, 1900.
Govt. printing office
Washington 1900
8pp.
240mm   H
Title recorded at Library of Congress.

Sutherland (W. S.) – South African Sketches, Parodies, And Verses, Up-To-Date.
Midland Printing and Publishing Co.
Cradock (1901?)
96pp. Illustrated.
210mm   SABIB
Humorous sketches, verses, etc. connected with the author's experiences in Aliwal North while the town was occupied by Boers (Nov. 1899 – Mar. 1900).

Swaan (W.) (Printer) – An Address By Dutch Christian Ministers Of Religion To All English Clergymen And Other Ministers Upon The War In South-Africa.
W. Swaan/printer

Arnhem (1900?)
17pp.
220mm   SABIB
An appeal for the cessation of war.

Swinton (Sir Ernest) – The Defence Of Duffer's Drift, Etc. See entry under BACKSIGHT FORETHOUGHT.

(Swiss & Co.) (Army Printers) – 2nd Battalion South Wales Borderers. South African War 1899–1902.
Swiss & Co.
Devonport nd. (c.1902)
125pp. With folding map.
137×110mm   p.77

(Swiss & Co.) (Printers) – 1st Battalion Loyal North Lancashire Regiment. South African War 1899–1902.
Swiss & Co.
Devonport nd. (1903)
142pp.
138×108mm

Sykes (Harold Pratt) – Diary Of The Relief Of Mafeking, May, 1900. Printed For Private Circulation Only.
(No other information)
(c.1900)
16pp.
16mo.   M

Sykes (Jessica) – Side Lights On The War In South Africa Being Sketches Based On Personal Observation During A Few Weeks Residence In Cape Colony And Natal.
T. Fisher Unwin
London 1900
vii+156pp.
189×127mm   p.99

(Syme. David and Co.) – The 'Leader' Souvenir. Etc. See entry under PACKER (J. W.)

Symonds (Dr. H.) – Siege Of Kimberley Oct. 1899.
Dr. H. Symonds
Printer/publisher not shown
Dorchester nd. (c.1900)
14pp. (Printed rectos.)
255×205mm
A record of events during the siege being an extended letter from Dr. Symonds to his brother addressed as My dear E. – The letter is headed Kimberley Club and the final entry dated Feb. 24 (1900). The printed sheets are bound by Henry Ling of Dorchester. Possibly privately printed and limited to a few copies.

T

(T.) – An American View Of The South African Situation: How Australasia Might Help Great Britain, By 'T'.
(Published by the author?)
New York 1901
64pp.
200mm   SABIB
Author's name, E. T. Hargrove. An exposure of Britain's mistakes in connection with the war and in dealings with the Boer Republics.

Tainton (Clifton F.) – The War And Its Lessons. The Fighter Of The Future.
'African Review' Military Special.
African Review
London 1899?
20pp. Illustrated.
340mm   SABIB
Catalogued from cover. Author's name from end of text. M dates volume 1889?

Tait (Samuel) – A Siege Experience Etc. See – 'HIPPOPHAGIST'.

Tallichet (Ed:) – Europe And The Transvaal War. Translated By The Rev. Canon St. John. (With Denial By The Right Hon. Arthur J. Balfour.)
John Bellows
Gloucester nd. (1900?)
37pp.
183×121mm   RCSL

Tamplin (H. T.) – The Voyage Of The S.S. Bavarian, Which Sailed From Liverpool On March 25th, 1901. By H. T. Tamplin K.C.M.G. Lieut.-Colonel.
The London and Counties Publishing Co., Ltd.
London 1901
40pp.
Cr.8vo.   M
A description of life on board a transport.

Tamplin (H. T.) – The Voyage Of His Majesty's Transport 'Bavarian', Which Sailed From Liverpool On March 25th, 1901.
London & Counties Publishing Co.
London 1904
40pp.
180mm   SABIB
A copy of the 2nd Impression.

Taylor (D.) – Souvenir Of The Siege Of Mafeking. From Original Photographs By D. Taylor, Photographer, Mafeking, 1899–1900.
Sir W. C. Leng & Co. printers
Sheffield nd. (c.1900)
Double plate panoramic view together with plates numbered 1–114.
279×400mm

(Taylor, Garnett, Evans, & Co., Ltd.) (Publishers) – A Short History Of The 3rd Battalion The Prince Of Wales's Volunteers (South Lancashire Regiment) Formerly 4th Royal Lancashire (The Duke Of Lancaster's Own) Light Infantry Militia, Being Principally Extracts From The Regimental Records.
Author not shown
Taylor, Garnett, Evans, & Co., Ltd.
Manchester: Reddish and London 1909
112pp.
225×185mm
Much of the content concerns the war in South Africa.

Teller (Henry M.) – Papers Relating To War In South Africa. (Compilation)
Publisher/printer not shown
Washington 1900
36pp.
Size not shown   H
U.S. Senate, Document No.386, 56th Congress, 1st Session.

Tempelhof (Dr. W. G.) – With The Boers Round Kimberley. Being A Personal Narrative Of Scenes And Occurrences In The Enemy's Laagers During The Siege Of Kimberley, 1899–1900. By Dr. W. G. Tempelhof, Late Of Wolmaranstad, And Formerly Of Beaconsfield. Reprinted From 'The Diamond Fields Advertiser'.
'Diamond Fields Advertiser'
Kimberley (c.1900)
17pp.
215×140mm   CC
First published in the 'Diamond Fields Advertiser'. SABIB dates both original and reprint pamphlet, 1902.

Thackwell (Carrie) – Weaving In Wartime, And Earlier Poems.
R. F. Houlston/Bath
Houlston & Sons/London
1900
32pp.
135×195mm

Collection of poems on the war dedicated to 'A gentleman in kharki ordered south'.

('Theta') – The Situation In South Africa. A Historical Sketch By 'Theta'. Proceeds Given To Transvaal Relief Fund.
Dinwiddie, Walker & Co., Ltd.
Napier 1900
32pp.
8vo.   M
An account of the Boers down to the war of 1899–1902. Quotations are given from leading New York newspapers concerning President Kruger's ultimatum to Great Britain.

Thomas (C. H.) – Origin Of The Anglo-Boer War Revealed. The Conspiracy Of The 19th Century Unmasked.
Hodder & Stoughton
London 1900
viii+215pp.
200×132mm

(Thomas. R. E. & Co.) (Printers) – St. Paul's Cathedral. Form Of Prayer To Be Used On Friday, January 12, At 8 P.M., At A Farewell Service Attended By The City Of London Imperial Volunteers, Before Embarking For South Africa.
Printed by R. E. Thomas & Co.
(London 1900?)
8pp.
210mm   SABIB

Thompson (Col. C. W.) & Others – Seventh (Princess Royal's) Dragoon Guards. The Story Of The Regiment (1688–1882) And With The Regiment In South Africa (1900–1902).
'Daily Post' Printers
Liverpool 1913
xiv+168pp. Maps and plates
290×228mm
A volume in two parts. The South African War record, which forms the greater part of the book, is by Major N. D. H. Campbell, Capt. W. S. Whetherly & Capt. J. E. D. Holland.

Thompson (G. C.) – The Country And The War. A Paper Read At A Meeting Of The Cardiff Impartial Society, March 5th, 1900. With An Added Chapter On The Question Of The Suzerainty.
'Western Mail' Limited
Cardiff 1900
51pp.
8vo.   M

Thompson (H. M.) – General Election, 1900. Should The Electors Support The War Policy Of The Present Government?
Wm. Lewis
Cardiff (1900)
60pp.
8vo.   M

Thomson (Ada) – Memorials Of Charles Dixon Kimber, Lieut. 48th Co. Imperial Yeomanry. By His Sister, Ada Thomson.
James Nisbet & Co., Ltd
London 1902
viii+249pp. Plates and map.
198×130mm

Thomson (Ada) – 'Promoted': The Memorials Of Charles Dixon Kimber, Lieut. 48th Co. Imperial Yeomanry, By His Sister, Ada Thomson.
South Africa General Mission
Wimbledon 1915
x+187pp. Illustrated.
185×124mm
Card covered, copy of 6th edition.

Thomson (H. C.) – The Supreme Problem In South Africa. Capital And Labour. With Suggestions For The Basis Of An

Enduring Peace. Reprinted from the *Investors Review.*
John Paterson
London nd. (1900)
31pp.
210mm   SABIB

Thomson (Lieut.-Col. S. J.) – The Transvaal Burgher Camps South Africa.
Pioneer Press
Allahabad 1904
74pp. Folding plans.
180×125mm
Author was director of the Transvaal Burgher Camps.

Tilly (Olive) – 'The Battle Angel' Dedicated To The Memory Of The New Zealanders Who Have Fallen In The Transvaal.
J. B. Berry
Auckland 1901
6pp. Illustrated.
255mm   BIM
Title from cover. War poetry.

('Times Of Ceylon') (Publishers) – Our Boer Prisoners. Supplement To The 'Times Of Ceylon'. Special Edition.
'Times Of Ceylon' Printing Dept.
(Colombo 1900?)
2+7+1pp. Portraits, plates and facsimiles, no text except captions.
170×250mm   SABIB
Catalogued from cover.

Tod (Noel Moir) – Letters From Ladysmith.
Privately printed
Publisher/printer not shown
np./nd. (c.1900)
28pp. Map and illustrations.
245×160mm
In memory of Lieut. Tod, of the Cameronians, killed in action at Ladysmith. Paper covered.

Toogood (Arthur) – A Battle Ode.
H. I. Jones, printer
Wanganui 1900
16pp.
205mm   BIM
Title from cover. War poetry.

(Toronto Printing Co.) (Publisher?) – Souvenir Toronto Contingent Of Volunteers For Service In Anglo-Boer War.
Toronto Printing Co.
Toronto 1899
46pp. Illustrated. (Printed rectos.)
150×225mm   WS

(Townshend & Son) (Publisher) – The Mafeking Mail Special Siege Slip.
Townshend & Son
Mafeking 1900
152 issues. (Complete set.)
400×265mm
Reprint of newspapers published in Mafeking Nov. 1, 1899 to May 31, 1900. The volume includes a preface and list of defending forces.

(Townshend & Son) (Printers) – Concise Diary, First Division South African Field Force Under Command Of Lieut.-General Lord Methuen.
Townshend & Son, printers
Vryburg 1902
13pp.
210mm   SABIB
Oct. 21, 1899 to March 20, 1902, when Major-Gen. Sir J. G. Maxwell assumed command.

(Townshend, Taylor & Snashall) (Printers) – Reprint Of The Principal Army Orders And Lines Of

Communication Orders Since Outbreak Of Hostilities To 31st January, 1900. (For Reference.)
Townshend, Taylor & Snashall, printers
Capetown (1900?)
70pp. Tables.
250mm   SABIB

(Townshend, Taylor and Snashall) (Printers) – Additional Reprint Of The Principal Army Orders, Lines Of Communication Orders And Base Orders From 1st February, 1900 To 31st March, 1900. (For Reference.)
Townshend, Taylor and Snashall (Printers)
(Capetown 1900?)
51pp.
230mm   SABIB

(Townshend, Taylor and Snashall) (Printers) – Additional Reprint Of The Principal Army Orders And Lines Of Communication Orders, From 1st August 1900, To 30th September, 1900. (For Reference.)
Townshend, Taylor and Snashall (Printers)
(Capetown 1900?)
55pp.
250mm   SABIB

(Townshend, Taylor & Snashall) (Printers) – South Africa. Revised Reprint Of The Principal Army Orders, Lines Of Communication Orders And Cape Colony District Orders From Outbreak Of Hostilities To The End Of July, 1901, With The Principal Headquarters' Circular Memos. For 1900 & 1901. (For Reference.)
Townshend, Taylor & Snashall, printers
Cape Town (1901?)
238+1pp. With tables.
320mm   SABIB
No title page. Catalogued from cover.

(Townshend, Taylor & Snashall) (Printers) – Protest Of The Refugee Committee, Cape Town, Against Capitalistic Legislation In The Transvaal.
Townshend, Taylor & Snashall, printers
Cape Town 1900
24pp.
244×154mm   RCSL

(Townshend, Taylor and Snashall) (Printers) – The Capitalist & The Empire In The Transvaal. Issued By The Refugee Committee Of The Uitlanders, Cape Town, 15th October, 1900.
Townshend, Taylor and Snashall, printers
Cape Town 1900
16pp.
241×151mm   RCSL
Reference to the resumption of business activity in the colony following hostilities.

(Townshend, Taylor and Snashall) (Printers) – District Aliwal North. Martial Law Regulations. August 15, 1901. In English And Dutch (With Index).
Townshend, Taylor and Snashall (Printers)
Cape Town 1901
viii+28pp., viii+30pp.
110mm   SABIB
English and Dutch text. Signed F. G. Stone, Major R. G. A., Commandant Aliwal North District. No title page. Catalogued from cover.

(Townshend, Taylor & Snashall) (Printers) – Martial Law Regulations For Cape Ports, 1901.
Townshend, Taylor & Snashall
Cape Town 1901
iii+12pp.
120mm   SABIB
No title page. Catalogued from cover.

(Townshend, Taylor & Snashall)
(Printers) – Important Truths About The
War In South Africa. Reprint From
The Banner Of Israel.
Townshend, Taylor & Snashall, printers
(Cape Town 1902?)
16pp.
210mm   SABIB
*Comments on the war from the standpoint
of British Israelites.*

(Townshend, Taylor & Snashall)
(Printers) – Martial Law In Cape Colony.
1901–2. 3rd ed.
Townshend, Taylor & Snashall, printers
Cape Town 1902
vi+89pp.
180mm   SABIB
*'The present edition embodies martial law
circulars nos. 1–17 issued since the
publication of the 1st edition dated 1st
May 1901, etc.'*

(Transatlantic Society Of America)
(Publisher) – The South African War:
A Word Of Truth.
The Society
Philadelphia 1902
26pp.
190mm   SABIB
*Case presented from a pro-British point
of view.*

(Transvaal Colony) – Proclamation By
Lord Kitchener, High Commissioner,
Dated August 7th, 1901. Letter From
Lord Kitchener, To Comdt.-General
Louis Botha, Dated August 6th, 1901.
Letter From Lord Kitchener To Mr.
M. T. Steyn, Dated August 6th, 1901.
The Following Letters, Which Were
Captured By The British Forces At
Reitz, O.R.C., Are Also Included:
Letter From Mr. Reitz To The
Government Secretary, O.F.S. Dated
May 10th, 1901. Letter From Mr. Steyn
To Mr. Reitz, Dated May 15th, 1901.
Printer/publisher not shown
nd. (1901)
10pp.
380mm   SABIB
*Pamphlet in English and Dutch.
Pagination includes covers.*

(Transvaal Colony) (Proclamations) – See
entries under GOVERNMENT PRINTING
WORKS and WATERLOW and Sons.

(Transvaal Colony) (Surveyor-General's
Office) – Register Of Soldiers' Graves In
The Transvaal. See entries under
(GRAVES)

(Transvaal Committee/London)
(Published By) – Pamphlets issued
London 1899/1900. Some titles are listed
under author. List extracted from SABIB
and M.
General size 220mm.

Shall We Destroy The Transvaal
Republic And Cause Civil War In South
Africa? (1899)   2pp.
*No title page. Catalogued from caption
title.*

Sir William Harcourt On The Objects Of
The War. (1899)   2pp.

South African History (Reprinted From
The 'Morning Leader') (1899)   4pp.

A Summary Of The Controversy
Between Great Britain And The
Transvaal. (1899)   4pp.

The Transvaal Crisis. Report Of A Public
Meeting Held In St. Martin's Town Hall
On Monday, July 10th, 1899, 'To Protest
Against Reckless Threats Of War With
The Transvaal'. (1899)   25pp.

Speech In The House Of Commons On
February 7th, 1900, By Dr. G. B. Clark,
M.P., In Support Of Mr. Redmond's
Amendment. (1900)   8pp.

Our Boer Policy: An Historical Sketch.
By Dr. G. B. Clark, M.P. (Formerly
Consul-General Of The South African
Republic) (1900)   32pp.

The Transvaal Question. Some Views Of
Mr. Frank Watkins, Late Member Of
The Transvaal Second Volksraad.
(1900)   8pp.
*No title page. Catalogued from caption
title.*

Two Wars Of Independence. America,
1775–1782. Africa 1899. (1900?)   4pp.
*No title page. Catalogued from caption
title.*

The War. An Appeal To The Patriotism
Of Members Of Parliament Against The
Brutal And Cowardly Policy Of The
Government.(1900)   7pp.
Entered under PRO PATRIA.

Report Of Six Months Work. (1900) 4pp.
*No title page. Catalogued from caption
title.*

('Transvaal Leader' Office) (Publisher) –
South African Irregular Forces
Sustentation Fund. Report Of The
Administrative Committee From The
Establishment Of The Fund In
November, 1899, To The 30th April,
1905.
'Transvaal Leader' Office
Johannesburg 1905
10+1pp.
320mm   SABIB

(Transvaal Leader Printing And
Publishing Syndicate) (Printers) –
Re-print Of Circulars Issued By The
Director Of Supplies, Army
Headquarters, South Africa, 1902.
Transvaal Leader Printing and Publishing
Syndicate
Johannesburg (1902?)
99+iv.pp. Illustrations/tables.
240mm   SABIB
Illustrations consist of specimen forms.

Treleaven (W. W.) – The Truth About
The Transvaal. A Short History Of The
Boers. Reprinted From The 'Manchester
Courier' September 30, 1899.
Thos. Sowler & Sons, Ltd.
16pp.
8vo.   M
*The Transvaal troubles re-stated.
A retrospect and a forecast. Published on
the eve of war.*

Tremayne (Capt. J. H.) – XIII Hussars.
South African War. Etc. See entry under
MAY & Co. Printers.

Treves (Sir Frederick) – The Tale Of
A Field Hospital.
Cassell and Company, Limited
London, Paris, New York & Melbourne
1900
viii+109pp. Illustrated.
196×164mm
*Various editions published 1900–1912
bound in limp morocco or cloth.
A clothbound edition of 1912 lacks
all plates apart from a portrait frontispiece
of author.
Clothbound edition of 1902, 203×165mm
Clothbound edition of 1912, 194×128mm*

Trimble (W. C.) – The Royal Inniskilling
Fusiliers At The Battle Of Inniskilling
Hill, Fought In South Africa, February
23 And 24, 1900, As Told In Verse....

With Illustrations Of The Battlefield, The
Officers Who Fell, &c.
'Impartial Reporter' Office
Enniskillen (1901?)
24pp. Illustrated.
260×380mm   SABIB

(Trimble, W. M.) (Printer) – A Short
Account Of The Part Played By The First
Battalion The Royal Inniskilling Fusiliers
During The South African Campaign
October 1899–May 1902. Published By
The Regiment As A Memento Of The
Campaign.
W. M. Trimble (Printer)
'Impartial Reporter' Office
Enniskillen 1903
109pp.
210×136mm   p.101

('True American') – The South African
Republics *vs.* Great Britain.... By
A True American.
Printer/publisher not shown
New York 1900
37pp. (Addenda inserted 9pp.)
210×180mm
*SABIB lists author as J. F. Sleeper. See
other entries under Sleeper.*

(T. T. & S.) (Printers) – The War In
South Africa. The Terms Of Peace.
Reprinted From The 'Spectator' March
3rd, 1899.
T. T. & S. (Townshend, Taylor &
Snashall)
(Cape Town) (1900)
8pp.
8vo.   M
*A pamphlet printed in English and Dutch
advocating equality between the races after
the war. 'March 3rd, 1899' is changed to
March 3rd, 1900 in SABIB. The latter
states the title, in both English and Dutch,
is taken from the cover.*

(T. T. And S.) (Printers) – Addenda And
Corrigenda, No. 2, To Fifth Printed List
Of Casualties From The 1st July To The
31st December, 1901.
T. T. And S. printers
Cape Town 1902
xvii pp.
327×215mm   CC
*See entries under CASUALTIES and
CASUALTY LISTS/WAR OFFICE.*

Tucker (Lt. Gen. C.) – Report On
Organisation And Equipment Of
Infantry. See WO. 89.

Tullibardine (The Marchioness of)
(Editor) – A Military History Of
Perthshire 1899–1902 With A Roll Of
The Perthshire Men Of The Present Day
Who Have Seen Active Service Under
The British Flag Compiled By The Editor
& Jane C. C. Macdonald.
R. A. & J. Hay/Perth
J. Maclehose & Sons/Glasgow
William Brown/Edinburgh
1908
xxi+316pp. Maps, portraits and
illustrations.
252×190mm   p.99

Turner (David) – A Schoolmasters
Experience Of Life Amongst The Boers,
Before And During The War.
Central Educational Co./Derby, &
Simpkin Marshal/London
(1901?)
58pp.
180mm   SABIB
Probably Simpkin Marshall/London.

Twain (Mark) – To The Person Sitting
In Darkness.
Anti-Imperialist League of
New York

Reprinted by permission from the
North American Review 1901
16pp.
171×110mm
*Reference to the South African, and
other conflicts.*

Twisleton (Corporal F.) – With The
New Zealanders At The Front: A Story
Of Twelve Month's Campaigning In
South Africa.
Edmondson and Co.
Skipton nd. (c.1901)
iv+187pp. Frontispiece.
186×120mm
*Volume published in cloth binding and
limp card. Card covered edition
180×122mm.*

(Tydeman J. R.) (Printer) – A Protest
Against The Cooking Up And
Dissemination Of Old And Stale News
As To The Present War In South Africa.
J. R. Tydeman, printer
Horsham 1901
4pp.
8vo.   M
Writer signs himself 'B'.

U

(Uitlander) – Letters From An Uitlander,
1899–1902. See entry under MURRAY
John.

Unger (F. W.) – With 'Bobs' And Kruger
Experiences And Observations Of An
American War Correspondent In The
Field With Both Armies.
Henry T. Coates and Company
Philadelphia 1901
x+412pp. Illustrated.
210×140mm

(Unionist Party) (Publisher) – Election
pamphlets printed London 1900 by
McCorquodale & Co. 2–4pp. Fifteen
titles listed in SABIB Vol.4 p.580. Some
relate to the present war.
220mm

'Stop The War'.	2pp.
Friend Or Foe, Briton Or Boer.	2pp.
Peace: Who Can Make It?	2pp.
Kruger And Arbitration.	2pp.
The War In South Africa, Who Began It? Why, The Boers Did!	2pp.
The Discovered Letters, Three Pro-Boer English M.P.'s.	4pp.
Who Provoked The War?	2pp.

**(United States) (Adjutant General's
Office)** (Publisher) – Notes Of Military
Interest For 1901. No. XXXVI. [& 1902.
No. XXXVIII.]
Government Printing Office
Washington 1902–1903
2 vols. Pagination not shown. Folding
maps and diagrams.
230mm   SABIB
*Observations made throughout on
apparatus, conduct and techniques of
South African War.*

**(United States) (Congress. House Of
Representatives)** (Publisher) – Horses,
Mules, Etc. Shipped To South Africa.
Message From The President Of The
United States, Transmitting Report And
Accompanying Papers Concerning
Shipments Of Horses, Mules, And Other
Supplies From Louisiana To The Seat Of
War In South Africa.

Government Printing Office
Washington (1902?)
27pp.
230mm   SABIB

(United States War Dept.) (Publishers) –
Reports On Military Operations In South
Africa And China. See entry under
GOVERNMENT PRINTING OFFICE.

(United States War Department)
(Publishers) – Selected Translations
Pertaining To The Boer War. See entry
under GOVERNMENT PRINTING
OFFICE.

(University Press) (Publisher) – The
Knapsack Bible South African Field
Force 1899–1900.
University Press
Oxford 1899
983pp.
12mo.   L/W 485
*Pocket bible issued to troops in South
Africa.*

(University Press) (Publisher) – South
Africa 1900 The Gospel According To
St. John.
University Press
Oxford 1900
80pp.

(Unwin. T. Fisher) (Publisher) – How To
Read War News A Vade-Mecum Of
Notes And Hints To Readers Of
Despatches And Intelligence From The
Seat Of War With A Coloured War Map
And A Glossary Of Military Technical
Terms, Local, African And Dutch
Phrases, Etc. Also A Supplementary
Chapter On The Situation By Dr. G. M.
Theal.
T. Fisher Unwin (publisher)
London 1900
140pp. With folding map.
147×96mm   p.58

V

(Vacher & Sons) (Printers) – Mr. Lloyd-
George, M.P., And Concentration
Camps. (By A Welsh Barrister Who Has
Served In The Ranks.)
Vacher & Sons, Printers
Westminster (1902)
12pp.
211×138mm   CC
*Catalogued from cover. At end of text –
A Welsh barrister who has served in the
ranks. The writer questions the truth of
Lloyd-George's reference in a speech to
the slaughter of thousands of children in
South Africa.*

Valintine (H. P.) – Ten Weeks A Prisoner
Of War.
Geddis and Blomfield
Wellington, N.Z. 1901
29pp. Folding plan.
250mm   SABIB
*Description of life at the prisoner-of-war
camp at Waterval, Tvl.*

Vander Byl (C. F.) – Patrolling In South
Africa. Illustrated.
Gale & Polden
London (1901?)
vii+43pp. With diagrams.
130mm   SABIB
*Author belonged to the 16th Lancers. No
other information.*

Vander Byl (Captain C. F.) – Patrolling
In South Africa, With Hints On Training
Scouts At Home. (Second Edition.
Illustrated.)

Gale & Polden Ltd.
London/Aldershot 1902
79pp. Illustrated.
Minimo.   M

Van Der Hoogt (C. W.) – A Century Of
Injustice. Synopsis Of A Message To The
People Of U.S.A. Sent By The
Government Of The S.A. Republic.
Printer/publisher not shown
Baltimore 1899
119pp. Illustrated.
8vo.   M

Van Der Hoogt (C. W.) – The Story Of
The Boers, Narrated By Their Own
Leaders. Prepared Under The Authority
Of The South African Republics By
C. W. Van Der Hoogt. Illustrated.
Preceded By The Policy Of Mediation,
By Montagu White, Late Consul-General
To The South African Republics.
Harper & Brothers, Publishers
New York/London 1900
ix+284pp. Maps and illustrations.
190×125mm

(Van de Sandt de Villiers & Co.)
(Printers) – The People's Congress.
Worcester, 6th December, 1900.
(Reprinted From The *'South African
News'.*) Het Volks Congres. Worcester,
6 December, 1900. (Overgedrukt uit
'Ons Land'.)
Van de Sandt de Villiers & Co., printers
Cape Town 1900
36pp.
250mm   SABIB
*Catalogued from cover. Pamphlet in
English and Dutch. – A continuation of
discussions held by Afrikaners in Cape
Colony after annexation of O.F.S. See
also – (Volkskongres) – Report of the
proceedings, etc.*

Van Siclen (George W.) – American
Sentiment. A Plebiscite Upon The
Boer War.
(Printer/publisher not shown)
(New York 1900?)
22pp.
230×145mm

Van Warmelo (D.) – On Commando.
Methuen & Co.
London 1902
viii+183pp. Portrait frontispiece.
198×130mm   p.63

Varley (H.) – God's Settling Day
Recent National Events And The South
African War.
Alfred Holness
London nd. (c.1900)
24pp.
185×105mm
*Hope expressed for a British victory in the
present war to end slavery in South
Africa.*

Vaughan (E. L.) (Compiler) – List Of
Etonians Who Served In South Africa
Between October 11, 1899, And May 31,
1902.
Spottiswoode and Co., Ltd.
Eton College 1908
viii+64pp.
200×142mm

Verner (Lieut.-Colonel Willoughby)
(Compiled and edited by) – The Rifle
Brigade Chronicle For 1900. (Eleventh
Year). Centenary Number.
John Bale, Sons and Danielsson, Ltd.
London 1901
xvi+409pp. Folding maps and plates.
216×139mm
*Much on the war in South Africa,
including events at Ladysmith.*

Verner (Lieut.-Colonel Willoughby)
(Compiled and edited by) – The Rifle
Brigade Chronicle For 1901.
John Bale, Sons and Danielsson, Ltd.
London 1902
xii+184pp. Illustrated.
220×140mm
*Contains reference to 2nd Batt. in
South Africa.*

Vernon-Harcourt (F. C.) – The Bible On
The Battlefield.
Marshall Brothers
London nd. (c.1901)
xvi+329pp. Illustrated.
195×130mm
Cover title – The Bible In The Battlefield.

Viljoen (Gen. Ben) – My Reminiscences
Of The Anglo-Boer War.
Hood, Douglas, & Howard
London 1902
542pp. Maps and illustrations.
191×127mm

Viljoen (Gen. Ben) – My Reminiscences
Of The Anglo-Boer War. (Popular Ed.)
Hood, Douglas, & Howard
London 1903
313pp. Frontispiece.
230×145mm

Viljoen (Ben J.) – An Exiled General.
A. Noble Printing Company
St. Louis 1906
62+pp.5–312. With frontispiece and
plates.
220×147mm
*Volume published to raise funds for
destitute Boer families emigrating to the
United States. Two parts. The first relates
to the early history of South Africa and
the second relates to the author's war
experiences.*

Villebois-Mareuil (Count Georges De) –
War Notes. The Diary Of Colonel De
Villebois-Mareuil, From November 24th,
1899, To March 7th, 1900. Authorised
Translation From The 'Paris Liberte' By
Frederic Lees. With A Preface By E. M.
De Vogüé Member Of The Académie
Française.
Adam & Charles Black
London 1901
xx+283pp.
197×130mm   p.83

Villebois-Mareuil (Count Georges De) –
War Notes. The Diary Of Colonel De
Villebois-Mareuil From November 24th,
1899, To April 4th, 1900; Etc. (Copy of
the 2nd Ed.)
Adam & Charles Black
London 1902
xx+352pp.
190mm   SABIB

Vincent (Sir Howard) – In A Boer
Concentration Camp (From 'The
Times'.)
Geo. J. Cosburn
Newbury nd.
Pagination not shown.
Pamphlet listed in THB.

Vincent (Sir C. E. Howard) – The British
Volunteers In South Africa. What They
Did, And How They Did It. Extracts
From The Orders Of General Officers
And Colonels Commanding The Regular
Battalions, Under Whom They Served.
Vacher & Sons
London 1901
15pp.
8vo.   M

Vincent (Sir Charles Edward Howard) –
Lessons Of The War. Royal United

Service Institution, Whitehall. Special
Address By Colonel Sir Howard Vincent,
K.C.M.G., C.B., M.P., Commanding
Queen's Westminster Volunteers.
'Personal Observations And Impressions
Of The Forces And Military
Establishments Now In South Africa'.
General Maurice, C.B., R.A.,
Commanding Woolwich District, In The
Chair. . . .
Geo. J. Cosburn, printer
Newbury (1900?)
35pp.
210mm   SABIB

Vincent (Sir Charles Edward Howard) –
Lessons Of The War. Royal United
Service Institution. . . . Special Address
By Colonel Sir Howard Vincent,
K.C.M.G., C.B., M.P., Commanding
The Queen's Westminster Volunteers.
'Personal Observations And Impressions
Of The Forces And Military
Establishments In South Africa'. Major-
General Sir Frederick Maurice, K.C.B.,
R.A., Commanding Woolwich District,
In The Chair. Republished By Request
And Permission Of The Council.
Printed and published by
Geo. J. Cosburn
Newbury (1900?)
36pp.
210mm   SABIB
*Revised and brought up to date –
16-6-1900.*

Vincent (Sir Charles Edward Howard) –
Special Address. Royal United Service
Institution, Whitehall, On Wednesday,
January 29th, 1902. The Situation In
South Africa. Further Personal
Observations And Impressions By
Colonel Sir Howard Vincent, K.C.M.G.,
C.B., V.D., M.P., Aide-De-Camp To
The King, In Continuation Of The
Address Of April 9th, 1900.
Printed and published by
Geo. J. Cosburn
Newbury (1902?)
64pp.
220mm   SABIB
Catalogued from cover.

(Virtue & Company Limited. H.)
(Publishers) – War With The Boers.
Illustrated.
H. Virtue & Company Limited
London nd. (c.1902)
20 parts.
259×193mm
*Paper covers. A history of the war in 20
parts, supplied to subscribers only. Title
and imprint details from cover. See entry
under BROWN, H. and GREW, E. Sharpe
– War With The Boers, etc.*

Vivers (R. W.) – Letters From South
Africa, March To September, 1902.
To Which Is Added A Selection Of
Original Verses.
Privately printed
London 1902
111pp.
8vo.   M
*Reference to political state of the country
at the end of the war.*

(Volkskongres) (Graaff-Reinet) – Report
Of The Proceedings Of the People's
Congress Held At Graaff-Reinet, Cape
Colony, 31st May, 1900.
('The Congress'?)
(Graaff-Reinet 1900?)
pp.5–20.
210mm   SABIB
No title-page. Catalogued from cover.

(Volkskongres) (Worcester) – See VAN
DE SANDT DE VILLIERS & Co., Printers
– The People's Congress, etc.

**(Vredes Comité's In De Oranje Rivier
Kolonie)** – See ARGUS Co., Printers –
Report Of The Deputation, Etc.

W

Wakinshaw (J. W.) – The Editor Edited.
The *Newcastle Daily Chronicle* And The
South African War.
William H. Robinson
Newcastle-on-Tyne (1902?)
32pp.
210mm   SABIB
Name of author from text.

Waldegrave (John) – Papers By
John Waldegrave.
Printed for private circulation (Printer
not shown.)
London 1903
5+128pp.
230mm   SABIB
*Author joined the British Army in South
Africa in 1901. He died at Lichtenburg
April 4, 1901. Several papers relate to his
experiences at the front.*

Walker (John & Co.) (Publishers) –
Commanders Of The Empire Nos. 1–3.
Soldiers.
London (c.1900)
240mm   SABIB
*3 vols. Each contains 12 brief biographies
and portraits of British officers, most of
whom served in South Africa. SABIB
states parts 1–3 published by (Piccadilly,
Bradford, Views, Limited 1900?).*

Walker (J. S.) – Copy Of A Letter To
'The Times', August 29th, 1899, On The
Transvaal Military Organization.
Chas. J. Thynne
London (1899?)
8pp.
120×90mm   SABIB

Walker (Capt. R. S.) – Interim Report
On Searchlights, Etc. See WO. 125.

Wallace (Edgar) – War! And Other
Poems.
Townshend, Taylor & Snashall,
printers for *Eastern Press*
Cape Town (1899?)
10pp.
210mm   SABIB
*Poems for the period. Eastern Press series
No. 1. Poems on the South African War.
(No. 2 in the series see – JOE, Dennison).
Series 1 & 2 paged continuously, i.e.,
1–10+ii+11–18. Part 2 illustrated.*

Wallace (Edgar) – Unofficial Dispatches.
Hutchinson & Co.
London nd. (c.1900)
viii+pp.9–327. With double frontispiece.
192×125mm
*Some copies have cover title – Unofficial
Despatches.*

Wallace (Edgar) – Writ In Barracks.
Methuen & Co.
London 1900
121pp.
Cr.8vo.   M
*M. – A volume of poems, the majority of
which are written on subjects connected
with the British army in the South African
War.*

Wallace (D) and Boyd (F. D.) (Editors) –
Report Of The Work Of The Edinburgh
And East Of Scotland South African
Hospital.
Oliver and Boyd
Edinburgh 1901
x+193pp. Folding plan, charts and plates.
226×180mm   p.118

Walsh (Walter) – Boers Wha Hae Wi'
Botha Bled. See – MATHEW, James P.,
printers.

Walsh (Walter) – The Briton And The
Boer: An Appeal From Philip Drunk To
Philip Sober. (4th ed.)
James P. Mathew
Dundee (1900?)
16pp.
220mm
*Pro-Boer pamphlet. SABIB lists date of 1st
ed. 1899. 4th and 5th ed. (1900?). 6th ed.
(1901?). No title page. Catalogued from
cover.*

(War Pictures) – See (PEARSON, C.
Arthur).

Walter (Maj. J. M.) – Rules For
Guidance Of Press Censors In
South Africa; By Maj. J. M. Walter,
May, 1901.
Military Intelligence Directorate
Army Headquarters
Pretoria 1901
10pp.   MOD
Item from War Office library. WO. ref. –
WH Loc: ID21; SA58; Camps Boer.

(Walters. W.) (Publisher) – The New
Testament Of Our Lord And Saviour
Jesus Christ. Illustrated From Original
Drawings Made In The Holy Land, By
H. A. Harper And J. Clark.
W. Walters
London (1900?)
400pp. Illustrated.
*Cover title – Soldier's New Testament:
South Africa 1900.*

Ward (Rev. H.) – The Pulpit And
The War, A Paper Read At A Meeting
Of The 'Malton Clerical Society'
On February 19, 1900, By The Rev.
H. Ward, Vicar Of Appleton-Le-Street.
John Sampson
York (1900)
15pp.
8vo.   M

(War Office) – Publications are listed in
two groups. Titles numbered 1–162 are
extracted from a list supplied by the
Ministry of Defence Library, London,
and are entered hereunder together with
library reference. Other War Office
entries are drawn from various sources.

[1] Memorandum [On South Africa] By
Gen. Sir R. H. Buller, With Comments
By F. M. Viscount Wolseley, July 1899.
WO. 1899
3pp.
WH Loc: SA65.

[2] Memorandum [On South Africa] By
F. M. Viscount Wolseley, Aug. 1899.
WO. 1899
3pp.
WH Loc: SA65.

[3] Reports On Magersfontein, Dec.
1899.
WO. 1900
5pp.
WH Loc: SA65.

[4] Responsibility For The Occupation Of
Ladysmith, The Defence Of Kimberley
And The Occupation Of Mafeking,
Jan. 1900.
WO. 1900
3pp.
WH Loc: SA65.

[5] Report On The Delay In Bringing
Force From Beira To The Front; By
Lt.Gen. Sir F. Carrington, Aug. 1900.
WO. 1900
2pp.
WH Loc: SA65.

[6] Journal Of The Principal Events
Connected With South Africa. Parts
1–16, May 1899–July 1902.
WO. 1901–02
Bound in 2 vols. (Var. pag.)
WH Loc: ID22; SA9; Cc295.

[7] Correspondence On The Action By
Lt.Col. Thorneycroft In Withdrawing
From Spion Kop.
WO. 1902
7pp.
WH Loc: SA65.

[8] Lt.Gen. Lord Methuen's Report On
The Engagement Which Took Place On
7 Mar. 1902 Between Tweebosch And
Leeuwkuil In The Lichtenberg District.
WO. 1902
5pp.
WH Loc: SA20.

[9] Recommendations By Various
Military Authorities During Last Summer
As To Reinforcements For South Africa
And Principal Events Which Led Up
To War.
WO. 1902
3pp.
WH Loc: SA65.

[10] Translations From Foreign Journals
Relating To The Recent War In South
Africa, Oct. 1902.
WO. Intelligence Division, 1902
56pp.
324×203mm
WH Loc: SA36A; SA40.

[11] Military Retrospect Of The War In
South Africa Translated From *Beiheft
Zum Militar Wochenblatt*, 1901; By Maj.
J. E. Edmonds.
WO. Intelligence Division, 1902
19pp.
WH Loc: SA36B.

[12] South Africa War, 1899–1900: Home
And Oversea Correspondence By F. M.
Lord Roberts. Vol. I. – From 12 Dec.
1899 To 4 June 1900 (Nos. 1–651).
WO. 1904
xxv+134pp.
WH Loc: SA66.

[13] South Africa War, 1899–1900: Home
And Oversea Correspondence By F. M.
Lord Roberts. Vol. II. – From 5 June To
5 Sept. 1900 (Nos. 652–1122).
WO. 1904
xv+76pp.
WH Loc: SA66.

[14] South Africa War, 1899–1900: Home
And Oversea Correspondence By F. M.
Lord Roberts. Vol. III. – From 5 Sept.
1900 To 1 Jan. 1901 (Nos. 1124–1663).
WO. 1904
xix+108pp.
WH Loc: SA66.

[15] Correspondence With Boer Leaders.
WO. 1901
28pp.
WH Loc: SA65.

[16] List Of Transvaal Commandos And
Their Approximate Strength On 1 May
1901; Prepared By Field Intelligence
Department, South Africa.
WO. 1901
7pp.
WH Loc: SA59.

[17] Boer Organisation In Orange River
Colony.
WO. 1901
5pp.
WH Loc: SA59.

[18] Translations Of Boer Documents
Forwarded To The War Office By
Director Military Intelligence, South
Africa.
WO. 1901–2
(Var. pag.)
WH Loc: SA65.

[19] Boer Forces In The Field [Strengths];
By Lt.Col. David Henderson, Mar. 1902.
WO. 1902
2pp.
WH Loc: SA65.

[20] Translation Of Consular
Correspondence And Other Official
Documents Of The Late Orange Free
State Found Buried In The Orange River
Colony, Apr. 1902.
WO. 1902
49pp.
WH Loc: SA65.

[21] Memorandum On Cavalry, Artillery
And Infantry Drafts During The South
African Campaign, 1899–1901; By Col.
F. S. Robb, Sept. 1902.
WO. 1902
15pp.
WH Loc: SA50.
Item marked – Confidential.

[22] South African Garrisons, May 1903.
(WO. 1903?)
2pp.
WH Loc: SA50.

[23] South African Garrison.
(WO. 1903?)
3pp.
WH Loc: SA50.

[24] South African Surrenders, Being
Some Account Of The Recorded
Surrenders Of British Troops Which
Took Place During The South African
War, 1899–1902 And Of The Action
Subsequently Taken In Connection
Therewith.
WO. Apr. 1905
viii+261pp.
WH Loc: SA7A.

[25] Report On Adjutant General's
Department; By Maj.Gen. W. F. Kelly,
July 1900.
(WO.?) 1902
8pp.
*WH Loc: SA39M/PRO Loc: WO.
108/260.*

[26] Auxiliary Forces For Service In
South Africa. Royal Warrants And Army
Orders, Feb. 1903.
WO. 1903
66pp.
WH Loc: SA43.

[27] South African Colonial Irregular
Corps: Approximate Strength, Jan. 1901.
WO. 1901
2pp.
WH Loc: SA50; SA65.

[28] South Africa, 1899–1900. Colonial
And Indian Contingents For Operations
In South Africa [Strengths] Apr. 1900.
WO. 1900
23pp.
WH Loc: SA61.

[29] Detail Of 6 Infantry Division For
Service Abroad, Dec. 1899.
(WO.?) 1899
3pp.
WH Loc: SA50.

[30] Detail Of 7 Division For Service
Abroad, Dec. 1899.
(WO.?) 1899
3pp.
WH Loc: SA50.

[31] Detail Of 8 Infantry Division For
Service Abroad, Dec. 1899.
(WO.?) 1899
3pp.
WH Loc: SA50.

[32] Report On The Imperial Yeomanry
In South Africa; By Maj.Gen. J. P. B.
Brabazon, Oct. 1900.
(WO.?) 1902
12pp.

WH Loc: SA39S/PRO Loc: WO.
108/263. See entries under IMPERIAL
YEOMANRY.

[33] Report Of Col. A. G. Lucas, Deputy
Adjutant General Of The Force
Regarding The Raising Of Drafts And
New Battalions For The Imperial
Yeomanry.
(WO.?) 1902
287pp.
WH Loc: SA11B.

[34] Scheme For An Indian Contingent
For Operations In South Africa; By
Brig.Gen. Alfred Gaselee, Office Of
QMG, India, Aug. 1899.
WO. 1899
12pp.
WH Loc: SA65.

[35] Telegrams On Employment Of
Natives As Troops Or Police, Mar. 1902.
(WO.?) 1902
2pp.
WH Loc: SA65.

[36] Reports From Ordnance Officers In
South Africa On The Working Etc. Of
The Army Ordnance Department.
(WO.?) 1901
92pp.
WH Loc: SA30/PRO Loc: WO. 108/245.

[37] Reports From Ordnance Officers In
Natal, South Africa On The Working
Etc. Of The Army Ordnance
Department.
(WO.?) nd.
27pp.
WH Loc: SA31.

[38] Report On Army Ordnance
Department; By Col. R. F. Noel Clarke.
July 1900.
(WO.?) 1902
8pp.
WH Loc: SA39T/PRO Loc: WO.
108/244.

[39] Answers To Questions From Various
Branches Of The Quartermaster-
General's Department By Officers
Employed In South Africa.
(WO.?) 1901
207pp. Maps. Illustrations.
WH Loc: SA32; Cttee. Rpts.

[40] Natal Field Force [Staff List]
Oct. 1899.
WO. 1899
2pp.
WH Loc: SA50.

[41] Lines Of Communication [Staff List]
Oct. 1899.
WO. 1899
3pp.
WH Loc: SA50.

[42] Staff Of 1 Army Corps, Oct. 1899.
WO. 1899
6pp.
WH Loc: SA50.

[43] Staff 5 Division, Dec. 1899.
WO. 1899
1p.
WH Loc: SA50.

[44] Staff 6 Division, Dec. 1899.
(WO.?) 1899
1p.
WH Loc: SA50.

[45] Staff 7 Division, Dec. 1899.
(WO.?) 1899
1p.
WH Loc: SA50.

[46] Staff 8 Division
WO. 1900
1p.
WH Loc: SA50.

[47] Detail Of 12th, 13th, 14th, And 15th
Brigades Royal Field Artillery For

Service Abroad, Jan. 1900.
WO. 1900
3pp.
WH Loc: SA50.

[48] Papers Laid Before The Committee
On Horse And Field Artillery, 1901.
Reports On Artillery Equipments In Use
In South Africa (i) Horse Artillery,
12 pdr. (ii) Field Artillery 15 pdr. And
12½ pdr. (iii) Field Artillery, 5 Inch
Howitzer.
(WO.?) 1901
430pp.
WH Loc: SA33A.

[49] Reports On Artillery Equipment In
South Africa; Heavy Artillery.
(WO.?) 1901
163pp.
WH Loc: SA33B/PRO Loc: WO.
108/266.

[50] Reports On Artillery Equipment In
South Africa: Vickers Maxim 1 pdr.
Automatic Gun.
(WO.?) 1901
77pp.
WH Loc: SA33C/PRO Loc: WO.
108/265.

[51] Report On Work Done By 3rd
Balloon Section, R.E. In South Africa;
By Lt. R. B. D. Blakeney.
(WO.?) 1901
4pp.
WH Loc: SA40G.

[52] South Africa. Engineer Arm.
Balloon Section, Remarks On
Recommendations By Lt. Blakeney In
His Report; By Capt. H. S. Jones, July
1901.
WO. 1901
2pp.
WH Loc: SA40H.

[53] South Africa. Engineer Arm,
Balloon Section, Remarks On Lt.
Blakeney's Report; By Maj. G. M.
Heath, July 1901.
WO. 1901
3pp.
WH Loc: SA40H.

[54] Detail Of 3rd Cavalry Brigade For
Service Abroad, Jan. 1900.
(WO.?) 1900
3pp.
WH Loc: SA50.

[55] Detail Of 4th Cavalry Brigade For
Service Abroad, Feb. 1900.
(WO.?) 1900
3pp.
WH Loc: SA50.

[56] Report On The Organisation
And Equipment Of Cavalry; By Lt.Gen.
J. D. P. French.
(WO.?) 1902
13pp.
WH Loc: SA39H/PRO Loc: WO.
108/250.

[57] Censorship Of Cables: South Africa.
Reports From Censors At Maritzburg
Forwarded By General Hildyard To The
War Office, July 1901.
WO. 1901 [A690]
14pp.
WH Loc: ID19.

[58] Telegraphic Censorship During The
South African War 1899–1902, June
1903.
Publisher/printer not shown
np./June 1903 [A815]
iv+72pp.
WH Loc: ID18.

[59] Report On Army Chaplain's
Department (Church Of England); By
H. T. Coney, Chaplain To The Forces,
Army HQ, July 1902.

(WO. 1902?)
2pp.
WH Loc: SA39E/PRO Loc: WO.
108/255.

[60] Concentration Camps And
Correspondence With Miss Hobhouse.
May 1901.
WO. 1902
15pp.
WH Loc: SA35.

[61] Report From Notes Of Lord
Kitchener's Speech To The Burghers In
The Camps At Belfast, Middleburg And
Balmoral On 18 Dec. 1901.
WO. 1902
WH Loc: SA65.

[62] Demobilization Regulations. South
Africa, July 1902.
(WO.?) 1902
42pp.
WH Loc: SA44B.

[63] Undesirable Aliens Expelled From
South Africa.
WO. 1900
32pp.
WH Loc: SA38C; SA65.

[64] South Africa. Despatches, Vol. I. –
1 Nov. 1899–1 Aug. 1900.
WO. (1900?)
400pp.
WH Loc: SA19.

[65] South Africa. Despatches, Vol. II.
Aug. 1900–Nov. 1900.
WO. 1901
203pp.
WH Loc: SA19.

[66] South Africa. Despatches, Vol. III.
Dec. 1900–June 1902.
WO. 1902
vi+560pp.
WH Loc: SA19.

[67] Despatches From Lt.Gen. Lord
Methuen In Connection With The Action
at Magersfontein, 11 Dec. 1899.
Dec. 1899.
WO. 1900
6pp.
WH Loc: SA65/PRO Loc: WO. 132/14.

[68] Appendices To Gen. White's
Despatches Dated 23 Mar. 1900
Describing The Defence Of Ladysmith
From 2 Nov. 1899 To 1 Mar. 1900.
WO. 1901
18pp.
WH Loc: SA20.

[69] Report On Office Of Provost
Marshal; By Maj. R. M. Poore, July
1900.
(WO.?) 1902
11pp.
WH Loc: SA39J/PRO Loc: WO.
108/259.

[70] Telegrams Regarding Allegations Of
Murder Against Bushveldt Carbineers.
(WO.?) 1902
2pp.
WH Loc: SA65.

[71] Memorandum On Proposal That
A Military Officer Who Meets With
A Reverse On Service Should Be Tried
By Court Martial As Is Done In The
Navy When An Officer Loses His Ship;
By F. M. Lord Roberts. May 1902.
WO. 1902
13pp. Maps.
WH Loc: SA65.

[72] Letter Regarding Proposal That
A Military Officer Who Meets With
A Reverse On Service Should Be Tried
By Court Martial As Is Done In The
Navy When An Officer Loses His Ship;
By Lt.Gen. Sir Ian Hamilton. May 1902.
WO. 1902
3pp.
WH Loc: SA65.

[73] Special Report On Organisation And Equipment Of The Engineer Arm In South Africa; By Maj.Gen. Elliott Wood, July 1900.
WO. 1900
87pp. With diagrams.
WH Loc: SA40A / PRO Loc: WO. 108/246.

[74] Special Report On Organisation And Equipment Of The Engineer Arm (Auxiliary Forces) In South Africa.
WO. 1901
10pp.
WH Loc: SA40B / PRO Loc: WO. 108/248.

[75] Extracts From Reports By Officers Commanding Units In South Africa During 1899–1901. Vol. I:- Subjects, Rifle, Magazine, Lee-Metford And Lee-Enfield; Carbine, Magazine Lee-Metford And Lee-Enfield; Small Arm Ammunition; Sword Bayonet.
(WO.?) 1901
227pp.
WH Loc: SA29–I.

[76] Extracts From Reports By Officers Commanding Units In South Africa During 1899–1901. Vol. II:- Subjects, Sword, Cavalry And Lance; Pistols And Pistol Ammunition.
(WO.?) 1901
62pp.
WH Loc: SA29–II.

[77] Extracts From Reports By Officers Commanding Units In South Africa During 1899–1901. Vol. IV:- Subjects, Mule-Harness; Harness; Saddlery; Saddle Blankets; Horseshoes; Forage Nets; Picketing Pegs; Ropes.
(WO.?) 1901
176pp.
WH Loc: SA29–IV / PRO Loc: WO. 108/275.

[78] Extracts From Reports By Officers Commanding Units In South Africa During 1899–1901. Vol. V:- Subjects, Water Carts; Scotch Carts; Maltese Carts; Ammunition Carts And Wagons; Wagon Ambulance; Wagon General Service.
(WO.?) 1901
227pp.
WH Loc: SA29–V.

[79] Extracts From Reports By Officers Commanding Units In South Africa During 1899–1901. Vol. VI:- Subjects, Blankets; Waterproof Sheets; Artificers Tools; Camp-Kettles; Entrenching Tools; Tents; Filters.
(WO.?) 1901
205pp.
WH Loc: SA29–VI / PRO Loc: WO. 108/277.

[80] Extracts From Reports By Officers Commanding Units In South Africa During 1899–1901. Vol. VII:- Subjects, Signalling Equipment; Telescopes; Binoculars.
(WO.?) 1901
77pp.
WH Loc: SA29–VII / PRO Loc: WO. 108/278.

[81] Extracts From Reports By Officers Commanding Units In South Africa During 1899–1901. Vol. VIII:- Subjects, Guncotton Detonators; Bicycles; Other Articles Brought To Notice.
(WO.?) 1901
45pp.
WH Loc: SA29–VIII / PRO Loc: WO. 108/279.

[82] Extracts From Reports By Officers Commanding Units In South Africa During 1899–1901. Vol. 10:- Subjects, Clothing.

(WO.?) 1901
96pp.
WH Loc: SA29–10 / PRO Loc: WO. 108/280.

[83] The Supply Of Meat To The Troops On Active Service In South Africa.
WO. 1902
16pp.
WH Loc: SA65.

[84] Report On Remount Department; By Lt.Col. W. H. Birkbeck, July 1900.
(WO.?) 1902
21pp.
WH Loc: SA39N / PRO Loc: WO. 108/261.

[85] Remounts: Replies To The QMG's Questions By Col. W. H. Birkbeck, Sept. 1902.
(WO.?) 1903
8pp.
WH Loc: SA39P.

[86] Report Of The Inspector-General Of Remounts From The Conclusion Of The South African War, June 1902, To March 1904; By Maj.Gen. F. W. Benson.
(WO.?) 1904
16pp.
WH Loc: SA39Q.

[87] Reports On N. American, Russian, S. American, Canadian, English, Indian, Australian And Hungarian Horses And Cobs.
(WO.?) 1902 [A749]
15pp.
WH Loc: SA39R.

[88] Report On Organisation And Equipment Of Infantry; By GOC 11th Division, July 1900.
(WO.?) 1902
12pp.
WH Loc: SA39C / PRO Loc: WO. 108/253.

[89] Report On Organisation And Equipment Of Infantry; By Lt.Gen. C. Tucker, GOC 7th Division, July 1900.
(WO.?) 1902
12pp.
WH Loc: SA39C / PRO Loc: WO. 108/254.

[90] Report On Intelligence Department; By Lt.Col. C. V. Hume, July 1900.
(WO.?) 1900
8pp.
WH Loc: SA39Y / PRO Loc: WO. 108/270.

[91] South Africa: Supplementary Reconnaissance Reports, Sept./Nov. 1899.
WO. Intelligence Division 1899 [A611]
234pp. Maps.
WH Loc: 6B21.

[92] Report On Field Intelligence From 29 Nov. 1900 To The Cessation Of Hostilities; By Lt.Col. David Henderson, June 1902.
(WO.?) 1902
3pp.
WH Loc: SA39Z / PRO Loc: WO. 108/269.

[93] Ladysmith Intelligence Reports: Precis Of Intelligence 12 Oct. 1899– 1 Mar. 1900.
(WO.?) 1903
85pp.
WH Loc: SA41.

[94] Correspondence Etc. Between British And Boer Generals Concerning Matters Relating To The Usages Of War Etc.
WO. 1901
70pp.
WH Loc: SA65.

[95] Report On Lines Of Communication; By Lt.Gen. Frederick Forestier-Walker,

July 1900.
(WO.?) 1902
3pp.
WH Loc: SA39U / PRO Loc: WO. 108/251.

[96] Notes On The Working Of The Line Of Communication In Natal, By Col. J. Wolfe-Murray.
(WO.?) 1902
12pp.
WH Loc: SA39V.

[97] Report On Survey And Mapping Section In South Africa; By Bvt.Lt.Col. H. M. Jackson And Capt. P. H. Du P. Casgrain, Sept. 1902.
WO. 1903
30pp. With maps.
WH Loc: SA40J.

[98] Memorandum For Debate On Martial Law By The Law Officers Of The Crown, Jan. 1902.
(WO.?) 1902
3pp.
WH Loc: SA65.

[99] Report On The Organisation And Working Of The South African Permit Office.
(WO.?) 1903
26pp.
WH Loc: SA39D.

[100] Medical Report On The Campaign In Natal, 1899–1900; By Col. T. J. Gallwey.
(WO.?) 1901
23+12pp.
WH Loc: Cttee. Rpts.

[101] Report On The Organisation And Equipment Of Medical Units; By Surg.Gen. W. F. Stevenson, July 1900.
(WO.?) 1902
13pp.
WH Loc: SA39L / PRO Loc: WO. 108/252.

[102] Detailed Reports On The Sanitary Conditions Relating To Proposed Cantonments And Encampments For The Troops In South Africa; By Lt.Col. W. G. Macpherson, Nov. 1902.
WO. 1903
285pp. Maps, plans.
WH Loc: SA34E.

[103] General Report On The Sanitary Conditions Likely To Affect The Health Of Troops In Cantonments And Encampments In South Africa; By Lt.Col. W. G. Macpherson, Jul. 1903.
WO. 1903
55pp. Illustrated.
WH Loc: SA34D.

[104] Regulations For The Mobilisation Of A Field Force For Service In South Africa.
WO. 1899
24pp.
WH Loc: SA44A.

[105] Precis Of Reports Furnished By The GOC's Commanding Districts On The Mobilisation Of 1899–1900 In Compliance With The War Office Letter No. 40116/6910 Of 9 Mar. 1900.
(WO.?) 1901
127pp.
WH Loc: Cttee. Rpts.

[106] South Africa, Revised Orders By Lt.Gen. Sir George White, Commanding In Natal.
(WO.?) 1899
29pp.
WH Loc: SA45; Camps Boer.

[107] South Africa, 1900, F. M. Lord Roberts. 1. Proclamations. 2. Army Orders. 3. Circular Memoranda. [Text Of

Proclamations Taken From Command
Paper CD 426.]
WO. 1902
xvii+71pp.
WH Loc: SA42A.

[108] South Africa, Circular Memoranda
Issued By Chief Of Staff And Adjutant
General. Nos. 1-61, Jan. 1900-Feb.
1902.
(WO.?) 1900-1902
(Var. pag.)
WH Loc: SA14.

[109] Report On The Military Postal
Service; By Lt.Col. J. Greer, July 1900.
(WO.?) 1902
5pp.
*WH Loc: SA39F/PRO Loc: WO.
108/257.*

[110] Military Pigeon Post Cape Colony.
Report Of Operations, Sept. 1901 To
Aug. 1902; By Lt. Eustace H. Abadie.
(WO.?) 1902
18pp. Map, diagram.
*WH Loc: SA39G/PRO Loc: WO.
108/271.*

[111] Prisoners Of War In Ceylon:
Nominal Roll Of Foreigners.
WO. 1900
5pp.
WH Loc: SA6B.

[112] Treatment Of British Prisoners Of
War At Pretoria.
WO. 1900
38pp.
WH Loc: SA7B.

[113] Prisoners Of War At Pretoria: The
Roll Call; Reprinted From *Standard and
Diggers News.*
WO. 1900
24pp.
WH Loc: SA7B.

[114] Prisoners Of War. St. Helena.
WO. 1901
20pp.
WH Loc: SA65.

[115] Lines Of Communication, Cape
Colony. Working Of Midland Section
During South African Campaign 1899-
1900; Notes By Maj. W. E. Fairholme.
June 1900.
WO. 1900 [A636]
10pp.
WH Loc: SA39B; DMO6; Bd. A Papers.

[116] Imperial Railways [Financial
Aspects]; By G. Fleetwood Wilson.
WO. 1901
15pp.
WH Loc: SA17D.

[117] Report On The Provision And
Working Of A Full And Sufficient
Number Of [Telegraph] Wires For The
Use Of An Army Corps Operating On
A Trunk Line Of Communication;
By Lt.Col. R. L. Hippisley And Lt.Col.
E. P. C. Girouard, Jan. 1902.
WO. 1902
8pp.
WH Loc: SA40F.

[118] South Africa, Report On Siege
Railway Plant; By Lt. David Lyell,
Feb. 1902.
WO. 1902
4pp. With diagram.
WH Loc: SA40E.

[119] Transport And Freight Ships For
South Africa: Dates Of Arrival At Cape
Town, July 1900.
WO. 1900
11pp.
WH Loc: P765.

[120] Transport And Freight Ships For
South Africa: Approximate Dates Of

Arrival, July 1900.
WO. 1900
2pp.
WH Loc: P765.

[121] Embarkation Of Field Force For
South Africa. Feb. 1900.
WO. 1900
viii+60+vii.pp.
WH Loc: P765.

[122] Embarkation Of Field Force For
South Africa. Apr. 1900.
WO. 1900
45pp.
WH Loc: P765.

[123] Embarkation Of Field Force For
South Africa. Aug. 1900.
WO. 1900
25pp.
WH Loc: P765.

[124] Report On Searchlight Equipment
Taken To South Africa, By Capt.
Dumaresq. May 1901.
WO. 1901
2pp.
WH Loc: SA40C.

[125] Interim Report On Searchlights In
South Africa; By Capt. R. S. Walker.
Nov. 1901.
WO. 1902
9pp.
WH Loc: SA40D.

[126] Report On Signalling; By Lt.Col.
T. E. O'Leary. July 1900.
(WO.?) 1902
6pp.
*WH Loc: SA39K/PRO Loc: WO.
108/256.*

[127] Reports On Artillery Equipment In
South Africa: Machine Guns.
(WO.?) 1901
65pp.
WH Loc: SA33D.

[128] Reports From Ordnance Officers In
South Africa On The Working Etc. Of
The Army Ordnance Department.
(WO.?) 1901
92pp.
WH Loc: SA30.

[129] Reports From Ordnance Officers In
Natal, South Africa On The Working
Etc. Of The Army Ordnance
Department.
(WO.?) nd.
27pp.
WH Loc: SA31.

[130] Documents Prepared By The War
Office For The Royal Commission On
War Stores In South Africa.
WO. 1906
(Var. page.)
WH Loc: SA28.

[131] Royal Commission On War Stores
In South Africa. Resume Of References
To The War Office, Members Of The
War Office 1902-4, Officers And
Soldiers In The Report Of The Royal
Commission On War Stores In South
Africa And In Appendices Vols. II And
IV Together With (1) Note Of The
Decision Of The Army Council Or Of
Action Being Taken In The Case Of
Each Individual (2) Statements By Those
Concerned On The Allegations (3) Copy
Of The Communication To The Press
Dated 15 Oct. 1906 (4) Statement As To
Action In Regard To The Institution Of
Criminal Or Civil Proceedings.
WO. 1906
150pp.
WH Loc: SA25.

[132] Indian Telegrams On South Africa,
July 1899 To Jan. 1900.
WO. 1900
56pp.
WH Loc: SA55; Bd. in SA56.

[133] Indian Contingents For South
Africa: Telegrams July 1899-Oct. 1900.
WO. 1901
viii+101pp.
WH Loc: SA61A.

[134] South Africa. Telegrams. Vol. I.
Containing Telegrams Nos. 1 To 2000
Ending 22 Dec. 1899.
WO. 1900
xxxv+746pp.
WH Loc: SA52/PRO Loc: WO. 108/229.

[135] South Africa. Telegrams. Vol. II.
Containing Telegrams Nos. 2001 To 3800
Ending 9 Mar. 1900.
WO. 1900
xlix+793pp.
WH Loc: SA52/PRO Loc: WO. 108/229.

[136] South Africa. Telegrams. Vol. III.
Containing Telegrams Nos. 3801 To 5000
Ending 24 April 1900.
WO. 1900
xxxvii+548pp.
WH Loc: SA52/PRO Loc: WO. 108/230.

[137] South Africa. Telegrams. Vol. IV.
Containing Telegrams Nos. 5001 To 6000
Ending 6 June 1900.
WO. 1900
xv+556pp.
WH Loc: SA52/PRO Loc: WO. 108/230.

[138] South Africa. Telegrams. Vol. V.
Containing Telegrams Nos. 6001 To 7000
Ending 21 July 1900.
WO. 1900
xxii+612+21pp.
WH Loc: SA52/PRO Loc: WO. 108/231.

[139] South Africa. Telegrams. Vol. VI.
Containing Telegrams Nos. 7001 To 8250
Ending 18 Sept. 1900.
WO. 1900
xviii+729pp.
WH Loc: SA52/PRO Loc: WO. 108/231.

[140] South Africa. Telegrams. Vol. VII.
Containing Telegrams Nos. 8251 To 9600
Ending 4 Dec. 1900.
WO. 1900
xxx+753pp.
WH Loc: SA52/PRO Loc: WO. 108/232.

[141] South Africa. Telegrams. Vol. VIII.
Containing Telegrams Nos. 9601 To
10600 Ending 1 Feb. 1901.
WO. 1901
xxvi+668pp.
WH Loc: SA52/PRO Loc: WO. 108/232.

[142] South Africa. Telegrams. Vol. IX.
Containing Telegrams Nos. 10601 To
11600 Ending 2 April 1901.
WO. 1901
xxvi+634pp.
WH Loc: SA52/PRO Loc: WO. 108/233.

[143] South Africa. Telegrams. Vol. X.
Containing Telegrams Nos. 11601 To
12600 Ending 28 May 1901.
WO. 1901
xxv+634pp.
WH Loc: SA52/PRO Loc: WO. 108/233.

[144] South Africa. Telegrams. Vol. XI.
Containing Telegrams Nos. 12601 To
13600 Ending 30 July 1901.
WO. 1901
xxii+643pp.
WH Loc: SA52/PRO Loc: WO. 108/234.

[145] South Africa. Telegrams. Vol. XII.
Containing Telegrams Nos. 13601 To
14600 Ending 1 Oct. 1901.
WO. 1901
xx+536pp.
WH Loc: SA52/PRO Loc: WO. 108/234.

[146] South Africa. Telegrams. Vol. XIII.
Containing Telegrams Nos. 14601 To
15600 Ending 3 Dec. 1901.
WO. 1901
xv+603pp.
WH Loc: SA52/PRO Loc: WO. 108/235.

[147] South Africa. Telegrams. Vol. XIV.
Containing Telegrams Nos. 15601 To
16600 Ending 10 Feb. 1902.
WO. 1902
xiii+471pp.
WH Loc: SA52/PRO Loc: WO. 108/235.

[148] South Africa. Telegrams. Vol. XV.
Containing Telegrams Nos. 16601 To
18600 Ending 25 June 1902.
WO. 1902
xxix+585pp.
WH Loc: SA52/PRO Loc: WO. 108/236.

[149] South Africa. Telegrams. Vol. XVI.
Containing Telegrams Nos. 18601 To
19022 Ending 11 Sept. 1902.
WO. 1902
xi+262pp.
WH Loc: SA52/PRO Loc: WO. 108/236.

[150] Telegrams Between Commander-In-
Chief And Lt.Gen. Sir Ian Hamilton,
Nov.–Dec. 1901.
(WO.?) 1901
4pp.
WH Loc: SA65.

[151] South African War, 1899–1902.
Telegrams Relating To Censorship,
Prisoners Of War Etc.
WO. 1902
xix+358pp.
WH Loc: SA57/PRO Loc: WO. 108/306.

[152] South African War, 1899–1902.
Confidential Telegrams 12 Oct. 1899 To
1 Oct. 1902.
(WO.?) nd.
lx+510+xxvi.pp.
WH Loc: SA56.

[153] South Africa. Vol. I. Telegrams
And Letters Sent By F. M. Lord Roberts
From 23 Dec. 1899 To 19 Apr. 1900.
(Nos. C1 To C1214).
WO. 1903
xxiv+122pp.
WH Loc: SA64/PRO Loc: WO. 108/238.

[154] South Africa. Vol. II. Telegrams
And Letters Sent By F. M. Lord Roberts
From 19 Apr. To 18 June 1900. (Nos.
C1216 To C2146).
(WO.?) 1903
xiv+124pp.
WH Loc: SA64/PRO Loc: WO. 108/239.

[155] South Africa. Vol. III. Telegrams
And Letters Sent By F. M. Lord Roberts
From 19 June To 7 Aug. 1900. (Nos.
C2149 To C3376).
WO. 1903
xxviii+144pp.
WH Loc: SA64/PRO Loc: WO. 108/240.

[156] South Africa. Vol. IV. Telegrams
And Letters Sent By F. M. Lord Roberts
From 8 Aug. 1900 To 13 Sept. 1900.
(Nos. C3378 To C4599).
WO. 1903
xxxiv+148pp.
WH Loc: SA64/PRO Loc: WO. 108/241.

[157] South Africa. Vol. V. Telegrams
And Letters Sent By F. M. Lord Roberts
From 14 Sept. To 31 Oct. 1900. (Nos.
C4600 To C5900).
WO. 1903
xxxvi+141pp.
WH Loc: SA64/PRO Loc: WO. 108/242.

[158] South Africa. Vol. VI. Telegrams
And Letters Sent By F. M. Lord Roberts
From 1 Nov. To 26 Dec. 1900. (Nos.
C5908 To C6683 & C1 To C101).
WO. 1903
xxi+76pp.
WH Loc: SA64/PRO Loc: WO. 108/243.

[159] South Africa. Telegrams, Dec. 1903
To Mar. 1904.
WO. nd.
58pp.
WH Loc: SA54.
*War Office library. Listed with South
African War telegrams.*

[160] South Africa. Telegrams Between
25 May 1902 And 31 March 1905 Dealing
With Supplies Etc.
WO. 1905
139pp.
WH Loc: SA53/PRO Loc: WO. 108/320.
*War Office library. Listed with South
African War telegrams.*

[161] Report On Transport Services; By
Maj.Gen. W. G. Nicholson, July 1900.
(WO.?) 1902
12pp.
*WH Loc: SA39W/PRO Loc: WO.
108/258.*

[162] Report On Army Veterinary
Department; By Vet.Col.
I. A. Matthews.
(WO.?) 1902
3pp.
WH Loc: SA39A.

(War Office) (Publisher) – Secret.
Military Notes On The Dutch Republics
Of South Africa. Compiled In Section B,
Intelligence Division, War Office.
Revised June 1899.
War Office
London 1899
119pp. Folding maps and plans in
separate pocket.
*A summary of information gathered by
British agents in South Africa published a
few months prior to the outbreak of war.*

(War Office) (Publisher?) – Notes On
The Lines Of Communications In The
Cape Colony. Collated By Major
E. A. Altham.
(HMSO?)
London 1899
69pp. Folding maps, tables.
240mm
*Listed from SABIB. Item marked – War
Office Intelligence Division.*

(War Office) (Publisher?) – Secret. South
African Telegrams.
Publisher/printer not shown
Possible War Office document
np./nd. (c.1901)
176+20pp.
327×207mm
*Orange wrap. Title from cover. Telegrams
numbered 1–475 from 13th Oct. 1899 to
12th Feb. 1901. With 20pp. – Table of
Contents.*

(War Office) (Publisher?) – Secret.
A Supplement To – South African
Telegrams.
Publisher/printer not shown
np./nd. (c.1901)
pp.173–202+pp.17–23.
325×209mm
*Telegrams numbered 463–543 from 28th
Jan. 1901 to 11th June 1901.*

(War Office) (Publisher) – Departure Of
Troops From South Africa. (From 15th
November, 1899, To 31st July, 1901.)
Part I.
War Office
London 1901
ix+62pp.
324×198mm
WO. ref: – WH Loc: SA12B.

(War Office) (Publisher) – Departure Of
Troops From South Africa. (From 1st
August, 1901, To 31st August, 1903.)
Part II.
War Office
London 1904
xx+88pp.
323×197mm
WO. ref: – WH Loc: SA12B.

(War Office) (Publisher) – Militia
Embodiment, 1899–1902.

War Office
London 1902
8pp.
*Notes concerning Militia units engaged in
the war.*

(War Office) (Publisher) – Embarkations
In Connection With The South African
Campaign, 1899–1901.
(Up To 19th October 1900.) Volume I.
War Office
London 1901
xxix+166pp.
320×206mm   p.49
WO. ref: – WH Loc: SA12A.

(War Office) (Publisher) – Embarkations
In Connection With The South African
Campaign, 1899–1902.
Volume II (October, 1900, To June,
1902.)
War Office
London 1903
xv+3+158pp.
329×210mm
WO. ref: – WH Loc: SA12A.

(War Office) (Publisher) – Embarkations
In Connection With The South African
Campaign, 1899–1902.
Supplement To Volume II. (July, 1902,
To December, 1902.)
War Office
London 1903
16pp.
329×210mm
WO. ref: – WH Loc: SA12A.

(War Office) (Intelligence Branch, Etc.) –
Statement Of The Intelligence Division
(On The Work Done In Preparation For
The War In South Africa).
WO. 1902
15pp.
Ref. WO. Cat./1912.

(War Office) (Publisher) – Return Of
Death Sentences Inflicted, Penal
Servitude Sentences Confirmed, And
Other Penalties Awarded By Military
Courts In South Africa During 1902.
WO. 1902
61pp.
Ref. WO. Cat./1912.

Warren (S. Hazzledine) – Britain To
Arms! Verses On The Transvaal War,
November, 1899.
Eden Fisher and Co.
London 1899
14pp.
8vo.   M

Wason (Rigby) (Editor) – Some
Volunteer Verse.
Printed for private circulation by
Hazell, Watson & Viney, Ld.
London and Aylesbury 1905
103pp.
200×145mm
*Poems by and for members of the C.I.V.
with reference to the war.*

('Waterfall Wag') – The Pretoria
Prisoners' Paper, Etc. See entry under
CLEMENTS PRINTING WORKS.

(Waterlow And Sons) (Printers) –
Transvaal Colony Proclamations From
1900–1902 (Revised To 30th November,
1902). (2nd ed.)
Waterlow and Sons, printers
London 1902
viii+538pp.
240mm   SABIB

Waters (Colonel W. H. H.) (Translator) –
The War In South Africa Prepared In
The Historical Section Of The Great

General Staff, Berlin.
John Murray
London 1904
ix+280pp. Folding maps and plates.
226×146mm   p.104
*The German Official account of the war
in South Africa. (See DU CANE. Col. H. –
The War In South Africa, Etc., a
continuation of the German Official
account of the South African war.)
Editions were published in 1905 and 1907.*

Waterston (Jane Elizabeth) – War
Telegrams To The Lovedale Library,
From Dr. Jane Waterston, Capetown.
Oct. 12, 1899 To Oct. 31, 1900.
Institution Press
Lovedale 1900
299 leaves/pages?
220mm   SABIB

Watkins (Owen Spencer) – Chaplains
At The Front. Incidents In The Life Of
A Chaplain During The Boer War,
1899–1900.
S. W. Partridge & Co.
London 1902
334pp. Illustrated.
189×124mm   p.10
SABIB & M list edition printed 1901.

Watkins Yardley (Lt.Col. J.) – With The
Inniskilling Dragoons, Etc. See entry
under YARDLEY.

Watson (J. Hannan) – A Trooper's
Sketch Book Of The Boer War.
James Brown & Son
Glasgow nd. (1902)
80pp. (Unnumbered.) Illustrated
throughout.
215×280mm   p.65

Watt (J. A.) – The Official Diary.... Of
The 5th. And 6th. South Australian
Imperial Bushmen's Contingents In
South Africa.
Jennings' Print (Printer)
Rose Park? (19—?)
24pp. With portrait.
210mm   SABIB

Wauchope (Capt. A. G.) – A Short
History Of The Black Watch (Royal
Highlanders) 1725–1907. To Which Is
Added An Account Of The Second
Battalion In The South African War,
1899–1902.
William Blackwood & Sons
Edinburgh/London 1908
xiii+241pp. With maps.
223×145mm
*Various maps to the South African
section.*

Webb (Rev. Allan B.) – Some Questions
On The Settlement In South Africa.
Skeffington & Son
London 1900
27pp.
8vo.   M

Webster (R. E.) (Viscount Alverstone) –
Speech By Lord Alverstone, 24th April,
1902, On The South African War
(Martial Law In Cape Colony).
Wyman & Sons, for H.M.S.O.
London (1902?)
6pp.
250mm   SABIB
*House of Lords. Session 1902. Reprinted
from the parliamentary debates, etc.*

(Weeks Ltd.) (Printer) – Soldiers Of The
Queen, New Zealand's Contingent To
The Front. October, 1899.
Weeks Ltd.
Christchurch nd. (1899?)

32pp. Illustrated.
139×222mm   CC
*A pictorial souvenir of the First N.Z.
Contingent leaving for South Africa
aboard S.S. 'Waiwera'. Title from cover.*

(Weeks Ltd.) (Printers) – Third
Contingent And New Zealand Rough
Riders. Soldiers Of The Queen February
17th 1900.
Weeks Ltd.
Christchurch 1900
16pp. Illustrated.
140×260mm   BIM
Title from cover.

Weir (Charles James) – The Boer War
A Diary Of The Siege Of Mafeking.
Spence & Phimister/Printed for private
circulation
Edinburgh 1901
ii+107pp. Illustrated.
196×134mm   CC

Wellington (Hon. George L.) – The War
In South Africa. Speech Of The Hon.
George L. Wellington, Of Maryland, In
The Senate Of The United States,
Monday, May 28th, 1900.
Printer/publisher not shown (Govt.
printing office?)
Washington 1900
20pp.
Roy.8vo.   M

(Wertheimer, Lea & Co.) (Printers) –
Prayer And Thanksgiving To Almighty
God For The Restoration Of Peace In
South Africa, To Be Used In The
Synagogues Of The United Kingdom On
Wednesday, June 11th, 5662–1902.
Wertheimer, Lea & Co., printers
London (1902)
7pp.
220mm   SABIB
Text in Hebrew and English.

(Wertheimer, Lea & Co.) (Printers) –
Thanksgiving Service On The Occasion
Of The Cessation Of Hostilities In South
Africa And The Conclusion Of Peace, To
Be Held On The First Day Of Shebuoth,
Wednesday, 11th June, 1902, In The
Synagogues Of The Spanish And
Portuguese Congregations Of Great
Britain.
Wertheimer, Lea & Co. (Printer)
London 1902
7pp.
210mm   SABIB
Text in Hebrew and English.

(West Kent Regt.) – 2nd Battn. The
Queens Own West Kent Regt. South
Africa, 1900–2.
(No other information)
*Listed under military histories, records,
etc., in THB.*

(West Riding Regt.) – The Duke Of
Wellington's (West Riding Regiment).
Publisher/printer not known
York 1904
30pp. Illustrated.
220×142mm
*Card cover. Ceremony on the occasion of
the unveiling of the South African War
Memorial at York Minster 20th September
1904. With a list of names borne on the
memorial and photographs of some South
African war memorials.*

(West Yorkshire Regt.) – Extract From
Digest Of Service, Etc. See YORKSHIRE
HERALD Newspaper Co., Ltd.

Westcott (B. F.) (Bishop Of Durham) –
The Obligations Of Empire, By The

Bishop Of Durham.
Macmillan
London 1900
14pp.
180mm   SABIB
*Address given at service of intercession for
sufferers from the war in South Africa.*

**(Western Morning News Company,
Limited. The) (Publisher)** – Devonshire
Infantry Volunteers In The Boer War.
Services In The Campaign.
The Western Morning News Company,
Limited
Plymouth 1901
12pp. Illustrated.
178×242mm   RCSL

Westlake (J.) – The Transvaal War
A Lecture Delivered In The University
Of Cambridge On 9th November, 1899.
C. J. Clay & Sons, Cambridge University
Press Warehouse.
London 1899
iii+35pp.
215×140mm
M lists copy of 56pp.

(Westwood & Son. A.) (Publishers) – The
Fifes In South Africa, Etc. See entry
under STURROCK, J. P.

Wetton (Thomas Charles) – With
Rundle's Eighth Division In South
Africa, Being A Volunteer's Experience
With The Division, 1900–1902.
Henry J. Drane
London nd. (c.1902)
vii+pp.8–580. Illustrated.
185×126mm   p.98
SABIB lists date of publication – 1904.

Wetton (Thomas C.) – Reminiscences Of
The 34th Battalion, Imperial Yeomanry.
Sidey and Bartlett
London nd. (1907)
viii+259pp. Illustrated.
185×126mm

Whales (G. N. H.) (Editor) – The
Mafeking Mail Special Siege Slip. See –
TOWNSHEND & SON.

Wheildon (Frank) (Printer?) – Royal
Opera House, Covent Garden. Grand
Concert, Thursday, February 22nd 1900,
At 8.30. Arranged By The Marchioness
Of Lansdowne's Committee. In Aid Of
The Officers Wives' And Families' Fund.
Frank Wheildon
London nd. (1900)
13pp.
266×196mm
*Concert programme together with a list of
Regiments represented in the Military
Tableau. – Single sheet inserted. Title
from cover.*

(Whitcombe & Tombs Ltd.) (Printers) –
The Veldt Lyre. Published At Rhenoster
Kop Christmas Day 1900.
Whitcombe & Tombs Ltd.
Wellington (nd.)
34pp. Illustrated.
250×185mm   BIM
*Publication incorporating the 'Second
N.Z. Contingent Chronicle'. Contributors
include E. A. Rees, L. Price &
R. Johnstone.*

(White. A. J. Limited) (Publisher?) – Our
Friends The Enemy.
A. J. White Limited
London nd. (1902?)
32pp. Illustrated.
186×120mm
*Advertising booklet for Mother Seigel's
Curative Syrup and other medical*

products, being a calendar for 1903 and a Boer War diary from 1899 to the conclusion of peace. Title from cover.

White (F. M. Sir G. S.) – Orders By Lieut.-General Sir G. S. White.
London (1899)
No other information.
THB
Possibly orders by Gen. White commanding at Ladysmith. SABIB (Vol. 2./p.406.) lists Natal Field Force orders – 16th November 1899 – 2nd March 1900. 8 leaves of varying size, unbound. Issued at Ladysmith during the siege.

(White. R. T.) (Printer) – The Great Boer War Tales Told By A Trooper. I.Y. R. T. White (printer)
Dublin nd. (c.1902)
26pp.
206×100mm   CC   p.82
Title from cover.

(Whitehead. E.) (Printer) – Souvenir Of The Melbourne Celebration, May 23rd 1900.
E. Whitehead
Melbourne (1900)
12pp. Illustrated.
SABIB
Souvenir booklet in celebration of the relief of Mafeking.

(Whitehead. E. & Co.) (Printer) – Souvenir Of The First Victorian Contingent To The Transvaal, October 1899.
E. Whitehead & Co.
Melbourne 1899
(Pagination not shown.)
ALH

(Whitehead. E. & Co.) (Printer) – Souvenir Of The Second Victorian Contingent To The Transvaal, January 1900.
E. Whitehead & Co.
Melbourne 1900
(Pagination not shown.)
ALH

(Whitehead. E. & Co.) (Printer) – Souvenir Of The Third Victorian Contingent To The Transvaal, The Bushmen's Corps, March 1900.
E. Whitehead & Co.
Melbourne 1900
12pp.
RCSL

(Whitehead & Co.) (Publisher?) – Australian Imperial Regiment: Souvenir Of The Victorian Contingent, April 1900.
Whitehead & Co.
Melbourne 1900
(Pagination not shown.)
ALH

(Whitehead & Co.) (Publisher?) – Souvenir Of The Welcome Home To Col. T. Price, Officers And Men On Their Return From Active Service In South Africa, Melbourne, December 4 1900.
Whitehead & Co.
Melbourne 1900
(Pagination not shown.)
ALH

Wigg (H. V.) – Pro-Boer Slanders: A Reply, Speech By Mr. H. V. Wigg, At The Oddfellows' Hall, Grenfell, 27th February 1902.
W. B. Howarth, printer
Grenfell (1902)
5pp.
8vo.   M
Copy from BM Library.

(Wilkie & Co.) (Printers) – Our Boys A Souvenir Of The Otago And Southland Contingent, March 24th 1900. Wilkie & Co., for the Otago and Southland Patriotic Committee
Dunedin 1900
16pp. (Unnumbered.) Illustrated.
ROTE
A pictorial record of local volunteers in the 4th N.Z. contingent.

Wilkins (T.) – Facts And Thoughts On The Transvaal War.
London (1900)
No other information.
8vo.   THB

Wilkins (Thomas) – The Why And Wherefore Of The Transvaal War.
Cooper & Bidd
Peckam ? 1899
2pp.
8vo.   M
Item from British Museum Library. SABIB lists item published by Cooper & Budd, Peckham 1899.

Wilkinson (Caroline) – With The Notts Militia In South Africa.
The Author's Association. London Provincial Office. Darlington
1904
150pp. Illustrated.
SM.Quarto.   M
Experiences of an Officer's wife in South Africa during the war.

Wilkinson (Frank) – Australia At The Front: A Colonial View Of The Boer War.
John Long
London 1901
xi+286pp. Folding map and illustrations.
196×125mm   p.51

Wilkinson (Frank) – Australian Cavalry The New South Wales Lancer Regiment And First Australian Horse.
Angus and Robertson
Sydney and Melbourne 1901
x+64pp. Coloured frontispiece and other plates.
250×186mm   p.15

Wilkinson (S.) – War And Policy (The South African War.)
Publisher/printer not shown
np. 1900
Pagination not shown. (Maps.)
Ref. WO. Cat./1912.

Wilkinson (Spenser) – The Illustrated London News Record Of The Transvaal War, Etc. See – ILLUSTRATED LONDON NEWS AND SKETCH, LIMITED.

Wilkinson (Spenser) – Lessons Of The War Being Comments From Week To Week To The Relief Of Ladysmith.
Archibald Constable
London 1900
xi+204pp.
197×130mm

Will (William) – A Record Of Northern Valour. How The Volunteers In The Counties Of Aberdeen, Banff And Kincardine, And The London Scottish Regiment Rose In A National Crisis.
Aberdeen Journal
Aberdeen 1901
52pp. With portraits.
181×251mm   W

Willcocks (Sir W.) – Three Months In South Africa. . . . A Lecture Delivered At The Century Club, Cairo, On The 28th January, 1902.

National Printing Department
Cairo 1902
46pp.
Roy.8vo.   M
Lecture relating to the war in South Africa.

Williams (Basil) – Record Of The Cape Mounted Riflemen.
Sir Joseph Causton & Sons, Limited
London 1909
v+138pp. Map and plates, many in colour.
215×140mm
A regimental record including substantial Boer War content.

Williams (Charles) – Hushed Up: A Case For Inquiry Into Some Suppressed Facts Concerning The Conduct Of The War In South Africa.
Grant Richards
London 1902
106pp.
180mm   H

Williams (F. J.) – Account Of Siege Of Ookiep In Report Of The Cape Copper Co., Ltd., 1902. See – CAPE COPPER COMPANY LIMITED, The.

Williams (Basil) and Childers (Erskine) (Edited By) – The H.A.C. In South Africa, A Record Of The Services Rendered In The South African War By Members Of The Honourable Artillery Company.
Smith, Elder & Co.
London 1903
x+234pp. Folding map.
199×130mm   p.12

Williams (H.) and Hicks (F. C.) (Editors) – Selected Official Documents Of The South African Republic And Great Britain. A Documentary Perspective Of The Causes Of The War In South Africa.
American Academy of Political and Social Science
Philadelphia 1900
72pp.
Roy.8vo.   M

(Willis A. D.) (Printer) – The Collegiate School Wanganui In South Africa 1899–1900. Illustrated With Photos Of Former Pupils Who Served In New Zealand United Kingdom South African Irregular Units.
A. D. Willis, printer
Wanganui (c.1902)
48pp. Illustrated.
140×250mm   BIM

(Wills. W. D. & H. O. Ltd.) (Publishers) – British Commanders In The Transvaal War 1899–1900.
W. D. & H. O. Wills Ltd
London nd. (c.1900)
48pp. Illustrated.
206×144mm

Wilson (Capt. C. Holmes) – The Relief Of Ladysmith. The Artillery In Natal.
William Clowes & Sons, Limited
London 1901
xii+114pp. With plans.
183×123mm

Wilson (G. Fleetwood) – Imperial Railways, Etc. See WO. 116.

Wilson (H. W.) – With The Flag To Pretoria. A History Of The Boer War Of 1899–1900.
Harmsworth Brothers, Limited
London 1900/1901
Two vols.

Vol. 1. – viii+364pp. Folding map and illustrations throughout.
Vol. 2. – viii+pp.365–716. Folding map and illustrations throughout.
330×247mm   p.18

Wilson (H. W.) – After Pretoria: The Guerilla War. The Supplement To 'With The Flag To Pretoria'.
The Amalgamated Press, Limited
London 1902
Two vols.
Vol. 1. – viii+528pp. Illustrated throughout.
Vol. 2. – vi+pp.529–1008. Illustrated throughout.
328×247mm

Wilson (H. W.) – With The Flag To Pretoria, Etc. & After Pretoria The Guerilla War, Etc.
Issued in 72 parts.
Parts 1–30 With The Flag To Pretoria.
Parts 31–72 After Pretoria The Guerilla War.
Illustrated wraps.
335×250mm

Wilson (J.) – In The Fighting Line With Buller (Clearing Lang's Nek Tunnel) By J. H. Wilson (Tug Wilson) Of Johannesburg.
P. Davis
Durban 1900
50pp.
210mm   SABIB
Catalogued from cover. Account of author's experiences during the war.

Wilson (R.) – Cecil John Rhodes And His Work, With An Account Of The Siege & Relief Of Kimberley, 1899–1900 Also Sectional Maps Of The War Areas.
Townshend, Taylor & Snashall
Cape Town (1900)
iv+36pp. Portrait, map.
8vo.   M
Limited Boer War content.

Wilson (Lady Sarah) – South African Memories Social, Warlike & Sporting From Diaries Written At The Time.
Edward Arnold
London 1909
xii+331pp. Illustrated.
227×150mm

Wilson (Sir W. D.) – Report On The Medical Arrangements In The South African War By Surgn.Gen. Sir W. D. Wilson.
Harrison & Sons for H.M.S.O.
London 1904
395pp. Illustrations, maps and plans.
Folio
Report by Surgeon-General Sir W. D. Wilson late Principal Medical Officer, South African Field Force.

Wilson (William L.) – England And The Transvaal: The Case For Intervention. An Englishman's Appeal And Address To The English People.
The Grosvenor Press
London 1899
52pp. With a map.
8vo.   M
Political aspects of the present crisis examined. SABIB lists 2nd, 4th, and 5th editions.

(Wilter. Frank) (Publisher) – An English Translation Of All Dutch Official Telegrams Received In Vryheid During Boer War Up To The Time When British Troops Occupied Vryheid.
Frank Wilter

Vryheid, Transvaal Colony 1901
96pp.
220×140mm
Title from cover.

(Wilter. Frank) (Publisher) – The History Of The Vryheid District. Diary Of The Boer War. Calendar For 1902.
Frank Wilter, printer and publisher
Vryheid/Transvaal (1901?)
46+2pp.
210mm   SABIB
No title page. Catalogued from cover. Diary of the South African War extends to Sept. 1901.

Winnington-Ingram (Right Rev. A. F.) – The Blessing Of Peace. A Sermon Preached Before Their Majesties The King And Queen, In St. Paul's Cathedral, At The Thanksgiving Service For Peace, On Sunday Morning, June 8, 1902.
Wells Gardner, Darton & Co.
London 1902
14pp.
8vo.   M

Winton (David Gullan) – A Diary Of The Siege Of Ladysmith From The First To The Finish.
For private circulation
Daily Journal Office
Newcastle-Upon-Tyne 1901
62pp.
182×125mm

Wisser (John P.) – The Second Boer War, 1899–1900.
Hudson-Kimberley Publishing Company
Kansas City, Mo. 1901
270pp. With separate portfolio of maps.
8vo.   M
An account of the war with reference to the 'Journal of the United States Artillery' and the European military periodicals 'Militar Wochenblatt' and 'Revue du Cercle Militaire'.

Witton (Lieutenant George R.) – Scapegoats Of The Empire The Story Of The Bushveldt Carbineers.
D. W. Paterson Co.
Melbourne 1907
x+240pp. Illustrated.
190×126mm   p.6
Second edition published the same year.

Wolfe-Murray (Col. J.) – Notes – Line Of Communication In Natal. See WO. 96.

Wolseley (F. M. Viscount) – Memorandum On South Africa, Etc. See WO. 2.

Wood (Maj.Gen. Elliott) – Special Report, Engineer Arm In South Africa. See WO. 73.

Woodford (Walter) – C.I.V.M.I. South Africa 1900. 'L' Co. (Queens Westminster Rifle Volunteers) At The Front.
Publisher/printer not shown
nd. (c.1900)
55pp.
213×138mm
A card covered volume without title page. The title is drawn from the cover and the authors name from p.55. A diary of events from Jan. 1 to Oct. 17, 1900. The narrative relates to a detachment of 'L' Co. (Q.W.R.V.) selected to serve with the C.I.V. in South Africa. The men were employed by the firm of Jas. Shoolbred & Co.

(Woodfall & Kinder) (Printers/ Publishers?) – A Militia Unit In The

Field, Being A Brief Account Of The Doings Of The Sixth Battalion Lancashire Fusiliers In The South African War During The Years 1900 And 1901.
Printed for private circulation by Woodfall & Kinder
London 1902
viii+182pp.
189×125mm

(Woodhill Printing Works) (Publisher?) – Transvaal War: Illustrated Record Of The Departure Of The NSW Contingent, November 1899.
Woodhill Printing Works
Sydney 1899
(Pagination not shown.)
                    ALH

Worsfold (W. Basil) – Lord Milner's Work In South Africa, From It's Commencement In 1897 To The Peace Of Vereeniging In 1902, Containing Hitherto Unpublished Information.
John Murray
London 1906
viii+620pp. Portraits and map.
225×145mm
M lists John Murray ed. of viii+583pp.

Worsfold (W. Basil) – Lord Milner's Work In South Africa, Etc.
Kegan Paul, Trench, Trübner/London
E. P. Dutton/New York
1913
viii+620pp. Folding map and plates.
220mm   SABIB
Cheaper re-issue.

(Wright. George Edward) (Publisher) – Great Britain And The Dutch Republics. Reprinted From 'The Times' London.
George Edward Wright at 'The Times' Office
London 1900
60pp.
16mo.
Entered under South African War in M. English and French editions listed.

Wroughton (Captain J. B.) – A Short Account Of The 1st (Hertfordshire) Volunteer Battalion The Bedfordshire Regiment In South Africa.
Publisher/printer not shown
Privately printed
Hertford 1905
27pp.
190×130mm

Wyndham (The Rt. Hon. George) – House Of Commons – Session 1900. Debate On The Queen's Speech. The War In The Transvaal. Speech By Mr. George Wyndham, M.P., On Thursday, 1st February, 1900. Reprinted From The 'Parliamentary Debates'.
Wyman & Sons Ltd.
London (1900?)
16pp.
8vo.   M

Wyndham Malet (Major Guilbert E.) – The History Of 'J' Battery Royal Horse Artillery (Formerly A Troop, Madras Horse Artillery) Compiled From Private And Official Records.
Charles Good and Co., Printers
London nd. (c.1903)
x+133pp. Frontispiece and folding map.
220×140mm   p.28

X

('X') – The War In South Africa, By X. The Boers As Seen By Those On The Spot.

Transvaal Committee
London 1900
15pp.
8vo.   M
See Transvaal Committee.

(X. C.) – Everyday Life In Cape Colony
In Time Of Peace. By X. C.
T. Fisher Unwin
London 1902
127pp. Illustrated.
Cr.8vo.   M
*Experiences of an agriculturist in Cape
Colony together with notes on affairs in
the district during the early stages of war.
BM lists author – Richard Cadbury.*

(XXX+LIX) – Unfounded Attacks On
British Officers Made In 'An Absent
Minded War' By 'An Army Staff
Officer'. A Refutation By XXX and LIX.
Skeffington
London 1901
xiv+104pp.
182×123mm   p.57
SABIB lists author – J. E. Goodwyn.

Y

(Y) – How A Nation Went To War: By
Y. Their Christianity, Self-Restraint,
And Bravery.
Publisher/printer not shown
(London 1900?)
14pp.
210mm   SABIB
Pro-Boer pamphlet.

Yaldwyn (W. B.) – British & Boer.
(No. 1). Satirical And Patriotic Verses.
Printed and published for the author
by Mitchley & Sinclair
Port Elizabeth (1900?)
7pp.
220mm   SABIB

Yaldwyn (W. B.) – British & Boer.
(No. 2). Satirical And Patriotic Verses
And Dialogues.
Printed and published for the author
by Mitchley & Sinclair
Port Elizabeth (1900?)
7pp.
220mm   SABIB

Yaldwyn (W. B.) – British & Boer.
(No. 3). Our Three Victories, &c., &c.
Paardeberg! Colenso!! Ladysmith!!! On
The Anniversary Of Majuba, 27th
February, 1900.
Printed and published for the author
by Mitchley & Sinclair
Port Elizabeth (1900?)
7pp.
220mm   SABIB

Yardley (Lieut.-Colonel J. Watkins) –
With The Inniskilling Dragoons The
Record Of A Cavalry Regiment During
The Boer War, 1899–1902.
Longmans, Green, and Co.
London 1904
xiv+365pp. Folding map and
illustrations.
235×160mm

Yate (A. C.) – The Army And The Press
In 1900, Etc. See – ROBINSON (F. E.) &
Co.

Yates (R. E.) (Editor) – Diary Of
Trooper Fielding (Late Of The 18th
Hussars) During The South African War.
Printed privately

'Gazette' Co., Ltd.
Darwen 1904
120pp.
185×120mm   CC   p.12

Yelverton (R. D.) – The Invasion Of The
Transvaal. An Address Delivered At The
Public Meeting At Lee, On Thursday,
October 12th, 1899, By R. D. Yelverton,
Esq., Ex-Chief Justice Of The Bahama
Islands. (Second Edition.)
Printed and published by
F. Longman & Sons
8pp.
8vo.   M

Yorke-Davies (Dr. N. E.) – The Feeding
Of The Soldier. The Lesson Of The
Great Boer War. . . . Reprinted From An
Article In *'The Gentleman's Magazine'*,
1902, With Opinions Of The Press,
Letters, References To Military
Authorities, &c., Relating To Emergency
Rations And Portable Food During The
War.
Chatto and Windus
London 1903
37pp.
Quarto   M

(Yorkshire Herald Newspaper Company,
Ltd. The) (Publishers) – Extract From
Digest Of Service Of The 2nd Battalion
The Prince Of Wales's Own (West
Yorkshire Regt.) In South Africa From
October 30th 1899, To August 4th, 1902.
The Yorkshire Herald Newspaper
Company, Ltd.
York 1903
106pp.
212×137mm   p.45

(Yorkshire Post. The) (Publisher) –
England And The Boers. The Short
History Of A Long Strife.
The Yorkshire Post
Leeds 1899
19pp.
180×125mm
*Reprinted from The Yorkshire Post
Sept. 1899.*

(Yorkshire Post. The) (Publishers) –
England And The Boers. The Short
History Of A Long Strife And The Case
For The Outlanders.
The Yorkshire Post
Leeds 1899
30pp. Folding map.
180×120mm
*Enlarged edition. Excerpts reprinted from
Sept. and Oct. 1899.*

Young (Filson) – The Relief Of Mafeking
How It Was Accomplished By Mahon's
Flying Column; With An Account Of
Some Earlier Episodes In The Boer War
Of 1899–1900.
Methuen & Co.
London 1900
xii+293pp. Illustrated.
198×130mm

Yule (G. Pratt) – Refugee Camps
Mortality Statistics. See entry under
PRATT YULE.

Z

('Z') – The War In South Africa, By Z.
Women And Children Dying. Worse
Horrors Than Death. Mr. Kruger's
'Malicious Lies'?
Publisher/printer not shown
(1900?)
16pp.
8vo.   M

*Pamphlet in reference to alleged atrocities
committed by British troops in South
Africa.*

Zietsman (L. F.) – An Afrikander
M.L.A. Supports The Treason Bill. Mr.
Zietsman's Attitude. Abused By The
Dutch Party.
Cape Times
Cape Town 1900
11pp.
160mm   SABIB
*No title page. Catalogued from caption
title. Reprinted from 'Cape Times' of
August 13 (1900). Speech of Mr.
Zietsman in support of a bill dealing with
Cape Colony rebels against the Crown.*

ADDENDA

HMSO

(Cd.466.) – Committee On The
Organization, Arms, And Equipment Of
The Yeomanry Force.
London 1901
16pp.

(Cd.468.) – Yeomanry Cavalry Training
Return, 1900.
London 1901
Folded sheet.

(Cd.519.) – Army And Militia. Annual
Report Of The Inspector-General Of
Recruiting For The Year 1900.
London 1901
44pp. Folding chart.

(Cd.1463.) – South Africa. Further
Correspondence Relating To Affairs In
South Africa (In Continuation Of
Cd.1163.)
London 1903
vi+79pp.
*Contents relate to Emigration of Women,
Land Settlement, Repatriation and the
refugee situation.*

Morton (Alf C.) (Editor) – 'The Gymeric
Times'.
Indian Ocean
24th April 1900
15pp.
335×215mm
*A magazine edited by Alf C. Morton of
the New Zealand 'Times' & 'Mail'
Wellington. Published for the amusement
of members of the New Zealand 4th and
5th Contingents being conveyed from
Lyttelton to Beira aboard HM Troopship
'Gymeric'. This cyclostyle copy of the
'Gymeric Times' is issue No.1 published
on the Indian Ocean, Tuesday 24th April
1900.*

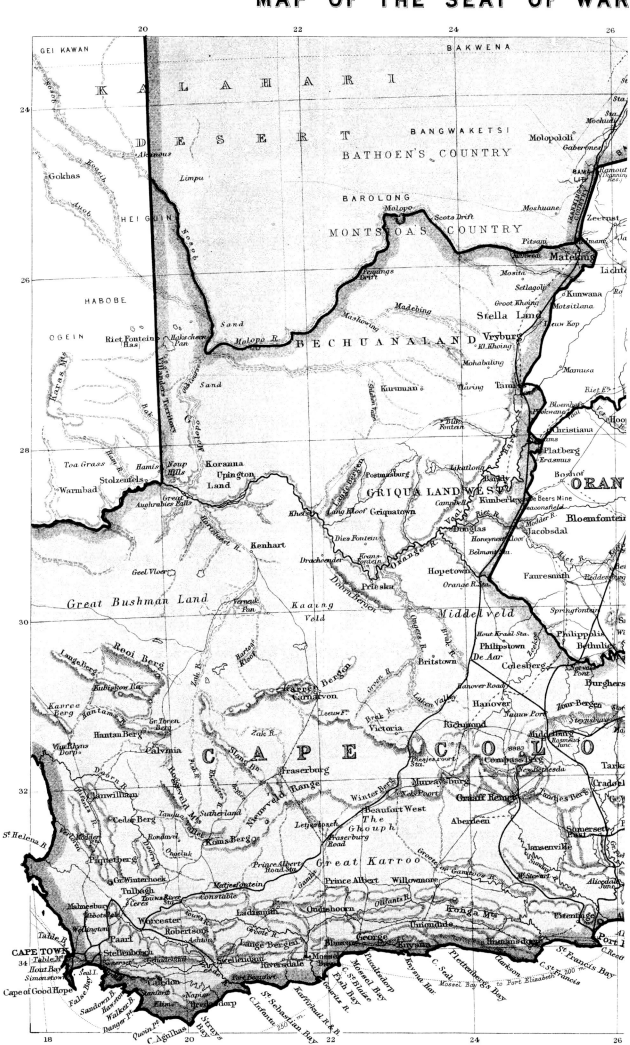

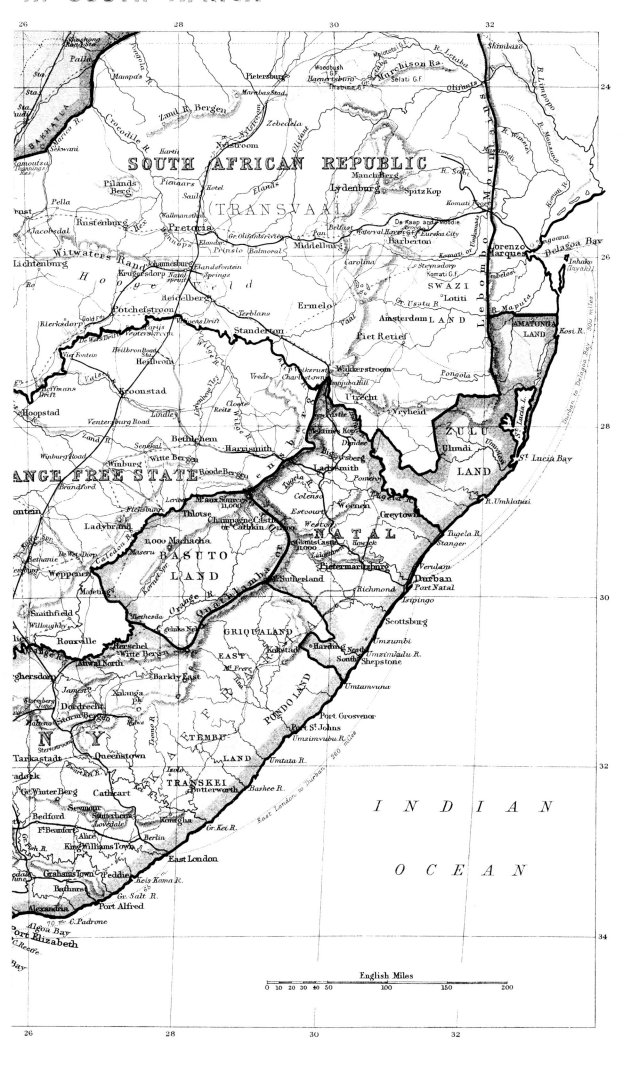

Printed by
Lund Humphries Limited
Bradford